THE CAMBRIDGE

THE PRE-RA

The group of young painters and writer:
movement in the middle years of th
influential in the development not only of literature and painting, but also
more generally of art and design. Though their reputation has fluctuated over
the years, their achievements are now recognized and their style enjoyed and
studied widely. This volume explores the lives and works of the central figures
in the group: among others, the Rossettis, William Holman Hunt, John Everett
Millais, Ford Madox Brown, William Morris and Edward Burne-Jones. This is
the first book to provide a general introduction to the Pre-Raphaelite movement
that integrates its literary and visual art forms. The *Companion* explains what
made the Pre-Raphaelite style unique in painting, poetry, drawing and prose.

ELIZABETH PRETTEJOHN is Professor of History of Art at the University
of York.

A complete list of books in the series is at the back of this book.

THE CAMBRIDGE
COMPANION TO
THE PRE-RAPHAELITES

THE CAMBRIDGE COMPANION TO

THE
PRE-RAPHAELITES

EDITED BY
ELIZABETH PRETTEJOHN

CAMBRIDGE
UNIVERSITY PRESS

CAMBRIDGE
UNIVERSITY PRESS

University Printing House, Cambridge CB2 8BS, United Kingdom

Cambridge University Press is part of the University of Cambridge.

It furthers the University's mission by disseminating knowledge in the pursuit of
education, learning and research at the highest international levels of excellence.

www.cambridge.org
Information on this title: www.cambridge.org/9780521719315

© Cambridge University Press 2012

First published 2012
Reprinted 2013

A catalogue record for this publication is available from the British Library

Library of Congress Cataloguing in Publication data
The Cambridge companion to the Pre-Raphaelites / [edited by] Elizabeth Prettejohn.
p.   cm. – (Cambridge companions to literature)
Includes bibliographical references and index.
ISBN 978-0-521-89515-6 (hardback) – ISBN 978-0-521-71931-5 (paperback)
1. Pre-Raphaelitism – England.   2. Arts, English – 19th century.   I. Prettejohn, Elizabeth.
NX454.5.P7C36 2012
700.942′09034–dc23
2012006885

ISBN 978-0-521-71931-5 Paperback

CONTENTS

List of illustrations   *page* ix
Notes on contributors   xi
Acknowledgements   xv
List of abbreviations   xvii
Chronology   xix
LOUISE HUGHES

Introduction   1
ELIZABETH PRETTEJOHN

PART ONE. PRE-RAPHAELITISM

1   The Pre-Raphaelites and literature   15
    ISOBEL ARMSTRONG

2   Artistic inspirations   32
    JENNY GRAHAM

3   Pre-Raphaelite drawing   47
    COLIN CRUISE

4   The religious and intellectual background   62
    MICHAELA GIEBELHAUSEN

5   *The Germ*   76
    ANDREW M. STAUFFER

PART TWO. PRE-RAPHAELITES

6   The poetry of Dante Gabriel Rossetti (1828–1882)   89
    JEROME MCGANN

7   The painting of Dante Gabriel Rossetti   103
    ELIZABETH PRETTEJOHN

8   William Holman Hunt (1827–1910)   116
    CAROL JACOBI

9   John Everett Millais (1829–1896)   133
    PAUL BARLOW

10 Ford Madox Brown (1821–1893)   148
    TIM BARRINGER

11 Christina Rossetti (1830–1894)   164
    LORRAINE JANZEN KOOISTRA

12 Elizabeth Eleanor Siddall (1829–1862)   183
    DEBORAH CHERRY

13 The writings of William Morris (1834–1896)   196
    JEFFREY SKOBLOW

14 The designs of William Morris   211
    IMOGEN HART

15 Edward Burne-Jones (1833–1898)   223
    CAROLINE ARSCOTT

16 Algernon Charles Swinburne (1837–1909)   236
    CATHERINE MAXWELL

17 William Michael Rossetti (1829–1919)   250
    ANGELA THIRLWELL

18 Envoi   265
    ELIZABETH PRETTEJOHN

    Appendix 1. The contents of The Germ   273
    Appendix 2. The Pre-Raphaelite 'list of Immortals'   277
    Guide to further reading and looking   279
    Index   291

ILLUSTRATIONS

1 William Holman Hunt, *The Lady of Shalott*, 1886–1905,
  oil on canvas, 185 × 143.7 cm, Wadsworth Atheneum, Hartford,
  Connecticut. The Ella Gallup Sumner and Mary Catlin Sumner
  Collection Fund. 1961.470©2011. Wadsworth Atheneum
  Museum of Art/Art Resource, NY/Scala, Florence   *page* 43

2 Dante Gabriel Rossetti, *Dante Drawing an Angel on the
  First Anniversary of the Death of Beatrice*, 1849, pen and
  black ink (inscriptions outside drawn frame in brown ink),
  39.4 × 32.6 cm, Birmingham Museums & Art Gallery   52

3 Simeon Solomon, *Babylon Hath Been a Golden Cup*, 1859,
  pen and black and brown ink over traces of pencil on paper,
  26.6 × 28.3 cm, Birmingham Museums & Art Gallery   59

4 John Everett Millais, *Christ in the House of His Parents*,
  1849–50, oil on canvas, 86.4 × 139.7 cm, Tate, London.
  © Tate, London, 2011   65

5 William Holman Hunt, *The Light of the World*,
  1851–3, retouched 1858, 1886, oil on canvas over panel,
  125.5 × 59.8 cm (arched), Warden and Fellows of Keble
  College, Oxford   68

6 Dante Gabriel Rossetti, *The Girlhood of Mary Virgin*,
  1848–9, oil on canvas, 83.2 × 65.4 cm, Tate, London.
  © Tate, London, 2011   97

7 Dante Gabriel Rossetti, *Proserpine*, 1873–7, oil on canvas,
  116.8 × 55.9 cm, private collection, photo © Christie's
  Images/The Bridgeman Art Library   112

8 William Holman Hunt, *The Hireling Shepherd*, 1851–2, oil
  on canvas, 76.4 × 109.5 cm, City of Manchester Art Galleries   121

9 William Holman Hunt, *The Shadow of Death*, 1869–73, oil
  on canvas, 214.2 × 168.2 cm, City of Manchester Art Galleries   126

10 John Everett Millais, *Isabella*, 1848–9, oil on canvas,
102.9 × 142.9 cm, © Walker Art Gallery, National Museums
Liverpool/The Bridgeman Art Library   134

11 John Everett Millais, *A Huguenot, on St Bartholomew's
Day, Refusing to Shield Himself from Danger by Wearing the
Roman Catholic Badge*, 1851–2, oil on canvas, 92.7 × 62.2 cm
(arched), © The Makins Collection/The Bridgeman Art Library   140

12 Ford Madox Brown, *Geoffrey Chaucer Reading the 'Legend
of Custance' to Edward III and His Court, at the Palace of
Sheen, on the Anniversary of the Black Prince's Forty-Fifth
Birthday*, 1845–51, oil on canvas, 372 × 296 cm (arched),
Art Gallery of New South Wales, Sydney/The Bridgeman
Art Library   152

13 Ford Madox Brown, *An English Autumn Afternoon*, 1852–4,
oil on canvas, 71.8 × 134.6 cm (oval), © Birmingham
Museums and Art Gallery/The Bridgeman Art Library   157

14 Double-page spread from *The Germ*, no. 1, showing Christina
Rossetti's 'Dream Land' opposite Dante Gabriel Rossetti's
'My Sister's Sleep'. Courtesy of Toronto Public Library   172

15 Elizabeth Siddall, *Clerk Saunders*, 1857, watercolour,
bodycolour and coloured chalks on paper, 28.4 × 18.1 cm,
The Syndics of the Fitzwilliam Museum, Cambridge/The
Bridgeman Art Library   184

16 Elizabeth Siddall, *Self-portrait*, c. 1853–4, oil on canvas,
20.3 cm (diameter), whereabouts unknown   193

17 Morris, Marshall, Faulkner & Co., *Jasmine* wallpaper,
designed by William Morris and printed by Jeffrey & Co.
from 1872. Photo © Victoria and Albert Museum, London   215

18 Edward Burne-Jones, *The Beguiling of Merlin*, 1873–4, oil
on canvas, 186 × 111 cm, © Lady Lever Art Gallery, National
Museums Liverpool/The Bridgeman Art Library   228

19 Edward Burne-Jones, *King Cophetua and the Beggar Maid*,
1880–4, oil on canvas, 290 × 136 cm, Tate, London.
© Tate, London, 2011   232

20 Julia Margaret Cameron, *William Michael Rossetti*, 1865,
albumen photographic print from wet collodion negative,
25.5 × 20 cm, private collection. Inscribed on verso by William
Michael Rossetti: 'The hand with umbrella is Browning's'   257

NOTES ON CONTRIBUTORS

ISOBEL ARMSTRONG FBA is Emeritus Professor of English at Birkbeck, University of London. She has written widely on the poetry and culture of the long nineteenth century and on feminism and aesthetics. Her books include *Victorian Poetry: Poetry, Poetics and Politics* (1993), *The Oxford Anthology of Nineteenth-Century Women's Poetry* (1996), *The Radical Aesthetic* (2000) and *Victorian Glassworlds: Glass Culture and the Imagination* (2008).

CAROLINE ARSCOTT is Professor of Nineteenth-Century British Art and Head of Research at The Courtauld Institute of Art. She is the author of *William Morris and Edward Burne-Jones: Interlacings* (2008), co-editor of *Manifestations of Venus: Essays on Art and Sexuality* (2000), and has published widely on Burne-Jones, Morris, Luke Fildes, William Powell Frith, George Scharf, James McNeill Whistler and the Victorian representation of childhood and the city. She was a member of the Editorial Board of the *Oxford Art Journal* from 1998 to 2008 and is an editor for the *RIHA Journal*.

PAUL BARLOW is Senior Lecturer in Art and Design History at Northumbria University. He is the author of *Time Present and Time Past: The Art of John Everett Millais* (2005) and has written widely on Victorian art and artists, including Frederic Leighton, George Frederic Watts and Thomas Woolner. He is co-editor of *Victorian Culture and the Idea of the Grotesque* (1999) and *Governing Cultures: Art Institutions in Victorian London* (2000) and a member of the Editorial Board of *Visual Culture in Britain*.

TIM BARRINGER is Paul Mellon Professor of the History of Art at Yale University. His books include *Reading the Pre-Raphaelites* (1998), *Men at Work: Art and Labour in Victorian Britain* (2005) and co-edited collections including *Colonialism and the Object* (1998), *Frederic Leighton* (1999, with Elizabeth Prettejohn), *Art and the British Empire* (2007) and *Writing the Pre-Raphaelites: Text, Context, Subtext* (2009, with Michaela Giebelhausen). His exhibitions include *American Sublime: Landscape Painting in the United States 1820–1880* (2002), *Art and Emancipation in Jamaica* (2007), *Opulence and Anxiety* (2007) and *Before and After Modernism: Byam Shaw, Rex Vicat Cole, Yinka Shonibare, MBE* (2010).

xi

DEBORAH CHERRY is Professor of Modern and Contemporary Art at the University of Amsterdam, where she is completing *The Afterlives of Monuments*, a special edition of *South Asian Studies*. Her work on Elizabeth Siddall initiated the study of the women artists of the Pre-Raphaelite movement. She is the author of *Painting Women: Victorian Women Artists* (1993) and *Beyond the Frame: Feminism and Visual Culture, Britain 1850–1900* (2000).

COLIN CRUISE teaches at the School of Art, Aberystwyth University. He has published widely on nineteenth-century art, writing on Rossetti, Burne-Jones, Pater and Wilde. He curated two major exhibitions: *Love Revealed: Simeon Solomon and the Pre-Raphaelites* (2005) and *The Poetry of Drawing: Pre-Raphaelite Designs, Studies and Watercolours* (2011), both for Birmingham Museum and Art Gallery. His book *Pre-Raphaelite Drawing* was published in 2011.

MICHAELA GIEBELHAUSEN is Senior Lecturer in the Department of Art History and Theory and co-director of the Centre for Curatorial Studies at the University of Essex. She is a corresponding member of the Centre André Chastel, Université Paris-Sorbonne (Paris IV). She is the author of *Painting the Bible: Representation and Belief in Mid-Victorian Britain* (2006), editor of *The Architecture of the Museum: Symbolic Structures, Urban Contexts* (2003), and co-editor (with Tim Barringer) of *Writing the Pre-Raphaelites: Text, Context, Subtext* (2009). Her recent research focuses on the nineteenth-century destruction and transformation of Paris as manifested in photography and popular prints.

JENNY GRAHAM is an Associate Professor in Art History at the University of Plymouth, specializing in the reception of the Renaissance during the modern period. She is the author of *Inventing Van Eyck: The Remaking of an Artist for the Modern Age* (2007) and is now working on a study of the later reception of Vasari's *Lives of the Artists*, entitled *Afterlives: Giorgio Vasari and the Rise of Art History in the Nineteenth Century*.

IMOGEN HART is Assistant Curator in the Department of Exhibitions and Publications at the Yale Center for British Art, where she was co-curator of the exhibition *Paintings from the Reign of Victoria: The Royal Holloway Collection, London* (2009). She is the author of *Arts and Crafts Objects* (2010) and co-editor of *Rethinking the Interior, c.1867–1896: Aestheticism and Arts and Crafts* (2010). Other publications include an essay on William Morris's patterns in *William Morris and the Art of Everyday Life* (2010) and a chapter on Arts and Crafts magazines in *The Oxford Critical and Cultural History of Modernist Magazines* (2009).

LOUISE HUGHES completed her Ph.D. in 2010 at the University of Bristol and specializes in European Modernism, the painter Chaim Soutine (1893–1943) and the reception of medieval sources in French Modernism of the interwar period.

Forthcoming publications include a monograph on Soutine and a study of the use of fiction in academic art history. She is also interested in public engagement with art history and has lectured for diverse audiences at the University of Oxford, the Royal West of England Academy and Tate Britain.

CAROL JACOBI teaches at Birkbeck College and the Courtauld Institute, specializing in revisionist approaches to modern British art. She is the author of *William Holman Hunt: Painter, Painting, Paint* (2006), and co-curated the international exhibition *Holman Hunt and the Pre-Raphaelite Vision* (2008–9). Her monograph *Isabel Rawsthorne: Out of the Cage* is forthcoming.

LORRAINE JANZEN KOOISTRA is Professor of English at Ryerson University in Toronto, Canada. She is author of *Poetry, Pictures, and Popular Publishing: The Illustrated Gift Book and Victorian Visual Culture 1855–1875* (2011), *Christina Rossetti and Illustration: A Publishing History* (2002) and *The Artist as Critic: Bitextuality and Fin-de-Siècle Illustrated Books* (1995). She is co-editor of *The Culture of Christina Rossetti: Female Poetics and Victorian Contexts* (1999) and *The Yellow Nineties Online* (www.1890s.ca).

JEROME MCGANN is John Stewart Bryan University Professor at the University of Virginia. He is founder and co-director (2003–8) of NINES (Networked Infrastructure for Nineteenth-Century Electronic Scholarship) and general editor of *The Complete Writings and Pictures of Dante Gabriel Rossetti: A Hypermedia Archive*, a pioneering online research archive. Among his more than thirty books are *Swinburne: An Experiment in Criticism* (1972), *Black Riders: The Visible Language of Modernism* (1993) and *Dante Gabriel Rossetti and the Game That Must be Lost* (2000).

CATHERINE MAXWELL is Professor of Victorian Literature at Queen Mary, University of London. She is the author of *The Female Sublime from Milton to Swinburne: Bearing Blindness* (2001), *Swinburne* in the British Council series Writers and Their Work (2006) and *Second Sight: The Visionary Imagination in Late Victorian Literature* (2008). She has edited a collection of Swinburne's poetry (1997), and co-edited Vernon Lee's *Hauntings and Other Fantastic Tales* (2006) and a collection of essays, *Vernon Lee: Decadence, Ethics, Aesthetics* (2006). She is guest editor of a special issue of *Victorian Review* on 'Victorian Literature and Classical Myth' (2008), and of a double issue of the *Yearbook of English Studies* on 'The Arts in Victorian Literature' (2010). She is currently co-editing a collection of essays on Swinburne.

ELIZABETH PRETTEJOHN is Professor of History of Art at the University of York. Her books include *The Art of the Pre-Raphaelites* (2000), *Beauty and Art 1750–2000* (2005) and *Art for Art's Sake: Aestheticism in Victorian Painting* (2007). She co-curated the exhibitions *Imagining Rome* (1996), *Sir Lawrence Alma-Tadema*

(1996–7), *Dante Gabriel Rossetti* (2003–4) and *John William Waterhouse: The Modern Pre-Raphaelite* (2008–10).

JEFFREY SKOBLOW is Professor of English Language and Literature at Southern Illinois University Edwardsville. He is the author of *Paradise Dislocated: Morris, Politics, Art* (1993) and *Dooble Tongue: Scots, Burns, Contradiction* (2001), along with numerous articles on writers including Morris, Burns and more contemporary Scottish writers.

ANDREW M. STAUFFER is an Associate Professor of English at the University of Virginia, where he also directs the NINES digital initiative (www.nines.org). He is the author of *Anger, Revolution, and Romanticism* (2005) and the editor of works by Robert Browning and H. Rider Haggard. He has published widely on Romantic and Victorian subjects and is currently working on a project related to the troubled archive of nineteenth-century literature.

ANGELA THIRLWELL read English at St Anne's College, Oxford, and lectured for the Faculty of Continuing Education at Birkbeck College, University of London. She is the author of *William and Lucy: The Other Rossettis* (2003), *Into the Frame: The Four Loves of Ford Madox Brown* (2010) and 'The Game of Life', a character study of Ford Madox Brown for the exhibition on the artist at Manchester and Ghent (2011–12). She edited the *Folio Anthology of Autobiography* (1994) and *The Pre-Raphaelites and Their World* (1995).

ACKNOWLEDGEMENTS

I owe special thanks to Jerome McGann, who gave valuable advice in the planning stages of this volume, and to Charles Martindale whose support was untiring throughout. Louise Hughes joined me at a crucial moment to help with the minutiae of editing, and I am grateful for her good humour and resourcefulness. I would like to thank all those at Cambridge University Press who have helped with the volume, in particular Linda Bree and Maartje Scheltens for their great patience as well as their skill and expertise. Thanks to Jamie Carstairs, Juliet Edwards, Karin Kyburz, the Courtauld Institute of Art and the Faculty of Arts Research Fund at the University of Bristol for help with the illustrations, and to Richard Shone for advice and permission to quote from *The Burlington Magazine*. Many others have given generous advice and support of various kinds, including Jason Rosenfeld, Rachel Sloan, Sam Smiles, Alison Smith, Julian Treuherz and numerous colleagues at museums and galleries with Pre-Raphaelite holdings.

ABBREVIATIONS

DGR *Correspondence*	*The Correspondence of Dante Gabriel Rossetti*, ed. William E. Fredeman and others, 9 vols. (Cambridge: D. S. Brewer, 2002–10). The first two digits of the letter number (given in parentheses) indicate the year of writing (for example, letter 48.7 is the seventh extant letter from 1848).
Germ	*The Germ: Thoughts towards Nature in Poetry, Literature and Art: Being a Facsimile Reprint of the Literary Organ of the Pre-Raphaelite Brotherhood, Published in 1850* (London: Elliot Stock, 1901). Page numbers are to the facsimile text of the magazine except where the (separately paginated) 'Introduction by William Michael Rossetti' is specified.
Hunt	William Holman Hunt, *Pre-Raphaelitism and the Pre-Raphaelite Brotherhood*, 2 vols. (London and New York: Macmillan, 1905–6).
PRB	'Pre-Raphaelite Brotherhood' or 'Pre-Raphaelite Brother'.
The Rossetti Archive	*The Complete Writings and Pictures of Dante Gabriel Rossetti: A Hypermedia Archive*, ed. Jerome J. McGann, www.rossettiarchive.org/.
Ruskin	*The Works of John Ruskin (Library Edition)*, ed. E. T. Cook and Alexander Wedderburn, 39 vols. (London: George Allen, 1903–12).

CHRONOLOGY

1819	Birth of John Ruskin
1821	Birth of Ford Madox Brown
1825	Births of James Collinson (PRB), Thomas Woolner (PRB)
1827	Births of William Holman Hunt (PRB), Maria Francesca Rossetti
1828	Births of Dante Gabriel Rossetti (PRB), Frederic George Stephens (PRB)
1829	Births of John Everett Millais (PRB), William Michael Rossetti (PRB), Elizabeth Eleanor Siddall
1830	Birth of Christina Georgina Rossetti
1833	Birth of Edward Burne-Jones
1834	Destruction of the Palace of Westminster by fire; birth of William Morris
1837	Accession of Queen Victoria; birth of Algernon Charles Swinburne
1839	Birth of Jane Burden (later Morris)
1840	Birth of Simeon Solomon
1842	National Gallery (London) acquires Jan van Eyck's *Portrait of Giovanni Arnolfini and His Wife* (1434)
1843	Ruskin, *Modern Painters*, Vol. I; Wordsworth becomes Poet Laureate; competitions begin for decorative art at the new Palace of Westminster (−1847)

1845	The Great Famine, Ireland (–1852); D. G. Rossetti begins translating Dante and early Italian poets
1846	Ruskin, *Modern Painters*, Vol. II
1848	Year of European revolutions; Chartist demonstrations and petition; formation of the Pre-Raphaelite Brotherhood; Hunt and D. G. Rossetti compile the list of Immortals (see Appendix 2); Marx and Engels, *Manifesto of the Communist Party*
1849	First PRB paintings appear at exhibition: D. G. Rossetti's *The Girlhood of Mary Virgin* (Figure 6) at Free Exhibition, Hunt's *Rienzi Vowing to Obtain Justice for the Death of His Young Brother*, Millais's *Isabella* (Figure 10) and Collinson's *Italian Image-Makers* at Royal Academy (all signed with 'P. R. B.' initials); W. M. Rossetti begins to keep the *P. R. B. Journal*; D. G. Rossetti and Hunt tour France and Belgium
1850	*The Germ* published January–May; second PRB exhibition season: Rossetti's *Ecce Ancilla Domini!* at National Institution, Millais's *Christ in the House of His Parents* (Figure 4) and Hunt's *A Converted British Family* at Royal Academy; Hunt, Rossetti and Stephens paint outdoors in Kent; W. M. Rossetti begins career as art critic for *The Critic*, then *The Spectator*; Tennyson becomes Poet Laureate
1851	Great Exhibition at the new Crystal Palace in Hyde Park; Brown's *Geoffrey Chaucer* (Figure 12) at Royal Academy; Ruskin writes to *The Times* in defence of the PRB; Hunt and Millais paint outdoors at Ewell, Surrey
1852	Opening of the new Palace of Westminster; Brown begins important modern-life paintings: *Work* (–1865), *The Last of England* (–1855), *An English Autumn Afternoon* (–1854, Figure 13); Hunt's *The Hireling Shepherd* (Figure 8), Millais's *Ophelia* and *A Huguenot* (Figure 11) at Royal Academy; Woolner emigrates to Australia to prospect for gold
1853	Crimean War begins (–1856); Burne-Jones and Morris become friends as undergraduates at the University of

Oxford; Millais paints Ruskin's portrait at Glenfinlas in Scotland, and is elected Associate of the Royal Academy

1854   Hunt tours the Middle East (–1856) and shows *The Awakening Conscience* and *The Light of the World* at the Royal Academy; Working Men's College founded (teachers will include Ruskin, Rossetti, Brown and Burne-Jones)

1855   Exposition Universelle, Paris, includes important works by Brown, Hunt and Millais; Burne-Jones and Morris travel to France in the Long Vacation and decide to become artists; W. M. Rossetti writes art criticism for new American periodical, *The Crayon* (succeeded by F. G. Stephens in 1856)

1856   The *Oxford and Cambridge Magazine* publishes twelve issues

1857   Matrimonial Causes Act conditionally allows women to divorce; Pre-Raphaelite Exhibition, Russell Place, with seventy-one works by PRBs and associates including Siddall; W. M. Rossetti helps to organize an Exhibition of British Art which introduces Pre-Raphaelite art to the United States; Ruskin, *The Elements of Drawing*; publisher Edward Moxon's edition of Tennyson's *Poems* includes illustrations by Hunt, Millais and D. G. Rossetti; project to decorate the Oxford Union (under D. G. Rossetti's leadership, with paintings by Burne-Jones, Morris and others) brings Algernon Charles Swinburne into Rossetti's circle

1858   Founding of the Hogarth Club (–1861); William Morris, *The Defence of Guenevere, and Other Poems* (dedicated to D. G. Rossetti)

1859   Charles Darwin, *On the Origin of Species*; D. G. Rossetti paints *Bocca Baciata*; marriage of Jane Burden and William Morris

1860   Publication of *Essays and Reviews*, which controversially presents a view of the Bible based on scientific, linguistic and historical investigation; Hunt shows *The Finding of the Saviour in the Temple* in a special exhibition at the

German Gallery; marriages of Elizabeth Eleanor Siddall and Dante Gabriel Rossetti, Georgiana Macdonald and Edward Burne-Jones; Stephens becomes regular art critic for *The Athenaeum* (–1900); Ruskin, *Modern Painters*, Vol. V (the last); Swinburne, *The Queen-Mother and Rosamond* (dedicated to D. G. Rossetti)

1861   American Civil War (–1865); death of Prince Albert; abolition of serfdom in Russia; independent kingdom of Italy established; founding of Morris, Marshall, Faulkner & Co. ('the Firm'); D. G. Rossetti, *The Early Italian Poets* (dedicated to Elizabeth Siddall, now Rossetti)

1862   London International Exhibition, with exhibit by 'the Firm'; death of Elizabeth Eleanor Siddall (now Rossetti); Christina Rossetti, *Goblin Market and Other Poems* with two illustrations by D. G. Rossetti; Swinburne reviews Baudelaire in *The Spectator*; D. G. Rossetti moves to Tudor House, Cheyne Walk, Chelsea, with W. M. Rossetti and Swinburne as lodgers

1863   Ernest Renan, *Vie de Jésus*, a biography of Christ casting doubt on his divine status; Alexander Gilchrist, *Life of William Blake, 'Pictor Ignotus'* (completed by the Rossetti brothers and Anne Gilchrist)

1864   Burne-Jones elected Associate of the Old Water-Colour Society

1865   Abolition of slavery in North America; birth of W. B. Yeats; Brown holds solo exhibition of *Work* and other paintings, for which he writes his own catalogue; Dudley Gallery formed by a committee of artists; Swinburne, *Atalanta in Calydon*

1866   Christina Rossetti, *The Prince's Progress and Other Poems* with two illustrations by D. G. Rossetti; Swinburne, *Poems and Ballads* (dedicated to Burne-Jones)

1867   Morris, *The Life and Death of Jason*; W. M. Rossetti, *Fine Art, Chiefly Contemporary* (dedicated to Frances Mary Lavinia Rossetti)

1868	Morris, *The Earthly Paradise* (–1870, 3 vols., dedicated to Jane Morris); Swinburne, *William Blake* (dedicated to W. M. Rossetti)
1869	Ruskin appointed Slade Professor of Art at the University of Oxford; Hunt paints *The Shadow of Death* (–1873, Figure 9); exhumation of poems by D. G. Rossetti from Siddall's coffin
1870	D. G. Rossetti, *Poems* (dedicated to W. M. Rossetti); Burne-Jones resigns from Old Water-Colour Society following objections to the male nude in his *Phyllis and Demophoon*
1871	Paris Commune; Rome becomes capital of a united Italy; Swinburne, *Songs before Sunrise* (dedicated to Giuseppe Mazzini); Ruskin founds School of Drawing at Oxford
1872	Christina Rossetti, *Sing-Song* with illustrations by Arthur Hughes
1873	Solomon arrested and tried for sodomy; D. G. Rossetti begins *Proserpine* (–1877, Figure 7); Morris, 'Love Is Enough'; Walter Pater, *Studies in the History of the Renaissance*
1874	William Michael Rossetti and Lucy Madox Brown marry
1875	'The Firm' reformulated as Morris & Co. under Morris's sole proprietorship; Swinburne, *Essays and Studies*
1876	Morris, *The Story of Sigurd the Volsung and the Fall of the Niblungs*
1877	First exhibition of Grosvenor Gallery, with important work by Burne-Jones including *The Beguiling of Merlin* (Figure 18; D. G. Rossetti declines to exhibit); Ruskin, *The Laws of Fésole*
1878	Exposition Universelle, Paris, including Burne-Jones's *The Beguiling of Merlin* (Figure 18); Frederic Leighton elected President of the Royal Academy (–1896); Swinburne, *Poems and Ballads: Second Series*

1880	First Anglo-Boer War (–1881); Swinburne, *The Heptalogia*
1881	Death of James Collinson; Christina Rossetti, *A Pageant and Other Poems*; D. G. Rossetti, *Poems: A New Edition* and *Ballads and Sonnets*
1882	Death of Dante Gabriel Rossetti; memorial exhibitions in the winter of 1882–3 reveal his paintings to the public; Morris, *Hopes and Fears for Art*; Swinburne, *Tristram of Lyonesse and Other Poems*; birth of Virginia Woolf
1883	Swinburne, *A Century of Roundels* (dedicated to Christina Rossetti)
1886	Hunt paints *The Lady of Shalott* (–1905, Figure 1)
1888	Morris, *Signs of Change* and 'A Dream of John Ball'; first exhibition of the Arts and Crafts Exhibition Society
1889	Swinburne, *Poems and Ballads: Third Series* (dedicated to William Bell Scott)
1890	Death of Vincent van Gogh; Morris, *News from Nowhere*
1891	Morris founds the Kelmscott Press
1892	Death of Thomas Woolner
1893	Death of Ford Madox Brown; Christina Rossetti, *Verses*
1894	Death of Christina Georgina Rossetti; Swinburne, *Astrophel and Other Poems* (dedicated to Morris)
1895	Radio communication begins; Oscar Wilde imprisoned for homosexual offences
1896	Deaths of John Everett Millais, William Morris; Christina Rossetti, *New Poems* (collected by W. M. Rossetti); Swinburne, *The Tale of Balen*
1898	Death of Edward Burne-Jones
1899	(–1902) Second Anglo-Boer War
1900	Death of John Ruskin
1901	Death of Queen Victoria; accession of Edward VII; facsimile edition of *The Germ* published

ELIZABETH PRETTEJOHN

Introduction

'I cannot compliment them on common sense in choice of a *nom de guerre*', wrote John Ruskin in a letter to the editor of *The Times* published on 13 May 1851, the first time he commented on the work of the Pre-Raphaelite Brotherhood.[1] The reservation came in the context of a stirring defence of the controversial group, and in one way Ruskin was right: the word 'Pre-Raphaelite' has caused problems for the group's reputation ever since. Arguably the allusion to the art of a pre-modern age has prevented the artists and writers who adopted the label from being given their due as the first of the modernist avant-gardes. Moreover, the word can be criticized for over-complexity. It refers to the art of an age not precisely before Raphael himself, but rather before his followers and imitators, the 'Raphaelites'. To be 'Pre-Raphaelite', then, is not just to look back to an archaic past; it is also defiantly to reject the idea of following in the footsteps of a master or school. The word thus carries a modernist implication difficult to disentangle from its archaizing one, something that has caused critical problems throughout the century and a half from the formation of the PRB to the present day.

Yet in another sense Ruskin was spectacularly wrong. The word 'Pre-Raphaelite' is perhaps the most successful label ever devised for an English artistic movement, still more widely familiar than such labels as 'Vorticism', or even 'the YBAs'; it makes an effective brand name across the spectrum from scholarly journal articles through museum exhibitions to greetings cards. So familiar, indeed, is the label that we may forget to notice how strange it is. It is not easy to pronounce, and there is a flavour of jargon about it; it sounds like a term of scholarly art history rather than the slogan for a group of young rebels. In that respect, however, it was brilliantly calculated to capture the attention of an age that was just beginning to organize its discussions of art and literature historically. It is the obvious precursor of the many style labels that adopt a temporal prefix, from Roger Fry's coinage of 1910, 'Post-Impressionist', through to 'Pre-Columbian', 'Neo-Romantic' or 'Postmodern'. In a famously waspish review of 1850,

Charles Dickens ridiculed the ungainliness of the prefix along with its 'retro-gressive' implications. He invents a 'Pre-Newtonian Brotherhood' for civil engineers who reject the laws of gravity, a 'Pre-Harvey-Brotherhood' of sur-geons who refuse to acknowledge the circulation of the blood, a 'Pre-Gower and Pre-Chaucer-Brotherhood' (or 'P. G. A. P. C. B.') who wish to restore old English spellings.[2] Dickens's wit calls attention to another function of the name, a kind of subversive analogue for a professional association; the initials 'P. R. B.', appended to a painter's signature, mock the conventional sign of academic status, 'R. A.' (for Royal Academician, a full member of the Royal Academy of Arts).

Neither Ruskin in the Pre-Raphaelites' defence, nor Dickens on the attack, succeeded in mitigating the label's polemical edge, which indeed their vivid responses may have helped to publicize. Both texts also interpret the word unequivocally as an intervention into contemporary debates about paint-ing. This is logical enough, in view both of the primary designation of the word and of its extended connotations, yet it raises a question scarcely less significant than that of the relation of archaism to modernism in the move-ment's endeavours. As the chapters in this *Cambridge Companion* demon-strate, Pre-Raphaelitism as we now understand it designates a movement in English literature as much as it does the corresponding movement in the visual arts. How then should we interpret the relationship between the vis-ual and the literary arts, between drawing and painting on the one hand and reading and writing on the other, in a movement that takes its name so obviously from the history of painting?

One way of addressing the question is an appeal to history, something that the Pre-Raphaelites' own historical consciousness would seem to sanc-tion. A preliminary analysis might award the primacy to painting, not just in the choice of name, but also in the composition of the original Brotherhood, six of whose seven members were aspiring artists: James Collinson, William Holman Hunt, John Everett Millais, Dante Gabriel Rossetti and Frederic George Stephens had met one another as painting students in the Royal Academy Schools, where Thomas Woolner trained as a sculptor. The first documents of the group are drawings made in the earliest days of their association, and they made their first public appearance as painters, in the London exhibitions of 1849, the first exhibiting season after the group was formed, apparently in the autumn of the previous year.

Yet these first paintings, like the group's early drawings, were literary – not just in the simple sense that they drew their subject matter from literary sources such as the English Romantic poets, Dante and Boccaccio, but also because they were steeped in the young artists' reading; even their know-ledge of Italian painting before Raphael came as much through the growing literature of art history as it did from the study of visual sources. While the first paintings were on display the seventh Brother, William Michael Rossetti (also the real brother of Dante Gabriel), began to keep a journal of the group's activities, the earliest sign of a determination to write the movement into the historical record. The very first entry, made on 15 May 1849, shows the group engaged in reading and writing alongside drawing and painting. Millais was writing a poem, while Stephens sat to him for the figure of Ferdinand in his subject from Shakespeare's *The Tempest* (*Ferdinand Lured by Ariel*, The Makins Collection). On the same day D. G. Rossetti completed his drawing from Dante's *Vita Nuova*, intended for presentation to Millais (Figure 2), and recited a poem of his own as well as one by Coventry Patmore, which the assembled Brothers 'minutely analyzed'. William himself was contemplating a subject from Patmore, for a drawing or painting, on which Millais advised him.[3] The entry gives a vivid sense of the collaborative spirit within the group; it also shows all of the Brothers trying their hands at both literary and visual media. Christina Rossetti, regarded from the start as a 'sister' to the Brotherhood, also tried drawing and painting as well as poetry, and throughout the journal the artist-Brothers engage in intensive discussions of literature, past and present.

It was not long before they introduced their writing, both critical and creative, to the public, in a magazine that ran for just four issues early in 1850, under William's editorship. Some such title as 'Pre-Raphaelite Journal' or 'P. R. B. Journal' was contemplated and rejected – not, apparently, because the word 'Pre-Raphaelite' was thought inapplicable to writing, but rather because the contributors included a wider circle of friends and associates as well as the members of the PRB proper.[4] The eventual title, *The Germ*, emphasized the forward-looking over the retrogressive aspect of the movement, and the publication anticipated the 'little magazines' of later avant-garde movements not only in its manifesto character but also in its utter failure to cover its costs. As William later put it, the magazine was 'a most decided failure' in commercial terms.[5] As part of a rescue attempt, the third issue re-launched the project under a new title, *Art and Poetry: Being Thoughts towards Nature: Conducted principally by Artists*, and with a clearer statement of how writing was to function within the project: 'With a view to obtain the thoughts of Artists, upon Nature as evolved in Art, in another language besides their *own proper* one, this Periodical has been established.'[6]

This would seem to suggest that the Pre-Raphaelites thought of themselves first as visual artists, and only secondarily as writers. That was how the critic David Masson took the project in 1852, when he reviewed *The Germ* alongside the paintings exhibited that year: 'As might be expected,

Pre-Raphaelitism expresses itself far better on canvas than on paper.'[7] Masson traced the primary impulse back to the poetic innovation of Wordsworth, the desire to strip away the conventions of established literary practice by 'looking directly to Nature' (75). Yet it was the effort to 'apply the same theory to art' that led to the distinguishing feature of Pre-Raphaelitism, its adoption of models from painting before the age of Raphael as a way of stripping away the conventions of later art. Pre-Raphaelite writing, in Masson's account, simply borrows this procedure from painting: 'Now, if the Pre-Raphaelites were to write prose or verse, the very same feeling which makes them Pre-Raphaelites in painting, would lead them to outdo even the simplicity of Wordsworth, by a return to the more archaic simplicity of the writers of the time of Dante'; 'what strikes us most', in the writings of *The Germ*, 'is the archaic quaintness of their style, which is precisely such as would be formed now-a-days by a passionate study of the *Vita Nuova* of Dante, or of parts of the *Decameron* of Boccaccio' (80). Painting, in this account, is the primary Pre-Raphaelite art form, and Pre-Raphaelite writing may be said to deserve the name because it borrows its basic procedure from the sister art.

It may not be so easy, however, to distinguish among the primary sources for Pre-Raphaelite style in the two arts: by 1852 the *Vita Nuova* of Dante and the stories of Boccaccio's *Decameron* had already inspired drawings and paintings by the Pre-Raphaelites, and the mission statement in the third issue of *The Germ* provides a different rationale for the primacy of paint-ing. The magazine's distinctive characteristic, or selling point, was that its contributors were practising artists rather than professional writers. This was not, however, a matter of being specially qualified, by virtue of their artistic training, to write about visual art. A generation later, James McNeill Whistler would argue that only practitioners were competent to comment on the art form they practised, but that is not the emphasis in *The Germ*. While there were notable contributions on the visual arts, such as F. G. Stephens's 'The Purpose and Tendency of Early Italian Art' or Ford Madox Brown's 'On the Mechanism of a Historical Picture', poetry and literary criticism accounted for the large majority of the contents (see Appendix One). The artists' writings were to be valued precisely because they were 'in another language than their *own proper* one' – something like the opposite of Whistler's later argument.[8] The adoption of an unfamiliar 'language' can be seen as an alternative method of starting afresh from first principles. As unprofessional writers, the artists could claim to bypass the conventions of established literary practice, just as they attempted to renounce the con-ventions of the art schools by looking to 'Pre-Raphaelite' models for their visual works. When Masson called several of the contributions to *The Germ* 'juvenile and immature' (84), he meant it as a criticism; yet the words indicate some kind of success in casting off the polish and sophistication of current literary convention.

The obvious corollary would be that someone untrained in painting might bring a special freshness to that medium, and indeed a notable feature of the PRB was that a relative beginner such as Dante Gabriel Rossetti was able to produce striking results in the very first oil paintings he made, *The Girlhood of Mary Virgin* (Figure 6) and *Ecce Ancilla Domini!* (Tate). The ideal Pre-Raphaelite might be someone untrained in either painting or poetry, who could work unfettered by existing conventions in either medium. Elizabeth Siddall, who entered the Pre-Raphaelite circle in late 1849 or early 1850, came close to fitting that description, and her poems and drawings were admired for an imaginative power that seemed to come across the more directly in that it was expressed in a simplified technique. Later in the 1850s, the ideal was still in place when Edward Burne-Jones and William Morris took up the visual arts without the benefit of an art school training (as undergraduates, they were also involved in a successor project to *The Germ*, another short-lived 'little magazine' called *The Oxford and Cambridge Magazine*).

Both the stylistic archaism to which Masson called attention and the unprofessional writing of *The Germ* are referred to a more basic aim, that of stripping away conventions in an effort to start afresh from first principles. Both Masson (with reference to Wordsworth) and *The Germ* describe this as a return in some sort to 'Nature', in formulations that seem typical of the nineteenth century, but the underlying idea remains powerful in later modernisms. Stéphane Mallarmé puts it well in his article of 1876 on a movement that is often seen as the originary avant-garde in painting, French Impressionism:

> In extremely civilized epochs the following necessity becomes a matter of course, the development of art and thought having nearly reached their far limits – art and thought are obliged to retrace their own footsteps, and to return to their ideal source, which never coincides with their real beginnings. English Praeraphaelitism, if I do not mistake, returned to the primitive simplicity of medieval ages.[9]

The Pre-Raphaelites might also remind us of a parallel to a much earlier modernism, that of the turn of the fourteenth century: in Canto XXIV of the *Purgatorio* (the central book of the *Divine Comedy*), Dante describes the 'sweet new style' (*dolce stil novo*) of his own poetic circle as an exact record of the dictation of Love.[10]

The idea of starting afresh from first principles is the most classic, then, of modernist moves. As R. H. Wilenski put it in his defence of the modernist sculptors in 1932, 'they began by assuming, for the moment, that no one had ever made sculpture before and that it was their own task to discover the nature of the activity in which they were about to be engaged.... They began, that is to say, at the beginning'.[11] Both of the Pre-Raphaelite procedures, stylistic archaism and writing or painting as a beginner, are means to a similar end, but unlike Wilenski's and many other formulations of the later modernist avant-gardes they are not medium specific. Despite the apparent priority of painting in the history of Pre-Raphaelitism, and even in its chosen name, the project belonged no more properly to painting than to literature, or rather its ways of starting afresh from first principles were equally applicable to both arts. Either the writer or the painter might take inspiration from models that dated from before the conventions had (putatively) set in, or the beginner in either medium might work untrammelled by academic convention.

The first procedure is vulnerable to the charge of archaism, the second to that of amateurism, and both have been levelled at the Pre-Raphaelites. Yet from the perspective of twentieth-century modernism there is a more damning charge. Pre-Raphaelitism would seem to be a classic example of what the great American critic of modernist painting, Clement Greenberg, called the 'confusion of the arts' – where painting is contaminated by narrative or literary allusion – and the Pre-Raphaelites duly appear in his list of artists who represent an 'all-time low'.[12] Although the Pre-Raphaelite procedures are perfectly cogent ways of starting afresh from first principles, they became unrecognizable as such for most of the twentieth century.

Perhaps, though, the Pre-Raphaelite project is better understood not as a 'confusion of the arts', but rather as an attempt to break down the boundaries between them, boundaries that had themselves come to seem conventional. The enthusiasm for trying one's hand at any medium, already apparent in the first entry of the *P. R. B. Journal*, doubtless reflects the reckless confidence of youthful inexperience, but it is also closely related to a distinctive feature of Pre-Raphaelitism, to which several of the contributors to this *Companion* call attention, its readiness to transgress the conventional boundaries between art forms, and moreover between the creative arts and those activities more usually considered scholarly, art-historical or critical. Thus we have not only 'literary' painting and 'pictorial' poetry, but also art criticism by poets, literary criticism by artists, and works in a variety of media that engage with the emerging scholarly discipline of art history, or that conduct criticism through creative means. Most of these boundary-crossing forms were already present in the writings of *The Germ* and in the earliest drawings and paintings of the PRB, albeit sometimes in 'juvenile and immature' forms.

This brings us back to the question posed at the outset: How then should we interpret the relationship between the visual and the literary arts, between drawing and painting on the one hand and reading and writing on the other, in a movement that takes its name so obviously from the history of painting? The answer must be a capacious one. Neither the literary nor the visual arts can be said to have taken chronological precedence; still less did Pre-Raphaelitism set up any kind of hierarchy between them. Nor did it prescribe the forms their cross-currents and reciprocities might take. Pre-Raphaelitism was both a literary and an artistic movement; or perhaps it would be better to say that it was neither, in that it refused to recognize the difference as meaningful.

That makes the study of the Pre-Raphaelites important in the scholarly disciplines of both art history and English literature, not to mention a multitude of related fields and sub-disciplines – museum studies, comparative literature, the histories of taste and criticism, for example. Hence the remarkable proliferation in the scholarly literature on the Pre-Raphaelites in the past half-century, what William E. Fredeman, himself one of the most productive of Pre-Raphaelite scholars, has called a 'growth industry'.[13] Yet the disciplinary arrangements in our universities and art galleries also tend to segregate the studies of Pre-Raphaelite art and Pre-Raphaelite literature from one another. Pre-Raphaelite literature is the province of university English departments and scholarly journals; its focus is on criticism, with an emphasis on individual poets or poems rather than on the wider collaborations within the group as a whole. Pre-Raphaelite visual art, on the other hand, has been explored most extensively in exhibitions and their accompanying catalogues, as well as the catalogues of the museum collections that house Pre-Raphaelite works and catalogues raisonné on individual artists; these provide superb venues for exploring the inter-relationships among visual works, but divorce them misleadingly from the web of literary relationships without which they may make little sense. The prejudice against the Victorians, evident in both literary and art-historical scholarship throughout much of the twentieth century, has been more persistent in art history, and studies of Pre-Raphaelite art have been slow to percolate from the museum world (where the Pre-Raphaelites have been perennially popular with wider audiences) into the scholarly journals.

A particularly interesting case is that of Dante Gabriel Rossetti, a figure of commanding importance in both art and literature, but whose reputation is curiously different in the two fields. In literary studies his star has soared, and the intellectual sophistication of his poems as well as his translations from Dante and the other Early Italian poets now seems securely established. Rossetti's high reputation owes much to the endeavours of Jerome McGann, whose essay of 1969, 'Rossetti's Significant Details', has itself attained a lasting fame, and who writes on Rossetti for the present volume; he has now been joined by a new generation of serious Rossetti scholars in what is now another 'growth industry' within Pre-Raphaelite studies.

In art history Rossetti's reputation has been much more equivocal, and perhaps even damaged by the popularity of his paintings in reproduction; a taint of lubriciousness or vulgarity lingers, and his remarkable experimental techniques in drawing and painting can still be misunderstood as indicating deficient skill. The exhibition on Rossetti, held in 2003 at the Walker Art Gallery, Liverpool, and the Van Gogh Museum, Amsterdam, received far more sympathetic, and intelligent, reviews from continental critics, who were often seeing his work for the first time, than from British critics too bored, or patronizing, to question their own received opinions. The exhibition catalogue, on which I collaborated with distinguished curatorial colleagues from the two exhibiting institutions, is inadequate in its coverage of Rossetti's literary work, despite the manifest importance of the latter to the visual works on display. Although it is, in compensation, much the most up-to-date treatment of Rossetti's work in visual media, it has been largely ignored in subsequent writing on Rossetti from a literary perspective. Now the magnificent web-based archive, *The Complete Writings and Paintings of Dante Gabriel Rossetti*, under McGann's editorship, provides superb coverage of Rossetti's work in all media, with facilities for cross-referencing (it is a good source, too, for Pre-Raphaelitism in general).[14] This, perhaps, is the ideal scholarly medium for Pre-Raphaelitism as a movement both visual and literary, although the digital image remains a poor substitute for the original works in their visual media (including books and manuscripts, whose physical and material presence is always crucial in Rossetti's work).

Rossetti is an extreme case. Nonetheless, there is still a regrettable segregation between the studies of Pre-Raphaelite literature and Pre-Raphaelite art, despite growing recent interest in interdisciplinary scholarship. If the ideal Pre-Raphaelite may be someone equally untrained in either poetry or painting, the ideal Pre-Raphaelite scholar would presumably be someone equally expert in both – a tall order indeed. The more practical alternative, and one more in the Pre-Raphaelites' own spirit of collaboration, is the one adopted in this *Companion*, which brings together leading scholars in the two fields. This seems an obvious course of action, and it is remarkable that it has not been tried before. Although several recent scholarly collections have included contributors from both fields, they are based in one or the other; for example, David Latham's *Haunted Texts* of 2003 and *Writing the Pre-Raphaelites* of 2009, edited by Michaela Giebelhausen and Tim Barringer (both contributors to the present volume), are fine interdisciplinary collections, but the former clearly emanates from a literary perspective, the latter from an art-historical one.[15] Moreover, these and similar volumes are clearly designed to address specialized areas within Pre-Raphaelite studies, rather than serving as general introductions to Pre-Raphaelitism.

Yet a general introduction, covering art and literature together, is just what the student new to Pre-Raphaelitism most needs; it may also be just what the more advanced student or scholar in either art or literature needs, to acquaint herself or himself with the other field. The present volume does not attempt to analyze all of the myriad, and fascinating, interconnections among the Pre-Raphaelite media, or indeed to cover all of the diverse media practised by the Pre-Raphaelites; those are areas for more specialized studies. Its task is simpler and more basic: it aims to explore the whole movement, art and literature together, at an introductory level. Each of the contributors has something fascinating to say about media other than their '*own proper one*', and often they have been able to provide novel insights from the perspective of another discipline. In the main, though, each scholar writes in her or his specialist area. It is rather through the juxtaposition of the essays within the volume as a whole that the *Companion* achieves its aim of presenting Pre-Raphaelite art and literature as integral parts of a collaborative enterprise. The emphasis is on the earlier phase of the movement, from the formation of the PRB through to the 1860s; although all of the contributors suggest the directions in which the artists, writers or themes of their respective chapters would move after this initial period, there is no attempt to cover the more diverse and diffuse developments of the later decades of the nineteenth century, or the many artists and writers of later generations who allied their work in some way to that of the earlier Pre-Raphaelites.

Part One opens the volume with five general chapters on concerns shared widely among the Pre-Raphaelites. The first two form a pair, which deals with the sources and inspirations on which the Pre-Raphaelites drew, from the literature of the past (in Isobel Armstrong's chapter) and the art of the past (in Jenny Graham's). Michaela Giebelhausen's chapter concerns the intellectual background for the movement, with particular emphasis on religion, an area traditionally considered crucial to Pre-Raphaelitism but which has been relatively neglected in recent years. Colin Cruise's chapter on Pre-Raphaelite practices in drawing and Andrew Stauffer's on *The Germ* form a more informal pairing, since they deal with the group's very first experiments in visual and literary production respectively.

Part Two includes chapters on the main protagonists of Pre-Raphaelitism in both arts. The figures chosen for inclusion make a very conventional canon of Pre-Raphaelites. In a volume twice or three times as long, it would no doubt be interesting to include a wider variety of the fascinating 'minor' figures associated with the group, and quite possibly some of them would emerge as not so minor after all. Here, though, the primary aim has been to provide chapters on the most famous figures, the ones that someone coming to the movement for the first time, or someone coming to either the literary or the artistic side of it from a principal expertise in the other side, most needs to know about. The chapters are arranged in a rough chronology, in the order in which each figure became involved with Pre-Raphaelitism. In two cases, Rossetti and Morris, chapters on both their literary and their artistic work have been deemed necessary. Part Two therefore opens with paired chapters on Rossetti, by Jerome McGann and myself. These are followed by chapters on two of the other PRBs, William Holman Hunt (by Carol Jacobi) and John Everett Millais (by Paul Barlow), and on another painter who was of great importance as colleague and mentor to the group from its inception although he never became a PRB, Ford Madox Brown (by Tim Barringer). Next come two figures who might be called Pre-Raphaelite Sisters, involved from the start in the case of Christina Rossetti (by Lorraine Janzen Kooistra) or within a couple of years in that of Elizabeth Siddall (by Deborah Cherry). Paired chapters on Morris, by Jeffrey Skoblow and Imogen Hart, move to what has sometimes been called the 'second phase' of Pre-Raphaelitism, the new group that formed around Dante Gabriel Rossetti in the later 1850s; Morris himself, Edward Burne-Jones (by Caroline Arscott), and Algernon Charles Swinburne (by Catherine Maxwell) had all been Oxford undergraduates, and their involvement shifted the social centre of the group. A final chapter deals with a figure who had in fact been a PRB and of the utmost importance since the earliest days, William Michael Rossetti (by Angela Thirlwell). He appears at the end in acknowledgement of his equally crucial role as chronicler and historian of Pre-Raphaelitism. Painters slightly outnumber poets in this sequence (with Rossetti, Morris and Siddall counted as both), and they predominate in the earlier chapters; starting with Christina Rossetti, there is a more equal balance between poetry and painting. The volume ends with a brief editorial Envoi, which reflects on the Pre-Raphaelites' legacy and proposes some directions for future study.

Many of the contributors have found it useful to make reference to a document from the earliest days, the 'list of Immortals' drawn up in a 'studio conclave' (Hunt's words) in 1848. This is one among many unplanned interconnections that have emerged in the course of writing, but perhaps it is significant that so many of the contributors have found this somewhat eccentric text relevant to the approach of the volume. Mentioned in a letter from Dante Gabriel to William Michael Rossetti of 30 August 1848, the list itself has been transmitted through Holman Hunt's autobiography, where Hunt admits to having omitted the names of a number of contemporaries no longer well-known.[16] Even in its edited form, though, it is further evidence of the interdependence of literature and painting not only to Rossetti, but also to Hunt (usually considered the most singleminded of painters), and it served as some kind of rallying point for their other friends and associates. It includes scientists and political figures as well as artists and writers, and they are freely interspersed, so that the Early English Balladists appear just before Giovanni Bellini, and Leonardo before Spenser (see Appendix Two). The order is broadly, but not slavishly chronological; it ranges from Isaiah and Pheidias to Browning and Flaxman. There is something 'juvenile and imma-ture' about this act of hero worship (along with two heroines, Joan of Arc and Elizabeth Barrett Browning), but also something scholarly and erudite.

The list of Immortals presents a schematic map of the entire history of the arts, in which the PRB has as yet no place, but in relation to which it would shortly begin to position itself. The name 'Pre-Raphaelite', which may still have been under discussion at the time the list was drawn up, does not naively take up a position before Raphael (who appears almost exactly halfway through), but rather implies a perspective on the whole history, 'Raphaelite' as well as 'pre-Raphael'. This is a more complex act of self-positioning than either the simple retrogression that infuriated Dickens, or the modernist claim to begin at the beginning. The following chapters show how persistently, and how variously, Pre-Raphaelite art and literature inter-twined not only with one another, but also with the longer histories in which they strove to take their places.

NOTES

1 Ruskin, vol. XII, p. 321.
2 Charles Dickens, 'Old Lamps for New Ones', *Household Words*, 1 (15 June 1850), pp. 266–7.
3 William E. Fredeman (ed.), *The P. R. B. Journal: William Michael Rossetti's Diary of the Pre-Raphaelite Brotherhood 1849–1853: Together with Other Pre-Raphaelite Documents* (Oxford: Clarendon Press, 1975), p. 3.
4 Ibid., pp. 17, 204–5.
5 *Germ*, 'Introduction by William Michael Rossetti', p. 11.
6 Ibid., printed on end wrappers for nos. 3 and 4 (following pp. 144, 192).
7 David Masson, 'Pre-Raphaelitism in Art and Literature', *The British Quarterly Review*, 16 (1852), repr. in James Sambrook (ed.), *Pre-Raphaelitism: A Collection of Critical Essays* (Chicago and London: The University of Chicago Press, 1974), p. 84 (page references hereafter in text).
8 See 'Mr. Whistler's "Ten O'Clock"' (1888), in James Abbott McNeill Whistler, *The Gentle Art of Making Enemies*, 2nd edn (1892), facsimile reprint (New York: Dover Publications, 1967), pp. 131–59.

9 Stéphane Mallarmé, 'The Impressionists and Edouard Manet', *The Art Monthly Review and Photographic Portfolio*, 30 September 1876, repr. in Charles S. Moffett and others, *The New Painting: Impressionism 1874–1886*, exhibition catalogue (San Francisco: The Fine Arts Museums of San Francisco, 1986), p. 34.

10 *The Divine Comedy of Dante Alighieri*, Italian text with translation and comment by John D. Sinclair, vol. II: *Purgatorio* (Oxford: Oxford University Press, 1971), pp. 310–11 (Canto XXIV, lines 52–60).

11 R. H. Wilenski, *The Meaning of Modern Sculpture* (1932) (Boston: Beacon Press, 1961), p. 84.

12 Clement Greenberg, 'Towards a Newer Laocoon' (1940), *Clement Greenberg: The Collected Essays and Criticism*, ed. John O'Brian, 4 vols. (Chicago and London: The University of Chicago Press, 1986–93), vol. I, pp. 23, 27.

13 William E. Fredeman, 'The Great Pre-Raphaelite Paper Chase: A Retrospective', in David Latham (ed.), *Haunted Texts: Studies in Pre-Raphaelitism in Honour of William E. Fredeman* (Toronto: University of Toronto Press, 2003), p. 211.

14 www.rossettiarchive.org

15 Latham, *Haunted Texts*; Michaela Giebelhausen and Tim Barringer (eds.), *Writing the Pre-Raphaelites: Text, Context, Subtext* (Farnham, Surrey and Burlington, Vermont: Ashgate, 2009).

16 DGR *Correspondence*, vol. I, p. 71 (letter 48.10); Hunt, vol. I, pp. 158–60.

PART ONE

Pre-Raphaelitism

I

ISOBEL ARMSTRONG

The Pre-Raphaelites and literature

A list of Immortals

> Hunt and I have prepared a list of Immortals, forming our creed and to be pasted up in our study for the affixing of all decent fellows' signatures. It has already caused considerable horror among our acquaintance: I suppose we shall have to keep a hairbrush.[1]

At the end of August 1848, at the height of his friendship with William Holman Hunt, and just as Pre-Raphaelite theories were beginning to emerge among a group of artist friends, Dante Gabriel Rossetti wrote about this iconoclast project to his brother, William. The list of 'Immortals' was intended to make people's hair stand on end (Dante Gabriel was alluding to the Latin sense of 'horror'). Hence the need for a hairbrush. The list, on the principle of a Michelin Guide, gave star ratings on a scale of four to none to fifty-seven writers and artists, including Jesus, and a few political figures. 'The first class consists only of Jesus Christ and Shakespeare', Rossetti wrote. Hunt, who reproduced the list in his memoir of the Pre-Raphaelites, actually assigns four stars to Jesus (the only figure to receive four) and three to Shakespeare and 'The Author of Job'.[2] Two-star figures are Homer, Dante, Chaucer, Leonardo da Vinci, Goethe, Keats, Shelley, Alfred (the Saxon king), Landor, Thackeray, Washington and Browning. Boccaccio, Fra Angelico, Elizabeth Barrett Browning, Patmore, Raphael, Longfellow, Tennyson and the 'Author of *Stories after Nature*' (Charles Jeremiah Wells) get one star. Among those who get none are Pheidias, Rienzi, Spenser, Hogarth, Byron, Wordsworth, Michael Angelo, Early English Balladists, Titian, Tintoretto, Cromwell, Poe and Columbus. But their inclusion is intended to signify their importance (see Appendix Two for the complete list).

There does not seem much that is shocking here. No Baudelaire or Sade, authors who became prominent in the much later time of Rossetti's friendship with Algernon Charles Swinburne, Edward Burne-Jones and William Morris. There is no Blake, who was known to Rossetti, but who did not

seem to have been taken up by his friends. But Hunt glossed the iconoclastic intentions behind the list not immediately evident from Rossetti's
letter: it was a 'manifesto of our absence of faith in immortality, save in that
perennial influence exercised by great thinkers and workers'. He quoted
Rossetti's blasphemous 'Creed', which was intended to be a fresh reading of
Christianity as well as a book list and roll call of PRB celebrities:

> We, the undersigned, declare that the following list of Immortals constitutes
> the whole of our Creed, and that there exists no other Immortality than what
> is centred in their names and in the names of their contemporaries, in whom
> this list is reflected:– (vol. I, p. 159)

Hunt, in this much later memoir, hurriedly closed down the possibility that
he might be seen as an infidel, and assured the reader of both his own and
Rossetti's Christian orthodoxy and innate morality. Despite his wilful mis-
recognition of Rossetti's project, this was to some extent an attempted act
of generosity to Rossetti, from whom he had become thoroughly alienated
later in the 1850s. Nevertheless, the 'Immortals' list is invaluable. It points
up the character of the subversiveness of early Pre-Raphaelite thinking. It
is also a way into mapping the networks of reading that underlay the first
phase of Pre-Raphaelite activity, and into understanding what literature and
literary culture meant to the group. It is Rossetti, however, who leads us to
networks of reading in the PRB circle.

I explore the 'Immortals' list as a springboard to understanding the literary
in the movement. Some figures leaned more towards literature than others,
and it is important to understand which core figures are comprehended in
the early phase of Pre-Raphaelitism, to which the list primarily relates, and
which in its second and later phase. Dante Gabriel Rossetti, William Michael
Rossetti, William Holman Hunt, John Everett Millais, Thomas Woolner,
James Collinson and Frederic George Stephens were of course the founding
members of the PRB, circulating round *The Germ*, its aesthetic manifesto.
The poets, Christina Rossetti, William Bell Scott and William Allingham,
and the painter, Ford Madox Brown, were all imaginatively committed to
Dante Gabriel Rossetti, by far the most voracious reader of the set. Coventry
Patmore was also a figure in his circle. After the Brotherhood dissolved in
the early 1850s, it was Rossetti who continued to explore Pre-Raphaelite
thought. His friendships and aesthetic life turned towards Morris, Burne-
Jones and Swinburne. Their periodical was the *Oxford and Cambridge
Magazine*. We can see the link between the first and second phases of Pre-
Raphaelitism in the reprinting of Rossetti's poem, 'The Blessed Damozel',
from *The Germ* by the *Magazine* in 1856. John Ruskin was critic and mentor of both groups, regarded variously with suspicion and enthusiasm. He

took a strong interest in the group's writings, particularly those of Dante Gabriel Rossetti and Elizabeth Siddall, though it is his views on painting that were of course influential and sometimes irritating. The iconoclastic list illuminates the first phase of Pre-Raphaelite activity, with which I am mainly concerned here. But it also contains the seeds of the second phase, to which I will turn briefly at the end of this discussion.

Several significant strands of Pre-Raphaelite reading emerge in the list. Three trends, not always associated with the group, are apparent. First, the list is an indicator of political ideology, so muffled in later memoirs. The political figures – Rienzi, Cromwell, Hampden and Washington – signify a republican and democratic strand of thought, stretching from Renaissance Europe to modern America. Hunt later excused this radicalism: 'like most young men', the group was 'stirred by the spirit of freedom'; the 'tyranny exercised over the poor and helpless' moved them, but this was only a phase of youth (vol. I, p. 114). Later he spoke of the distorting influence of Ford Madox Brown's 'extreme revolutionary ideas' (vol. II, p. 434). Brown had indeed rejoiced in the revolutions of 1848.[3]

Second, the list, featuring Joan of Arc as well as Elizabeth Barrett Browning, is also an indicator of the group's sexual politics and a muted but perceptible feminism. (To live on free and sexually open terms with women was, of course, a male prerogative, but it also meant the granting of certain freedoms to women.) Rossetti 'picked up' copies of the volume *Improvisatrice* by 'L.E.L.' (the initials under which Letitia Elizabeth Landon published) in 1848, and asked William about two of her poems, '"Violet" and "Bracelet"', with respect.[4] He thought that his sister Christina should join the Pre-Raphaelite Brotherhood.[5] He was friend to the feminists, Barbara Bodichon and Bessie Parkes. He asked Robert Browning to thank Elizabeth Barrett Browning for the 'wonderful' *Aurora Leigh*,[6] and dismissed the sexual conventionality of Patmore's *Angel in the House*,[7] as did Brown.

Third, the list demonstrates the Pre-Raphaelite attempt to unite an English literary tradition with a continental tradition, where a pictorial and textual history pre-dated Raphael and brought Italian and Germanic writing together. Dante and Boccaccio come together with Chaucer, the Early English Balladists, Spenser, Shakespeare and Milton. As the inclusion of Alfred shows, the list consolidates a thoroughly 'English' tradition, but at the same time this Protestant tradition reached for hybrid alliances with continental source material. This group was fascinated by cultural transmission and the assimilation and transformation of texts. Rossetti admired Brown's *Wycliffe Reading his Translation of the New Testament to John of Gaunt* (1847–8, Cartwright Memorial Hall, Bradford).[8] Hunt, not in general an admirer of Brown, nevertheless mentions his *Chaucer Reading* the 'Legend of Custance' to Edward III and his Court (Figure 12) in his memoir (vol. I, p. 123). The interest follows through to William Morris's Kelmscott Chaucer (1896). It is manifested in the use of Germanic material, from Arthurian to Norse legend, that characterizes the later phase of Pre-Raphaelite writing in particular. But there was also an eager hybridizing that rejoiced in mixing literary forms and traditions. Keats's 'Isabella and the Pot of Basil', for instance, combining a Boccaccian story with a form that develops from English ballad narrative, loosened to the short legend or tale, attracted Hunt and Millais as a subject for painting. The eclecticism of this movement is deliberate. They were determined to be transgressive, hybridizing genres and mixing styles both in literature and art.

These three trends could well do with more extended discussion. However, the list is above all an indicator of the fractured nature of Pre-Raphaelite aesthetic theory and of the texts – often the same texts – that held the group together and broke it apart. The way the group thought about modern poetry, particularly the poetry of Keats and Tennyson, is one aspect of this fissure. 'Ut pictura poesis': the poem might be a picture, but the picture was itself a poem. Transgressive hybridity extended from mixed genres to mixed art forms, as painting and poetry were crossed with one another. The pressing question was how the picture poem and the poem picture could be developed out of the work of Keats and Tennyson, pictorializing poetry and textualizing painting. Yet if the idea of the contemporary was a problem, so too was the meaning of the past. How Dante came to figure for the group posed equally difficult problems. Here Rossetti's strange interest in Charles Jeremiah Wells (a little-known writer and friend of Keats, who seemed to Rossetti to hold the key to his aesthetic, but an anomalous presence among poets such as Shakespeare and Dante) begins to make sense. I will return to Wells later in this discussion.

Arguably the list represents the effort of Rossetti's troubled but searching sacrilegious sacramentalism to come up with a reading of modernity that would incorporate an earlier tradition by revising its historical meaning, including the meaning of Christianity. If we foreground the importance of the contemporary and historical text for the Pre-Raphaelites, the rather banal issue of the return to nature, enshrined in the Pre-Raphaelite creed by Hunt and Millais, and the association of the group with microscopic detail, initiated by Ruskin, takes on a different aspect.

Modern and contemporary writing

To turn to two-star Keats and one-star Tennyson, the moderns who dominate the pictorial themes of the Pre-Raphaelites, their peculiar importance can begin to be understood through the absence of images drawn from novels in most Pre-Raphaelite works. There is only one novelist in the list, Thackeray: Millais became the great friend of the novelist later in his life;[9] Brown read *The Newcomes* to see what Thackeray had to say about artists' lives (he was sceptical).[10] Hunt recalls his early delight in Dickens's *Barnaby Rudge* (vol. I, p. 23), and Rossetti also read the novel as a boy.[11] Rossetti read Walter Scott, Edward Bulwer Lytton and the French novelist Eugène Sue (*Le Juif errant*) avidly. (He asked his brother not to give away the ending of Sue's *Barbe-Bleue*.[12]) He read George Sand and other Dickens works,[13] liked *Adam Bede*,[14] and, in 1854 – 'the first novel I've read for an age' – admired *Wuthering Heights*. 'But it is a fiend of a book – an incredible monster, combining all the stronger female tendencies from Mrs. Browning to Mrs. Brownrigg. The action is laid in Hell – only it seems places & people have English names there' (Elizabeth Brownrigg, a midwife, murdered a workhouse inmate and was hanged at Tyburn in 1767).[15] Rossetti loved murders and the darkness of the Gothic.[16] The *Castle of Otranto* was among the earliest books he read. The darkness was real. Just before the Immortals list he tells his brother half-jokingly of another scandalous club, a 'Mutual Suicide Association' he and Hunt created for those 'weary of life'.[17]

But it was not a question of placing an ideal Keatsian or Tennysonian poetic world over against the harsh realism of the novel, or pitting the past against the contemporary. The presence of Poe in the list, poet and storyteller, shows that the dark and nightmare world could inhabit poetry and prose, an imagined past or modern scene. When John Lucas Tupper (a sculptor and Pre-Raphaelite associate) wrote in *The Germ* that art could comprehend battles, murders and executions, he was not confining this material to the modern subject only, or only to novels. Paintings and poems alike must exploit such material.[18] What Rossetti was seeking was a form of writing in which the everyday was transvalued, imbued with intense sacramental meaning at the same time as remaining the everyday, whether that meaning reached into heaven or hell. Except in rare cases, such as *Wuthering Heights*, the novel was not capable of achieving this transvaluation, for him at least. For instance it was Scott's ballad poems rather than his novels that he preferred.[19] He was critical of the Spasmodics and Alexander Smith, poets though they were, because he thought they remained with the realism of psychological display only, rather than achieving the fusion of immediate sensuous experience and sacralized feeling, the one generating the other, for which he sought. Criticizing William Allingham's 'The Music Master' in a letter to the poet of June 1855, he confessed to a 'need, in narrative dramatic poetry … of something rather "exciting," & indeed I believe something of the "romantic" element, to rouse my mind to anything like the moods produced by personal emotion in my own life.... Keats's narratives would be of the kind I mean'.[20] The fact that he first wrote 'schoolgirl' for 'romantic' shows the sort of risks Rossetti's sensuous sacramentalism took. Allingham's poem, he went on to say, chiefly awakens contemplation, 'like a walk on a fine day with a churchyard in it, instead of rousing one like a part of one's own life and leaving one to walk it off *as one might live it off*' (my emphasis).[21] The transvaluation he sought was not transcendental but enabled one to 'live it'. In a letter to Patmore later that year he wrote of the '*spiritual* type', and of Millais's 'trifling fancy' in *Christ in the House of His Parents* (Figure 4), in which 'the symbolism is not really inherent in the fact, but merely suggested or suggestible, & having had the fact made to fit it'.[22] Symbolism 'inherent in the fact' was a modern or secular form of the Incarnation, arising out of what Tupper called 'sensory-organic' experience.[23]

It was over Keats that the Pre-Raphaelites bonded. They also bonded over Tennyson, particularly 'The Lady of Shalott', and here the different emphases of their aesthetic can be seen, as we shall explore at the end of this section. Coventry Patmore's poems were of less intense interest to them, though Millais painted a scene of foreshadowed seduction from Patmore's 'The Woodman's Daughter' (1850-1, Guildhall Art Gallery, London). Byron, but not Wordsworth, was a favourite (though Ruskin gave Elizabeth Siddall a copy of Wordsworth's poetry[24]). 'He's good, you know, but unbearable', Rossetti wrote to Allingham of Wordsworth in 1859.[25] We must assume that he shared Keats's view of Wordsworth as the 'egotistical sublime'. He sought out Keats's contemporary, Leigh Hunt. Rossetti in particular adored Browning. Famously, he wrote the fan letter of 1847 that brilliantly connected Browning with the anonymously published *Pauline* (1830), the first poem Browning published.[26] It testifies to Rossetti's capacity for research as well as his critical flair that he identified the poem while reading in the British Museum Library. He was thrilled when Browning quoted part of his own poem, 'The Blessed Damozel', when they at last met.[27] He made enthusiastic plans to go with Holman Hunt, Woolner and his brother to Browning's incest play, *A Blot in the Scutcheon*, in 1848: 'real, intrinsic, and unconventional purity ... never fails to excite the moral execration of the enlightened Briton [but] virtue is less sensitive at Islington' (it was played at Sadler's Wells).[28] Rossetti's unfinished painting, '*Hist!' said Kate the Queen*, is taken from *Pippa Passes*, the love of a page for a high-born lady. Yet at the famous reading, by Browning of 'Fra Lippo Lippi' and by Tennyson of *Maud*, sketched by Rossetti in 1855, his admiration for Tennyson, in spite of the repetitious grumbling of that poet, almost equalled that for Browning.[29] For Browning never entered the Pre-Raphaelite imaginary as fully as Tennyson. For them Tennyson inherited the Keatsian mode. Tennyson was the poet who made possible what Ruskin asked for – a poet on canvas: 'a poet on canvas is exactly the same species of creature as a poet in song'.[30] And Tennyson generated the agonistic sexuality the PRB saw as a product of Victorian modernism.

A 'common enthusiasm for Keats brought us into intimate relations', Hunt wrote of himself, Millais and Rossetti in the late 1840s (vol. I, p. 107). Hunt and Millais argued over whether 'The Eve of St Agnes' or 'Isabella' was the greater poem (vol. I, p. 79). Rossetti's favourite was 'The Eve of St Agnes' (vol. I, p. 105). The escape of Porphyro and Madeline was a key moment for the Brotherhood. Hunt described it, rather unconvincingly, as the 'sacredness of honest responsible love' (vol. I, p. 85). But like 'Hyperion' it was a model of what it meant to break away from antecedents – and from conventional morality – in a 'progressive' move (vol. I, p. 88). The group read Monckton Milnes's *Life and Letters of Keats* together on a trip up the Thames to Greenwich (vol. I, p. 114). Keats, Rossetti wrote to his brother in 1848, speaking of Milnes's *Life*, was a 'glorious fellow', who had, like the Brotherhood, concluded that the early Italian painters 'surpassed even Rafael himself!!!'.[31]

They painted from Keats and returned to Keats. For when they spoke of modern subjects the Pre-Raphaelites comprehended in this not only the use of contemporary subjects, breaking away from historical and genre painting, but the *modern materials* offered by contemporary culture, including literary culture, and whatever histories modernity drew upon. This is what Ruskin meant when, quoted by Hunt, he wrote of the power in 'modern life' (vol. II, p. 428). That is why Millais could portray the violence of Lorenzo in his *Isabella* of 1849 (Figure 10), for the Boccaccio story was mediated by a modern, Keats. For this group the sexual liberation of Porphyro and Madeline stood for the sensuous immediacy that emancipation could achieve.

When Hunt spoke of 'Nature's principles of design' (vol. I, p. 112), 'Nature's' poetics meant painting out of doors, 'direct on the canvas itself, with every detail I can see, and with the sunlight brightness of the day itself' (vol. I, p. 91). This kind of painting achieved, he thought, the immediate sensory experience absent from the conventional post-Raphaelite rules, abstractly quantifying proportions of light and shade, grouping and architectural balance, pilloried in Ruskin's pamphlet on Pre-Raphaelitism.[32] It did not necessarily mean 'microscopic' detail, an element that Ruskin introduced into the debate in what was actually a critique of Millais, for Ruskin always believed in painting what the eye, not the microscope, could see.[33] It *did* mean sensuous plenitude. That's why it was not Wordsworthian, though the doctrine of 'Nature' might suggest that it should be. Keatsian plenitude is what Rossetti had in mind when he wrote to Christina in 1853 asking her to render sentiment or narrative 'from real abundant Nature' rather than from 'dreamings'.[34] (She did this, of course, in the confounding 'Goblin Market', her long fairy-tale poem published in 1862.) Hunt tells how he sat up all night learning the doctrine of nature from Ruskin's *Modern Painters* like a revelation. But Hunt, when he later allied himself and Millais against Rossetti, speaking of 'our principles', interpreted 'Nature' with a narrow literalism (vol. I, p. 112). For him, sanitizing Pre-Raphaelite principles from a distance in time, this meant mimetic exactitude and perspective, as also for Millais (professedly not the intellectual of the group), who was Hunt's faithful echo – we 'must take Nature as [our] only guide'.[35]

But if one thinks of the Pre-Raphaelite poem as picture, and the picture as poem, through Keats's work, then both art forms 'read' textually through image, scene and narrative. At the same time both repudiate the disembodied eye, the abstract scopism of their culture; both attempt to represent a sensory state where eye and touch are not severed. The eye feels, touch sees. Eye and touch mediate image or scene by reading each other. This is how the embodied transvaluation of the actual occurs and this is what 'nature' is. The paradigm for this is sexual experience. There is a politics here as the political is the private.

Moxon's illustrated Tennyson of 1857, the volume to which Hunt, Millais and Rossetti contributed illustrations, shows what fissured the group. Hunt took 'The Lady of Shalott' and the line 'The Mirror cracked from side to side' as the subject of his wood engraving, later to become a painting (Figure 1). Rossetti also illustrated 'The Lady of Shalott' and chose the final part of the poem, where Sir Lancelot muses, 'She has a lovely face'. Among Millais's Tennysonian subjects, mostly in modern dress, 'Mariana' is typical.[36]

Each illustration figures foiled desire. Hunt's turbulent image has the Lady standing in the centre of her mirrored chamber, caught in the toils of her own web, the circular rhythms of the engraving suggesting how she is physically caught in the circle of repetitious exchange between image and representation. Much later Hunt glossed his painting in terms of psychology and symbol (and in a way much less interesting than the actual picture) rather than the alienated eye: 'The parable, as interpreted in this painting, illustrates the failure of a human soul towards its accepted responsibility.'[37] Abrogating her task of portraying the Christian court of Arthur, with its many emblems of the religious life, the soul's act of rebellion, moral and sexual, is destructive. This kind of symbolism was what Hunt constantly sought. Ruskin's symbolic reading of Tintoretto's *Annunciation*, in which the ruined stable represented the ruined Jewish church, delighted him (vol. I, p. 90). But it was exactly this kind of mistakenly literary symbolic narrative that Rossetti deprecated. Symbol was the other side of Hunt's literalism. It split the world between body and soul, material and immaterial, real and unreal, and created a dualism that banished true sacramental materialism from the everyday and located it in an abstract, disembodied spirituality. Even at the height of their friendship he joked about Hunt's metaphysical tendencies – 'the metaphysico-mysterioso-obscure'.[38]

Rossetti's own engraving abandons perspective (over which he and Hunt had a 'constant argument'),[39] and presents the immensely elongated, angular figure of Lancelot looming obliquely above the lady's undulating form. Lancelot's misprision and the gap between the man and the woman are incorporated into the picture through line and through this perspective, askance and distorting as they are. There is no detached symbol here. Lancelot's form seems built into the insistent angularity of the architecture itself, becoming a part of its heavily bent and crooked lines, whereas the Lady floats free from it. Rossetti's need to bring symbol and fact together is at work here, as touch is structurally estranged from sight. The illustrations caused him much pain. He was always worried that the artist's own 'allegory' might be 'killing' a 'distinct idea of the poet's'.[40]

Millais's illustrations are different again. They foreground a single figure at the crisis of a narrative. His are highly plotted pictures, implying a story, novelistic in a way that Hunt's and Rossetti's are not. The despairing Mariana, in modern dress (she is wearing a hat), has hurled herself forward on a padded window seat. The contours of her body have the same tactile quality as the cushions, trapped in the cell-like space. Isolated modern subjects recur: 'Locksley Hall' figures two lovers kissing in a lonely seascape.

Thus, in its use of contemporary materials, the group fractures into three forms of the literary – symbol (Hunt), narrative (Millais) and the icon that fuses meaning and materiality (Rossetti). What they still explore, though, are the visual and tactile possibilities of their subjects.

Writers of the past

Two-star Dante and one-star Wells come to the fore in this section. Just as Rossetti's interest in Blake and in *Songs of Innocence and of Experience* was not shared by Hunt and Millais, neither was his delight in Dante. Indeed, the mistaken 'medievalism' – 'of knights rescuing ladies, of lovers in mediæval dress' – of which Hunt accused Rossetti, a serious deviation from the truth to nature of his own and Millais's practice, he thought, derived seemingly from Rossetti's reading of such authors (vol. I, p. 106). Dante Gabriel's commitment to Dante was shared by his two sisters, Christina and Maria. It was of course a family steeped in Dante. Rossetti's father worked on interpreting hidden meanings in Dante's poetry. He was a friend of the Rev. H. F. Cary, who translated the *Divine Comedy* and advised Rossetti senior to publish his work on Dante's secret codes. Maria wrote on Dante.[41] We know that the sisters read John Keble's sacred verse.[42] James Collinson, with his verse tale for *The Germ*, 'The Child Jesus', followed their religious preoccupations.[43] Yet Rossetti himself did not derive conventionally religious poetry from Dante. And in this practice he influenced two other friends, Thomas Woolner and William Bell Scott.

It was Dante's *Vita Nuova* that profoundly shaped Rossetti's thinking. He was translating the *Vita Nuova* as early as 1848 and in 1854 wrote to Allingham of his plans.[44] This work became the volume of 1861, *The Early Italian Poets ... Together with Dante's Vita Nuova*.[45] In it Rossetti presented translations not only of Dante but also of Dante's contemporaries, the sonnets that reply to Dante and answer one another – perhaps the first intertextual anthology. In some ways this volume presents a sublimed understanding of the kind of interpersonal group that Rossetti longed for the Pre-Raphaelites to be. His translations of the sonnets have powerful affinities with those in his own later sonnet sequence, *The House of Life*. At the book's core is Dante's autobiography. Rossetti described its 'extreme sensitiveness': the figure of Beatrice, he said, was 'less lifelike than lovelike': the loved woman, 'the glorious lady of my mind', whom Dante falls in love with at the age of nine and sees again nine years later, is a prototype of almost all Rossetti's female figures.[46] '[F]rom that time forward Love quite governed my soul':

> At that moment, I say most truly that the spirit of life, which hath its dwelling in the secretest chamber of the heart, began to tremble so violently that the least pulses of my body shook therewith ... the animate spirit, which dwelleth in the lofty chamber whither all the senses carry their perceptions, was filled with wonder, and speaking more especially unto the spirits of the eyes, said these words: *Your beatitude hath now been made manifest unto you ... Alas! How often shall I be disturbed from this time forth* [Rossetti's translation of the Latin].[47]

The 'animate spirit': 'spirits of the eyes', presaging 'disturbed' passion; it was from passages like this that Rossetti derived the sacramental eroticism that so troubled his contemporaries (and still troubles us). Visionary and sensuous, addressing the eyes as spirit and the spirit through the eyes, this account of experience saw symbol and fact as one, the lover not as 'lifelike' but as ontologically 'lovelike', 'rousing one like a part of one's own life', as he said to Allingham, so that one 'might walk it off *as one might live it off*.'

The 'glorious lady of my mind', though an object of longing and desire, is not a transcendental figure. She is sought for as the moment of fulfilment when 'Hand and Soul', to use the title of Rossetti's story for *The Germ*, come together. We can trace her in this story and in the poems of Rossetti's contemporaries, Woolner and Bell Scott.

'I am an image, Chiaro, of thine own soul within thee', the mystical lady of 'Hand and Soul' tells the artist.[48] Capable of imagining the 'glorious lady', but betraying the image in a number of ways, through 'cold symbolism' or through an unthinking, demotic existence, Chiaro's physical union with her is no ideal experience, as, tangled in her hair, he literally tastes his tears of shame. These meetings are rarely beatific, simply because the unions of sacramental sexuality are rare and thus constantly betrayed: 'And Chiaro held silence, and wept into her hair which covered his face; and the salt tears that he shed ran through her hair upon his lips; and he tasted the bitterness of shame'.[49] This is a variant of Dante's vision of the death of Beatrice, who is taken up by a weeping figure – 'and as he wept he gathered the lady into his arms'.[50]

The transfiguring woman is a motif in the work of both Woolner and Bell Scott. The title poem of Woolner's *My Beautiful Lady* was first published in *The Germ* and finally published in his collection of 1863.[51] Bell Scott's *Poems*, published in 1854 and described as 'Poems by a Painter', contains, like Woolner's collection, poems that celebrate women whose presence changes the everyday and brings a sensuous spirituality into being.[52] None of these are remarkable poems. They lack the verbal experiment of Rossetti's *House of Life* sonnets, where he learned to make the Dantesque vision belong to an intimate quotidian landscape. But their very lack of complexity exposes the needs of this kind of lyric writing, the need to bring the sexual and the visionary together, to make them interact, and to invest both with a greater depth of passional feeling than convention allows. That is why they are disturbing and often embarrassing – a 'schoolgirl' effect (to recall Rossetti's term that itself recalls the 'cockney' Keats), I believe, however, to be intentional.

In 'Her Shadow', Woolner plays in a painterly way with the hallmark Pre-Raphaelite purple and green, and with the 'leafy mimicry' of shadows and the beauty of the woman's shadow as she walks with the lover. The poem moves from the shadows that can only be made by a physical body to the possibility of the severance of shadow and body. Playing on the ambiguity of 'pass' (passing by and passing away), there is the possibility that the woman will become a 'shade', a ghost, and not the living body that makes a living shadow.

> At matin time when creepers interlace
> We sauntered slowly, for we loved the place,

And talked of passing things; I pleased to trace
Through leafy mimicry the true leaves made
The stateliness and beauty of her shade;

A wavering of strange purples dimly seen,
It gloomed the daisy's light, the kingcup's sheen,
And drank up sunshine from the vital green;
That silent shadow moving on the grass
Struck me with terror it should ever pass (lines 1–10)[53]

Bell Scott's long poem, 'A Dream of Love', moves from a city landscape where the population suffer 'obstruction in their eyes, not death … They lived, yet lived not' (lines 23–5), into the plenitude of a dream wood and the song of a visionary woman. Pain and grief create life: 'Oh Lady, thou art beautiful: and now / The dark hair of thy song doth shade its eyes, / The eyelid of thy music droops: it plains / Slowly and saturated with sweet pain, / carries my soul into a sphered realm / Of everlasting melancholy' (lines 156–61).[54]

The sign of a consummation between material and immaterial, flesh and feeling, for these poets is the kiss. It was so for Rossetti and the kisses of *The House of Life* against which he defended himself years later in the 'fleshly school' controversy.[55] There is much kissing in the poems of Woolner and Bell Scott: 'kissing clung, / Close kisses, stifling kisses … one long, sighing kiss';[56] 'He thought to catch her limber waist, / And another kiss repay'.[57] In such kisses sight reads through touch, touch sees – a kind of Braille of the body.

For the modern reader, used primarily to a simple sexual register in physical contact, these passages are either embarrassingly erotic or comic, and tend to be seen as mystification called forth by the fractures of Victorian culture's increasingly economic subject. They certainly explicitly point to a crisis in sexuality and as explicitly explore it. The fusion of material and immaterial that comes under the sign of the erotic in this poetry is an important aspect of the aesthetic, evolved from Rossetti's reading of Dante, that valued symbol 'inherent in the fact'. Dante and Keats come together here. This reading of symbol was also valued by Swinburne, another 'fleshly poet', and is one of the continuities between first and second-phase Pre-Raphaelitism.

It is here that Rossetti's continued interest in the now obscure Charles Jeremiah Wells, whose anomalous presence in the 'Immortals' list has been mentioned, comes into focus. Wells, friend of Keats (the Keats connection again) and the donor of the roses in Keats's sonnet, 'To a friend who sent me some roses', wrote a series of short chivalric-romantic narratives of war and love that capture the sensory abundance the Pre-Raphaelites looked for. His *Stories after Nature*, inflecting 'nature' as the plenitude of the sensuous, also figure the visionary fleshly woman who later haunted the work of Rossetti and others. An example paralleling the lovers' flight in 'The Eve of St Agnes' is 'Christian and his Companions'.[58] From such tales – not allegories, not symbolic stories, but figuring out meaning by (as Rossetti put it) *'living it off'*, through narrative and fusing fact and meaning – emerge a unique genre of prose fable that we see in Rossetti's 'Hand and Soul', in his sister's fairy tales, in the prose romances of Morris and in the work of Walter Pater. It is a little examined genre of Victorian modernism, making a decision to *live out* aesthetic and philosophical ideas through non-discursive fictions.[59]

The later phase

Wells enables us to make a further genealogical connection. His *Stories*, first published in 1822, were edited in 1891 by W. J. Linton, the engraver of two of Rossetti's designs for the Moxon Tennyson. And there is a further connection. Swinburne edited Wells's drama of 1824, *Joseph and his Brethren*, in 1876. He praised above all the 'life and heat of blood' in Praxanor, Potiphar's wife, set against the 'sentimental chastity' of her maidservant, as the equal of Cleopatra. 'All women in literature after these two seem coarse or trivial when they touch on anything sensual': 'the written words bite and burn'.[60] Praxanor is indeed remarkably Swinburnian: 'The flame rejected by this wall of ice / Returns for ever to consume myself, / Withering in my own remorseful fire'.[61] But she prefigures a violent sexuality very unlike the fleshly visionary woman of the earlier phase.

The turn to Swinburne, to Burne-Jones and Morris, marks a different or more extreme form of the transgressive aesthetic that developed earlier. When he wrote to Swinburne in 1864 about *Atalanta in Calydon* and other planned publications, Rossetti remarked that these would make 'a few not even over particular hairs to stand on end, to say nothing of other erections equally obvious'. The results of reading Baudelaire's 'suppressed poems' would require 'an emetic' to 'relieve the outraged British nature'.[62] These explicit sexual and cloacal puns contrast with the innocent hairbrush required to assuage the shock of the list of 'Immortals' and the 'unconventional purity' earlier attributed to Browning, and suggest why Hunt and Millais distanced themselves from Rossetti. In a letter to Swinburne of 1866, discussing the Moxon English Poets series, it is Byron and Shelley, and above all Blake, who feature now as powerful figures in Rossetti's pantheon.[63] Keats and Wells still have their place (with the eccentric poet Ebenezer Jones), but are less prominent. Blake absorbed his energies when he assisted Anne Gilchrist with the completion of the two-volume *Life of Blake*, which appeared in 1863. Rossetti had acquired a manuscript notebook of Blake's in the late 1840s, but though Blake meant a good deal to him, Blake was not one of the poets that occasioned *group* feeling, as Keats did for the first-phase Pre-Raphaelites. Perhaps the only poet of the first phase who absorbed and developed the almost confounding simplicity of Blake's *Songs of Innocence and of Experience* was Christina Rossetti. She alone understood how to create a crystal lyric that sounded complexity. Blake's prophetic books pre-occupied Rossetti now, not, as earlier, the *Songs*.[64] There is a perceptible shift to the supernatural. Rossetti seems to have reintegrated his early reading of works such as Perrault's *Contes de Fées*[65] and Keightley's *The Fairy Mythology*[66] into his work. In the same letter to Swinburne he mentions 'an admirable fairy tale by my sister' (*Hero. A Metamorphosis*). He was working on 'the design of *Aspecta Medusa*' in 1868.[67] Swinburne's *Notes on the Royal Academy Exhibition, 1868* single out Rossetti's *Lady Lilith* and *Sibylla Palmifera* as 'types of sensual beauty and spiritual, the siren and the sibyl'.[68] The Dantesque vision had mutated.

The death of Elizabeth Siddall in 1862, Rossetti's commitment to the firm of Morris, Marshall, Faulkner & Co., perhaps the publication of Christina Rossetti's *Goblin Market and Other Poems* in 1862, all these mark a shift to what we might think of as late Pre-Raphaelitism, or its second phase. And besides these internal changes, a later stage of capitalism and empire, the strengthening of socialism and a more vehement aestheticizing of the artist in the culture provided the external context for the noticeable shifts in second-phase Pre-Raphaelitism. The reading networks of the second phase were no less complex and fissured. They fall out of the remit of this essay, but cannot be understood without some knowledge of the reading passions of the first phase of Pre-Raphaelitism. It is as if the concerns of the first phase intensified in the 1860s. At once more agonistic and more confident – if not hubristic – the politics became more radical, the reading of sexuality both more flagrant and more conflicted, the experiment with genre more deconstructive. What dominates the second phase is the long poem, and the ambition to deal with these problems on a large scale. We may think of this as an experiment with epic, a genre Herbert Tucker has recently brought into prominence, wholly redefining the genre for the nineteenth century.[69] But these are paradoxical avant-garde epic poems. Implicitly, for this reason, Milton meant more to the second phase than to the first. That is why Rossetti's *House of Life* sonnet sequence must be seen as an attempt to create an epic monument out of the 'moment's monument' of the sonnet, constructing the longest poem from the shortest poems. The avant-garde epic can again be seen in the two 'Tristram' epics by Swinburne and Morris, *Tristram of Lyonesse* and *Tristram and Isolde*. The two phases share a profoundly experimental energy, a willingness to work at the edge of orthodoxy and beyond.

NOTES

1 DGR *Correspondence*, vol. I, p. 71 (letter 48.10).
2 Hunt, vol. I, p. 159 (volume and page numbers hereafter in text).
3 William Michael Rossetti (ed.), *Praeraphaelite Diaries and Letters* (London: Hurst and Blackett, 1900), pp. 86, 136–7; compare Woolner's and W. M. Rossetti's republicanism, p. 225. For D. G. Rossetti's familiarity with revolutionary thought, see DGR *Correspondence*, vol. I, p. 36 (letter 44.3).
4 DGR *Correspondence*, vol. I, p. 70 (letter 48.10).
5 Ibid., p. 66 (letter 48.7).
6 DGR *Correspondence*, vol. II, p. 271 (letter 59.36).
7 Ibid., p. 19 (letter 55.8).
8 DGR *Correspondence*, vol. I, p. 58 (letter 48.3).
9 John Guille Millais, *The Life and Letters of Sir John Everett Millais*, 2 vols. (London: Methuen & Co., 1899), vol. I, pp. 276–8.
10 W. M. Rossetti (ed.), *Praeraphaelite Diaries and Letters*, p. 114.
11 DGR *Correspondence*, vol. I, p. 12 (letter 42.1).
12 Ibid., p. 33 (letter 44.1).
13 Ibid., p. 36 (letter 44.3, Sand); vol. I, p. 32 (letter 44.1, Dickens).
14 DGR *Correspondence*, vol. II, p. 263 (letter 59.27).
15 DGR *Correspondence*, vol. I, p. 381 (letter 54.63).
16 Ibid., p. 126 (letter 49.19).
17 Ibid., p. 71 (letter 48.10).
18 *Germ*, pp. 17–18, 118–25 (John Lucas Tupper, 'The Subject in Art', nos. I and II).
19 DGR *Correspondence*, vol. I, pp. 13–14, 23 (letters 42.2, 43.2).
20 DGR *Correspondence*, vol. II, p. 46 (letter 55.32).
21 Ibid.
22 DGR *Correspondence*, vol. II, p. 73 (letter 55.54).
23 *Germ*, p. 17.
24 DGR *Correspondence*, vol. II, p. 64 (letter 55.46).
25 DGR *Correspondence*, vol. II, p. 282 (letter 59.47).
26 DGR *Correspondence*, vol. I, pp. 45–6 (letter 47.3).
27 DGR *Correspondence*, vol. II, p. 66 (letter 55.48).
28 DGR *Correspondence*, vol. I, p. 79 (letter 48.14).
29 DGR *Correspondence*, vol. II, pp. 80–1 (letter 55.8).
30 Ruskin, vol. XII, p. 352 (from Ruskin's pamphlet, *Pre-Raphaelitism*, 1851).
31 DGR *Correspondence*, vol. I, p. 68 (letter 48.9).
32 Ruskin, vol. XII, p. 353.
33 Ruskin, vol. XII, pp. 359–60; compare Ruskin's letter to *The Times* of 5 May 1854 (Ruskin, vol. XII, pp. 328–32).
34 DGR *Correspondence*, vol. I, p. 293 (letter 53.57).
35 Millais, *Life and Letters*, vol. I, p. 49.
36 Alfred Tennyson, *Poems* (London: Edward Moxon, 1857, and frequently reprinted). For reproductions see *Pre-Raphaelite Illustrations from Moxon's Tennyson* (London: Academy Editions, 1978), plates 1 (Millais), 6 (Hunt), 7 (Rossetti).
37 William Holman Hunt, '*The Lady of Shalott*' by *Holman Hunt*, exhibition catalogue (London: Arthur Tooth & Sons' Galleries, 1905), p. 3.

38 Dante Gabriel Rossetti, *Letters of Dante Gabriel Rossetti*, ed. Oswald Doughty and John Robert Wahl, 4 vols. (Oxford: Clarendon Press, 1965–7), vol. I, p. 40; cf. DGR *Correspondence*, vol. I, p. 69 (letter 48.9; in this edition the reading is 'metaphysico-mysterioso-obscene').

39 Hunt, vol. I, p. 118.

40 DGR *Correspondence*, vol. II, p. 7 (letter 55.4).

41 Maria Francesca Rossetti, *A Shadow of Dante: Being an Essay towards Studying Himself, his World and his Pilgrimage* (London: Rivingtons, 1871).

42 The range of Christina Rossetti's reading, sometimes overlapping with Dante Gabriel's, can be seen in *The Letters of Christina Rossetti*, 4 vols., ed. Antony H. Harrison (Charlottesville and London: University Press of Virginia, 1997–2004).

43 James Collinson's *The Child Jesus* (32 pp.) was published anonymously by the Religious Tract Society in 1855; a version was published in the second number of *The Germ*, pp. 49–57. Rossetti described it as a parable of incarnation, DGR *Correspondence*, vol. I, pp. 73–4 (letter 48.11).

44 DGR *Correspondence*, vol. I, p. 381 (letter 54.63).

45 *The Early Italian Poets: From Ciullo d'Alcamo to Dante Alighieri: (1100–1200–1300): In the Original Metres: Together with Dante's Vita Nuova: Translated by D. G. Rossetti* (London: Smith, Elder and Co., 1861). The book is reproduced in full (images and transcript) in *The Rossetti Archive*.

46 Ibid., pp. 191, 223.

47 Ibid., pp. 224–5.

48 *Germ*, p. 30.

49 Ibid., p. 31.

50 *Early Italian Poets*, p. 227.

51 Thomas Woolner, *My Beautiful Lady* (London: Macmillan and Co, 1863).

52 William Bell Scott, *Poems* (London: Smith, Elder, & Co, 1854; frontispiece illustration inscribed 'Poems by a Painter').

53 Woolner, *My Beautiful Lady*, p. 45.

54 Scott, *Poems*, pp. 138, 145.

55 Isobel Armstrong, *Victorian Poetry: Poetry, Poetics and Politics* (London: Routledge, 1993), pp. 385–7.

56 Woolner, *My Beautiful Lady*, p. 55 ('Tolling Bell', lines 46–9).

57 Scott, *Poems*, p. 73 ('A Bridal Race', lines 17–18).

58 Charles Wells, *Stories after Nature* (1822), with a preface by W. J. Linton (London: Lawrence and Bullen, 1891).

59 For the prose romance and William Morris as a practitioner see Jeffrey Skoblow in this volume, pp. 196–213.

60 Charles Wells, *Joseph and his Brethren: A Dramatic Poem*, with an introduction by Algernon Charles Swinburne (London: Chatto and Windus, 1876), pp. xvi, xiv, xiii, xvi.

61 Ibid., p. 145.

62 DGR *Correspondence*, vol. III, p. 216 (letter 64.161).

63 Ibid., p. 373 (letter 66.3).

64 DGR *Correspondence*, vol. II, pp. 490–1 (letter 62.60).

65 DGR *Correspondence*, vol. I, p. 36 (letter 44.3).

66 Ibid., p. 368 (letter 54.57).

67 DGR *Correspondence*, vol. IV, p. 69 (letter 68.92).
68 William Michael Rossetti and Algernon Charles Swinburne, *Notes on the Royal Academy Exhibition, 1868* (London: John Camden Hotten, 1868), p. 46 (in Swinburne's section).
69 Herbert Tucker, *Epic* (Oxford: Oxford University Press, 2008).

2

JENNY GRAHAM

Artistic inspirations

When Burne-Jones died in 1898, his obituarist in *The Times* lamented that an age of legend, magic and mystery had died with him.[1] 'The tide is running away from Botticelli and Van Eyck, towards Velasquez', explained the newspaper, drawing a neat but predictable line between two epochs of taste: the revivalism of the nineteenth century on the one hand and the incipient modernism of the *fin de siècle* on the other. Then, as now, the Pre-Raphaelites were chiefly associated with the art of the fifteenth century, art before Raphael, which became fashionable with the Victorians. By the time of Burne-Jones's death, another revival was under way, as the *fin de siècle* embraced Velázquez, the old master whose broad, painterly realism had inspired Manet, Whistler and other modern painters. But while Pre-Raphaelitism has rightly retained its place in the cultural imagination as a project inspired by the fifteenth century, its sphere of interest regarding the art of the past was actually broader, its intersection with past and present canons more complex. Indeed, Pre-Raphaelitism was itself a product of the growth of art history in the nineteenth century, the movement's shifting reference points closely allied to developments in the new field. Not only that, but the Pre-Raphaelites influenced that discourse, as crucial a cog in the canon-making machine during the nineteenth century as the museums and old masters that inspired them. Far from dying with Burne-Jones as *The Times* predicted, for example, the interest in Botticelli that he and Rossetti, in particular, had helped to kindle became a serious art-historical effort among scholars between 1900 and 1920, when more books were published on the Italian quattrocentist than on any other old master.[2]

The Pre-Raphaelites were no slavish followers of art-historical fashion, however. At the beginning they knew less at first hand than the previous generation about the early art their name evoked, which had gained ground with British connoisseurs after the Napoleonic Wars fostered a new continental culture of museums. There is no evidence that the group even visited an exhibition in London boasting so-called Giottos, Fra Angelicos and van

Eycks at the British Institution in 1848, the very year of their formation. That is not to say they did not see it, since so little documentation for the group survives from this date. But the anecdote is often repeated by scholars, and has become entangled with an image of the group's youthful folly. It prompted Francis Haskell, for example, the pioneer historian of collecting and taste, to remark during the 1970s, 'I sometimes feel that before 1848 every painter in England had admired the works of the artists preceding Raphael – except those who were to become the Pre-Raphaelites.'[3]

The group's choice of name was a particular problem, then, for critics past and present, because it is extremely unlikely that the group had seen many examples of early Renaissance art at all. Properly understood in the context of the group's inexperience, however, the name serves as a powerful reminder of the extent to which the general principles of revivalism were already at large in the cultures of the nineteenth century. We should also recognize that the Pre-Raphaelites were artists before antiquarians, their allegiance to a notion of the past at first a manifesto against the academic principles of the present. In choosing the name, the group were aligning themselves with a more general air of dissent in the mid-nineteenth-century art world against the traditional worship of Raphael, Reynolds and high academicism. In an age that was already witnessing a full-scale turn by museums and popular book-writers to artists before Raphael, Pre-Raphaelitism represented the culmination rather than the origin of those influences and notoriously ignited a critical backlash against both the group's own and pre-1500s art. This was not simply because the idea of a brotherhood founded on the principles of early art smacked of Catholicism, as scholars have usually pointed out, but also because the group turned what was previously tolerated as a quaint fashion for the 'primitives', inoffensive within the nascent art history, into a polemical form of modern painting.

Modern painters or old masters?

By the time the Brotherhood was formed in 1848, the issue of revivalism was already sufficiently a part of the zeitgeist that it had entered the press. The currency of such ideas followed the acquisition in 1842 of the National Gallery's first primitive, Jan van Eyck's *Portrait of Giovanni Arnolfini and his Wife*, then simply titled 'Portraits of a Gentleman and a Lady', and in the wake of the Westminster fresco competitions of the 1840s.[4] Revivalism could be lampooned in the pages of *Punch*, where the medievalist tendency of designs for the decoration of the new Houses of Parliament was routinely mocked. Revivalism could be the object of savage attack and a subject for serious debate and dissemination. 1848 itself saw the *Illustrated London*

News reporting on a new esteem among collectors for the school of Giotto, his style no 'longer classed with the efforts of South-Sea Islanders',[5] while *Punch*, making fun of the Westminster designs in 1845, advised young artists against the examples of Raphael and Michelangelo, 'their style being a great deal too free and easy, and not at all cramped, stiff, and wooden enough for high art'.[6] From these and other contexts Pre-Raphaelitism emerged in its first form, the tangible manifestation of old and new influences on the modern British school as they were brought into dialogue.

In their earliest encounters with the old masters, Hunt and Millais followed convention, copying at the Dulwich Picture Gallery and the National Gallery from the Netherlandish, Spanish and Italian Baroque revered by Regency collectors: Rubens and Rembrandt, Murillo, the Carracci family and Guido Reni. In 1905, perhaps keen to distance himself from what had become a cliché, Hunt relates how his first idea for the brilliant colours of Pre-Raphaelitism did not come from a fifteenth-century primitive but from the experience of copying another kind of painting in the National Gallery, the early nineteenth-century British artist David Wilkie's *The Blind Fiddler* (1806, Tate). While we would not usually associate with Pre-Raphaelitism a fireside scene inspired by Dutch and Flemish genre painting of the seventeenth century, in a chance encounter in front of the painting Hunt was inspired by a former pupil of Wilkie himself – the fancifully named Claude 'Lorraine' Nursey – to notice its areas of glassy, vivid colour. Only then, Hunt tells us, did he, as a student, drill down to the roots of that inclination by looking at van Eyck's *Arnolfini Portrait*, or two works by Francia, an Italian working a generation before Raphael, which had entered the National Gallery collection in 1841. Hunt also read about quattrocento fresco painting in Luigi Lanzi's *History of Painting in Italy*, a fount of information for would-be revivalists, first translated in the 1810s but reissued in 1847 as a Bohn's Standard Library edition – a series which made scholarly works widely accessible in English – at a time when interest in early Italian art was growing.[7]

Rossetti's formative experience of the old masters likewise began conventionally, by copying a cast at the Royal Academy of Ghiberti's so-called 'Gates of Paradise' (1425–52, Baptistery, Florence), which Academy students had been copying since the time of Sir Joshua Reynolds, first President of the Royal Academy (1723–92).[8] Accordingly, Ghiberti was one of only two genuinely 'Pre-Raphaelite' artists in the list of 'Immortals' drawn up in 1848 when the Brotherhood was founded (see Appendix Two). The other was Fra Angelico, as yet unrepresented at the National Gallery, and whose work Hunt and Rossetti did not know until they saw his *Coronation of the Virgin* at the Louvre during their tour of France and Belgium in 1849.[9] The group's source for their initial admiration of Fra Angelico was literary, one of the many pen portraits popular at this time which presented Vasari's friar in terms entirely sympathetic to the Pre-Raphaelite credo. Fra Angelico's image as a monkish artist free from the corruption of the market, his career an 'unbroken tranquil stream of placid contentment and pious labours', was so described, for example, in Anna Jameson's *Memoirs of the Early Italian Painters* of 1845, which Rossetti was given as a student by his godfather Charles Lyell.[10] Such was the general fashion for Fra Angelico that he was the first artist to be published in 1848 by the Arundel Society, a learned body founded the same year as the Pre-Raphaelite Brotherhood, with the aim of popularizing Italian art before Raphael through cheap prints.[11]

Hence Pre-Raphaelitism was the product of these converging art-historical influences at the mid-century, and encounters with literary and textual sources preceded the group's experience of particular works of early Renaissance art. The second volume of Ruskin's *Modern Painters* (1846) prompted Hunt's admiration for old master works that especially displayed a sense of truth to nature, among them passages of detail to be found in two National Gallery pictures which were post- rather than pre-Raphaelite, the purple irises of Titian's *Bacchus and Ariadne*, for example, or the dandelion clocks of a *St Catherine of Alexandria* by Raphael himself.[12] Similarly, it was Ruskin's account of *The Annunciation* in the Scuola di San Rocco, Venice, by Tintoretto, another post-Raphaelite painter, which gave Hunt his first introduction to the concept of symbolic realism, and not van Eyck's *Arnolfini Portrait* as we might assume.[13]

Rossetti could be equally broad church, in his high regard for Raphael's *Portrait of Baldassare Castiglione* at the Louvre in 1849, say, or in his prose story 'Hand and Soul' (first published in *The Germ*, 1850) which contrasted the modern-day reputations of two imaginary works in Florence's Pitti Palace, a so-called primitive and a Raphael, both of which, it was acknowledged, had their merits. Rossetti's satire on the polarization of early and later art, and those who blindly followed that fashion, reveals a sophisticated understanding of the wider battle which raged at mid-century over Raphael's place in the canon. Influenced by revivalist debates, writers including Ruskin and Anna Jameson began to divide Raphael's oeuvre into early and late phases which, broadly defined as chaste and degenerate, straddled a moment of corruption wrought by the onset of the High Renaissance in Rome.

Rossetti's admiration for a range of early and later Renaissance works is apparent in his series of poems on pictures he saw at home and abroad in 1849, fifteenth-century works by Memling and Mantegna, to be sure, but also Leonardo's *Madonna of the Rocks* (now in the National Gallery) and Giorgione's *Concert Champêtre* at the Louvre, now sometimes attributed to Titian. Rossetti's mode of writing poems about paintings reflects not only Pre-Raphaelitism's aim to combine the arts of word and image, but also the influence, again, of a larger literary culture, echoing Shelley's poem after a so-called Leonardo *Medusa* in the Uffizi Gallery (now thought to be seventeenth-century Flemish) or Robert Browning's verses on 'Old Pictures in Florence' (1845).[14] Rossetti's interest in the image of the old masters as cultish personalities, imbued with special powers, is also evident in his sketches during the 1850s of celebrated artists at work. These include the fashionably monkish Fra Angelico kneeling devoutly before his easel, representing perfectly Pre-Raphaelitism's devotion to both fifteenth-century sincerity and the act of art-making itself; Giorgione painting a Venetian model in the same languid vein of Rossetti's sonnet after the Louvre's *Concert Champêtre*; and a gothic-style genre scene of van Eyck in his studio, now lost.

Pre-Raphaelitism was fundamentally concerned, then, with old masters of many kinds, reference points for particular endeavours, yes, but also as a general category, the means for the group's negotiation of their own place in the canon. This interest in the renewed dialectic between the art of the past and present, thrashed out by the critics of the day, is caught particularly nicely in Rossetti's quip to Ruskin, who was dragging his heels in 1855 over the third volume of his magnum opus, that his modern painters 'will be old masters before the work is ended'.[15]

Giottesque or grotesque?

A visual source, rather than a text, which influenced the Pre-Raphaelites was Carlo Lasinio's *Pittura a fresco del Campo Santo di Pisa* (1828). This book of engravings, after frescoes attributed to Giotto, Benozzo Gozzoli and others in the monumental burial cloister at Pisa, had a devout following among British enthusiasts of early Italian art. Certainly when Millais showed Hunt and Rossetti his copy in 1848, the flat angular character of the frescoes provided them with something of an epiphany, a visual identity to suit their ideas at the time of the Brotherhood's formation, which Hunt later attributed entirely to 'the finding of this book at this special time'.[16] Although Pre-Raphaelitism grew out of other influences as well, the group's identification with early Italian art intensified after this experience in particular.

The style of the frescoes, and especially the linear form of the engravings themselves, was most closely taken up in Millais's early work, notably *Isabella* (Figure 10) and his pen and ink drawings from the same period. Similarly, where previously Hunt had borrowed the prone figure in his *The Eve of St Agnes* (1848, Guildhall Art Gallery, London) from a copy after

Poussin's seventeenth-century *The Plague at Ashdod* at the National Gallery, he now turned to an earlier work in the collection, Francia's *Pietà*, for the more rangy figure of the corpse with pointy, upturned toes in *Rienzi* (1849, private collection).[17]

Not unnaturally, the Pre-Raphaelites' turn to early Italian art for inspiration was increased by new additions in this field to the collections they saw. It has been convincingly argued that both Millais's and Rossetti's first Pre-Raphaelite paintings were influenced, for example, by the wing panels of Lorenzo Monaco's *The Coronation of the Virgin*, painted around 1400, which entered the National Gallery in 1848.[18] The unusual composition of Millais's *Isabella*, with its many figures seen in profile, seated side by side, echoes the distribution of Monaco's saints, positioned in rows to face the centre rather than the viewer, customary in fifteenth-century altar-pieces. In particular, Isabella's silhouette pose in delicate grey, her hand at ease on the dog's head, and the posture of her lover who turns earnestly towards her, recall the two saints in the foreground of Monaco's right-hand panel. Rossetti likewise seated Mary and her mother St Anne in the same position in *The Girlhood of Mary Virgin* (Figure 6). The biblical symbolism of Mary's lily, like St Peter's key in the Lorenzo Monaco, and Rossetti's replication of the tiled floor in tilted perspective, reinforces the association with the earlier image. After all, the Gallery's purchase of the primitive, then attributed to Giotto's pupil Taddeo Gaddi, had also caught the attention of the *Illustrated London News* in November 1848, where it was engraved shortly after the Brotherhood's formation. The accompanying description even contained the buzzword of the day for describing art's embryonic beginnings – 'we now see in the early school of painting *the germ* of all the light and life and loveliness which was so refulgent under Raphael and Titian' – which the group would adopt a month later as the name for their short-lived literary organ.[19]

Since Oxford was an important centre for the Pre-Raphaelites and their circle, it is not surprising that they were also influenced by the early Italian art to be seen there in the Christ Church Picture Gallery. It has been suggested, for example, that Ford Madox Brown's *Our Lady of Good Children* (1847–61, Tate) drew stylistic inspiration from a so-called Filippo Lippi at Christ Church, now attributed to a minor Tuscan painter,[20] while the regimented perspective lines of the trees in Millais's *The Woodman's Daughter* (1851, Guildhall Art Gallery, London) clearly derive from Paolo Uccello's *The Hunt in the Forest* (c.1470) which was donated to the University Gallery, Oxford in 1850.[21] Similarly, the motif of Jesus kissing Mary's proffered cheek in another important work by Millais, *Christ in the House of His Parents* (Figure 4), comes from a *Virgin and Child with Six Saints* by

Sano di Pietro at Christ Church, then attributed to Duccio, which Ruskin had sketched as early as 1842.[22]

Yet the case of Millais's *Christ in the House* demonstrates the diversity of old master references employed by the group from the beginning. Another source has been suggested for the picture, from a very different kind of Italian painting at Christ Church, the Baroque setting of Annibale Carracci's *The Butcher's Shop* (c.1585).[23] Like Millais's painting, Annibale's showed a group of figures, probably also a family, assembled around a workbench, a composition which Millais adapted for his scene depicting the young Christ in Joseph's carpentry shop. Millais borrows from Annibale, for example, the bent body of Joseph's assistant, the head-dress and compositional arrangement of St Anne, and he appropriates generally for his own setting something of *The Butcher's Shop*'s realism. Neither Annibale's nor Millais's depictions shy away from the essential facts of a workplace, be it hung with animal carcasses or for woodworking.

But why this particular old master, this picture? Millais's turn to a source so seemingly antithetical to Pre-Raphaelitism, to the work of an artist revered by tradition, indeed by Reynolds as President of the Royal Academy, conveys a deeper truth about the movement. It reminds us that the group was not just interested in the style or subjects of past art, but used it to make a point, usually to criticize the more conventional forms of painting for its contrivances. Thus the influence of *The Butcher's Shop* may be especially ideological if what is also being borrowed is the grittiness of Annibale Carracci's own insubordination – the Italian's elevation of the lowly genre subject of a butcher's shop to the scale of a history painting – in support of Millais's most powerfully anti-academic statement. Like Annibale's butchers, Millais's is a real-world Holy Family, but inspired also by the down-to-earth appearance of early Flemish painting. As Malcolm Warner has pointed out, expectations of a Madonna and Child at this time were based on gentle, Raphaelesque paradigms.[24] Sure enough, the ensuing critical backlash against Millais's painting – most famously in Dickens's remark that the Virgin Mary would lower the tone of even the worst gin shop in England – echoed the *Art Journal*'s general complaint against Pre-Raphaelitism in 1850, that 'truly between the Giottesque and the grotesque there is but a step'.[25]

Pre-Rubenses, Pre-van Eycks

While the Pre-Raphaelites' taste for the Italian primitives joined up with a ready-made context, then, their interest in early Flemish painting was less orthodox. For a start, the fledgling art history in England was slower to respond to the Flemish primitives, whose warts-and-all realism was deemed ungainly and awkward, out of step with an aesthetics that only tolerated early Italian art, after all, as the seed – the germ – of art's full bloom during the High Renaissance. If Pre-Raphaelitism was criticized for bringing those influences into modern painting, supposedly arresting the progress of four centuries, the reaction to the early Flemish strain in their work was yet more hostile because the style was seen as the root of their work's quotidian turn. By marrying the unflinching realism of early Flemish painting with modern life subjects the Pre-Raphaelites had entered uncharted territory, going beyond ground covered by their revivalist predecessors, William Dyce, or the Nazarenes (a group of nineteenth-century German Romantic painters), whose work remained chastely Italianate.[26] It was the *Art Journal*, again, which voiced conventional taste when it regretted that the Pre-Raphaelites were nothing like the Baroque Flemish school, not 'Pre-Rubenses' but rather 'Pre-Van Eycks'.[27]

Thus the Flemish primitives had less of a following, even in revivalist circles, than the early Italians. It was not until 1868 that the Arundel Society finally made prints after van Eyck's famous *Ghent Altar-piece*, decades after it had published Fra Angelico or Giotto, and the Society never regarded van Eyck's *Arnolfini Portrait* as a suitably earnest subject for popular reproduction, even though the painting had been championed by Ruskin in the *Quarterly Review* as early as 1848.[28] Of all the old masters, however, it was this particular van Eyck which most comprehensively influenced the development of Pre-Raphaelitism, appealing principally, as Malcolm Warner has put it, to their 'belief in the painter as eyewitness rather than creator of beauty', and to their revival of the mode of realistic symbolism.

According to Warner, of all the Pre-Raphaelite works Hunt's *Awakening Conscience* (1854, Tate) offers the most direct engagement with van Eyck's original. In Warner's reading, Hunt's well-known story of a kept woman, seized by a moment of epiphany, is told through a parallel set of symbols to those which convey the gravity of van Eyck's married couple. In Hunt's picture, gravity gives way to parody. Van Eyck's dog, symbolic of marital fidelity, becomes a cat tormenting a bird, while the carefully removed clogs of the original, a sign of bourgeois respectability in the home, are replaced by a soiled glove, tossed aside to signal the woman's lost virtue.[29] Ford Madox Brown's *Take your Son, Sir!* (1851–92, Tate) seems to offer a similar social comment on extra-marital strife. Brown makes van Eyck's mirror a device to show the reflection of a mutton-chopped man presented with his illegitimate child, in another contrasting, it would seem, of Victorian and van Eyckian morals. William Morris tackled a similar theme in *La Belle Iseult* (1858, Tate), where he turned van Eyck's respectably curtained bed into the rumpled site of Arthurian adulteress Iseult's infidelity with Tristram.[30] And while not all scholars agree on the detail of these interpretations – some see nothing in Brown's painting to suggest a narrative about illegitimacy; others believe that Morris's painting represents Guinevere's adultery with Lancelot – the ubiquity of the van Eyck reference for all of these artists is beyond doubt.

Morris's medievalizing homage to van Eyck's *Arnolfini Portrait* is a reminder that the style of early Flemish art represented other contexts for the Pre-Raphaelites than the realist gaze favoured by Hunt and Brown. For the movement's Romantics, Rossetti, Morris and Burne-Jones, the Flemish primitives offered rich materials for emulation of the kind of mystical representation of nature they also admired in the German Renaissance artist Albrecht Dürer (1471–1528). Like Giotto and Fra Angelico, early Northern artists became ancestral figures, their works key points of reference for the Pre-Raphaelite vision of the Middle Ages. Morris, for example, was drawn to the chivalric character of van Eyck's motto *Als Ich Kan* – 'If I/Eyck can', or, more properly, 'as best I/Eyck can' – inscribed upon the frame of his red-turbaned self-portrait which entered the National Gallery in 1851. Around 1862, van Eyck's dictum was adopted by Morris for a wallpaper design for Red House, the Arts and Crafts Movement home he built in Bexleyheath ('but I can't', added prankster Burne-Jones, creeping downstairs one morning at dawn).[31] For others in the Pre-Raphaelite circle, Dürer became an important model for the close depiction of nature, with William Bell Scott visiting Nuremberg to perfect the details of his historical picture, *Albrecht Dürer on the Balcony of his House* (1854, National Gallery of Scotland), and John Brett, better known for his *The Stonebreaker* (1857–8, Walker Art Gallery, National Museums Liverpool), depicting himself in the image of a Dürer self-portrait.

It was Rossetti who sustained the strongest interest in the Northern Renaissance, kindled particularly by his trip to France and Belgium with Hunt in 1849 during which they bought Dürer prints in Paris. Rossetti later borrowed the domestic setting of a Dürer woodcut, *The Birth of the Virgin* (1502–3), especially the left-hand detail of the water fountain, for his *Mariana in the South* in the Moxon Tennyson of 1857.[32] In Belgium, so taken was Rossetti with the works of van Eyck, and especially with those of van Eyck's follower Hans Memling, that in 1863 he went again with his brother William Michael. In embracing the new cultural tourism to Flanders enabled by the expansion of the railways, the Pre-Raphaelites were not only experiencing but spreading new art-historical fashions as they took root. When Rossetti became fascinated by Memling's paintings in the Hospital of St John at Bruges, writing two sonnets on the artist for *The Germ* in 1850, he followed in the footsteps of Thackeray who had earlier contrasted the sincerity of Memling at Bruges with the 'swaggering canvases' of Rubens of which he tired during his travels through Belgium in 1840.[33] Rossetti continued the trend during the 1850s, borrowing the medieval townscape of van Eyck's *Rolin Madonna* (1436, Louvre) for his drawing of Taurello (1850–2, Tate), a character from Browning's troubadour poem, *Sordello*; adding pipe organs in the style of van Eyck and Memling to several of his works, including his *St Cecilia* for the Moxon Tennyson; and collaborating with Elizabeth Siddall on the decoration of a jewel casket in the style of Memling's celebrated St Ursula Shrine at Bruges (St John's Hospital, 1489).[34]

The meeting of Rossetti's early Flemish and early German influences is particularly evident in one of the last drawings of this period of high revivalism, *Mary Magdalene at the Door of Simon the Pharisee* (1858–9, Fitzwilliam Museum, Cambridge). While it recalls the composition and building types of Memling's religious paintings at Bruges, and the detailed plant life of Dürer's engravings, the opulent figure of Mary Magdalene, with her flowing locks, points forward to the taste for the Venetians – Giorgione, Titian and Veronese – then emerging through the influence of Ruskin and the museum world. We are reminded once more of the complexity of the sources for Pre-Raphaelitism even at its most medievalist.

Post-Raphaelitism

From the 1860s, the group's artistic inspirations, and indeed the canon itself, diversified into a more explicit communion of pre- and post-Raphaelite art. The earlier division between 'Christian art' and the High Renaissance was replaced in a budding age of aestheticism, of art for art's sake, with a common interest in art which was unashamedly about the senses, surface and texture. This materialism could be admired simultaneously in the patterned delicacy of Botticelli, the vivid luxury of Titian's women or the realism of Velázquez, three old masters whose stars were in the ascendant during this decade. Indeed, as Pre-Raphaelitism itself diversified after the 1850s, it reflected this increasing diversity of the art-historical landscape, with the influence of post-Raphaelite art becoming a particularly strong feature. Rossetti famously entered his Venetian period with the painting *Bocca Baciata* (1859, Museum of Fine Arts, Boston), followed by pictures such as *Fazio's Mistress* (1863, Tate), a work that paid homage to Titian's *Woman With a Mirror* (c.1513–15) which he saw at the Louvre. Millais studied van Dyck at Genoa and Rembrandt in Holland, turning to Rembrandt again in 1888 for a discussion of modern art and the old masters in an article for *The Magazine of Art*.[35] The group's art collecting reflects a similar eclecticism. Millais owned a genuine Holbein portrait, a van Dyck bought from

Blenheim Palace and Sweerts's *Men Playing Checkers*, a seventeenth-century Flemish genre painting now in the Rijksmuseum, Amsterdam.[36] And as well as the fashionable early Italian paintings and relief sculptures that Hunt bought during his stay in Florence between 1866 and 1869, he counted a 'Titian', a 'van Dyck' and a 'Velázquez' amongst his collection.[37]

Indeed, the visual example which best illustrates the shifting artistic inspirations between the first and last eras of Pre-Raphaelitism is Hunt's late painting, *The Lady of Shalott* (1886–1905, Figure 1). In it, the early interest in van Eyck, still present, and appropriate for the chivalric subject of Tennyson's poem, gives way to Venetian colouring and the Titianesque female form of the Lady trapped in her tower, cursed never again to look upon the outside world. Condemned to weave upon her loom, she is forced to seek inspiration only in the scenes and passers-by she sees reflected in a mirror. Several times in his career Hunt wrought this moment of her down-fall, another archetypal fallen woman, perhaps, whose ordered world turns to chaos – 'The mirror crack'd from side to side' – when she abandons her task to gaze out upon Sir Lancelot riding towards Camelot. Hunt had started thinking about this composition as early as 1850, making a draw-ing in black chalk, pen and ink, now in the National Gallery of Victoria, and a design for a wood-engraving in the Moxon Tennyson of 1857. The changing points of reference, regarding old master taste, can be readily dis-cerned in the early and late versions. In 1850 the Lady was a damsel in a van Eyckian dress, and indeed her story is told, in homage to van Eyck's *Arnolfini Portrait*, in a series of roundels which surround the mirror. By con-trast, the composition of the 1905 painting uses a more elaborate symbol-ism to construct a narrative about the now decadently clad Lady's neglect of duty, which is tied together by a different reference point, a series of dec-orative art objects of the sort made fashionable by the Aesthetic Movement, classical and Renaissance bas-reliefs.

A quintessential late work, Hunt's picture necessarily revisits the begin-ning, the defining features of the original Pre-Raphaelitism. There is the sub-ject drawn from literature, the van Eyck clogs of the *Arnolfini Portrait* and the typological symbolism of the flowers discarded to the right foreground, symbols of the Madonna which contrast with the Lady's own negligence. But there is also a later, more modish emphasis on beauty and the beautiful object. The auburn flashes in the Lady's hair and the deep satin sleeves of her dress are those of Titian, while the relief tondos on either side of the mirror are carriers of meaning and fabulous possessions in equal parts. The fash-ion for Italian relief sculpture was closely tied to the taste for the decorative qualities of Botticelli and Donatello in the 1870s, not the moralizing charac-ter of earlier Pre-Raphaelitism. Yet Hunt characteristically marries old and

Figure 1 William Holman Hunt, *The Lady of Shalott*, 1886–1905, oil on canvas, 185 × 143.7 cm, Wadsworth Atheneum, Hartford, Connecticut. The Ella Gallup Sumner and Mary Catlin Sumner Collection Fund. 1961.470©2011. Wadsworth Atheneum Museum of Art/Art Resource, NY/Scala, Florence.

new values by making these reliefs speak to his subject's meaning. Both the Madonna adoring the child on the left, and the Hercules in the garden of the Hesperides to the right, are paragons of duty. While Hercules completes his Labour, claiming the golden apples, the guardian daughters of the garden are negligent, asleep, sisters to the Lady of Shalott in their abdication of responsibility. Always the master storyteller of the original Brotherhood, Hunt's interest in relief sculpture – the Madonna and child depicted here is based on his own Andrea della Robbia[38] – was no doubt enhanced by its narrative possibilities.

Thus Hunt's image bookends early and late Pre-Raphaelitism, Christian typological and decadent mythological symbolism, the movement's canons broader than the name alone implies. To return to the quotation with which we began, from the obituary of Edward Burne-Jones in *The Times* in 1898, the newspaper was quick to declare the rise of Velázquez's reputation as an end to Pre-Raphaelitism. However, what has seldom been recognized is the extent to which the Pre-Raphaelites were themselves agents of his rediscovery, decades ahead of the fact. In 1862, Millais was praising Whistler's *The White Girl* for its qualities of 'Old Seville'; by 1868 he had painted an English infanta of his own, entitled *Souvenir of Velasquez* (Royal Academy of Arts, London); while during the same period Rossetti wrote to the Burne-Joneses themselves of a 'Velasquez' he was keen to show off.[39] The prevailing narratives have privileged the rebellious and didactic nature of Pre-Raphaelitism's founding mission, making it difficult for us to look afresh at the associations of the term. But to map the diversity of the group's artistic inspirations is to appreciate the longevity of their careers during a formative period in the history of art history. We should rethink Pre-Raphaelitism as a conversation, not a rupture, with a canon in the making.

NOTES

1 *The Times*, 20 June 1898, p. 11.
2 Michael Levey, 'Botticelli and Nineteenth-Century England', *Journal of the Warburg and Courtauld Institutes*, 23 (1960), p. 291.
3 Francis Haskell, *Rediscoveries in Art: Some Aspects of Taste, Fashion and Collecting in England and France*, 2nd edn. (Oxford: Phaidon, 1980), p. 94.
4 Jenny Graham, *Inventing Van Eyck: The Remaking of an Artist for the Modern Age* (Oxford and New York: Berg, 2007), pp. 97–102. On the Palace of Westminster fresco competitions, see Michaela Giebelhausen, *Painting the Bible: Representation and Belief in Mid-Victorian Britain* (Aldershot, Hants. and Brookfield, Vermont: Ashgate, 2006), pp. 88–93.
5 *Illustrated London News*, 11 November 1848, p. 300.
6 'Advice to Aspiring Artists', *Punch* (1845), illustrated in Giebelhausen, *Painting the Bible*, p. 94.

7 Hunt, vol. I, pp. 53–4.
8 Hunt, vol. I, p. 106; Leonée Ormond, 'Dante Gabriel Rossetti and the Old Masters', *Yearbook of English Studies*, 36.2 (2006), p. 153.
9 Jane Langley, 'Pre-Raphaelites or Ante-Dürerites?', *Burlington Magazine*, 137 (August 1995), p. 504.
10 Ormond, 'Rossetti and the Old Masters', p. 154.
11 Robyn Cooper, 'The Popularization of Renaissance Art in Victorian England: The Arundel Society', *Art History*, 1 (September 1978), pp. 263–92.
12 Hunt, vol. I, p. 54.
13 Hunt, vol. I, p. 90; George P. Landow, *William Holman Hunt and Typological Symbolism* (New Haven and London: Yale University Press, 1979), pp. 2–6.
14 Ormond, 'Rossetti and the Old Masters', pp. 156–9.
15 DGR *Correspondence*, vol. II, p. 49 (letter 55.33).
16 Hunt, vol. I, p. 104.
17 Malcolm Warner, 'The Pre-Raphaelites and the National Gallery', *Huntington Library Quarterly*, 55 (1992), p. 3.
18 Ibid., pp. 3–5.
19 *Illustrated London News*, 11 November 1848, p. 300.
20 Giebelhausen, *Painting the Bible*, pp. 78–80.
21 Jason Rosenfeld and Alison Smith, *Millais*, exhibition catalogue (London: Tate Publishing, 2007), p. 50.
22 Illustrated in Gail S. Weinberg, '"First of All First Beginnings": Ruskin's Studies of Early Italian Paintings at Christ Church', *Burlington Magazine*, 134 (February 1992), p. 113. See also Giebelhausen, *Painting the Bible*, p. 113.
23 Giebelhausen, *Painting the Bible*, pp. 116–22.
24 Warner, 'The Pre-Raphaelites and the National Gallery', p. 6.
25 Giebelhausen, *Painting the Bible*, p. 88.
26 Giebelhausen, *Painting the Bible*, chapter 3.
27 Langley, 'Pre-Raphaelites or Ante-Dürerites?', p. 508.
28 John Ruskin, 'Eastlake on the History of Painting', *Quarterly Review*, 82 (March 1848), p. 394 (repr. Ruskin, vol. XII, pp. 256–7).
29 Warner, 'The Pre-Raphaelites and the National Gallery', pp. 8–9.
30 Graham, *Inventing Van Eyck*, pp. 112–14.
31 W. R. Lethaby, *Morris as Work-Master: A Lecture Delivered at the Birmingham Municipal School of Art* (London: John Hogg, 1901), p. 7.
32 John Christian, 'Early German Sources for Pre-Raphaelite Designs', *Art Quarterly*, 36 (Spring–Summer 1973), p. 58.
33 Ormond, 'Rossetti and the Old Masters', p. 162.
34 Julian Treuherz, Elizabeth Prettejohn and Edwin Becker, *Dante Gabriel Rossetti*, exhibition catalogue (London: Thames and Hudson, 2003), pp. 144, 176, 227.
35 Leonée Ormond, 'Millais and Contemporary Artists', in Debra N. Mancoff (ed.), *John Everett Millais: Beyond the Pre-Raphaelite Brotherhood* (New Haven and London: Yale University Press, 2001), p. 39.
36 Ellis Waterhouse, 'Holman Hunt's "Giovanni Bellini" and the Pre-Raphaelites' Own Early Italian Pictures', *Burlington Magazine*, 123 (August 1981), p. 474.
37 Diana Holman-Hunt, 'The Holman Hunt Collection: A Personal Recollection', in Leslie Parris (ed.), *Pre-Raphaelite Papers* (London: Tate Gallery, 1984), pp. 206–25.

38 Judith Bronkhurst, 'Holman Hunt's Picture Frames, Sculpture and Applied Art', in Ellen Harding (ed.), *Re-Framing the Pre-Raphaelites: Historical and Theoretical Essays* (Aldershot, Hants.: Scolar Press, 1996), p. 251, note 16.

39 Ormond, 'Millais and Contemporary Artists', p. 32; DGR *Correspondence*, vol. III, p. 435 (letter 66.96).

3

COLIN CRUISE

Pre-Raphaelite drawing

Paintings exhibited by members of the Pre-Raphaelite Brotherhood were criticized often for what was perceived as their badly drawn figures and faulty perspective as much as for their jarring colours and morbid subjects. The underlying drawing was perceived to be as much of a problem as the more painterly elements in their pictures. The awkward drawing of the human figures was viewed as wilful; it transgressed the sound and well-established academic conventions derived from the practices of the old masters. One example, from the *Quarterly Review* – representative of a mass of such criticism – will serve to illustrate this point:

> Whilst endeavouring to labour in the spirit of the old masters, the Pre-Raphaelites appear to have fallen into the grave error of believing that the correct drawing of the human frame is not essential, because it is not to be found in the works of the painters of the fourteenth century. Indeed they seem to think, and would lead the public to think, that its absence forms one of the claims of the old masters to our admiration, as if the fame of Chaucer was to be attributed to the quaintness of his spelling.[1]

Pre-Raphaelite drawing and academic convention

Knowledge of 'correct drawing' was acquired through the process of copying ancient sculptures using laborious hatching, stippling and rubbing techniques. The emphasis at the Royal Academy Schools was upon the acquisition of drawing skills. Students worked towards perfecting their understanding of anatomy, proportion, beauty and 'the Ideal' through drawing. There was virtually no formal training in painting, its methods or materials. We might usefully contrast the experience of Ford Madox Brown who had undergone a thorough academic grounding in Belgium before studying in Paris.[2]

The Pre-Raphaelite Brotherhood was formed at a time when the Royal Academy dominated the advancement of the professional careers of artists. Attendance at the Royal Academy Schools was the primary step in an artistic career and entrance was delayed until the correct standard of accomplishment in drawing had been obtained. In this, the Academy was following an implicit understanding of the process of picture-making outlined in the first of the Presidential *Discourses* of Sir Joshua Reynolds, delivered as an address to students at the Academy Schools in 1768, in which drawing was viewed as the foundation of all artistic endeavour. However, rather than studying detail and individual form, Academy students who progressed to the Life School were encouraged to use drawing as a process of selection and idealization that excluded the model's individuality and idiosyncrasy.

John Everett Millais, William Holman Hunt and Dante Gabriel Rossetti were introduced to the conventions of the prevailing academic system. Like all prospective Academy students they prepared for entrance in the prescribed manner, by the submission of a drawing to be inspected by the entrance committee. Millais's early career is a particularly striking example of the employment of the variety of educational options in drawing instruction of the time. His natural aptitude for art having been recognized early, he had lessons from a drawing master, Mr Bettall, from the age of eight. Moving to London from Jersey, Millais was enrolled at Sass's Drawing Academy, the most successful of the schools set up to help prospective students achieve the appropriate standard to be accepted as an Academy probationer. After the somewhat dry training at Sass's, at the age of eleven he became the youngest ever student to join the Academy Schools. At other times in his studies Millais drew independently and extensively in the sculpture galleries of the British Museum where he encountered Holman Hunt, similarly employed.[3]

For the Pre-Raphaelites, 'correct drawing' and idealization were not simply conventions but 'lies', at odds with the honesty that lay beneath the true artistic creativity they aimed for and which they identified in the works of painters working before the establishment of the tradition that followed Raphael. The academic training system encouraged a split between the practices of painting and drawing, both in the ways they were valued and in the way they were taught. Two types of graphic work characterize the group's different stylistic tendencies in the late 1840s and '50s. These are, first, a modified version of the 'outline style', used mainly in the earliest compositional drawings from 1848 to around 1852. This style is one that arose at the very inception of the Brotherhood. Its linearity challenged the orthodoxy of academic drawing techniques that emphasized form produced by shadow and reflected light. A second type was close drawing from nature, usually representing either a fragment of undergrowth or a landscape, as advocated by Ruskin. It became synonymous with his critique of both old master and contemporary art and his deep interest in drawing practices. That these are almost contradictory types of drawing is worthy of remark, indicating a diversity of influences and practices – perhaps, even, a fundamental split – in the Brotherhood at its formation. However, a third type of drawing, intensely composed and densely detailed, often independent of painting and not made specifically for book illustration, might be seen as a development from the original outline style. This kind of drawing is in some ways unique to the Pre-Raphaelites although it has some precedent in the works of Blake in its use of literary sources as the basis of a personal and expressive visual art. It became a trademark of Rossetti and his circle from the mid-1850s onwards and had huge influence upon the graphic arts in Britain through to the early twentieth century. It found its fullest expression in the works of Simeon Solomon and Edward Burne-Jones and other followers of the Pre-Raphaelites who further modified Pre-Raphaelite drawing by the addition of models from Renaissance art and other sources.

In these separate types of Pre-Raphaelite drawing there are issues of media as well as style and intention that are worth considering here. In rebelling against their Royal Academy training the Pre-Raphaelites re-evaluated drawing in several ways and for several reasons, most importantly in creating independent works in drawing media and, at times, in combining traditional monochromatic media with colour. However, their first drawings executed in the outline style are most often in pen and ink traced over a pencil outline. The style is akin to handwriting, properly 'graphic' in its proximity to penmanship, an effect enhanced by titles, quotations and dedications that appear under the images and, on occasion, around them. In their sharp linearity these outline drawings often appear to be engravings but, unlike commercial engraved illustration, they were unique rather than multiplied and personal rather than public. Ruskinian observational drawing, while dependent on pencil or chalk for its earliest exercises, encouraged the use of ink or watercolour wash in combination with pencil and pen drawing which allowed a greater range of marks and tones, imitative of effects in nature. Although Rossetti's watercolours are – as works on paper – arguably drawings, a full discussion of their qualities belongs elsewhere and I will not discuss them here.[4] His other, and equally influential, contribution, noted above, was in imaginative subject drawing and illustration, the original drawings for which were chiefly executed in pen and ink for translation into engraved form.

Outline style and its variations

The 'outline style' was somewhat old-fashioned by the 1840s. It had enjoyed a first vogue in the works of John Flaxman (1755–1826) whose designs for various classical texts, such as *The Odyssey* (1793), had been widely admired throughout Europe. It was later revived and changed for a new generation by the German artist, Moritz Retzsch (1779–1857). Retzsch's outline illustrations for Goethe's *Faust* (1816) and the plays of Shakespeare (published from 1828 onwards) enjoyed enormous popularity in Britain.[5] 'Outline style' eschewed the elaborate light and shade of academic drawing, with its stippled and rubbed effects, while allowing for invention, conveyed crisply through line alone; it is the style that all the original members of the Brotherhood used at one time or another.

Millais had developed his skills in outline drawing through copying prints. Some of this juvenilia shows the influence of Retzsch, a source he was to return to in his earliest Pre-Raphaelite works, such as the drawing for *Isabella* in pen and ink (1848, Fitzwilliam Museum, Cambridge) which borrows some of its compositional features from Retzsch's outlines for *Macbeth* (notably for Act 3 Scene iv).[6] Although he won the silver medal for drawing from the Antique at the Royal Academy Schools in 1843, Millais's rejection of the Academy is evident by his early adoption of the alternative drawing practices and styles that became identified with the Pre-Raphaelite Brotherhood. Their version of the 'outline style' seems deliberately designed to attract adverse criticism; their drawings moved away from that elegance of outline employed by Retzsch and his engravers into a reinterpretation of it where the lines are awkward, stiff and angular. They neglected not the beauty of line alone but the grace of proportion and gesture that Millais, for one, was only too skilled in producing. His drawing for *Christ in the House of His Parents* (1849, Tate) is an even more daring rejection of academic art than the controversial painting that followed it (Figure 4). The linear awkwardness of this drawing, and others, encodes their sincerity of purpose, evidence of their rejection of the 'lies' of conventional art.

What we might describe as a 'Pre-Raphaelite modified outline style' is directly related to that developed in the Cyclographic Society, formed in 1848. The Cyclographic was set up to encourage the production of designs by its members and to record their criticism. It was one of several such societies; Rossetti, for example, had joined a sketching society in 1843 as a student at Sass's Academy. The members of the Cyclographic, students of the Royal Academy, included Rossetti, Millais, Hunt and Walter Howell Deverell.[7] It was an important alternative to the Academy Schools and their teaching techniques and pointed a way forward from drawing into ambitious and complex subject paintings with serious subjects. However, in 1848 the members of the Brotherhood discovered the prints published by Carlo Lasinio in 1828 after the frescoes attributed to Giotto and Benozzo Gozzoli in the Campo Santo, Pisa. Although somewhat crude and inaccurate these prints played a major part in the Brotherhood's choice of an outline style.

The new, deliberately awkward linearity of an emerging Pre-Raphaelitism is realized in the etched illustrations contained in *The Germ*, the Pre-Raphaelite journal, in the contributions of Hunt, Deverell, Brown and Collinson.

In his first Pre-Raphaelite drawings Rossetti often employed a hard outline traced around all the figures and objects. This was not his only mode; his numerous drawings for poems by Edgar Allan Poe and for Goethe's *Faust*, which he worked on intermittently from 1846–8, use a freer, more expressive handling of pen and ink. One of his first works to bear the initials PRB and one of the most representative of the 'modified outline style', *Dante Drawing an Angel on the First Anniversary of the Death of Beatrice* (Figure 2), attempts to illustrate both the mind of the poet – as displayed in his 'automatic' work of art, the outline of a winged figure inscribed upon a tablet – and the minute externals of his everyday world, its chairs, books and bric-à-brac. The poet appears to have awakened from a deep trance. Rising from his desk he finds himself surrounded by friends who stare at him or examine his drawing with curiosity. The visionary and the familiar are united in this work which is a graphic expression of an idea about the power of drawing and its union with the poetic imagination. This was a subject dear to Rossetti who felt his loyalties divided between two art forms, poetry and visual art. The subject of this drawing, illustrating an episode recorded in Dante's autobiographical work *La Vita Nuova*, encapsulates the possibilities of being both poet and painter. Here, the poet draws, the artist writes poetry. The desire for artistic duality is accompanied by a solitary trance-like state in which creativity is achieved. It seems particularly important that the activity is drawing. Rossetti's self-identification with the medieval Italian poet is palpable. His depiction of Dante drawing anticipates the vogue for trance-drawing which moved from the inner circles of spiritualism in the mid-nineteenth century, reappearing in the psychoanalytically driven 'automatic drawing' of early twentieth-century modernism.

Rossetti's extensive use of drawing, rather than painting, points to the intimate relationship between the written word and the drawn line. His working processes in both poetic and pictorial composition allowed for constant changes of concept and expression, helping him to perfect all possible facets of the subject. His drawings act as drafts much in the same way as the worked and reworked versions of his poems. Often it is in the initial drawing that the most communicative kernel of his pictorial ideas resides and sometimes the idea was never realized pictorially to his satisfaction. Rossetti engaged deeply with the Romantic art of a previous generation, notably with the works of Flaxman, Fuseli and Blake, which were suffused with dramatic and poetic sources of inspiration. Arguably his later

Figure 2 Dante Gabriel Rossetti, *Dante Drawing an Angel on the First Anniversary of the Death of Beatrice*, 1849, pen and black ink (inscriptions outside drawn frame in brown ink), 39.4 × 32.6 cm, Birmingham Museums & Art Gallery.

drawings are more influenced by Blake than by early Italian art. Blake's work acted as a model for the ways in which poetry and the visual arts could be combined. Rossetti developed and modified further the outline style until it became a flexible and personal tool for the delineation of his complex poetic imagination.

Ruskin, drawing and 'truth to nature'

While the modified outline style was important in the development of novel ways of inventing figure compositions it was hardly useful in helping the Pre-Raphaelites realize their ambitions for 'truth to nature', an idea that they found championed by John Ruskin in the first volume of *Modern Painters* (1843). Ruskin advised young artists to go to Nature 'rejecting nothing, selecting nothing, and scorning nothing', a view of art that contradicted the academic 'Ideal' of selection and synthesis. Although written to defend the landscape painter J. M. W. Turner from the scorn of contemporary criticism, the book had a larger agenda in attacking conventionality in representing natural phenomena. Drawing is central to Ruskin's critical analysis of Turner whom he compares favourably to the old masters, chiefly the seventeenth-century landscape painter Claude Lorrain. Writing on the 'Truth of Vegetation', for example, Ruskin finds that Turner 'does not merely draw [upper branches] better than others, but he is the only man who has ever drawn them at all'.[8] Drawing is neither simply a preparatory task nor a demonstration of skill but a fundamental activity linked to the ability to 'see truly'.

Ruskin's influence upon the Pre-Raphaelites continued through personal contact with each artist as well as through his critical writings in the press and through personal correspondence. His initial defence of the Pre-Raphaelites, in his letter of 13 May 1851 to *The Times*, reflected upon their strengths in drawing. Rather than slavishly following academic practices or resorting to an imitation of early painting, he noted, approvingly, 'they will draw either what they see, or what they suppose might have been the actual facts of the scene they desire to represent'.[9] His observation that, in the paintings exhibited by the PRB at the Academy that year, 'there is not one single error in perspective in four out of the five pictures' is both an acknowledgement of their strengths as draughtsmen and an exposure of the common faults of academic painting. His concept of 'truth to nature' was vividly expressed in his critical notes on artists exhibiting at the Royal Academy between 1855 and 1859. For example, in the notorious critique of Daniel Maclise's *The Wrestling Scene in 'As You Like It'* (1855, private collection), Ruskin took issue with the artist's mistakes in the rendering of the Duke's garment. 'Imagine the errors which a draughtsman who could make such a childish mistake as this must commit in matters that really need refined drawing, turns of leaves, and so on!'[10] These opinions acted as something of a corrective to the adverse criticisms of Pre-Raphaelite drawing in the popular press which Ruskin regarded as 'scurrilous abuse'. At other times the Pre-Raphaelites themselves were not exempt from Ruskin's adverse criticism.

In his essay on 'Pre-Raphaelitism' he refers to 'certain qualities of drawing which they [the Pre-Raphaelites] miss from over-carefulness' and, at times, his reception of works by Millais and Hunt was harsh.[11]

Ruskin's own landscape and architectural drawings, most often executed in pen and ink, clearly move away from the pedestrian exercises of the amateur landscapist and begin to rival Turner in their technical achievements. His watercolour studies of plants and leaves, while lacking the complexity of his favourite artist in this genre, William Henry Hunt, have a sensitivity that comes from his acute understanding of the textures and structures of nature and the nuances of local colour. Perhaps his most original work as a draughtsman was in recording his interest in geology. His pen and wash drawings of rocks are an entirely new subject for art and unite drawing and scientific study.[12]

Ruskin wrote two books specifically devoted to the principles of drawing, *The Elements of Drawing* (1857) and *The Laws of Fésole* (1877).[13] Addressed not to professional artists but to amateurs and students, they are documents in the development of a Ruskinian Pre-Raphaelitism, of his vision of the underlying principles of art. At the time, published handbooks to drawing techniques were hugely popular. Ruskin's former drawing master, J. D. Harding (1797–1863), was particularly successful in his publishing ventures, as was the watercolourist Samuel Prout (1783–1852), one of his first draughtsman heroes. Prout's lithographs of Flanders and Germany, published in 1833, were formative in the development of Ruskin's skill in landscape and architectural drawing.

Ruskin was able to develop his skills as a teacher, as well as his particular view of the purpose of drawing, through his involvement with the Working Men's College from 1854–8 (the College was founded in 1854, with F. D. Maurice as its first principal, to provide a liberal education to workers). Ford Madox Brown and Rossetti taught there, too, and later Ruskin's assistant teacher was Edward Burne-Jones.[14] *The Elements of Drawing* was written in the context of debates around drawing that had been prompted by the curriculum created in 1853 by the new National Course of Instruction within the Schools of Design, a unified system of teaching drawing through basic but progressive exercises designed to help those training to be designers for industry to acquire drawing skills. The training systems initiated by both the Royal Academy and the Schools of Design were objectionable to Ruskin whose desire was to train the artist to 'see truly'. Indeed, in the Preface to the *Elements* he states his belief that 'the sight is a more important thing than the drawing; and I would rather teach drawing that my pupils may learn to love Nature, than teach the looking at Nature that they may learn to draw'.[15]

The Laws of Fésole was described by its author as being based upon the practice of 'the Tuscan Masters' which clearly allies his ideas on the subject to those of the Pre-Raphaelites in their return to simpler, more direct responses to nature. Here too, his writing on the teaching of drawing was chiefly directed to encourage the student to look closely and directly. However, he insisted on the completion of basic exercises in drawing lines and masses and grading tones before the commencement of more complex 'sketching from nature'. *The Laws of Fésole* was intended as a textbook for the schools of his visionary social and educational project, the Guild of Saint George, as well as recording the 'system of art-study' undertaken by undergraduates at Oxford where he was appointed Slade Professor of Art in 1869. Other ventures of Ruskin's at this time communicate the importance of drawing. The setting up of the collections of prints, drawings and watercolours for study purposes at the Guild of St George in 1871 was one of the more permanent of these. He founded the School of Drawing at Oxford in 1871 and, in 1875, presented drawings to the university, including works by Dürer and Turner, as well as those of contemporary artists such as Burne-Jones, to be used for educational purposes.[16]

Ruskin's emphasis upon looking closely led the student to understand the structure of nature, the basis of design and beauty, rather than the design of industrial goods. A holistic practice of looking, identifying and transcribing was the aim of Ruskin's instruction; the acquisition of a mere professional-seeming virtuosity – the goal of all other commercial drawing instruction – was not. It was not about imitation of nature for its own ends, nor for the acquisition of a polite skill to be paraded in society. Inculcating sound drawing practices, that trained both the eye and the hand, would affect the production of designed objects. In this way, Ruskin was to attack the concept of drawing as a skill valuable only for fine artists. The implications of skill, design and work as expressions of an artistic impulse were fully expounded in his appeal to invention and individual craftsmanship expressed in the most famous chapter of *The Stones of Venice*, 'The Nature of Gothic'.

Ruskin extended his influence from professional artists, such as the Pre-Raphaelites, to a wider and more general system for thinking about the role of drawing in education and, more generally, in national culture. Ruskin's ideas were to receive a warm response in the USA where his writings were to be almost as important for the promotion and acceptance of Pre-Raphaelitism as the work of the artists themselves. Through the writings of Charles Eliot Norton and others, close observational drawing was perceived as the central activity of an extended Pre-Raphaelitism, an emphasis not given to the movement in Britain.[17]

Later Pre-Raphaelite narrative and illustrative drawing

For all his insistence upon students acquiring manual skills through the performance of a series of exercises, Ruskin was keenly aware that drawing had other communicative qualities that had little to do with 'truth to nature' but were expressions of the 'signs of life and liberty' that he found in Gothic design. His appreciation of Rossetti and, subsequently, his encouragement of Burne-Jones indicate an engagement with more inventive and innovative drawing. His admiration for the work of Elizabeth Siddall suggests that he had an eye for talent that was not yet developed. Her work is particularly interesting for a study of Pre-Raphaelite drawing because she had escaped all of the formal training undergone by the Pre-Raphaelites. Instead, her emphasis is almost completely upon imaginative composition dealing with subjects derived from poetry, a direction encouraged by Rossetti as well as Ruskin.

In their earliest drawings the members of the Pre-Raphaelite Brotherhood engaged with literary texts. Their paintings, too, demonstrated a complex relationship between word and image. It is unsurprising that they used drawing for illustration, both as an inspiration for their complex compositions and as a way of earning money. Their drawings for illustration, however, were to have a wider influence and helped in the renewed identification of younger artists with the aims of the original movement. In 1856 Hunt, Millais and Rossetti were engaged, with other well-established artists, to illustrate Tennyson's poems for a volume now known as the 'Moxon Tennyson'. Rossetti's illustrations, such as *St Cecilia* for Tennyson's 'The Palace of Art', are innovative in that they use the text to present the reader with an almost independent visual experience. The volume contains Hunt's striking illustration for 'The Lady of Shalott' which revised his earlier hard-edged drawing of the subject from 1850 (National Gallery of Victoria, Melbourne). Subsequently, several of the Pre-Raphaelites and their associates were involved in the much delayed Dalziel illustrated Bible project. Millais's work for this was eventually published as a separate volume, *The Parables of Our Lord* (1864), and is one of his most significant contributions to contemporary illustration. In all of these works the underlying drawing communicates its clear graphic qualities even when mediated through the variable skills of wood engravers. This aspect of Pre-Raphaelite drawing was of great importance for the development of British art in the latter half of the nineteenth century.

Pre-Raphaelite drawing for illustration developed the outline style of the Brotherhood's earliest phase and, coming at a time of the expansion of both the illustrated periodical and literary press, disseminated the pictorial ideas of the new art movement. A 'second generation' of artists connected to the Pre-Raphaelite Brotherhood was directly influenced by these illustrations and related drawings and saw the potential they offered for the production of dramatic and poetic compositions constructed on an intimate scale. Rossetti's drawings were to enjoy a cult status for artists of the next generation. Highly elaborated pen-and-ink works such as *Mary Magdalene at the Door of Simon the Pharisee* (1858, Fitzwilliam Museum, Cambridge) set new standards for independent drawings with ambitious narrative goals.

Of the close associates of the Pre-Raphaelites who worked as illustrators the most significant was Frederick Sandys who developed his remarkable drawing skills in pencil, coloured chalk and pen-and-ink drawings. His drawings for reproduction in popular journals such as the *Cornhill* are astonishing in their precision of line and clarity of design. In several of his illustrations he included closely observed foreground vegetation which shows the influence of Dürer whose prints were collected by both Ruskin and Rossetti and were studied closely by Burne-Jones and William Bell Scott. Sandys's drawing for Christina Rossetti's poem 'If' (published in *Good Words*, October 1862), for example, is derived from Dürer's *Melencolia* (c.1513–14). Like Rossetti, Sandys consigned key pictorial elements to the edges of the composition or disguised them in a welter of detail, demanding the viewer's engagement with the picture as well as, and sometimes rather than, the text. The beauty of his illustration drawings led to the practice of preserving the original woodblock drawing which ordinarily would have been destroyed in the cutting process.

Pre-Raphaelite illustrations were appreciated as drawings and admired for their aesthetic qualities. When undergraduates at Oxford, both William Morris and Edward Burne-Jones were fascinated by Rossetti's drawings and watercolours. When Burne-Jones saw Rossetti's striking illustration of 'The Maids of Elfen-mere' drawn for William Allingham's *The Music Master* (1855) he thought it the most beautiful drawing for illustration that he had ever seen.[18] The rhythmic, repetitive simplicity of the figures of the Fates and the twisted, introspective shape of their victim is a powerful reinterpretation of several visual sources, among them Flaxman. The multiplicity of decorative patterns, such a strong feature of Rossetti's graphic work, is also present in Burne-Jones's early drawings in pencil and pen and ink, such as *Going to the Battle* (1858, Fitzwilliam Museum, Cambridge). Often, in these drawings the figures seem simply part of a decorative patterning although the faces, invariably abstracted in expression, give them an atmosphere of deep sadness, a constant feature of the artist's later work. The use of chevrons and chequerboard patterns is evidence of an interest in illuminated manuscripts that Burne-Jones shared not only with Rossetti and Morris but with Ruskin, too. In addition, Burne-Jones's mature work reveals a study of the drawings of Mantegna, Botticelli and Leonardo. He copied drawings by Michelangelo whose sophisticated handling of drawing materials, particularly in the production of a shadowy *sfumato*, augmented the stricter and 'purer' linearity of the earlier Pre-Raphaelite mode. As a result, Burne-Jones developed a penumbrous and sensual drawing style close in spirit to the new work of Symbolist artists working throughout continental Europe.

A tendency towards synthesis and eclecticism is also a feature of the drawings of Simeon Solomon. His juvenile compositions, awkward and quaint in style, were passed around at evening parties attended by the Pre-Raphaelites who praised them for their inventiveness. He was a prodigy, exhibiting drawings in commercial galleries in London from the age of fifteen. In the strongest of his early works he contrived to combine the 'modified outline style' with a technique of minute rendering of form and texture using tiny flecks of ink built up by hatching and cross-hatching. A good example is the drawing now known by the title *Babylon Hath Been a Golden Cup* (Figure 3), one of the first of the artist's works dealing with sexual ambiguity and desire.[19] Although he exhibited oil paintings at the Royal Academy exhibitions throughout the 1860s, Solomon presented some of his most daring and transgressive ideas as works on paper. His drawings and watercolours were exhibited at the Dudley Gallery (a London exhibiting society, established in 1865 by a committee of artists as an alternative to the more traditional exhibiting venues), where he was regarded as the head of a new Pre-Raphaelite school that included Walter Crane and Robert Bateman. After his arrest and trial for sodomy in 1873 Solomon continued to work although in much reduced circumstances, sometimes dependent upon the workhouse for shelter. His output for the remaining thirty years of his life consisted mainly of drawings of heads in chalk and pastel on themes derived from poetry and mythology displaying a variety of stylistic influences from Babylonian and ancient Greek art to Stothard and Blake. One of his favourite motifs was the head of Medusa, often depicted crying out in anguish. These repetitive images are frequently compared to works by his contemporary, the French artist Odilon Redon, as much for their mystical and literary subject matter as for their use of graphic media.

The drawings of Burne-Jones and Solomon departed from the aesthetic programme outlined by the Pre-Raphaelite Brotherhood at its formation. Indeed, in the promiscuous use of a diverse range of visual sources they introduce stylistic influences alien to the strictest interpretation of the term 'Pre-Raphaelite'. Their works show little interest, too, in the 'truth to nature'

Figure 3 Simeon Solomon, *Babylon Hath Been a Golden Cup*, 1859, pen
and black and brown ink over traces of pencil on paper, 26.6 × 28.3 cm,
Birmingham Museums & Art Gallery.

of the Brotherhood's earliest phase. On the other hand, in their pursuit of
themes of love, sexual passion and desire, their works expanded the agenda
of the earliest Pre-Raphaelite poetic compositions. Their adoption of drawing as a primary means of communicating ideas both subtle and ambitious
placed a new emphasis upon invention and immediacy which emulated
Rossetti at his most innovative and presaged key aspects of Modernism.

Although the Pre-Raphaelites presented some of their most radical
pictorial ideas in drawings and illustrations their work continued to be
criticized for poor draughtsmanship. The unfamiliar and challenging look
of Pre-Raphaelite drawing is not attributable either to an incomplete art
education or a misunderstanding of prevailing academic conventions.
Rather, it was a conscious rejection of convention at its most fundamental

level in order to create a more expressive and original art. Pre-Raphaelite drawing legitimized the direct, even close, study of nature above the academic tradition of the generalized, conventionalized and idealized. Through the translation of drawing into engraved illustrations the Pre-Raphaelites reached large audiences. They invented a new graphic style which was recognized for its strong visual qualities and originality. Arguably, after Pre-Raphaelitism, the collecting, valuation and exhibiting of drawings were never to be the same again.

NOTES

1 *Quarterly Review*, 100 (July 1857) p. 399.
2 Ford Madox Hueffer, *Ford Madox Brown: A Record of his Life and Work* (London and New York: Longmans, Green and Co., 1896), pp. 13–24.
3 John Guille Millais, *The Life and Letters of Sir John Everett Millais*, 2 vols. (London: Methuen and Co., 1899), vol. I, pp. 44–6.
4 For Rossetti's watercolours see Julian Treuherz, Elizabeth Prettejohn and Edwin Becker, *Dante Gabriel Rossetti*, exhibition catalogue (London: Thames and Hudson, 2003), pp. 156–80.
5 William Vaughan, *German Romanticism and English Art* (New Haven and London: Yale University Press, 1979), pp. 123–54.
6 Alastair Grieve, 'Style and Content in Pre-Raphaelite Drawings', in Leslie Parris (ed.), *Pre-Raphaelite Papers* (London: Tate Gallery, 1984), pp. 223–43.
7 Extant records of the Cyclographic Society are reprinted in William E. Fredeman (ed.), *The P. R. B. Journal: William Michael Rossetti's Diary of the Pre-Raphaelite Brotherhood 1849–1853: Together with Other Pre-Raphaelite Documents* (Oxford: Clarendon Press, 1975), Appendix 3, pp. 108–12.
8 Ruskin, vol. III, p. 586.
9 Ruskin, vol. XII, p. 322.
10 Ruskin, vol. XIV, pp. 11–12.
11 Ruskin, vol. XII, p. 388.
12 Stephen Wildman, 'Ruskin's Drawings 1844–1882', in Robert Hewison and others, *Ruskin, Turner and the Pre-Raphaelites*, exhibition catalogue (London: Tate Gallery Publishing, 2000), pp. 147–201.
13 Ruskin also published a manual on drawing and perspective, *The Elements of Perspective*; all three texts are reprinted in Ruskin, vol. XV.
14 Ray Haslam, 'Looking, Drawing, and Learning with John Ruskin at the Working Men's College', *Journal of Art and Design Education*, 7 (1988), pp. 65–79.
15 Ruskin, vol. XV, p. 13.
16 Robert Hewison, *Ruskin in Oxford: The Art of Education* (Oxford: Clarendon Press, 1996).
17 Theodore E. Stebbins, Jr., and Virginia Anderson, *The Last Ruskinians: Charles Eliot Norton, Charles Herbert Moore, and Their Circle*, exhibition catalogue (Cambridge, Mass.: Harvard University Art Museums, 2007).
18 Edward Burne-Jones, 'Essay on *The Newcomes*', *Oxford and Cambridge Magazine*, 1 (January 1856), p. 60.

19 The title and identification of this drawing have been disputed; see Gayle M. Seymour, 'The Old Testament Paintings and Drawings: The Search for Identity in the Post-Emancipation Era', in Colin Cruise and others, *Love Revealed: Simeon Solomon and the Pre-Raphaelites*, exhibition catalogue (Birmingham Museums & Art Gallery/London and New York: Merrell Publishers, 2005), pp. 17–18.

4

MICHAELA GIEBELHAUSEN

The religious and intellectual background

The list of Immortals is easily the movement's most intriguing document (see Appendix Two). Its fifty-seven names present an eclectic who's who which delineates the Pre-Raphaelite universe. It is as baffling as it is enlightening: a snapshot of hero worship taken in the early days of the Pre-Raphaelite Brotherhood. It has survived in an edited form and William Holman Hunt claimed that it originally 'included further names ... amongst them were many contemporaries now utterly forgotten'.[1] Looking at the list today, most of the names still ring bells or can be googled. Hunt's editing has stood the test of time. But what does the list tell us about the beliefs of the young men who first drew it up, one imagines, as a kind of party game or bonding exercise to classify and clarify their divergent notions of human greatness?

It contains twenty-nine poets and writers and a total of seventeen visual artists, including an unspecified number of early Gothic architects. There are eight historical figures who represent adventure, initiative and varying degrees of revolutionary persuasion, and two scientists. Most surprising perhaps are the names of several biblical figures: Jesus Christ, the author of the Book of Job and the prophet Isaiah. It is important to grasp what the document reveals about the predilections of the Brotherhood's members. First of all, it demonstrates a firm belief in a kind of secular immortality embodied in human endeavour. Given their chosen group name, Pre-Raphaelite Brotherhood, it seems obvious to find an emphasis on medieval Italian authors and visual artists. However, the canonical masters Raphael, Michelangelo, Titian and Tintoretto are also mentioned. Large indeed is the number of British Romantic poets and writers. In contrast, the very few British artists who make the list may serve as an indication of the Pre-Raphaelites' discontent with native artistic production. From this list, the Pre-Raphaelite project emerges as wide-ranging, eclectic and incongruous. It clearly favours writers over visual artists, possesses a revolutionary streak and doles out the top spot to Jesus Christ, awarding him the only four-star rating.

The reform of art

In 1848 revolutions swept across Europe, and in England seven young men, all aspiring artists, founded the Pre-Raphaelite Brotherhood. Their aim was to reform the state of the arts in England. William Michael Rossetti, the group's diarist, called theirs 'the temper of rebels: they meant revolt and produced revolution'.[2]

The revolutionary impact of their work has often been overlooked because the Pre-Raphaelites looked *back* to a time before 'the clear and tasteless poison of the art of Raphael' had seeped into artistic production.[3] What did the art critic John Ruskin mean by that tendentious remark? He shared with the Pre-Raphaelites the opinion that contemporary art had been dominated too much by the synthetic standards of the High Renaissance whose chief exponents were Raphael, in his mature style, and Michelangelo. In his *Discourses* (1769–90) Sir Joshua Reynolds, the first President of the Royal Academy of Arts, had upheld the work of both as a standard to which young artists should aspire. Their art remained the academic touchstone even in the days when four of the young Pre-Raphaelites, John Everett Millais, William Holman Hunt, Dante Gabriel Rossetti and Thomas Woolner, were students at the Royal Academy in the 1840s.

For the Pre-Raphaelites the artistic fault lines ran differently. In the words of William Michael Rossetti, the Pre-Raphaelites endeavoured 'to sympathize with what is direct and serious and heartfelt in previous art, to the exclusion of what is conventional and self-parading and learned by rote'.[4] They were interested in late medieval and early Renaissance art, that is to say the art *before* Raphael. To them the art of the young Raphael also displayed the freshness and sincerity that High Renaissance and academic art lacked. Theirs was a revolt that sought a way back to the sources, to reclaim long-lost purity and artistic sincerity. Such interests automatically brought them face to face with religious subject matter which had dominated the artistic production of the late Middle Ages. The Pre-Raphaelites were intrigued by the intricate iconography of medieval art which handbooks such as Anna Brownell Jameson's *Sacred and Legendary Art* (1848) had made available to mid-Victorian audiences. They pored over Carlo Lasinio's engravings of the Campo Santo in Pisa, which reproduced the revered frescoes of late medieval masters such as Benozzo Gozzoli and others.

The 1840s were an important decade in the history of British art. The destruction of the Palace of Westminster by fire in 1834 had generated an unprecedented opportunity for state patronage of the arts. The Westminster Cartoon Competitions were held to determine how the new Houses of Parliament should be decorated, and to select subjects and artists suitable for the task. They were instrumental in generating enthusiasm for a national art. The periodical press began to promote religious subject matter as one which could invest contemporary art with the power to inspire, educate and raise the moral standards of the day. Increasingly the walls of the Royal Academy and other exhibition venues teemed with works dedicated to heroism, nationalism and religion.

In this atmosphere of reform with its strong enthusiasm for a vibrant national school of art, the young Pre-Raphaelites staged their artistic revolt. The first works they presented to the public in 1849 broadly conformed to the subject categories set for the Westminster Cartoon Competitions: English history and literature, and the Bible. Rossetti showed a religious subject, *The Girlhood of Mary Virgin* (Figure 8). Hunt and Millais had both drawn inspiration from English literature. The former depicted a scene from Edward Bulwer Lytton's best-selling novel, *Rienzi: The Last of the Roman Tribunes* (1835), set in fourteenth-century Rome. Millais's *Isabella* (Figure 10) focused on reworking Keats's poem 'Isabella and the Pot of Basil' which was itself based on a story from Boccaccio's *Decameron*, a late medieval Italian collection of tales. Disparate themes perhaps, but all three hark back to the list of Immortals which featured Cola di Rienzi, the medieval tribune and proto-revolutionary, the Romantic poet John Keats, the Italian author Boccaccio and of course the four-star-rated Jesus Christ.

The three pictures shared an attention to natural detail, a light and luminous palette and a rich symbolic language. Hunt and Rossetti infused their works with references to Christian iconography. Hunt's arrangement of figures echoes that traditionally reserved for a lamentation of Christ, while Rossetti used a more detailed iconographical language which opened out the confines of the domestic scene to prefigure important moments in the life of Christ and the Virgin. Millais relied on the symbolic connotations of flowers and created his own visual references which resonate in the context of Keats's well-known poem of doomed love. Early Pre-Raphaelite painting combined deliberate stylistic archaisms borrowed from medieval art with a close observation of nature.

This is also evident in Millais's controversial work, *Christ in the House of His Parents* (Figure 4), which was shown at the Royal Academy in the spring of 1850. The painting's startling lack of idealism was regarded as unfitting for the elevated subject matter. The work drew vitriolic criticism. Charles Dickens famously attacked the painting as an exponent of the 'great retrogressive principle'.[5] For him the picture presented everything that was currently wrong in England. Its archaic style and the fact that it had been painted by a self-professed member of the Pre-Raphaelite Brotherhood

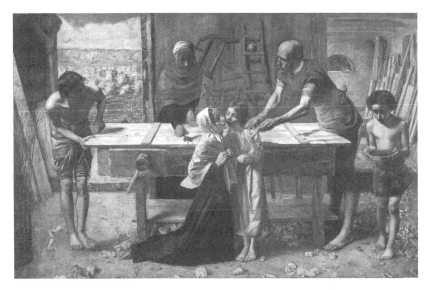

Figure 4 John Everett Millais, *Christ in the House of His Parents*, 1849–50, oil on canvas, 86.4 × 139.7 cm, Tate, London. © Tate, London, 2011.

seemed to suggest all sorts of religious connotations and a refusal of progress in all spheres of life. The alleged religious implications were especially pressing since several key members of the Oxford Movement, the high-church faction of the Anglican Church, had converted to Catholicism during the second half of the 1840s. The threat of Catholicism grew even more intensive in the autumn of 1850 when the Pope reinstated the Catholic hierarchy in England which had lapsed during the reign of Henry VIII. Religious tensions ran high, and the streets of London and elsewhere resounded with no-popery riots.

In this charged climate, some commentators regarded the unconventional style of Millais's painting as a sign of Catholic sympathies. Furthermore, disappointment was great because Millais had been the Royal Academy's precocious gold-medal student. His was to be a bright future in the service of art, not waylaid by fanaticism and sectarianism. But with *Christ in the House of His Parents* Millais had presented a work which flew in the face of accepted conventions. It combined elevated subject matter, the Holy Family, with an extraordinary attention to base physical detail such as Joseph's muscular arms and dirty toe-nails. Unlike the soft archaism and pale colours of Rossetti's *Girlhood of Mary Virgin*, Millais's work was packed with detailed anatomy and a forceful and unusual colour scheme. It was aggressively confident in conception and execution. Millais's artistic choices could not be argued away on grounds of immaturity and lack of technique. His work was highly original, competent and controversial. It brought an unprecedented degree of detail to a sublime and elevated subject which traditionally had received an idealized form of representation.

In Millais's treatment the members of the Holy Family are haggard and careworn and marked by hard physical toil. The figures are gauche, their poses awkward. They lack the grace customarily bestowed on them by painters since Raphael. The painting is also brimful with symbolism which prefigures the crucifixion. Jesus has torn his hand on a nail which is sticking out from the door that Joseph and his assistant have been working on. Blood from the wounded hand has dropped onto Jesus's foot and thus foreshadows the wounds inflicted on his body during the crucifixion. St Joseph and St Anne respond pragmatically to the incident. He pulls back Jesus's hand to inspect the wound and she extracts the offending nail from the unfinished door lying on the work bench. Mary, her face twisted in anguish, is the incarnation of grief; its marked exaggeration is triggered by a premonition of her son's fate, not the slight scratch on his palm. Millais freezes this mundane occurrence in the carpenter's shop in a tableau full of foreboding which is carried in the scene's innocuous details. Among the most resonant are: a half-finished basket whose whip-like reeds suggest the flagellation, a ladder leaning against the shop's back wall, reminiscent of that used in the deposition from the cross, and the pincers and nails on the work bench, further instruments of Christ's passion.

The painting's minutely observed details, deliberately awkward body language and rich symbolic references all ran counter to the established modes of representation and painterly decorum. The critics struggled to grasp the work's intent. Some thought Millais had pushed his practice to the verge of caricature. In an attempt to create an expressive and original pictorial language Millais had drawn on two contradictory sources of inspiration. He reached back in the history of art to late medieval painting and scrutinized nature. These sources stood in stark contrast to the academic practice which regarded the art of the High Renaissance as the unparalleled pinnacle of artistic achievement and worked with an idealized notion of nature. Millais's picture represents a deliberate rebuttal of academic values. In the tempestuous cultural climate of the time, riven with the threat of revolution and religious controversy, the critics recognized the painting as an act of defiance but suspected wider ramifications. As Charles Dickens had done, they saw in it a rejection of progress, suspected Catholicism and called the work a 'pictorial blasphemy'. As a result of Millais's experiment with available pictorial paradigms, which he wrested from their ideological signification, the work confounded expectation by radically refuting established conventions.

Towards a new Protestant painting

During the Brotherhood years (1848–53), the Pre-Raphaelites were mostly interested in religious subject matter because it chimed with their quest for earnestness and sincerity in art. They focused on art and not religious belief *per se*. They were drawn to the rich symbolic language of Christian iconography – a language that was being rediscovered and explained by authors such as Lord Lindsay and Anna Brownell Jameson.[6]

Jesus Christ, who topped the list of Immortals, was one of an idiosyncratic group of heroes much in the same fashion in which he seeped into the lines of Thomas Carlyle's lecture series *On Heroes, Hero-Worship and the Heroic in History* (1841). In these lectures, Carlyle conceived of history as the cumulative biographies of great men. It was they who shaped the course of history through a combination of circumstance and personality. The greatest of them all was Jesus Christ, so awe-inspiringly great in fact that Carlyle scarcely dared breathe his name. The Pre-Raphaelites shared this spiritual notion of Christ as a 'super-hero' figure. But it was not until the mid-1850s that one of them showed a serious interest in developing a new form of religious painting.

The doctrine of 'truth to nature' which the Pre-Raphaelites had adopted from Ruskin's writings presented an acute challenge for Hunt's representation of the risen Christ. *The Light of the World* (1851–3, Figure 5) is redolent with symbolism. Christ has stopped in front of an overgrown door, the hinges rusty from neglect. He is attired in priestly robes and wears the crown of thorns. The full moon rising behind his head endows him with a natural halo. This is a soothing night vision. The premise is simple: open your soul and let in the divine messenger. The artist aimed to ground the supernatural aspects of Christ in the minutiae of the everyday, here furnished by a moonlit English orchard with gnarled trees, bright green apples, brambles and weeds, all rendered with careful attention to detail. Yet the picture feels unreal: it is a vision, a fantasy.

George Bernard Shaw called it a 'childish conception' and wondered how 'a contemporary of Spencer, Comte and Darwin … should have painted that'.[7] Writing in 1886, he was also amazed by the picture's enduring popularity, stating that 'it must remain a treasure of English art' for as long as the British public refused to engage with the critical thinkers whose works had undermined the very fabric of Christian belief. In an age of religious doubt prompted by historical research and scientific discovery the painting achieved iconic status because it presented a soothing allegory of the omnipresence of the Christian faith. The work also marks the artist's private conversion and the turning point in his engagement with religious art. After

Figure 5 William Holman Hunt, *The Light of the World*, 1851–3, retouched
1858, 1886, oil on canvas over panel, 125.5 × 59.8 cm (arched), Warden and
Fellows of Keble College, Oxford.

a period of personal doubt, Hunt adopted a broad-minded Evangelicalism which upheld the divinity of Jesus Christ. He aimed to create a contemporary religious art relevant to mid-Victorian sensibilities which grounded a staunch Protestantism in realistic representation.

In 1854 Hunt embarked on his first journey to the Middle East. Like so many travellers before him, the artist was enraptured by the Orient's alleged timelessness. He seemed to have stepped back in time to the days when Jesus and his disciples inhabited the arid landscape of Galilee. It was here that he resolved the problem of painting the figure of Christ with Pre-Raphaelite attention to detail. Hunt imagined and reconstructed the historical circumstances of Christ's existence. For this, he turned to contemporary readings of the Bible which drew on historical investigation and textual criticism. Since the 1830s scholars had been treating the Scriptures no longer as the divinely inspired word of God but as a palimpsestical historical record that was open to interpretation. Out of such endeavours emerged a strong interest in the historical figure of Jesus which increasingly eroded his divine status.

In 1860, Hunt's breakthrough work, *The Finding of the Saviour in the Temple* (Birmingham Museums & Art Gallery), the result of his Middle Eastern sojourn, was first shown in London to great critical acclaim. That same year, the most important religious controversy of the age erupted over the publication of *Essays and Reviews*. The contributions presented a view of the Bible based on scientific, linguistic and historical investigation, focusing on contentious issues such as the historicity of the text, the impact of geology on the interpretation of Genesis and the precise nature of the supernatural in the biblical narrative. None of what the seven contributors had to say was strictly speaking new, but it was being said by churchmen and influential educators. The controversy over *Essays and Reviews* by far outstripped that over a nowadays far better-known book, Charles Darwin's *On the Origin of Species* (1859). It crystallized the belief of liberal Protestantism and was regarded as the manifesto of the Broad Church movement. In his essay, Frederick Temple urged the intrepid pursuit of knowledge for a deeper comprehension of the Bible: 'He is guilty of high treason against the faith who fears the result of any investigation, whether philosophical, or scientific, or historical.'[8] The authors of *Essays and Reviews* excelled at taking apart the frayed framework of Christianity. However, they were reluctant to propose answers to such pressing questions as the divinity of Jesus. Was he merely the son of man or indeed the son of God?

Hunt showed no such hesitation in his representation of Christ. The young Jesus who confronts the rabbis in the Temple is a figure inspired by his divine mission. And to his fretting parents who have been looking for him all over Jerusalem for days he calmly responds: 'I am about my father's business'.

Hunt presented this moment of divine revelation with meticulous attention to historical detail, hoping to capture it with an emotive immediacy which would make the biblical stories come alive for the contemporary viewer. He researched costumes and customs and scoured Jerusalem for Jewish models willing to sit for the rabbis. For the interiors of the temple, though, he sought inspiration from the reconstruction of the Moorish Alhambra at the Crystal Palace in South London. Despite such lapses in historical accuracy, his work brought an unusual rigour to the representation of the biblical narrative. He succeeded in substituting the worn-out conventions of religious painting with a sense of the Oriental and the authentic. He also created a figure of Jesus at once immediate, human and divine.

And as if in response to Temple's mournful observation, 'we have lost that freshness of faith which would be the first to say to a poor carpenter – Thou art the Christ, the Son of the living God',[9] Hunt's next major religious work represented Jesus in the carpenter's shop. In *The Shadow of Death* (1869–73, Figure 9) the artist gave his own version of the theme Millais had painted some twenty years earlier, in *Christ in the House of his Parents*. Hunt's Jesus is a young man with a distinctly Middle Eastern complexion, not the 'red-haired blubbering boy' at whom Charles Dickens had taken umbrage. The carpenter's son has finished his daily toil and assumed a pose for prayer. The late-afternoon sun casts Jesus's shadow on the back wall of the shop where the tools of the trade are fixed. Cross-bar and shadow meet in a sinister premonition of the crucifixion which is visible only to the viewer and the Virgin Mary. She is kneeling beside an open chest which contains the gifts the Magi once brought, together with the promise of Jesus's messianic future. Their rich splendour spills out into one corner of the carpenter's shop which speaks of mundane existence and toil. As Mary tries to reassure herself of the Magi's almost forgotten promise she is arrested by the sudden shadow on the wall and the fate it announces. Hunt thus makes visible Jesus's divinity in the detail of the everyday. Even the arcaded window doubles as an accidental halo. The image is crammed with objects that carry meaning. Jesus's bright red headband in the foreground prefigures the crown of thorns; the handle of the saw which aggressively points at his chest suggests the lance with which he is pierced while on the cross. The scrolls of the Torah on the window-sill point to his occupation as scholar, and the landscape of Lower Galilee seen through the window shows the key place of his ministry.

This carefully constructed scene was based on research conducted in Nazareth where Hunt had made drawings of a local carpenter's shop for Frederic William Farrar's enormously popular *The Life of Christ* (1874). The work of both men shared the ethnographer's historicizing gaze and the desire to ground Christ's divinity in fact. The figure of Christ had recently been the subject of a number of high-profile biographies. Of these, Ernest Renan's radical *Vie de Jésus* (1863) was perhaps the most controversial. The author had cast doubt on the divine status of Jesus Christ and deemed him an inspired preacher rather than the son of God. In the face of such 'heresy', Hunt and Farrar were keen to uphold in their work the notion of Jesus as unequivocally divine. Hunt combined first-hand knowledge of the Orient with a complex pictorial language which relied on detailed realism, pre-monition and typology, a system that connected events in the Old Testament with those in the New and provided a means of transcending the immediate timeframe of the scene.

Despite the considerable success of Hunt's brand of realist Protestant painting which combined a historical reading of the Bible with orientalist modes of representation and chimed with the beliefs of the Broad Church movement, it did not spawn a new school of painting or win him church commissions. His enterprise depended on the sale of his works and their copyright to art dealers who recouped their expenses through profitable one-picture touring shows, and print and catalogue sales. Hunt remarked in his autobiography how pleased he was that large numbers of England's working men had bought the engraving of *The Shadow of Death*.[10] In 1904, Hunt completed a third, much larger version of *The Light of the World* which toured parts of the British Empire for sixteen months and was seen by some four million people. It was permanently installed in St Paul's Cathedral in London – although the artist wanted the work to go to the National Gallery of British Art (now Tate Britain) – and prints have graced homes, vicarages and schoolrooms across the United Kingdom.

Religion as poetry

As early as 1822, James Marsh, the American editor of Coleridge's *Aids to Reflection*, detected a reversal in the relationship between religion and poetry, arguing that 'Poetry and history are no longer one … as our sober ancestors turned all their poetry into religion, so we are in danger of turning all our religion into poetry.'[11]

In fact, as history and scepticism began to scrutinize the biblical record they inadvertently helped to reaffirm the Bible's poetic potential. In his sem-inal *Das Leben Jesu* (1835), which was translated into English by George Eliot in 1846, David Friedrich Strauss refuted the established twin interpret-ations of the Scriptures, the supernatural and the rational. He plotted a third route instead: a mythical reading of the record.[12] Similarly, Ernest Renan's *Vie de Jésus*, although much maligned for its outright denial of Christ's divinity, offered a highly original and poetical re-imagining of Jesus, the man and inspirational orator. The historicizing of the Bible played itself out in the various biographies of Jesus Christ as well as in travel guides to the Holy Land. Biblical criticism aimed to read the Scriptures like any other book, admitting to a fallible and fragmentary record of events and probing their status as the inspired word of God. Whilst such processes challenged more traditional forms of belief, they also firmly placed the Bible in the ranks of world literature and pure poetry.

John Ruskin claimed that 'to Rossetti, the Old and New Testaments were only the greatest poems he knew' on par with such medieval masterpieces as Malory's *Morte d'Arthur* and Dante's *Vita Nuova*.[13] In his paintings and poems Dante Gabriel Rossetti treated biblical narratives and settings with a degree of poetic licence, as in his poem 'Ave'. When his brother pointed out that Nazareth was not a marine town, Rossetti replied: 'I fear the sea must remain at Nazareth.'[14] That is also where it was located in James Collinson's poem, 'The Child Jesus', which appeared in the second issue of *The Germ*. The poem offered a series of imaginary quotidian occurrences in the childhood of Jesus which prefigured scenes from the final days of his life, commonly referred to as the passion of Christ. In its use of prefigurative symbolism it resembled the popular poetry of John Keble, who was one of the leaders of the Oxford Movement and Professor of Poetry at Oxford (1831–41). Collinson was torn between his devotion to art and the Catholic faith. In 1850 he converted to Roman Catholicism and resigned from the Pre-Raphaelite Brotherhood.[15]

With its members he shared an interest in an imaginary reworking of biblical scenes from the life of the Virgin Mary and the infancy of Jesus. But the engraving which accompanied his poem, 'The Child Jesus', shows a formulaic approach to symbolism at odds with Millais's brilliant reworking of Christian iconography in the controversial *Christ in the House of His Parents*. Collinson's conversion also demonstrates that interest in Christian symbolism could indeed harbour affinities with the Catholic faith. In the preface to her authoritative exploration of Christian iconography, *Sacred and Legendary Art* (1848), Anna Jameson distanced herself from early art's religious lure: 'I have taken throughout the aesthetic and not the religious view of those productions of Art which ... informed with a true and earnest feeling, and steeped in that beauty which emanates from genius inspired by faith, may cease to be Religion, but cannot cease to be Poetry; and as poetry only I have considered them.'[16]

From the start, the Pre-Raphaelites were attracted to the poetry of the biblical records. Dante Gabriel Rossetti's *Ecce Ancilla Domini!* (1849–50, Tate) represents an entirely original and poetic rendering of the Annunciation which anticipated the Aesthetic Movement of the 1860s. Mary has been roused from her sleep by the sudden arrival of the archangel Gabriel, who announces her divine calling. The image is sexually charged and displays psychological empathy with the young woman who is at once startled and pensive. The colour scheme is strikingly reduced: almost a study in white such as those James McNeill Whistler would undertake in the next decade. Throughout the 1850s, Rossetti continued to produce a number of highly poetical watercolours of biblical characters and events. One such is *Mary in the House of St John* (1858, Delaware Art Museum). It shows mother and favourite disciple performing quiet acts of domesticity. The prominent window cross dominates the composition and reveals their shared thoughts which revolve around loss, pain and grief. Here the symbolism is not prefigurative but commemorative.

Rossetti's influence is perhaps best felt in the work of second-generation Pre-Raphaelites such as Arthur Hughes and Edward Burne-Jones. A prime example is Hughes's strikingly poetic *Nativity* (1858, Birmingham Museums & Art Gallery), which exudes a strong sense of spirituality. It is marked by a rich colour scheme and cramped claustrophobia which focus attention on Mary's tender gesture of swaddling her baby for the first time. Burne-Jones's design for the wood-engraving, *The Parable of the Boiling Pot*, depicts a rather obscure episode from the Old Testament book of Ezekiel (24:1–14): the Chaldean siege of Jerusalem. The evocative and ghoulish passage recounted the city's bloody fate. His rendition is imbued with the menacing and intensely poetic medievalism of Rossetti's watercolours.

While Hunt was finishing his first orientalist rendering of a biblical scene, *The Finding of the Saviour in the Temple*, Millais embarked on his designs for *The Parables of Our Lord* (1864). His illustrations often concentrate on single figures or the psychology of exchange between two figures. In the most striking of these, Millais has boldly updated the setting. In *The Foolish Virgins* the young women wear crinolines and cower in front of a cottage door in the driving rain. Others such as *The Good Samaritan* or *The Prodigal Son* show a mild period flavour which indicates another time and place without the frantic specificity displayed in Hunt's reconstructed biblical scenes.

The Parables of Our Lord constitutes the brothers Dalziels' most memorable venture into biblical illustration. In the 1860s, the influential printers and engravers also planned an edition of the Bible with illustrations by contemporary British artists of which Burne-Jones's *Parable of the Boiling Pot* was one. The project did not materialize, but in the 1880s they published *Dalziels' Bible Gallery* with over sixty illustrations to the Old Testament. These offer a wide range of styles, including old-masterly renditions and Nazarene idealism as well as heavily orientalized and purely poetic interpretations.

The poetic impetus in biblical illustration is perhaps best captured in the 1870s edition of *The Illustrated Family Bible* which contained stunning works by the Pre-Raphaelite sympathizer William Bell Scott. The editorial emphasized the novelty of Scott's contribution. The illustrations, it claimed, 'glowed with poetry' and 'address[ed] themselves to the understanding and the heart'.[17] Scott's most striking pieces concentrate on Christ's passion and resurrection. The artist deflects the painful physical aspects of the crucifixion. The crosses on Golgotha are visible in the distance, the emphasis is placed on the moment the veil in the Temple is rent and the sky darkens. Scott foregrounds the event's supernatural and spiritual elements. Likewise, he does not shy away from representing the resurrection. We are in fact invited to bear witness to it. The scene is set in the sepulchre. Two mourning angels watch over Christ who has just opened his eyes and is pulling back the shroud. The resurrection is made more immediate by the fact that Christ's two guardians have not yet realized the miracle.

From the 1860s onward, various forms of poetical representation of the Scriptures established themselves alongside Hunt's compelling orientalist realist mode. Walter Pater's *The Renaissance* (1873) perhaps best exemplified the emerging poetical sensibilities of the age. In its blatant eclecticism the collection of essays on individual artists, poets and scholars was somewhat reminiscent of the list of Immortals. In Leonardo da Vinci Pater celebrated 'the painter who has fixed the outward type of Christ for succeeding centuries' without relinquishing his innate scepticism or his relentless quest for beauty.[18] For Pater, Leonardo represented the quintessential modern artist who shared with the author 'the poetic passion, the desire of beauty, the love of art for its own sake'.[19] Implicit here is the new religion of beauty. Aestheticism has arrived and with it 'a new kingdom of feeling and sensation and thought'.[20]

The list of Immortals placed Jesus Christ in a secular pantheon of poets, painters and political figures. The four-star rating hinted at his exceptional status, perhaps his divinity even. Interest in religious subject matter remained a recurring theme of Pre-Raphaelite art. The Pre-Raphaelites were at the forefront of defining religious art for the age whether as ascetic reform of the worn-out conventions of painting, historicizing oriental realism or pure brilliant poetry which celebrated art as the new religion.

NOTES

1   Hunt, vol. 1, p. 160.
2   *Germ*, 'Introduction by William Michael Rossetti', p. 6.
3   Ruskin, vol. V, p. 83.

4 William Michael Rossetti (ed.), *Dante Gabriel Rossetti: His Family-Letters with a Memoir*, 2 vols. (London: Ellis and Elvey, 1895), vol. I, p. 135.

5 Charles Dickens, 'Old Lamps for New Ones', *Household Words*, 1 (15 June 1850), pp. 265–7.

6 Lord Lindsay, *Sketches of the History of Christian Art*, 3 vols. (London: John Murray, 1847); Anna Brownell Jameson, *Sacred and Legendary Art*, 2 vols. (London: Longman, Brown, Green & Longmans, 1848).

7 George Bernard Shaw, 'In the Picture-Galleries: The Holman Hunt Exhibition', *The World*, 24 March 1886, quoted from Mark Roskill, 'Holman Hunt's Differing Versions of the "Light of the World"', *Victorian Studies*, 6 (March 1963), p. 236.

8 Frederick Temple, 'The Education of the World', *Essays and Reviews* (London: John W. Parker and Son, 1860), p. 25.

9 Ibid., pp. 24–5.

10 Hunt, vol. II, p. 310.

11 James Marsh, 'Ancient and Modern Poetry', *North American Review* (1822), quoted from Jeffrey F. Keuss, *A Poetics of Jesus: The Search for Christ through Writing in the Nineteenth Century* (Aldershot, Hants.: Ashgate, 2002), p. 89.

12 David Friedrich Strauss, *The Life of Jesus Critically Examined* (1835), ed. Peter C. Hodgson (London: SCM Press Ltd, 1973).

13 Ruskin, vol. XXXIII, p. 271.

14 *Germ*, 'Introduction by William Michael Rossetti', p. 21.

15 On the vexed question of the reasons for Collinson's resignation see Ronald Parkinson, 'James Collinson', in Leslie Parris (ed.), *Pre-Raphaelite Papers* (London: Tate Gallery, 1984), p. 71.

16 Jameson, *Sacred and Legendary Art*, vol. I, pp. xi–xii.

17 *The Illustrated Family Bible* (London: A. Fullarton and Co., n.d. [1876]), p. 2 ('Publisher's notice').

18 Walter Pater, *The Renaissance: Studies in Art and Poetry: The 1893 Text*, ed. Donald L. Hill (Berkeley: University of California Press, 1980), p. 77.

19 Ibid., p. 190.

20 Ibid., p. 5.

5

ANDREW M. STAUFFER

The Germ

In the late summer of 1849 in London, the seven Pre-Raphaelite Brothers and a few of their friends began work on the first issue of a journal that would soon become *The Germ*. Other names were suggested at the time – *The P. R. B. Journal, Thoughts Towards Nature, First Thoughts, The Truth-Seeker* – but *The Germ* ultimately prevailed. As these several titles suggest, the journal was animated by philosophical and cultural ambitions. Like the PRB itself, *The Germ* aimed to resist the main currents of mid-Victorian aesthetics; it was published to give voice to a new school of art. In 1882, one critic called it 'the first, and indeed the only, official manifesto or *apologia* of Pre-Raphaelitism' with a distinct 'propagandist aim'.[1] Indeed, *The Germ* can be nominated as the first British periodical dedicated to a specific artistic programme. It therefore stands behind the many avant-garde journals or 'little magazines', such as *The Savoy* and *BLAST*, that would come to define aesthetic movements of later periods. In the event, *The Germ* had a very short run: only four issues appeared, from January through May 1850, each selling less than 100 copies. Yet these four issues maintained an influence over many artists and writers of the nineteenth century, and the journal continues to be read, imitated and reprinted. *The Germ* thus became a self-consciously foundational part of the Pre-Raphaelite legacy.

It was primarily Dante Gabriel Rossetti's idea, a collaborative monthly magazine that would be a venue for the Pre-Raphaelites' general aesthetic principles and early enthusiasms. In September 1849, Rossetti wrote to F. G. Stephens, 'it is my opinion that we may now make a very stunning thing indeed of this Magazine if we only like, and that it ought to be rigidly stuck to'.[2] From the first, *The Germ* was meant as a collective endeavour to bind the young men together as a true Brotherhood, which was itself the more serious inheritor of the 'Cyclographic' sketching society that many of them had belonged to the previous year. As a periodical 'conducted principally by artists' (its cover would eventually announce) and offering poetry, fiction, prose, reviews and a single etching per issue, *The Germ* required

literary output of the young painters and sculptors in the Pre-Raphaelite circle, and this too was one of Rossetti's goals. He plainly wanted to foster verbal and visual cross-over work in keeping with his own propensities. Yet this
also meant that authorial contributions were often delayed or abandoned,
sometimes having to be cajoled out of artists primarily occupied in the studio. Because of this aspect of its composition, the actual contents of *The
Germ* are somewhat miscellaneous. However, there is a discernible spirit to
the journal, and its history and contents help us understand this formative
phase of the careers of a number of the Pre-Raphaelites.

Ernest Radford calls *The Germ* 'the respiratory organ of the Brethren'.[3]
It contains interesting work by James Collinson, F. G. Stephens, Thomas
Woolner and William Holman Hunt, as well as by PRB associates such as
Ford Madox Brown, Walter Deverell, Coventry Patmore and William Bell
Scott. Yet it was the Rossetti family that dominated the journal – Dante
Gabriel, William Michael and Christina contributed among them about half
of its total contents, with William Michael serving as editor. In this regard,
The Germ looks back to the private, hand-drawn magazines produced by
the Rossetti household: the *Hodge Podge; or Weekly Efforts* which they
wrote sporadically in the summer of 1843, and its short-lived successor,
the *Illustrated Scrapbook*. William Michael reports that both 'The Blessed
Damozel' and an early version of 'The Portrait [On Mary's Portrait]' were
originally intended by his brother for one of these 'manuscript family
magazine[s]', which would mean that the family was still producing them
in 1846 or 1847.[4] Only two years later, *The Germ* was being drafted, and
'The Blessed Damozel' found a place there instead. 'The Portrait' (then
under a different title) was considered for the third issue, but Dante Gabriel
ultimately withdrew it on the grounds that *The Germ* had already featured
too many poems mourning dead women.[5] One of his other such contributions – 'My Sister's Sleep' – was printed under the heading 'Songs of One
Household', a seeming allusion to the intermural quality of *The Germ* and
its Rossettian contributions (see Figure 14).

At the time that *The Germ* was conceived, Dante Gabriel Rossetti was
channelling a number of very different literary influences, including primarily the early Italian poets, John Keats, Robert Browning and Edgar Allan
Poe. Many of these interests were shared by the PRB circle and formed the
basis of their association. In 1848, they even drew up a 'list of Immortals'
that they claimed 'constitutes the whole of our Creed'.[6] As Stephen Spender
has observed, the 'influence which the Pre-Raphaelites shared far more than
their pedantic formulae for the technique of painting were Keats's [poems]
"Isabella" and "La Belle Dame sans Merci" … The truest experience which
they shared was literary.'[7] It is certainly the case that the majority of the

names of the PRB 'Immortals' are authors, not painters; and at least half of those authors can be associated with Romanticism in some way (see Appendix Two). The resulting aesthetic programme found its centre in heroic imaginative effort, personal vision and a devotion to truth. In this view, medium mattered less than the springs and goals of art: paintings, sculptures and poems were all possible, equally valid expressions of an artist's thought.

Two prose contributions to *The Germ* stand out as representative summaries of the Pre-Raphaelite attitude towards art, and they are perhaps the best points of entry into an understanding of the early Brotherhood and their journal: D. G. Rossetti's serious hoax-story, 'Hand and Soul' (in issue one), and F. G. Stephens's essay 'The Purpose and Tendency of Early Italian Art' (in issue two). The only piece of prose fiction to appear in *The Germ*, 'Hand and Soul' serves as a kind of Pre-Raphaelite parable and is almost certainly the most important single contribution to the periodical. It tells the story of Chiaro dell'Erma, a fictional late-medieval Italian painter who struggles to find his true path as an artist, first pursuing fame for its own sake. His work becomes known and admired throughout Tuscany, but, in his dissatisfaction, Chiaro begins to believe that he 'had misinterpreted the craving of his own spirit' and turns instead to an art of religious faith and moral purity.[8] However, this results in 'laboured ... cold and unemphatic' pictures that do not please his former audiences. The story culminates as he witnesses a feud in Pisa break into a street battle right in front of his allegorical paintings of Peace on the walls of a church. Dismayed by the failure of his art and haunted by fears that he has betrayed himself, his viewers and painting itself, Chiaro is visited by an apparitional woman, 'clad to the hands and feet with a green and grey raiment, fashioned to that time'. She tells him, 'I am an image, Chiaro, of thine own soul within thee. See me and know me as I am' (553). Her message is one of comfort and direction: 'What [God] hath set in thine heart to do, that do thou; and even though thou do it without thought of Him, it shall be well done ... In all that thou doest, work from thine own heart, simply; for his heart is as thine, when thine is wise and humble ... Know that there is but this means whereby thou mayst serve God with man: – Set thine hand and thy soul to serve man with God' (554–5). The central part of the story ends with Chiaro painting a portrait of his visitant, and '[w]hile he worked, his face grew solemn with knowledge' (555). Thus fusing humility with egoism, the tale urges the painter towards a devotional mode of art in which his own soul serves as both inspiration and subject.

Such an allegory begins to reveal what was meant by the Pre-Raphaelite emphasis on 'truth to nature', a mode that need have little to do with objective clarity or pictorial realism. As Graham Hough writes of the story, 'This is a new kind of pre-Raphaelite creed – not fidelity to external nature, but fidelity to one's own inner experience … an art carried on in this spirit is itself a worship and service of God.'[9] While some Pre-Raphaelite artists, following Ruskinian principles, did attend closely to the minute details of the natural world, D. G. Rossetti was constantly pushing the concept of 'nature' towards an interior, imagined land. Along these lines, Roger Fry has written that 'Rossetti … could only paint at all under the stress of some special imaginative compulsion. The ordinary world of vision scarcely supplied any inspiration to him. It was only through the evocation in his own mind of a special world, a world of pure romance, that the aspects of objects began to assume aesthetic meaning.'[10] Such divisions within the Brotherhood would eventually become more apparent, but within *The Germ*, which was itself so much a product of Rossetti's influence, 'truth to nature' can be read as code for the expression of one's imagination. Like the Romantic poets before them, the early Pre-Raphaelites turned to the natural world as a mirror for their own self-projections; they hoped that the artistic mediations they enacted upon the world's particulars would reveal the truth of their hearts and souls.

Surrounding the tale of Chiaro is a contemporary frame narrative, set in the spring of 1847, which describes the experience of a visitor encountering Chiaro's painting of his soul during a visit to the Pitti Gallery in Florence. 'Hand and Soul' begins and ends in this frame, and the whole story mixes references to real and invented sources in a way that has led some readers to go looking for the fictional Chiaro dell' Erma's work or commentaries on it by the equally spurious 'Dr. Aemmster'. Coming across Chiaro's small painting of the feminine apparition of his soul, the narrator writes, 'As soon as I saw the figure, it drew an awe upon me, like water in shadow … the most absorbing wonder of it was its literality. You knew that figure, when painted, had been seen; yet it was not a thing to be seen of men' (555–6). Such an evaluation nicely exemplifies the Pre-Raphaelite desire for an art that would synthesize private vision and truth to nature. Chiaro's painting is both natural and supernatural, visually faithful to the details of his model and yet thoroughly predicated on self-projection that borders on magic conjuring. The painting also represents a pastiche of medieval style and nineteenth-century subject: thirteenth-century Italian paintings of women were almost exclusively of the Virgin or female saints, whereas Chiaro has rendered an image of his own soul. 'Hand and Soul' ends as the narrator's reverie is interrupted by the dismissive remarks on Chiaro's painting by a group of French and Italian art students, who call it mystical, impenetrable and insignificant. The frame story thus serves multiple functions: it brings the story into contemporary focus, augmenting its reality-effect and its hoaxing aspect; it allows D. G. Rossetti to stage the reception of 'pre-Raphaelite' art as a scene of 'awe' and 'wonder'; and it simultaneously casts this scene in an ironic light with the art students' commentary. We are left thinking that both Chiaro's painting and 'Hand and Soul' itself might be jokes or might be deadly serious, or – like much of the work of Poe for example – might be both at the same time.

F. G. Stephens's brief essay on early Italian art is an explicitly 'pre-Raphaelite' exordium, addressed to English artists. Stephens would go on to serve for several decades as regular art critic for the influential journal *The Athenaeum*, and so became a key figure in communicating Pre-Raphaelite principles to a wider audience, the *Germ* essay is an early warm up for that process. Written in defence of medieval painting, it moves rapidly towards general exhortations about the practice of art. Like other members of the Brotherhood in these early days, Stephens places a heavy emphasis on 'truth', a term used so vaguely that it evokes only a general sense of uncompromised devotion: 'Truth in every particular ought to be the aim of the artist. Admit no untruth: let the priest's garment be clean.'[11] The image of the artist as priest is in keeping with the religious, vaguely Catholic, atmosphere of *The Germ* more generally considered. The sentiment also reflects the influence of the Nazarenes, a group of early nineteenth-century German painters including Friedrich Overbeck who advocated a monastic devotion to art: another band of brothers who served as an important precedent for the PRB. With the Pre-Raphaelites, such an attitude typically turns aside from conventional Christianity in favour of a religion of art which must be pursued through one's own private vision. And yet this is a project to be conducted with 'humility', 'simplicity' and 'faith'.

In his essay, Stephens claims (echoing Rossetti's terms) that an artist's abilities as a draughtsman need only be 'maintained as a most important *aid*, and in that quality alone, so that we do not forget the soul for the hand'. The 'soul' here is the true source of art. Expanding upon this view, he makes clear that 'passion and feeling' are the crucial components, while 'mere technicalities of performance are but additions; and not the real intent and end of painting, as many have considered them to be'. In Stephens's view, the best artists always represent 'nature with more true feeling and love, with a deeper insight into her tenderness; ... it is the crying out of the man, with none of the strut of the actor ... Let us have the mind and the mind's-workings, not the remains of earnest thought which has been frittered away by a long dreary course of preparatory study, by which all life has been evaporated' (60). One can see the outlines of the Pre-Raphaelite programme in all of this, particularly in the essay's youthful confidence and disdain for preparation and 'mere' accomplishment. Stephens closes the essay by quoting a remark he attributes to the German philosopher and poet G. E. Lessing that 'the destinies of a nation depend upon its young men between nineteen and twenty-five years of age' (64), referring fairly precisely to the ages of his fellow conductors of *The Germ* and suggesting that the PRB have come to change the world.

Worth noting is the fact that both Stephens's essay and 'Hand and Soul' include mention of the art historian Jean-Baptiste-Louis-George Seroux d'Agincourt (1730–1814), whose multi-volume, massively illustrated *Histoire de l'art par les monumens* (1810–23) was a key sourcebook for the PRB as they developed their appreciation for medieval art. Seroux d'Agincourt is remembered now as one of the first modern historians to demonstrate a deep interest in the art of the Middle Ages, offering a wealth of illustrations meant to demonstrate art's various stages of decay and renewal from the fourth to the sixteenth century. An English translation of the *Histoire* was published by Longmans in 1847, just as the PRB was forming; Rossetti, Stephens and others took much of their knowledge of early Italian painting, sculpture and architecture from its hundreds of engraved plates. In their focus on the culture of the thirteenth and fourteenth centuries, both 'Hand and Soul' and 'The Purpose and Tendency of Early Italian Art' reflect Seroux d'Agincourt's influence on the artistic attitudes of the Brotherhood.

As mentioned, Poe's work was a major influence on the early Pre-Raphaelites and particularly on the contents of *The Germ*. One of the PRB list of 'Immortals', Poe had become a preoccupation of Dante Gabriel Rossetti's after 1846, when *The Raven and Other Poems* had appeared in London; it was the American author's poems, rather than the tales of mystery and suspense, that impressed the Pre-Raphaelites at this date. 'The Blessed Damozel' and 'The Portrait [On Mary's Portrait]' are both plainly indebted to 'The Raven', and Rossetti produced a series of remarkable illustrations inspired by Poe's poems, 'The Raven', 'The Sleeper' and 'Ulalume', between 1846 and 1848, apparently intended for an edition of Poe to be sponsored by the PRB. From one vantage, *The Germ* was the project that displaced that projected edition, while yet retaining some of the animating energies behind it. William Michael Rossetti confirms that 'The Blessed Damozel' derived from his brother's

> perusal and admiration of Edgar Poe's *Raven*. 'I saw' (this is Mr. Caine's version of Rossetti's statement) 'that Poe had done the utmost it was possible to do with the grief of the lover on earth, and I determined to reverse the conditions, and give utterance to the yearning of the loved one in heaven.' Along with *The Raven*, other poems by Poe – *Ulalume, For Annie, The Haunted Palace*, and many another – were a deep well of delight to Rossetti in all these years.[12]

Other contributions to *The Germ* evoke Poe's themes and language, such as Thomas Woolner's poem 'Of My Lady in Death', with its close attention to the hollow cheeks and sad eyes of his dying mistress and its closing line that echoes 'The Raven': 'No more; no more; oh, never any more.' Throughout his life, Poe himself dreamed of founding a magazine devoted to 'Independence, Truth, and Originality', and one might even say that *The Germ* emerged as a curious displaced homage to this desire.

Other important contributions to *The Germ* include Christina Rossetti's poems, most of which tend towards images of death or death-like sleep ('Dream Land' (Figure 14), 'An End', 'Repining', 'Song', 'Sweet Death') while evoking what would become her characteristic posture of self-abnegation and Anglican faith. William Michael Rossetti's reviews of Arnold, Browning and Clough mark the early emergence of a contemporary canon of Victorian poets through the eyes of the PRB; these comments on Arnold's self-consciousness or the extravagance of Browning's style show a perceptive critic at work. In addition, a number of poems by lesser-known figures are worth special attention, especially James Collinson's sentimental but weirdly harrowing series of vignettes, 'The Child Jesus: A Record Typical of the Five Sorrowful Mysteries', William Bell Scott's 'Morning Sleep' with its imaginative evocation of a state of reverie, and Walter Deverell's 'A Modern Idyl', with its quietly haunting vision of his little cousin playing in her white dress among the dry red leaves. Most of the essays are more like partial memoranda or rapid sketches and have little general interest, except as an index of the subjects and attitudes of the early PRB. An exception is John Orchard's posthumously published 'A Dialogue on Art', which, like Stephens's essay on early Italian art, offers a philosophical conversation about art's relation to nature, to thought, to spirituality and to purity, in ways that illuminate the terms of Pre-Raphaelitism.

One should also consider the four etchings of *The Germ* as a record of collaboration among members of the Brotherhood. William Holman Hunt's illustration for Woolner's 'My Beautiful Lady/My Lady in Death' is a two-panel picture showing first the narrator awkwardly grasping his beloved's arm as she leans towards a riverbank to pluck a flower, and then the narrator collapsed on her grave, with a procession of mourners in the background. Collinson's etching to accompany his poem 'The Child Jesus' recalls early Renaissance religious groups with its placement of Jesus at the centre of a pyramid of adorers, and yet here all are strangely children. A Latin epigraph quotes Psalm 8:2 ('Out of the mouth of babes and sucklings hast thou ordained strength'), alluding to the scene in his poem in which Jesus's childhood friends cast their little offerings at his feet. Ford Madox Brown's illustration 'Cordelia' (to accompany William Michael Rossetti's poem by that name) and Deverell's 'Viola and Olivia' (for John Tupper's poem) both turn to Shakespearean subjects, paying particular attention to details of wardrobe and architecture. Worth noting is the fact that Deverell's model for Viola was Elizabeth Siddall, who would soon become an integral part of the PRB circle and the wife of Dante Gabriel Rossetti. It was Deverell who introduced her to the circle, and this is the first known result of her modelling for the PRB. Taken together, the etchings provide a minor though evocative indication of Pre-Raphaelite artistic practice and interests, including character-driven literary and religious subjects and historical pastiche. They set forth a style of flat, intense representation quite at odds with the current scene of Victorian painting.

Part of the reason for the relative dearth of illustration in *The Germ* has to do with production costs: from the beginning, the journal was barely funded out of the pockets of its young contributors. *The Germ* was published by Aylott and Jones of Paternoster Row, who produced mostly ecclesiastical titles but who also had, in 1846, brought out the poems of 'Currer, Ellis and Acton Bell' – that is, Charlotte, Emily and Anne Brontë. The decision to take on *The Germ* seems to have followed closely on Aylott and Jones's relatively encouraging experiment with the Brontës. D. G. Rossetti wrote to his brother in September 1849, 'I believe we have found a publisher for the Magazine: viz: Aylott and Jones, 8 Paternoster Row. I was introduced to them about a week back by a printer, a friend of Hancock's. They seemed perfectly willing to publish for us.'[13] He went on to claim optimistically, 'I am certain that as soon as the prospectus is printed, we shall be able among the lot of us, to secure at least 250 subscribers before the thing is out at all, and this will be something.' These expectations were not met, however, and *The Germ* struggled to find subscribers and purchasers: the first issue sold seventy copies, and the second only forty. Publishing arrangements were changed as was the title, and the next two issues came out as *Art and Poetry: Being Thoughts towards Nature, Conducted principally by Artists*, with the publishing firm of Dickinson and Company subjoined. This change was the result of financial interventions by George Tupper and his brothers John and Alexander, members of the PRB circle and the printers of *The Germ*. The only palpable result was an increase in items in the journal written by the Tupper family, and it was soon clear that *The Germ* must fold. In June, D. G. Rossetti wrote, 'that unfortunate "star of the morning" [has] returned for ever into its natural firmament'.[14]

Yet the critics were kinder to *The Germ* than were purchasers, and it managed to get fairly widely noticed and praised in the reviews. *The Spectator* for 12 January 1850 found 'some (uncultivated) ability and freshness, or at least strangeness, in the publication', and the *Morning Chronicle* for 4

February remarked on the 'many original and beautiful thoughts in these pages' while yet hoping that the writers would get 'rid of those ghosts of medieval art which now haunt' their work. Reflecting on *The Germ* after its demise, *The Critic* (1 June 1850) judged that it 'was too good – that is to say, too refined and of too lofty a class, both in its art and in its poetry – to be sufficiently popular to pay even the printer's bill'. The reviewer went on to say, 'we cannot contemplate this young and rising school in art and litera-ture without the most ardent anticipations of something great to grow from it, something new and worthy of our age, and we bid them God speed upon the path they have adventured'. Much did grow from the Pre-Raphaelite *Germ*, not only as the individual careers of its members and wider circle progressed, but as Pre-Raphaelitism in art spread and evolved through the course of the century. Other literary periodicals in the nineteenth century emerged as part of this legacy as well, notably *The Oxford and Cambridge Magazine* (1856) and the American journals *The Crayon* (1855–61) and *The New Path* (1863–5), all of which pledged allegiance more or less explicitly to the example of *The Germ* and the Pre-Raphaelite themes and methods it discussed and demonstrated.

Looking back on *The Germ* at the turn of the twentieth century, an elderly William Michael Rossetti wrote, 'I am quite aware that some of the articles ... though good in essentials, are to a certain extent juvenile; but juvenility is anything but uninteresting when it is that of such men as Coventry Patmore and Dante Rossetti.'[15] Indeed, a great part of the con-tinuing appeal and historical importance of *The Germ* rests precisely in the view it allows of the earliest chapter of the Pre-Raphaelite movement and the initial works and writings of its founding members. In addition, it occu-pies a signal position in the history of English periodical culture as the first avant-garde magazine devoted to a set of aesthetic commitments. Indeed, its influence in this regard went beyond England to the French Symbolist magazines of the fin de siècle such as *La Plume* (1889–1913), *La Conque* (1891–2) and *Le Centaure* (1896). In an attempt to bring art to bear upon spiritual truth, and in their devotional attention to nature and to their inner selves, the early Pre-Raphaelites shifted the terms and practice of Victorian art. In producing *The Germ*, they made a record of their early collaborative efforts to these ends. We can glimpse now in the juxtaposition of subjects and styles some of the energetically various conversations that were shared by these young people as they began their careers. J. Ashcroft Noble tells the story that, soon after the publication of the first issue, one of the PRB over-heard a young man in a bookseller's shop reading the title as '*The Gurm*' with a hard G; this was found so humorous that the name stuck, and mem-bers of the circle often called their journal by that name[16]; D. G. Rossetti spells it that way, for example, in a letter to his brother of 3 September 1850.[17] It seems fitting that this note of mockery came to nominate a project that might, in other hands, have been overburdened with earnest self-importance. At its best moments, *The Germ* (or *Gurm*) seems to give us access to those early enthusiasms and high-spirited negotiations that lay behind the work of this extraordinary group of English artists and writers.

NOTES

1 J. Ashcroft Noble, 'A Pre-Raphaelite Magazine', *Fraser's Magazine* (May 1882), p. 569.
2 DGR *Correspondence*, vol. I, p. 89 (letter 49.8).
3 Ernest Radford, 'The Life and Death of "The Germ"', *Idler*, 13 (1898), p. 227.
4 William Michael Rossetti, *Dante Gabriel Rossetti as Designer and Writer* (London: Cassell and Company, 1889), p. 126.
5 William Michael Rossetti, *Pre-Raphaelite Diaries and Letters* (London: Ellis, 1900), pp. 258–9.
6 Hunt, vol. I, p. 159.
7 Stephen Spender, 'The Pre-Raphaelite Literary Painters' (1945), repr. in James Sambrook (ed.), *Pre-Raphaelitism: A Collection of Critical Essays* (Chicago and London: University of Chicago Press, 1974), p. 120.
8 *The Works of Dante Gabriel Rossetti*, ed. William M. Rossetti (London: Ellis, 1911), p. 551; page references hereafter in text.
9 Graham Hough, *The Last Romantics* (London: Methuen, 2007), p. 53.
10 Roger Fry, 'Rossetti's Water Colours of 1857', *Burlington Magazine*, 29 (June 1916), p. 100.
11 *Germ*, p. 61; page references hereafter in text.
12 William Michael Rossetti (ed.), *Dante Gabriel Rossetti: His Family-Letters with a Memoir*, 2 vols. (London: Ellis and Elvey, 1895), vol. I, p. 107.
13 DGR *Correspondence*, vol. I, p. 92 (letter 49.11).
14 DGR *Correspondence*, vol. I, p. 147 (letter 50.9).
15 *Germ*, 'Introduction by William Michael Rossetti', p. 27.
16 Noble, 'A Pre-Raphaelite Magazine', p. 569.
17 DGR *Correspondence*, vol. I, p. 151 (letter 50.15).

PART TWO

Pre-Raphaelites

6

JEROME MCGANN

The poetry of Dante Gabriel Rossetti (1828–1882)

At a time when poetic originality in England might seem to have had its utmost play, here was certainly one new poet more, with a structure and music of verse, a vocabulary, an accent, unmistakably novel, yet felt to be no mere tricks of manner adopted with a view to forcing attention – an accent which might rather count as the very seal of reality on one man's own proper speech; as that speech itself was the wholly natural expression of certain wonderful things he really felt and saw … That he had this gift of transparency in language – the control of a style which did but obediently shift and shape itself to the mental motion, as a well-trained hand can follow on the tracing-paper the outline of an original drawing below it, was proved afterwards by a volume of typically perfect translations from the delightful but difficult 'early Italian poets'; such transparency being indeed the secret of all genuine style, of all such style as can truly belong to one man and not to another.

Walter Pater, 'Dante Gabriel Rossetti' (*Appreciations*)[1]

The translation of culture

Published a year after Rossetti's death in 1882, Pater's essay remains perhaps the single best study of Rossetti's poetry we have. It is certainly the place to begin examining what Rossetti accomplished and why he was, as Ruskin and Pater thought, the most important aesthetic figure to emerge in the second half of the nineteenth century in England.[2]

Paradoxical though it may seem, Rossetti's poetic innovations and 'originality' are a direct consequence of the 'typically perfect translations from the delightful but difficult "early Italian poets"' that Rossetti published in 1861. Pater seems not to have known that these translations were produced before Rossetti wrote any of his celebrated 'original' poetry. But nearly all of Rossetti's verse before 1847, when he wrote his famous signature poem 'The Blessed Damozel', was translation work of some kind. The crucial period came in 1845–6 when he began translating Dante and other twelfth- and thirteenth-century Italian poets. He worked from the collections and resources he found in the library of his father Gabriele, a notable if somewhat eccentric scholar of Dante.

The mature and finished character of Rossetti's poetry, not least in this early period of its flowering, was achieved through the discipline he acquired translating Dante and the poets of the early *stil novisti* circle. These translations – probably begun as early as 1845 – plunged him into a study of Europe's most significant body of love poetry. The study was also an artistic practice, putting him through a rigorous course in writing technique. Rossetti became intimately involved with a group of writers – Dante, Cavalcanti and Cecco Angiolieri being the most eminent – who had established unsurpassed models for a poetry addressing itself to what Shelley would later call Intellectual Beauty. We rightly think of Rossetti as a poet of love and physical passion. Nonetheless, he is also (like Dante) an intellectual writer pursuing a definite set of ideas. The period 1848–51 is a distinctly programmatic one for Rossetti. His work and ideas inspired the founding of the original Pre-Raphaelite Brotherhood, along with its polemical theoretical organ *The Germ*, which appeared in four numbers in 1850.

Two aspects of this translation work are especially important. First, issues of prosody were a paramount concern. Italian verse is syllabic rather than accentual and it has much more flexible rhyming resources than English. Rossetti set out to explore what could be developed in English for Italian prosodic forms.

Distinguishing 'literality' from 'fidelity' in translation, he argued that a successful 'metrical translation' must develop verse equivalents for the prosodic features of the originals. In this kind of translation, semantic 'literality' is a secondary consideration since the poem's chief object is an act of *poetic* expression. Prosody is thus not ornamental or a service function for the poem's ideas, it is the proper form of ideas being called into a poetic (rather than a prose) expression. A prose translation – Rossetti called it 'paraphrase' – would deliver a different version of the ideas.[3]

Rossetti was also interested in translating Dante and his circle because their work supplied a model and example of a literary and cultural revolution. The key text here was Dante's *La Vita Nuova*, the autobiography in which Dante made his own life a poetical myth or exponent of the cultural changes he was prosecuting. This was the chief, and probably the first, of the 'early Italian' works Rossetti translated. Composing his translation *The New Life*, Rossetti was consciously trying to map Dante's life onto his own. He changed his name from Gabriel Charles Dante Rossetti to Dante Gabriel Rossetti while he was involved with this work. The formation of the Pre-Raphaelite Brotherhood in 1848–9 and the subsequent publication of

The Germ were both driven by Rossetti's commitment to his programme of literary, artistic and cultural transformation.

'Dante and his Circle', as Rossetti named the early Italian poets he was translating, thus looms over the entirety of his career and his self-conception. Dante's autobiography would exert a shaping influence on the structure and argument of his poetical masterwork, the sonnet sequence he titled *The House of Life*.[4] Because that argument is grounded in the 'unmistakably novel' style that Rossetti fashioned from his work with early Italian poetry, we must examine that style with attention and grasp its implications.

Two exemplary styles

Look at these passages from the first three stanzas of Rossetti's translation of Dante's canzone 'Gli occhi dolente per pieta del core' ('The eyes that weep for pity of the heart'):

> And because often, thinking, I recall
> How it was pleasant, ere she went afar,
>   To talk of her with you, kind damozels,
>   I talk with no one else,
> But only with such hearts as women's are.
>   And I will say, – still sobbing as speech fails, – (Lines 7–12)

> Beatrice is gone up to the high Heaven,
>   The kingdom where the angels are at peace;
> And lives with them: and to her friends is dead.
> Not by the frost of winter was she driven
>   Away, like others; nor by summer heats;
> But through a perfect gentleness, instead. (Lines 15–20)

> Wonderfully out of the beautiful form
>   Soared her clear spirit, waxing glad the while;
>   And is in its first home, there where it is.
> Who speaks thereof, and feels not the tears warm
>   Upon his face, must have become so vile
>   As to be dead to all sweet sympathies. (Lines 29–34)

Two of Rossetti's most notable innovations are in play here. First, he seeks out unusual rhymes: 'damozels', 'else', 'fails'; 'peace', 'heats'; 'form', 'warm'; 'is', 'sympathies'. This licentiousness assumes spectacular forms throughout his work. 'The Bride's Prelude', an astonishing technical performance in various respects, rhymes 'minute', 'into 't' and 'foot'; 'sconce', 'pleasaùnce' and 'swans'; 'err', 'wearier' and 'year'; 'haste' and 'last'; 'aggrieved' and 'lived'; 'paramours' and 'ours'. These freedoms draw the reader's attention to prosodic relationships that a more strict approach to end-rhyme would not so clearly exploit. The rhyme 'peace/heats' in the canzone, for example, throws into sharp relief the related rhymes 'Beatrice/gentleness', and that relation in its turn exposes the non-acoustic rhyme in the opening line, 'Beatrice/heaven'.

Of course all poetry depends upon these kinds of devices. What is important about Rossetti, as Pater clearly saw, is the programmatic character of the work. His irregular approach to end-rhyming exposes the reader to the formal resources of verse that go unmarked in more traditional approaches to prosody. The results are clear in a stanza like the following:

> But else, 'twas at the dead of noon
>> Absolute silence; all
> From the raised bridge to the guarded sconce
> To green-clad places of pleasaùnce
> Where the long lake was white with swans.
>> ('The Bride's Prelude', lines 262–6)

The three end-rhymes recuperate a set of linguistic relations that drive through the 'a' and 's' phonemes and proliferate through various secondary and tertiary relations. The immediate consonance of 'swans' and 'white with' sharpens the connection of the key phrase 'Absolute silence' to the final line, an effect complicated and further defined through the rhythmic rhyme 'white with/long lake'.

When readers comment on the 'painterly' character of Rossetti's verse, attention is drawn to sharply rendered pictorial details, as in this stanza. But the pictorial character of the work is at least as much owing to the way Rossetti visibilizes (so to say) his poetry's musical relationships. In poem after poem – 'For a Venetian Pastoral', 'For an Allegorical Dance of Women', 'Silent Noon' and 'The Monochord' are arresting examples – sound and silence acquire material presence, often, as in the above stanza from 'The Bride's Prelude', appearing a kind of mobile of alphabetic functions.

Rossetti's liberated approach to rhyme is closely connected to another prosodic feature of his translation work: the effort to educe a syllabic verse effect from accentual English forms. All the translations are grounded in patterns of monosyllabic words. Lines 29–34 of the canzone above exhibit the procedure in an especially clear way. Not only do the lines have few polysyllables, the insistent monosyllables completely transform the iambic and accentual patterns that English words naturally incline to. Consequently, formally polysyllabic words like 'Thereof', 'upon' and 'become' are virtually decomposed into monosyllabic units by the gravity field of the passage at large. At the same time, the focused polysyllables in the first line – 'Wonderfully' and 'beautiful' – attenuate the iambic urgencies of English, preparing the prosodic ground for the flattened syllablism that typifies this verse. When we arrive at line 34, the iambic pentameter pattern we would ordinarily read into the line seems now exactly *not* the pattern we want. For 'Wonderfully out of the beautiful form' of Rossetti's lines is emerging a new prosodic life for English verse, drawing 'true sympathies' from the inspiration of Dante and his circle.

Dante's *Vita Nuova* is a performative argument for a new poetry – a kind of drama in which Dante, observing and expressing himself 'in seconda persona', lays out his aesthetic *ragionamento*, his rationale of verse.[5] Rossetti's translations, in particular his translation of the *Vita Nuova*, recuperate Dante's aims for Rossetti's nineteenth-century world, most especially his English-speaking world. Pater recognized Rossetti's 'originality' partly because the programmatic character of Rossetti's work was so clearly displayed. The translation work has 'transparency of style' because it dramatizes its relation – its differences and similarities – with the work it is imitating ('a well-trained hand can follow on the tracing-paper the outline of an original drawing below it'). The translations assume that their reader will bear in mind the template of the syllabic language for which an English equivalent is being created. Rossetti's works are much less translations than demonstrated acts of poetic transformation.

That dialectic of language shows Pater how Rossetti's primary subject is not its semantic 'content' – ideas, themes, 'meanings' – but the possibilities of poetic expression as such. The translations and pastiche work are 'transparent' experiments with the English language. Remarkably, the work will evolve through two very different styles of 'new' writing. On the one hand is a so-called realistic style that gets developed in some of Morris's and Meredith's most interesting work and that certain Modernists will refashion – most notably Pound, Eliot and Reznikoff – often in free-verse forms. On the other hand is a variety of 'poetic' and consciously artificial styles that we associate with Swinburne, Yeats and Stevens as well as many of the aesthetes and decadents.

Although Rossetti mastered both of these styles, he was much more interested and involved in a poetry of high artifice. He pursues a realistic style almost exclusively in his earliest work – poems like 'My Sister's Sleep', 'The Woodspurge', 'On Refusal of Aid Between Nations' and the poems that he wrote during his trip with William Holman Hunt to Belgium and France (for instance, 'Antwerp and Bruges', which he published separately in *The Germ* [March 1850]). But all of his earlier poetry – 'The Blessed Damozel' and the *Sonnets for Pictures* are clear examples – is marked by an impulse towards exact detail. Moreover, the imitations and outright pastiche work so prevalent in his 1840s writing are directly related to this stylistic realism. In these texts – Browning's influence is apparent – Rossetti strove for a kind of historicist truth, a style that would efface the presence of Rossetti's personal identity. Poems like 'Ave' and 'Madonna Consolata', along with his various ballad imitations ('Dennis Shand' for instance), give the pattern, which is perhaps most spectacularly illustrated in the pastiche irregular sonnet, 'Piangendo star con l'anima smarrita'.[6]

This kind of realism was the hallmark of what Hunt understood as the 'true' impulse of the Pre-Raphaelite programme. Hunt's dismay that Rossetti's work, both artistic and literary, came to be identified with Pre-Raphaelitism was born of his awareness that Rossetti was not interested in realism of detail as such. It should be said in passing, therefore, that Rossetti's work in this style is not the outstanding example of Pre-Raphaelite realism. The palm here goes to his brother William Michael, whose narrative poem 'Mrs. Holmes Grey' is one of the most remarkable poetic innovations of the period. The parody newspaper report in the poem (lines 398–732) achieves, in a Victorian idiom and without free verse, nearly everything we value most in Modernist 'Objectivism', as is clear from the opening of that section of the poem:

'*Coroner's Inquest – A Distressing Case.*
An inquest was held yesterday, before
The County Coroner, into the cause
Of the decease of Mrs. Mary Grey,
A married lady. Public interest
Was widely excited.
    'When the Jury came
From viewing the corpse, in which are seen remains
Of no small beauty, witnesses were called.
"Mr. Holmes Grey, surgeon, deposed: 'I live
In Oxford, where I practise, and deceased
Had been my wife for upwards of three years ... '"' (lines 398–408)[7]

D. G. Rossetti's other style – highly artificial and, when it is least successful, mannered – is closely bound to his use of realist techniques. Both styles covet what Blake called 'minute particulars' where the particulars are elements of language-as-such, irrespective of their semantic value. Reference can be subordinated to phonetic demands, as it is in 'The Lady's Lament', Rossetti's early reprise on Poe's 'The Raven':

Never happy any more!
In the cold behind the door
That was the dial striking four:
One for joy the past hours bore,
Two for hope and will cast o'er,
One for the naked dark before.
    No, no more.   (Lines 22–7)

Many of Rossetti's late poems – for instance, 'Chimes', 'Adieu' ('Wavering whispering trees') and 'A Death-Parting' – are virtually abstract representations of phonological values. But the impulse to organize poems where the verbal units – lines, phrases, words, even (as we've already seen) individual letters – acquire a kind of absolute presence operates through all his work.

Here are three arresting – but also typical – examples:

> Could you not drink her gaze like wine?
>   Yet though its splendour swoon
> Into the silence languidly
>   As a tune into a tune,
> Those eyes unravel the coiled night
>   And know the stars at noon.
>
> ('The Card-Dealer', lines 1–6)

> It lies in Heaven, across the flood
>   Of ether, as a bridge.
> Beneath, the tides of day and night
>   With flame and darkness ridge
> The void, as low as where this earth
>   Spins like a fretful midge.
>
> ('The Blessed Damozel', lines 31–6)

> Look in my face; my name is Might-have-been;
>   I am also called No-more, Too-late, Farewell;
>   Unto thine ear I hold the dead-sea shell
> Cast up thy Life's foam-fretted feet between;
> Unto thine eyes the glass where that is seen
>   Which had Life's form and Love's, but by my spell
>   Is now a shaken shadow intolerable,
> Of ultimate things unuttered the frail screen.
>
> Mark me, how still I am! But should there dart
>   One moment through thy soul the soft surprise
>   Of that winged Peace which lulls the breath of sighs, –
> Then shalt thou see me smile, and turn apart
> Thy visage to mine ambush at thy heart
>   Sleepless with cold commemorative eyes.
>
> ('A Superscription')

In the first passage the 'coiled' pattern of musical relations is tuned as an explicit subject. As in the similar early poem 'For an Allegorical Dance of Women', a pictorial – indeed, a painterly – scene is deliberately set to musical figures that force our attention to the poem's phonological values.

The famous stanza from 'The Blessed Damozel' works towards similar ends through different means. The monosyllablism of Rossetti's Italian translations is clearly important to this verse. But the semantic urgency of the text is further dismantled by an aggressive use of enjambment and caesura. These come at semantic junctures that make the statement level of the verse far less apparent than the pure physique of its language. That kind of move rises to an extreme level of complexity in the sonnet 'A Superscription', written more than twenty years later. Added to the sonnet's echo-chamber of sounds are a series of difficult syntactic inversions beginning at line 4. Because the poem opens with a notable transparency of meaning – emphasized by its allegorical literality – the involuted syntaxes acquire special force. The sonnet also illustrates a typical Rossettian use of monosyllabic language. Octave and sestet ground themselves in monosyllablism until the final two lines, when polysyllabic words overwhelm both sections, closing each with a play of assonances and consonances that reach back to envelop the entire sonnet.

The productions of time

Translation, imitation, pastiche: in Rossetti's hands, these forms of writing expose a dialectical pattern that shapes his aesthetics, both artistic and literary. His signature formal innovation – the so-called 'double work of art' – is an explicitly dialectical event.[8]

The typical Rossettian double work develops in the manner of *The Girlhood of Mary Virgin*. That is to say, Rossetti executes a picture (Figure 6) and then writes a poem – usually a sonnet or a pair of sonnets – that comments and elaborates upon the pictorial work. The first of the two 'Girlhood' sonnets is an ekphrasis of the painting, the second an allegorical interpretation. (Only once – in the famous case of 'The Blessed Damozel' – did the textual work precede the pictorial work. In another case, the 'Introductory Sonnet' to the 1881 edition of *The House of Life*, the textual and visual elements are inseparably bound to each other in the manner of a Blake illuminated book.)

The meticulous attention to detail in the 'Girlhood' ensemble is a sign of conscious artifice. The 'realism' of these works is, like Browning's monologues, historicist: that is, the picture and the poems reference Rossetti's conception of how a medieval imagination would treat this subject. Consequently, Pater's remark about Rossetti's translations, that 'a well-trained hand can follow on the tracing-paper the outline of an original drawing below it', applies here as well. Rossetti's 'Girlhood' works are the tracings of an 'original' medieval way of representing the primitive Virgin Mary, who is 'gone … a great while' from the periods of the Middle Ages and the nineteenth century.

Figure 6 Dante Gabriel Rossetti, *The Girlhood of Mary Virgin*, 1848–9, oil on canvas, 83.2 × 65.4 cm, Tate, London. © Tate, London, 2011.

The special status of Rossetti's 'Introductory Sonnet' is useful for helping us understand these double works. Blake's 'composite art', as it has been aptly called,[9] had a profound influence on everything Rossetti did, not least on his double works. But the gap that stands between the composite parts of the Rossettian double work is one of its essential features. Blake does not develop or exploit this kind of gap to anything like the extent that Rossetti does. We know that Blake's work continually shifts the reader's or viewer's perspective, and we can see how much Rossetti learned from studying Blake's methods. But we can also see the difference.

Blake's programme was to cleanse the doors of perception in order to reveal the infinite world 'closed by your senses five':

If the doors of perception were cleansed every thing would appear to man as it is, infinite.
For man has closed himself up, till he sees all things thro' narrow chinks of his cavern.

(*The Marriage of Heaven and Hell*, Plate 14)

Infinity is obscured by the veil of phenomenal appearance, including the veils, artistic and literary, created by the arts of this world, which seduce us, Blake thought, with illusions of permanence. Blake's work is thus a kind of self-consuming artefact, an artistic project designed to carry one to another order of reality, beyond any conceivable set of apparitions, including the apparitions of Blake's own work.

Rossetti proceeds differently. His is not a transport to Eternity but a study of the House of Life in all its transformations and illusions. The situation is nicely defined in a notebook entry Rossetti wrote for a picture he projected but did not execute: 'Venus surrounded by mirrors, reflecting her in different views'. (A sketch of this picture survives.)[10] The idea defines what is involved in the Rossettian double work of art. Each part of the double work is a unique view of an ideal whose existence is posited through the different incarnate forms. The double work ensemble is an index, a momentary monument, of the process by which the visionary imagination sustains and develops itself. What is eternal in Rossetti is the transformational process itself – the 'productions of Time' that Blake's Eternals, situated elsewhere, are 'in love with'.[11]

While Rossetti's friend Swinburne glories in revelations of that process, Rossetti sees it through a glass darkly. Unlike Dante or Blake, Rossetti has no experience of a transmortal order except by historicist report. Dante and Blake both understand very well that they inhabit a world of illusions and that their work cannot render the world of Eternity. Their alienation is mitigated, however, because both distinguish a knowledge or experience of Eternity from the means of expressing it. The classic formulation of this faith is Dante's in the *Paradiso*, where he coins the word *trasumanar* to signal what cannot be signed:

> Trasumanar significar per verba
> non si poria; però l'essemplo basti
> a cui esperienza grazia serba.

> One cannot signify transhuman change in words; therefore
> let my poetic image serve for those who know the experience of divine grace.
>
> (*Paradiso* I. 70–2, my translation)

The point is that both Blake and Dante have had visionary experiences of a transhuman condition, as their work declares. Rossetti's experience – it is apparent in his signature poem 'The Blessed Damozel' – reports on a very different, a very mortal, paradise:

> And still she bowed herself and stooped
> Out of the circling charm;

Until her bosom must have made
  The bar she leaned on warm. (Lines 43–6)

Rossetti's art occupies what he called 'an inner standing-point', where this central Rossettian proverb holds: 'Thy soul I know not from thy body, nor / Thee from myself, neither our love from God' ('Heart's Hope', lines 7–8).[12] At once participant and observer of processes of radical transformation, knowing only human and not transhuman grace, Rossetti suffers perpetual bewilderment (a recurrent word in his writing, as in 'The Hill Summit', lines 10–11: 'I must tread downward through the sloping shade / And travel the bewildered tracks till night').

Another of Rossetti's touchstone poets, Browning, evades Rossetti's disillusion by standing aside from his historicist reports – that is to say, from his famous dramatic monologues, where Browning *in propria persona* plays no part. Rossetti does not insulate himself from his writing in that way, as a dramatic monologue like 'Jenny' demonstrates. The result is a poetry where hope is haunted by despair, disaster by strange signs of promise. Nothing illustrates the situation so well as the supreme poem of bewilderment of *The House of Life*, the sonnet 'He and I':

Whence came his feet into my field, and why?
  How is it that he sees it all so drear?
  How do I see his seeing, and how hear
The name his bitter silence knows it by?
This was the little fold of separate sky
  Whose pasturing clouds in the soul's atmosphere
  Drew living light from one continual year:
How should he find it lifeless? He, or I?

Lo! this new Self now wanders round my field,
  With plaints for every flower, and for each tree
  A moan, the sighing wind's auxiliary:
And o'er sweet waters of my life, that yield
Unto his lips no draught but tears unseal'd,
  Even in my place he weeps. Even I, not he.

Part of the climactic sequence of *The House of Life*, the sonnet marks a final crisis of consciousness. In one sense its disorienting pronouns record the literal dismemberment of the speaker's identity, defining thereby the nadir of the work's psychic drama. But because Rossetti's sonnet sequence has been driven to follow the logic of a *via negativa* since Sonnet XXVI ('Life-in-Love'), 'He and I' comes to represent that ultimate condition of emptiness required by the spiritual quest.

The fact that this sonnet is followed by the sonnets 'Newborn Death' and 'The One Hope' emphasizes its place in the sequence's dark logic. A secret promise enters with the allusion to Dante's *Vita Nuova* in line 9 of 'He and I'. This ghostly presence of a 'new self' remains obscurely pronominal – unnamed, like 'The One Hope' which it anticipates. It is the self that has discovered the 'lifeless' state (line 8) of the self that is dying of its desire, like St Teresa. It is the self that can 'weep for pity' at its other, bewildered self and in that very act generate what the last sonnet in the sequence calls 'the gift of grace unknown' ('The One Hope', line 11). Not, be it noted, the gift of a transhuman grace, but the gift of a grace known only through the sibylline leaves of a pagan poetics.

So while Rossetti is clearly invoking the formalities of Dante's myth at this pivotal moment in his poetic masterwork, his argument is very different. 'Grace' here emerges from a mortal order where change and uncertainty rule. The last four sonnets of *The House of Life*, from 'He and I' through 'The One Hope', are dominated by a series of unanswered questions that lead to a final, secular prayer for a 'word' that is both a 'name' and a 'spell'.

> When vain desire at last and vain regret
>   Go hand in hand to death, and all is vain,
>   What shall assuage the unforgotten pain
> And teach the unforgetful to forget?
> Shall Peace be still a sunk stream long unmet, –
>   Or may the soul at once in a green plain
>   Stoop through the spray of some sweet life-fountain
> And cull the dew-drenched flowering amulet?
>
> Ah! when the wan soul in that golden air
>   Between the scriptured petals softly blown
>   Peers breathless for the gift of grace unknown, –
> Ah! let none other alien spell soe'er
> But only the one Hope's one name be there, –
>   Not less nor more, but even that word alone.
>   ('The One Hope')

As Rossetti told his friend Alice Boyd in a letter of 22 March 1870, the sonnet expresses 'the longing for accomplishment of individual desire after death'. The pair of questions in the octave represent traditional alternative forms of 'accomplishment'. Privileging neither, the sonnet leaves these and all of its culminating questions unresolved, for the questions are important here not as problems to be solved but as emblems of living desire. So too for the prayer that completes everything (lines 12–14). It is the sequence's final figure and ultimate act of transformation – bewilderment appearing at last as a sacred form of desire. Like the questions posed in the last four sonnets of *The House of Life*, this prayer needs no reply, it needs only to be spoken.

To formulate these kinds of longing and uncertainties is the object of an art always moving *in medias res*. Thinking of the line of poets Rossetti all but created, Yeats would describe what is involved here in a useful prose paraphrase:

> We make out of the quarrel with others, rhetoric, but of the quarrel with our-selves, poetry. Unlike the rhetoricians, who get a confident voice from remem-bering the crowd they have won or may win, we sing amid our uncertainty; and, smitten even in the presence of the most high beauty by the knowledge of our solitude, our rhythm shudders.[13]

NOTES

1 Walter Pater, 'Dante Gabriel Rossetti', first published in Thomas Humphry Ward's 1883 edition of his anthology *The English Poets*, and reprinted with minor changes in Walter Pater, *Appreciations: With an Essay on Style* (London: Macmillan and Co., 1889), pp. 228–42 (quotation from pp. 229–30); cited here from the latter text in *The Rossetti Archive* (www.rossettiarchive.org/docs/pr99. p32.rad.html). All quotations from Rossetti's works are taken from the 'reading texts' supplied in *The Rossetti Archive*.

2 Jerome McGann, *Dante Gabriel Rossetti and the Game That Must Be Lost* (New Haven and London: Yale University Press, 2000), p. 2.

3 'Preface', Dante Gabriel Rossetti, *The Early Italian Poets: From Ciullo d'Alcamo to Dante Alighieri: (1100–1200–1300): In the Original Metres: Together with Dante's Vita Nuova: Translated by D. G. Rossetti* (London: Smith, Elder, and Co., 1861), p. viii; see www.rossettiarchive.org/docs/1–1861.yale.rad.html#1–1861.

4 The sonnet sequence, with details of its history and relation to Dante, can be found in *The Rossetti Archive* (www.rossettiarchive.org/docs/44–1869.raw.html). See also McGann, *Dante Gabriel Rossetti and the Game that Must Be Lost*, chapter 3.

5 Dante's move to cast his verse 'in seconda persona' – this is his formulation – is crucial, and he discusses it in relation to his poetry's 'ragionamento' ('rationale') in the prose parts of *La Vita Nuova*. See the prose that introduces his key can-zone 'Donne ch'avete intelletto d'amore'(www.rossettiarchive.org/docs/pq4308. a24.vol3.rad.html#p300); see also the discussion of the move in *The Rossetti Archive*'s commentary on Rossetti's translation of the canzone (www.rossettiar-chive.org/docs/10d-1861.raw.html).

6 Composed in Italian; for a discussion and translation see www.rossettiarchive. org/docs/17–1853.raw.html

7 Text from William E. Fredeman (ed.), *The P. R. B. Journal: William Michael Rossetti's Diary of the Pre-Raphaelite Brotherhood 1849–1853: Together with Other Pre-Raphaelite Documents* (Oxford: Clarendon Press, 1975), pp. 131–54.

8 See Maryan Wynn Ainsworth, *Dante Gabriel Rossetti and the Double Work of Art*, exhibition catalogue (New Haven: Yale University Art Gallery, 1976).

9 W. J. T. Mitchell, *Blake's Composite Art: A Study of the Illuminated Poetry* (Princeton, NJ: Princeton University Press, 1983).

10 See www.rossettiarchive.org/docs/f23.raw.html

11 *The Marriage of Heaven and Hell*, Plate 18.

12 Jerome McGann, 'D. G. Rossetti and the Art of the Inner Standing-Point', in David Clifford and Laurence Roussillon (eds.), *Outsiders Looking In: The Rossettis Then and Now* (London: Anthem Press, 2004), pp. 171–87.

13 William Butler Yeats, *Per Amica Silentia Lunae* (London: Macmillan, 1918), p. 29.

7

ELIZABETH PRETTEJOHN

The painting of Dante Gabriel Rossetti

In his memoir of his brother, William Michael Rossetti described the drawing of 1849, *The First Anniversary of the Death of Beatrice* (Figure 2), as 'more decidedly marked by the "Praeraphaelite" peculiarities of that date than anything else which Rossetti produced'.[1] What did William mean by this? The drawing is one of the very few works by members of the Brotherhood that include the 'P. R. B.' initials appended to the signature, and in the top right corner, outside the line that encloses the image, an inscription reads 'Dante G. Rossetti / to his P R Brother / John E. Millais'. On the literal level, then, the drawing is a Pre-Raphaelite artefact – not just a document of the friendships among the Brothers in the early days of their association, but a physical object handed from one Brother to another and invested with visible and legible signs of their collaboration within the wider Brotherhood.

On a second level, the image is 'Pre-Raphaelite' in subject and setting: it represents the early Italian poet Dante with a group of his friends, and another inscription marks the place and date, 'Florence, 9th June, 1291'. This seems to be the first time Rossetti represented a scene from Dante's story of his early life, the *Vita Nuova*, which he had just translated into English; the drawing makes a second translation, this time from word to image. By selecting the episode where Dante makes a drawing of an angel, on the first anniversary of Beatrice's death, Rossetti marks the transition from verbal to visual expression in his own exploration of Dante's art. At the same time, he gives the earlier poet a role, indeed a founding role (given the early date of the event), in the history of Italian visual art, as well as literature.

Rossetti had just begun to sign himself, as here, 'Dante G. Rossetti', altering the order of his own Christian names (he was christened 'Gabriel Charles Dante', and his family and friends continued to call him 'Gabriel'). His personal identification with the precursor poet is obvious, and it might even be said that, by showing Dante making a drawing, Rossetti causes his predecessor to identify, retrospectively, with himself as painter-poet. This suggests a third level of meaning for the drawing, which sets up an analogy between the historical 'Pre-Raphaelites' and the nineteenth-century ones. It is not quite possible to read the group represented in the drawing as a disguised group portrait of the nineteenth-century Brotherhood, for there are only six figures, yet the image captures something like the spirit of the early gatherings recorded in William's *P. R. B. Journal*.[2] Several friends have just entered the room, leaving the door ajar, and they crowd close, confident that they have the right not only to interrupt Dante at his work, but also to criticize it; one peers at the drawing, while two others, leaning on the back of Dante's chair, seem to share a comment, perhaps even a joke, as their mannered gestures hint. If the analogy is plausible, though, it does not make Dante (and therefore Rossetti) the centre of the artistic circle. The scene is composed instead as a confrontation, not without a sense of tension, between Dante and the next most significant poet of his circle, Guido Cavalcanti, the bearded figure in a long robe with whom he exchanges a serious glance. As much as the drawing reflects Rossetti's personal preoccupations, it is about artistic friendship and rivalry as much as it is about individual genius.

Perhaps, then, there is a fourth level of meaning, a programme or statement of artistic aims for the Brotherhood. Among these aims would be the interconnectedness of drawing and writing, and other arts are in evidence too: a sculpture of a saint affixed to the wall, a viol and bow on the floor below, and throughout the scene the arts of design, including a carved wooden chair and a stained-glass window. A curious geometrical figure is drawn on the wall of the window embrasure, and everywhere there are books and papers, evidence of scholarship or learning. Perhaps this gift to Millais, with its conspicuous PRB inscriptions, recommends Rossetti's programme for the Brotherhood: devoted to all the arts in concert, scholarly as well as convivial, defined by its affinity to the earlier artistic circle of Dante.

We cannot, of course, be certain that Rossetti intended the drawing to bear all of these meanings, or that his brother William interpreted it as doing so, but the subject matter is sufficient warrant, in itself, for proposing a sequence of interrelated levels of meaning, something central to Dante's practice with which Rossetti had to reckon when making his translation of the *Vita Nuova*. In the previous chapter, Jerome McGann shows how the translation formed Rossetti's poetic practice; here we shall see that it was no less important to Rossetti's practice as a visual artist. If he had to make 'his own language', in Ezra Pound's words, for rendering *stilnovista* poetry in English (like Pound, he also translated Cavalcanti),[3] he had also to make his own visual style for this second translation from word into image.

The style is new, though, in a special way, since it is also faithful to its original (which as McGann notes is not the same as being 'literal'). In this drawing of 1849 the distinctive style is already apparent: it translates into the pen-and-ink medium certain characteristics of the outline engravings through which Rossetti and his Pre-Raphaelite Brothers knew the visual art of the Early Renaissance painters, such as the frescoes of the Campo Santo in Pisa, engraved by Carlo Lasinio in the early nineteenth century (the volume they studied, according to tradition, when they formed the Brotherhood).[4] The angular figures, spasmodic gestures, profuse detail and flattened perspective are 'archaic' features, akin to the drawings of Millais and Hunt of similar date. Rossetti has often been accused of being an imperfect master of his craft, but the oddities of anatomy and perspective are 'mistakes' only in comparison with post-Renaissance conventions that would be anachronistic in the world of this drawing. In that light it would be more appropriate to marvel at the skill with which Rossetti invents a pictorial space and an array of figures that are rigorously consistent with one another, without falling back on art-school rules of thumb.

Anyway the control of Rossetti's pen-and-ink line gives the lie to any accusation of technical incompetence. Take, for example, the long parallel strokes that describe the folds of Cavalcanti's robe, or the more widely spaced but equally delicate graining of the chair: these have the verve of freehand drawing but never a glitch. There is no shading or smudging to create shadows among the drapery folds, only lines of equal weight, more or less close together to make forms darker or lighter. If Dante and Cavalcanti face one another in the represented image, Rossetti as giver and Millais as receiver of the drawing enter into similar rivalry. Rossetti may deserve his identification with Dante because he is also a poet, or simply as a birthright, but his draughtsmanship here can stand comparison with Millais, always considered the most dexterous of the Brothers.

The sheer painstaking of this drawing assorts oddly with a familiar anecdote, in which Rossetti abandons the technical exercise set him in 1848 by his first mentor, Ford Madox Brown, a study in oils of bottles or (as William more dismissively put it) 'pickle-jars', designed to teach skills in representing three-dimensional volumes on a two-dimensional surface.[5] According to Hunt, 'This discipline Rossetti had found so abhorrent that it had tormented his soul beyond power of endurance.'[6] The anecdote emphasizes what is certainly a fact, that Rossetti had less training in drawing and painting than his Pre-Raphaelite Brothers, which in Hunt's narrative tells against his claim to leadership of the group.

In an artistic project based on rejecting established techniques, though, it might be an advantage never to have been schooled in those techniques, a reason for the respect paid to Elizabeth Siddall's work a few years later. Rossetti is often said to have been 'self-taught', which may be true enough – but the drawing shows that, important as the word 'self' may be in this formulation, 'taught' should be taken with equal seriousness. The oil study of the pickle-jars survives, in the important Pre-Raphaelite collection at the Delaware Art Museum, and it is moderately competent, but it looks like a Rossetti mainly because the artist subsequently added a figure of a sleeping woman in his later, more famous style. If Rossetti could not learn to model three-dimensional volumes in 'correct' (i.e., post-Renaissance) perspective, that was perhaps because the exercise was imposed rather than self-motivated.

More importantly, though, it did not allow him to teach himself what he wanted to learn. A year later, *The First Anniversary of the Death of Beatrice* made a more effective technical exercise, in which volumetric form is by no means irrelevant; perhaps, indeed, the curious geometrical figure on the wall, with its flattened cylinder, alludes to the problem of representing volume in two-dimensional drawing. However, the crux of the exercise is to make a single drawing device, fine lines in parallel (although variously oriented) formations, serve to elaborate a highly complex populated space, one that persuades the viewer that it belongs to the Italian setting of five-and-a-half centuries ago. In one sense, this is an engraver's technique translated into the writer's medium of pen-and-ink, and verbal texts are at home within the image as well as around its framing line. In another sense, though, it thinks through the activity of drawing from scratch. It abruptly rejects the variety of effects cultivated by nineteenth-century engravers in favour of its single type of line: the exercise is to make this one type of line do the whole work of conveying the drawing's complex contents. Curves result from the different orientations of straight lines, and modelling from the different spacing of tonally equal lines on the white page, which remains much in evidence. Thus the drawing appears spare and lean, despite the density of its imagery.

At about the same time Rossetti made his first oil painting, *The Girlhood of Mary Virgin* (Figure 6), where again the representational level of meaning works together with the technique. The Virgin is learning to translate the visual appearance of a lily (her symbol) into a work of visual art, an embroidery. A recent technical analysis shows how consistently the painting was carried out. The colours do not overlap; instead, each stroke was placed into a space reserved for it in advance. The painting technique mimics the way an embroidery is composed of distinct coloured threads; the gold thread of the Virgin's needle was made like a real gold thread, with a core (in the painting, a green underpaint) overlaid with gold, and placed into a narrow space reserved for it within the red area that represents the fabric.[7] One way of explaining this laborious process would be to say that Rossetti was adapting his drawing technique to painting in oil colours; the technical analysis shows that everything in the image was carefully drawn before the colours were laid on. William Bell Scott observed Rossetti working on the painting with small watercolour brushes, to make strokes as distinct as pen lines rather than the blended volumes characteristic of contemporary oil painting.[8]

However, the experimental procedure is also a way of thinking through the activity of oil painting from scratch, in a fashion analogous to (rather than dependent on) Rossetti's simultaneous self-education in drawing. Just as he had taught himself to write by translating Dante, here he teaches himself to paint by imitating Jan van Eyck, the traditional inventor of oil painting. It is important, though, that this is not the kind of imitation recommended by Sir Joshua Reynolds in his *Discourses* and enshrined in the teaching of the Royal Academy and other art schools – that is, the adoption (and creative transformation) of specific elements from the prototype such as poses, gestures or compositional arrangements. Despite their antipathy to academic precept, the PRBs were not reluctant to use that method of imitation. As Malcolm Warner has pointed out, both Rossetti in the *Girlhood* and Millais in *Isabella* of the same year (Figure 10) adopted poses from figures of saints in an altarpiece by Lorenzo Monaco, the side panels from which entered the National Gallery in 1848 – the allusion was therefore very much up-to-date.[9] That procedure can perhaps be compared to the kind of translation that aims at 'literality'.

Rossetti's imitation of van Eyck is different, and much more like the practice of translation that he used for the *Vita Nuova*, one that aims at finding an equivalent for the poetic features of the original (such as metre and rhyme) rather than paraphrasing its ideas (see p. 90 above). As Ruskin remembered in 1865: 'I supposed, in old times, you were going to try to paint like that Van Eyck in the National Gallery with the man and woman and mirror.'[10] This refers to the painting now known as the *Arnolfini Portrait*, which entered the National Gallery in 1842, and which the Pre-Raphaelite Brothers (including Rossetti) often imitated in the older fashion – the circular mirror, in particular, recurs again and again in works of the extended Pre-Raphaelite circle through to the twentieth century.[11] In his first painting, though, Rossetti is concerned above all with teaching himself to 'paint like' van Eyck, not with borrowing any of its elements, nor even with copying the older artist's style – that too would be 'literal' rather than 'faithful', more like rote-learning than true self-teaching. Rossetti does make use of techniques attributed to van Eyck in recent accounts such as Charles Eastlake's *Materials for a History of Oil Painting* of 1847, in particular the pure white ground on which he lays his unmixed colours, and the reds and greens of the *Girlhood* recall those of the *Arnolfini Portrait*. However, this is not an exercise in historical reconstruction, and Rossetti does not attempt to replicate the complex sequence of layers that Eastlake observed in the work of the early Flemish painters.[12] Instead, he uses the white ground and unmixed colours to imagine the religious scene, which he further explores in two accompanying sonnets. For the next exhibition season, that of 1850, he clarified the process still further, in a scene of the Annunciation entitled *Ecce Ancilla Domini!* (the words of the Latin Bible with which Mary responds to the angel: 'Behold the handmaid of the Lord'; the painting is now in the Tate collection). Here the white ground becomes the presiding visual idea for the finished painting, predominantly white. Other colours are used sparingly and with ringing clarity. At the same time, they have symbolic force: white for the Virgin's purity, the blue traditionally used for her robe, here transferred to a background curtain. The embroidery from the *Girlhood* reappears, now completed; its searing red hints at the Passion to come.

Pace Hunt, who (at least in later years) thought Rossetti too devoted to the 'revivalist' side of the Pre-Raphaelite project, the paintings have nothing of pastiche about them; the figures' faces read as realistic portraits of individuals, like those in the contemporary paintings of Millais and Hunt, who were also experimenting with the white ground and pure colours of Early Flemish painting technique. Clearly this was a shared enterprise, instantly recognizable in the works of all three artists, and quickly taken up by other young artists as well; contemporary critics were in no doubt that the style was radically new, whether or not they approved. In one sense, it is pointless to speak of leadership in the development of what is so obviously a collaborative project. Yet Rossetti's experience of poetic translation provided an intellectual basis for the project – a 'theory', so to speak, although it manifested itself in poems and pictures, not a manifesto or treatise. Perhaps, paradoxically, it was his relative lack of experience as a painter that created the need to transform experimentation into something more programmatic. Thus Rossetti's first two oil paintings are at least as thoroughgoing in their demonstration of the new Pre-Raphaelite style as the works of his more experienced Brothers.

Yet Rossetti, unlike the other Brothers, made no more paintings of this kind. He was, indeed, the first of the PRBs to abandon the project in its initial form, and after 1850 he ceased to contribute to the annual public exhibitions; he showed his work only to friends and patrons, in his own studio, or (on rare occasions) at privately organized events. This withdrawal from the fray seems surprising on the part of the Brother who by all accounts was keenest on collaboration, and it has ordinarily been attributed to character failings. After the adverse criticism of the Pre-Raphaelite paintings in 1850, according to one line of argument, Rossetti became paranoid about showing in public. Alternatively, his lack of solid training, or his laziness, made him unable to continue in the painstaking procedure required for Pre-Raphaelite painting. Or his love-life intervened: obsessed first with Elizabeth Siddall, then with the disreputable Fanny Cornforth, finally with the wife of another man (Jane Burden, who married William Morris in 1859), he lost contact with his male colleagues and his art became merely a vehicle for his private passions. The tragic events of his later life – the death of Siddall in 1862, leading to unbridled grief, then drug addiction, and finally his death in 1882 – make compelling biography. They cast him as a pathetic figure, increasingly incapable of controlled artistic production.

These stories kept Rossetti's reputation alive throughout the twentieth century, when Pre-Raphaelite art was excluded from high culture, and in a sense they recognize his genius. A parallel would be the sensational life-story of Vincent van Gogh, who died in 1890, just eight years after Rossetti, and in both cases it is easy enough to debunk the romanticized, or fictionalized, aspects of the life-stories.[13] Yet van Gogh's art is permitted to transcend his personal tragedy. Rossetti's personal failure, on the other hand, has overwhelmed his artistic achievement: in the biographical literature he may appear as a genius, but a flawed one. It is only in very recent years that Rossetti has received serious attention from scholars of either literature or visual art, and this reappraisal has been led by literary scholars, most notably Jerome McGann. Rossetti's visual art, and particularly his work after the initial flourishing of the Brotherhood, remains more difficult to recuperate.[14]

In dramatic contrast is Rossetti's prominence in the popular media, based overwhelmingly on the paintings of women from the 1860s and 70s, familiar worldwide through endless reproduction on posters, greetings cards, picture books and the worldwide web. Perhaps, indeed, this is at the heart of the problem: Rossetti's later paintings seem too easily consumable to deserve serious scholarly attention. For the global public, moreover, these images have become the essence of Pre-Raphaelite visual style – the brand image, so to speak, of the Pre-Raphaelite movement. Rossetti's media celebrity threatens to obscure not only the sophistication of his own work, but the coherence of the Pre-Raphaelite movement as a whole.

It is by no means clear that media celebrity necessarily works in inverse proportion to quality (van Gogh would be an obvious counterexample). Even if it were, the problem remains: how can Rossetti's paintings of women be related to Pre-Raphaelite art, or indeed to his own poetic production in the later decades of his career? In the period of the Pre-Raphaelite Brotherhood, as we have seen, Rossetti's poetic and visual projects were intertwined, and in ways that had a formative impact on the movement as a whole. Did that cease to be the case, when he embarked on the paintings of women in 1859?

In one respect, these paintings can no longer be called 'Pre-Raphaelite': they take their inspiration no longer from the Early Flemish or Italian painters, but rather from masters of Raphael's own time. Thus they look very different from the *Girlhood* and *Ecce Ancilla Domini!*: full fleshy figures replace the ascetic, angular bodies of the earlier style, and complex paint layers of rich, blended pigment replace the fine individual brushstrokes of Rossetti's 'van Eyck' style. Yet the experimental procedure Rossetti used for creating this new style was precisely the one he had used in the earliest days of the Brotherhood. On a trip to Paris in 1860, he was carried away by Paolo Veronese's *Wedding Feast at Cana* (1562–3, Louvre): 'the greatest picture in the world beyond a doubt'.[15] He must also have been struck by the Louvre's Titian, *Woman with a Mirror* of about 1515, which he closely imitated in *Fazio's Mistress* of 1863 (Tate). Previously he had wanted to paint like van Eyck; now he was teaching himself to paint like the Venetians of the sixteenth century, Titian, Veronese and Giorgione. As before, he conceptualizes form and content together: the sensuous richness of his new 'Venetian' technique accompanies a sensuality or voluptuousness in the presentation of the female figure so powerful that it can repel viewers, if it does not enrapture them.

The pictures in this sequence, from *Bocca Baciata* of 1859 (Museum of Fine Arts, Boston) through to *Venus Verticordia* (Russell-Cotes Art Gallery and Museum, Bournemouth) and *Lady Lilith* (Delaware Art Museum), both finished around 1868, borrow the half-length figure seen in Titian's *Woman with a Mirror* and other Venetian paintings, and Rossetti tends to emphasize a potential of the half-length figure. By bringing the figure just a little closer than in the Venetian examples to the notional front plane of the picture, he breaks down the barrier between the depicted space and the space of the viewer. This obviously enhances the erotic force of the figure, bringing it into an intimacy that some viewers, then and now, experience as improper or indecorous. It also disrupts the normal perspective construction of the Post-Renaissance tradition; the figures do not occupy a coherent space on the other side of the picture plane, which ceases to divide the 'real' world from the depicted one. This is a different experiment from the perspectival irregularities of the PRB period, which draw more literally on the 'archaic' perspective systems of the period before the systematization of standard Renaissance practice. However, it is an alternative means of making what, for the art historian, is Rossetti's most radical move: to overthrow the tyranny of the perspectival system, with its privileged spectator, that had dominated Western painting since Brunelleschi.[16] Art historians attribute such radical moves almost exclusively to the painters of the modernist mainstream, in Paris and then New York. Yet Rossetti's painting, however much it was denigrated in the high modernist period, never went into oblivion: its influence on modernist artistic practice may have been far more significant than current art-historical orthodoxies acknowledge.

In 1867 Rossetti, always an obsessive collector, acquired a female portrait by Botticelli, a painter who was bound to be of special interest to him since he was known to have made an extensive series of illustrations to Dante's *Divine Comedy*.[17] The diaphanous draperies of the figure in this portrait (now in the Victoria and Albert Museum) are imitated in a number of Rossetti's works, and he also repeated the strangely oblique perspective of the setting. Early in the 1870s, he became interested in Michelangelo, whose sonnets he proposed to translate (a project that was never realized); here again there is a clear identification with the predecessor as painter-poet. Moreover, Rossetti saw a resemblance to Jane Morris in certain drawings by Michelangelo, which he believed to be portraits of Michelangelo's beloved friend in his later years, Vittoria Colonna; in a letter of 1878 he tells Jane that Vittoria Colonna was '*certainly* the original of those heads by M. A. which are portraits of you'.[18] For a third time, Rossetti reinvented his own style, in the same fashion as before, but now by inhabiting the styles of Botticelli and Michelangelo. The half-length figures of the earlier 1860s give way to three-quarter-length figures, predominantly based on Jane Morris.[19]

Rossetti probably designed the composition of *Proserpine* in 1871; the execution of the painting was beset by difficulties, and Rossetti began numerous versions of it, not all of which were brought to completion; he was working on the last replica, now in Birmingham Museum and Art Gallery, until a few days before his death in 1882.[20] In its prime versions (Figure 7 and Tate), the work is perhaps the most compelling example of his last phase: a three-quarter-length female figure in the diaphanous draperies of Rossetti's Botticelli, but with the strong physique of one of Michelangelo's Sibyls. It seems to epitomize the art-historical conception of a late style: a culminating masterpiece, which sums up the experimentation of a lifetime, and hints at mortality.[21]

Yet the painting also displays the multiple levels of meaning that had characterized Rossetti's work since the beginning, for example in *The First Anniversary of Beatrice*, or in the explications of Dante's poems in the *Vita Nuova*. On the literal level, this is a portrait of Jane Morris. While the bow-shaped lips, the wiry ripples of the hair, the long hands and the deep-set eyes appear mannered, the figure is startlingly like photographs of the real woman: the portrait-like realism of the PRB days is still active. The sway of the back and shoulder, which at first looks anatomically improbable, clearly recalls the attitudes Morris assumes in a series of photographs taken of her in Rossetti's garden in 1865.[22] Here the relationship of model to depicted

Figure 7 Dante Gabriel Rossetti, *Proserpine*, 1873–7, oil on canvas, 116.8 × 55.9 cm, private collection, photo © Christie's Images/The Bridgeman Art Library.

figure becomes complicated. Rossetti may have consulted the photographs when he was designing the pose for the figure. Presumably he also chose the poses for the photographs, which he commissioned from the photographer John Robert Parsons. Thus the painted figure is an imitation of the photographs, which are both a faithful record of the model's 'real' appearance and an artistic interpretation by Rossetti himself. Morris's uncanny likeness to the paintings for which she had modelled startled Henry James, when he first met her in 1869: 'It's hard to say whether she's a grand synthesis of all the pre-Raphaelite pictures ever made – or they a "keen analysis" of her – whether she's an original or a copy.'[23]

On a second level, the painting is a representation of the ancient goddess Proserpina, or in Rossetti's anglicized spelling 'Proserpine', which recalls famous lines from Milton's *Paradise Lost*: 'Not that fair field / Of Enna, where Proserpin gathering flowers / Herself a fairer flower by gloomy Dis / Was gathered, which cost Ceres all that pain / To seek her through the world' (Book IV, lines 268–71). Perhaps, indeed, these lines are a point of reference for Rossetti, for they recall, in turn, a passage from the *Purgatorio*, where

Dante sees Matilda gathering flowers, and addresses her: 'Thou puttest me in remembrance of what thing / Proserpine was, and where, when by mischance / Her mother lost her, and she lost the spring.'[24] Rossetti's Proserpine is not simply a character from ancient mythology but also the creation of many poets, including Rossetti himself: he wrote the accompanying sonnet twice, in English and Italian, each a translation of the other. Rossetti's earlier practice had been to inscribe the sonnets that accompanied his paintings on their gilded frames; in this late work, poem and painting come closer still, as the sonnet is painted on a scroll within the picture space.[25]

A third level of meaning might tie the first two together: Jane Morris may be imagined to be like Proserpina, trapped in an unhappy marriage with William Morris as the ancient goddess was doomed to union with Pluto in hell. Her hands, overlarge for the figure and instantly recognizable as Jane's own, assume their mannered gesture to grasp the pomegranate, the warmest colour note in the painting, cut open to display its luscious red seeds. The pomegranate is the sign of her relegation to Hades for half of every year: in the myth, she loses the chance of liberation when she consumes the seeds of a pomegranate. By extension, the fruit is also a symbol for Dante, alluding to his descent into Hell; Rossetti had represented Dante cutting into a pomegranate while Giotto painted his portrait, in a watercolour of 1852.[26] The painting is sombre in colour, and the accompanying sonnet emphasizes Proserpine's unhappy separation from the bright world above, with a four-fold repetition of the word 'Afar', each time at the beginning of a line. 'Afar away the light that brings cold cheer', the sonnet begins; 'Afar the flowers of Enna from this drear / Dire fruit'; 'Afar those skies from this Tartarean gray'. The moody palette of the painting is keyed to 'Tartarean gray', and the square of light from the upper world is in keeping, 'cold' indeed; but it is also bright. This enables a technical tour de force, the juxtaposition of the darkest tone in the picture, the figure's hair, with the brightest. The sestet moves away from the things depicted in the painting, first to Proserpine's musing, then to an unnamed interlocutor:

> Afar from mine own self I seem, and wing
>   Strange ways in thought, and listen for a sign:
>   And still some heart unto some soul doth pine,
> (Whose sounds mine inner sense is fain to bring
> Continually together murmuring,)
>   'Woe's me for thee, unhappy Proserpine!'[27]

This might be Proserpine speaking to herself from afar, or Rossetti speaking to Jane; the persons in Rossetti's late verse may always change places, like lover and beloved, viewer and depicted figure, or word and image. In the painting Proserpine is alone, but the sonnet is a physical presence, inscribed on its scroll at top right.

The biographical interpretation so prevalent in studies of Rossetti's visual art can be naïve, yet it responds to something important – only it is too limited. Rossetti's life and his art interpret one another, but they also interpret other lives, and other works of art, those of his Pre-Raphaelite Brothers and of the extended circle that he drew around him (and which only went on expanding after his death, from the artists and poets of the next generation, such as Pound, to ourselves). In this late double work the allusions to other poems and paintings reach an extreme of complexity, and surely invite the viewer-reader to extend what the painter-poet has suggested – to 'allegorize on one's own hook', as Rossetti put it much earlier when he spoke of illustrating Tennyson's poetry.[28] The visual style, concreted by this date from a bewildering array of imitations, has nothing eclectic about it: this is the Rossetti that viewers worldwide can now recognize at a glance. Yet in its intellectual range it is congruent with Rossetti's most 'Pre-Raphaelite' works of the beginning of his career. Easy it may be to love, or indeed to hate, the sheer look of it; it is not easy at all to exhaust its meanings, either literary or visual. It needs the skill of both the literary scholar and the art historian to interpret Rossetti, in a collaboration that would have delighted him.

NOTES

1 William Michael Rossetti, *Dante Gabriel Rossetti: His Family-Letters with a Memoir*, 2 vols. (London: Ellis and Elvey, 1895), vol. I, p. 158.

2 William E. Fredeman (ed.), *The P.R.B. Journal: William Michael Rossetti's Diary of the Pre-Raphaelite Brotherhood 1849–1853: Together with Other Pre-Raphaelite Documents* (Oxford: Clarendon Press, 1975).

3 Ezra Pound, *Make It New: Essays by Ezra Pound* (London: Faber and Faber, 1934), p. 399.

4 Hunt, vol. I, pp. 130–4.

5 W. M. Rossetti, *DGR: His Family Letters*, vol. I, p. 119.

6 Hunt, vol. I, p. 108.

7 Joyce H. Townsend, Jacqueline Ridge and Stephen Hackney, *Pre-Raphaelite Painting Techniques: 1848–56* (London: Tate Publishing, 2004), p. 82.

8 William Bell Scott, *Autobiographical Notes of the Life of William Bell Scott, and Notices of his Artistic and Poetic Circle of Friends 1830 to 1882*, ed. W. Minto, 2 vols. (London: James R. Osgood, McIlvaine, 1892), vol. I, p. 250.

9 Malcolm Warner, 'The Pre-Raphaelites and the National Gallery', *Huntington Library Quarterly*, 55 (1992), pp. 3–5 (the panels, NG 215 and 216, were then attributed to Taddeo Gaddi).

10 Ruskin, vol. XXXVI, p. 490.

11 Elizabeth Prettejohn, *The Art of the Pre-Raphaelites* (London: Tate Publishing, 2000), pp. 224–31, 261–2; Jenny Graham, *Inventing Van Eyck: The Remaking of an Artist for the Modern Age* (Oxford and New York: Berg, 2007), p. 112.

12 See Ruskin's summary of Eastlake's findings, published in the *Quarterly Review* for March 1848 as 'Eastlake on the History of Painting', in Ruskin, vol. XII, pp. 280–4.

13 Griselda Pollock, 'Artists, Mythologies and Media: Genius, Madness and Art History', *Screen*, 21 (1980), pp. 57–96.

14 In some accounts Rossetti's painting is treated as a commercial product, without the subtlety of Pre-Raphaelite poetry; see for example Kathy Alexis Psomiades, *Beauty's Body: Femininity and Representation in British Aestheticism* (Stanford University Press, 1997), pp. 94–133 (chapter 3: 'Hidden Just Behind Those Screens: Art Objects and Commodities').

15 DGR *Correspondence*, vol. II, p. 298.

16 On Rossetti's experimentation with perspective see Jerome McGann, *Dante Gabriel Rossetti and the Game That Must Be Lost* (New Haven and London: Yale University Press, 2000), pp. 110–18; Elizabeth Prettejohn, *Art for Art's Sake: Aestheticism in Victorian Painting* (New Haven and London: Yale University Press, 2007), pp. 206–8, 212–15, 228.

17 Gail S. Weinberg, 'D. G. Rossetti's Ownership of Botticelli's "Smeralda Brandini"', *Burlington Magazine*, 146 (January 2004), pp. 20–6.

18 Dante Gabriel Rossetti to Jane Morris (27 February 1878), in *Dante Gabriel Rossetti and Jane Morris: Their Correspondence*, ed. John Bryson in association with Janet Camp Troxell (Oxford: Clarendon Press, 1976), p. 54.

19 For a fuller account see Prettejohn, *Art for Art's Sake*, pp. 222–31.

20 For the complicated history (not yet satisfactorily resolved) see most recently Allan Life, 'The Oil Versions of Rossetti's *Proserpine*', in DGR *Correspondence*, vol. VI, pp. 588–604 (Appendix 2).

21 I am indebted for this idea to Sam Smiles, who explores the art-historical construction of 'late style' in his forthcoming monograph, *Turner's Last Paintings: The Artist in Old Age and the Idea of Late Style*.

22 See Julian Treuherz, Elizabeth Prettejohn and Edwin Becker, *Dante Gabriel Rossetti*, exhibition catalogue (London: Thames & Hudson, 2003), pp. 201–4.

23 Henry James to Alice James (10 and 12 March 1869), *The Complete Letters of Henry James, 1855–1872*, ed. Pierre A. Walker and Greg W. Zacharias, 2 vols. (Lincoln, Nebraska and London: University of Nebraska Press, 2006), vol. I, p. 237.

24 Canto XXVIII, lines 49–51, in Laurence Binyon's translation, *The Portable Dante*, ed. Paolo Milano (Harmondsworth: Penguin Books, 1977), p. 334.

25 See Richard Wendorf, *After Sir Joshua: Essays on British Art and Cultural History*, Studies in British Art 15 (New Haven and London: Yale University Press, 2005), pp. 96–7.

26 See Treuherz, Prettejohn and Becker, *Dante Gabriel Rossetti*, pp. 157–8.

27 *The Works of Dante Gabriel Rossetti*, ed. William M. Rossetti (London: Ellis, 1911), p. 253.

28 DGR *Correspondence*, vol. II, p. 7 (letter 55.4).

8

CAROL JACOBI

William Holman Hunt (1827–1910)

whilst I was painting ... in Rossetti's studio, there entered the greatest genius
that is on earth alive, William Holman Hunt – such a grand-looking fellow,
such a splendour of a man, with a great wiry golden beard, and faithful violet
eyes – oh, such a man.

So wrote Edward Burne Jones in 1856, eight years after the formation of
the Pre-Raphaelite Brotherhood.[1] Hunt was only twenty-nine and Burne-
Jones's breathless words show us that, like a modern celebrity, his activities
were mythologized as they occurred. All accounts of Hunt's career, then
and since, participate in this, but it is notable that the nineteenth-century
concept of 'genius', defiant originality and physical daring, remains recognizable today.

Hunt's art is best summarized as addressing extremes: both signification
and representation are taken to their absolute limit. His readiness to adapt
and combine narratives and allusions from all sorts of texts, ancient and
modern, pioneered a newly intense pictorial poetry. At the same time, on
the same canvases, investigations into artistic vision and experiments in
technique tested optical representation, and understandings of beauty and
truth were redefined. Hunt's success was won and maintained outside the
establishment. His radical self-stylization created a new kind of artist/hero
and confronted the problem of the role of art in a global, capitalist culture.
This was, however, only one aspect of his broader preoccupation with the
predicament of the individual within a modern, mass, materialist society.
Hunt's paintings and writings return again and again to the idea of the sub-
jective experience of the lover, the outsider or the leader in tension with the
collective values of family, establishment and crowd.

Overview: life and legacy

Hunt trained at the Royal Academy from seventeen and it continued to be
his venue for exhibition throughout the Pre-Raphaelite period, 1848–53.
The anti-establishmentarianism which brought him together with the other
Pre-Raphaelite Brothers also ensured his independence, however. By 1854
he was working on his own, pursuing adventure, aesthetic novelty and historical evidence in the Middle East. His interest in other cultures, and in

116

exceptional environments such as the Dead Sea, was another facet of his desire to explore boundaries. He returned to live in Jerusalem in the 1860s, 70s and 90s and also stayed for a time in Florence. The remainder of his career was spent in London, but the Academy was no longer his main platform. Instead, he developed the opportunities of expanding commercial markets and printing technologies to circulate his images to new audiences at home and abroad.

Despite Hunt's initial determination to succeed at the Royal Academy and reform art from within, he was, like Rossetti, never elected a member. In 1860, on Dickens's advice, he made the ground-breaking decision to by-pass the Academy's annual exhibition, the traditional stage for assessment, exposure and recognition of the year's art, and put his major Middle Eastern subject painting, *The Finding of the Saviour in the Temple* (1854–60, Birmingham Museums & Art Gallery), directly before the public. The dealer, Ernest Gambart, marketed it throughout the country as a solo exhibit, a kind of proto-cinema, top-lit in a darkened room. Although he paid Hunt a record-breaking 5,000 guineas for the picture and copyright, making the artist the equivalent of a millionaire in modern terms, ten times this amount was realized on ticket prices, merchandising and engraved reproductions, a practice which would soon dominate the marketing of art.[2] Twenty thousand guineas were paid for Hunt's next Eastern painting, *The Shadow of Death* (Figure 9). Hunt's was also an early example of a global career. He showed abroad from 1855 onwards and by the 1860s his major works were visiting America. In 1906 his life-sized, last version of *The Light of the World* (c.1900–4, St Paul's Cathedral, London) drew many million visitors in the southern hemisphere.[3] Countless reproductions, as well as quotations of the paintings in poetry, illustration, stained glass, tapestry, cartoons and advertising ('Fancy having a Light of the World shine on your electroplate!') still proliferate, creating a vast and often autonomous diaspora of Hunt images.

By the 1860s the failed warehouse manager's son was one of London's most eligible bachelors. Hunt's wry description of himself, 'the plebeian lion of the season',[4] illustrates his awareness that celebrity and status were no longer the preserve of land and name; a precarious version of them could be gained by achievement and wealth. Hunt pioneered the professionalization of his practice through publications, cooperative ventures such as the Hogarth Club and association with other areas of expertise like science and medicine. In 1880, he gave a substantial lecture to the Society of Arts on the science of artists' materials, later published in the *Architect*.[5] This adaptation of the practical role of the scientist is one facet of a lifetime of self-fashioning. Other models such as the swashbuckling adventurer and entrepreneur, as well as more traditional artistic tropes such as the sage, multiplied the myths that supported the success of his pictures. The very diversity of these, however, hints at an unsettled self-consciousness about identity that goes back to the Brotherhood.[6]

Hunt's heterogeneous public persona set up a tension between collective responsibility and independent non-conformism which is also a feature of personal accounts. His published work guarded his privacy, but surviving letters and journals reveal an experimental lifestyle.[7] He adopted bohemian domestic arrangements in Florence and Jerusalem as well as London. He preferred strong-minded friends of both sexes and exhibited little respect for the conventions of marriage, writing of it as a regrettable but necessary protection for women against social persecution, of less importance than educational and economic independence. In his twenties, he discarded considerations of class to pursue a partnership with an untaught working girl, Annie Miller, whom he encountered scraping a living in a pub. His priority was to encourage Annie towards a trade and the possibility of freedom in her choice of relationships. Annie's autonomy led her away from Hunt, however, and, by the late 1850s, the affair foundered. A decade on Hunt fell in love with Fanny Waugh (the writer Evelyn Waugh was descended from the same family), a cultured, self-reliant woman of similar age and sentiments to himself. They wed for the sake of her social position, but she was determined to accompany him on his travels, despite being pregnant. She died in childbirth in Florence. Hunt was desolate, and clung to his son, Cyril, for a year, an infatuated and anxious single father. In 1868 he relinquished him to Fanny's family and withdrew into work. Late in life he contravened the Table of Affinities to elope with the surrogate mother of his child, Edith Waugh, Fanny's much younger sister. Edith was a spirited companion, bringing up Cyril and another son and daughter in Jerusalem and London. The couple campaigned to change the law and their marriage was recognized just before Hunt's death in 1910.

Hunt's legacy remains unresolved. The twentieth-century tendency to simplify the seven members of the PRB to a trio with pleasingly complementary characteristics (Hunt earnest, Millais suave, Rossetti eccentric, for example, or red-head, blond and brunette) has led to a reductive view of all of the Brothers, not least the other four. Popular and scholarly writings unite in describing Hunt as the 'true' Pre-Raphaelite, alongside related terms such as dogged, dogmatic and inflexible. This narrative is usually accompanied by a story of religious fervour. As a result, Hunt's work has been represented as in two senses an act of faith, an unquestioning expression of Pre-Raphaelite *and* Christian creeds. This idea was consolidated by Hunt's last piece of autobiographical writing, *Pre-Raphaelitism and the Pre-Raphaelite*

Brotherhood. First published in 1905–6, this claimed to be the definitive history of the group and presented its author's five-decade career as a life-long expression of its ideals.

The twenty-first century has seen these myths fall away, however. Investigations of wider evidence are providing an increasingly complex picture of both Pre-Raphaelitism and Hunt's relation to it. The degree of fictionality of the autobiography, written in the artist's eighties, has become better understood, as has the variety of personas fabricated through his lifetime.[8] In the last decade, explanations of Hunt's pictures in his public writings have been supplemented and critiqued by a re-engagement with private writings, the works themselves and the circumstances surrounding their creation. Several exhibitions and a catalogue raisonné have accelerated this process.[9] Conservation science has supported a fresh appreciation of Hunt's aesthetic and technical innovations and drawn attention to his considerable work on painting materials.[10] Interdisciplinary approaches have provided new readings of Hunt's iconography and its engagement with social and political issues of his day. His religious beliefs, too, have been radically reassessed.[11] Hunt never denied being an atheist in his youth and an examination of unpublished writings has shown that his journey towards something like Christian conviction was later, less certain and less orthodox than some of the statements he made in later life would suggest.[12]

Pre-Raphaelitism: first principles

The City of London, where Hunt grew up, was the industrial and commercial heart of the largest and fastest modernizing city on earth.[13] He was from the beginning a habitué of the crowd, the context of strangers which distinguishes modern urban experience, and aware of the wider world through goods which converged from all corners of the empire. Hunt's engagements with this new society were more practical than those of the other PRBs. His father ran a warehouse and in 1839 withdrew his twelve-year-old son from school to work. Employment in the textile firm of Richard Cobden, radical politician and advocate of free trade, catalyzed a broader perspective on the new capitalist economy, while his family's bankruptcy and his own later losses in the banking collapse of 1866 instilled a life-long appreciation of its instability. At sixteen, Hunt left home to pursue painting full time. Struggling to support himself, he took three tries to satisfy the entrance requirements of the Academy Schools, succeeding in 1844. This experience of poverty and restrictive practices lent him sympathy for the revolutionary atmosphere of the 'hungry forties' and in 1848 he was probably a bystander at the last Chartist demonstration. His relationships with Annie Miller and outsider artists such as Ford Madox Brown and the Rossettis transgressed the fast-forming codes and boundaries of the middle classes. His rejection of his father's plans for him to secure success in trade, and his disregard for the middle-class regulation of sexual and social behaviour, paralleled his disdain for the academic values that could secure safe success in art. Pre-Raphaelitism was a spirited early expression of this youthful flirtation with reformist trends.

Hunt met the younger, more accomplished Millais at the Academy Schools and they attended the same avant-garde sketching club as Rossetti, the Cyclographic Society. Hunt was the first of the Brotherhood to go public in paint. Although his experimental picture for the Royal Academy exhibition of 1848, *The Flight of Madeline and Porphyro during the Drunkenness Attending the Revelry* (*The Eve of St Agnes*) (Guildhall Art Gallery, London) was painted side by side with Millais's *Cymon and Iphigenia* (Lady Lever Art Gallery, National Museums Liverpool), only Hunt's was selected. Their subjects were chosen to give literary anecdote, a respectable mainstay of Academy painting, a more radical edge. Both English sources (Keats and John Dryden respectively) told stories of love and kidnap derived from the tales of Boccaccio, whose bold plots transformed their Romantic themes into something more modern, in keeping with the energetic, radical atmosphere of the mid-century. Unlike the Romantic heroine, the female protagonists of these pictures reject their marriages and participate in their abduction from their families. Keats's medieval plot provided a means to question modern social and personal codes; the poem hints that the flight of Madeline and Porphyro has been prompted by sexual consummation justified by love rather than social, commercial or legal bonds. Hunt showed them creeping past drunken guards while the household carouses beyond, stressing mutuality and defiance. This anti-establishment subject matter complemented the Brothers' challenge to Academy teaching and structures. Hunt enthused about the eighteenth-century outsider artist William Hogarth, and Rossetti became his pupil. In 1849, Hunt and Rossetti visited Paris in the aftermath of the Revolution. Hunt's next major work, an image of an early Italian rebel, *Rienzi Vowing to Obtain Justice for the Death of his Young Brother, Slain in a Skirmish between the Colonna and the Orsini Factions* (1848–9, private collection), based on Bulwer Lytton's popular novel, *Rienzi: The Last of the Roman Tribunes* (1835), developed the theme of revolt again, moving away from poetry to the more tangible context of the historical novel. Portraits of the Pre-Raphaelite Brothers within the picture linked ancient events to modern European dissidents, especially the Rossetti family.

Hunt's radical style was equally indebted to precedents in the art of the past. Hunt had not shared the general dismay that greeted the brilliant colours revealed by the recent cleaning of Titian's *Bacchus and Ariadne*,

Figure 8 William Holman Hunt, *The Hireling Shepherd*, 1851–2, oil on canvas, 76.4 × 109.5 cm, City of Manchester Art Galleries.

at the National Gallery. He renounced the fashionable 'old master glow' that imitated the unifying tones of an aged brown varnish, and adopted a bright Renaissance palette. The rose madder cape fluttering from Porphyro's shoulders (fabulously juxtaposed with the hero's yellow hose, green cap, red feather and Madeline's purple dress) is a startling but somewhat literal response to the pink cloak of Bacchus in Titian's painting. Subsequent works such as *The Awakening Conscience* (1853–4, Tate) and *The Hireling Shepherd* (Figure 8) exhibit a more integrated use of the Venetian palette throughout setting and figures alike. Hunt's abandonment of centralized compositions and conventional post-Renaissance perspective also owed something to the more confrontational, frieze-like arrangements of Titian and the earlier Italian painters. The compositional emphasis on the foreground complemented the psychological immediacy of his post-Romantic subject matter. The emotional and ideological tension between the lovers and the drunken family, in *The Eve of St Agnes*, was revisited in later subject pictures such as *The Finding of the Saviour in the Temple*, where the Holy Family stand between a crowd of rabbis and the temple porch. This simple ploy was increasingly augmented by more complex negotiations of contradiction expressed through juxtapositions of individual characters: Christ is embraced by his parents, but he is preparing to leave.

Hunt's interest in tensions between individuals, families and society led him to make important developments to the figure group. Madeline and Porphyro modify the traditional linked stance of the strolling couple. Preliminary sketches show the couple in harmony, but the final painting fractures this; gazes and limbs are set at more awkward angles to each other. Dialogue of this kind is developed in *The Hireling Shepherd*. A shepherd flirts with a field girl seated in a meadow and the main confrontation now takes place between the lovers themselves. This tableau of temptation explores indecision. The man leans in but the field girl might be swaying back or away. Their two left hands match in shape but oppose in angle. Their two right hands, on the ground, do the same. They are flexed and uncomfortable: his, with splayed fingers and swollen veins, advances like the paw of an animal on all fours; hers props her body upright, but strays close to his crotch. The curled fingers of her free hand mirror his as he proffers a moth, but she may be accepting or refusing. Again, Hunt drew on the viewer's familiarity with conventional poses to add nuance to the figures' actions. The raised gesture registers as both the coy refusal conventional in pastoral courtship scenes, and the eager plucking characteristic of representations of the biblical Eve. On closer inspection it is neither of these. The field girl is running a skein of hair between forefinger and thumb, a vanitas motif that matches the moth. This motif, at once sensual, brooding and suggestive of entrapment, was a favourite of the Brotherhood. Such innovations derived from Hunt's unusually elaborate use of life models as well as his inventive attention to past art. Hunt emulated early painters' exploratory curiosity about the appearance of things, observing and transcribing, with fine brushes, even minor parts of figures, drapery and setting. Studies exist for a holly branch and the dogs in *The Eve of St Agnes*, for example. Encouraged by John Ruskin's hymn to the landscape painter J. M. W. Turner in the second volume of *Modern Painters* (1846), which proposed fidelity to optical perception as a basis for spiritual and artistic authority,[14] Hunt's research into vision became increasingly systematic, initiating a life-long scientific study of light, colour, pigment and paint. Luminosity and precision were enhanced by adapting fifteenth-century painting techniques. Hunt rejected the brown under-painting that had become conventional in the seventeenth century and painted over a white ground. He added varnish to his pigment and oil, so that if he laid the paint on thinly it was partially transparent. Light falling on the picture passed through the thin layer of colour, hit the white ground and reflected back again, illuminating it from behind. It is this that gives Hunt's pictures an almost uncanny intensity not recorded in photographic reproduction. Hunt introduced a new optical immediacy into the imitative genres of landscape and portrait painting, including complementarily coloured shadows, for example, but his most significant innovation was to extend these representational techniques to subject pictures. He began transcribing settings and models directly onto the canvas. *Rienzi* combined precise portraits of friends with the first landscape setting to be executed primarily outside in natural light. *The Hireling Shepherd* explored the dramatic potential of unconventional illumination and individualized faces to an even greater degree: the barbed highlight bisecting each blade of grass, the fringed purple shadow cast from the shepherd's lashes onto his cheek, the reddened flesh and bleached lips all record the vertical heat of a noonday sun.

The Hireling Shepherd was Hunt's first modern-life picture and marks his maturity as a painter. The poor press received by the Brotherhood during the initial years is well known, but it is important to note that it was not long-lived. *The Hireling Shepherd* attracted more than one buyer and Hunt painted a companion piece, of sheep only, which he called *Our English Coasts, 1852* (Tate). Fellow poets and painters such as Brown, William Dyce and Augustus Egg were quick to appreciate that Hunt's respect for medieval pictures was not slavish revivalism or regressive primitivism, as it was often labelled, but part of a search for new models of art which included Raphael, post-Raphaelite and contemporary painting as well as print-making, and which massively expanded expressive and formal possibilities. Hunt's eclectic engagement with literature from the Bible to blockbuster novels represented a parallel enrichment of iconographical potential. His revolutionary use of optical techniques chimed with the materialism of the age and addressed very pertinent issues about subjectivity, authority and truth. In 1855, more than a decade before 'Impressionism', Hunt's purple shadows and use of prismatic pigments to paint an èquivalent for perceptions of light bouncing off objects created a stir at the Exposition Universelle in Paris. Even Eugène Delacroix wrote ecstatically in his journal of *Our English Coasts* (diplomatically exhibited in Paris as *Strayed Sheep*).[15]

Mimesis and design

Hunt's curious and critical approach to his times and early attempts to educate himself developed into a lifetime of research. The fastidious observational component of his painting is only one example of this, and must not be separated from his travel, observations of human nature and eclectic reading. The memoir, *Pre-Raphaelitism and the Pre-Raphaelite Brotherhood*, bases the authority of its protagonist, his 'truth', on an understanding of both his life and his art as a fearless and insightful accumulation of data. Its celebration of evidence, experience and trial is of course an epistemological fantasy which plays down the insecurity of the 'first principles' approach. The struggle, contradiction and indecision of its practical implementation reveal themselves in Hunt's practice and private writings. Both betray battles to find firm meaning and values in inscrutable circumstance. It is a symptom of this continued experimentalism that the successes of the mid-1850s were followed by projects that were increasingly ambitious, punishing and time-consuming. A mere seven major pictures emerged from his Pre-Raphaelite period, but the next half-century would yield only seven more. *The Finding of the Saviour in the Temple* occupied five years on and off, *The Shadow of Death* required five years without a break and *The Triumph of the Innocents* obsessed him throughout his fifties.

Although an early work, *The Eve of St Agnes* demonstrates an aspect of Hunt's practical method that was to have far-reaching significance. Hunt brings about his new visual language by adapting many and varied liter-ary and visual sources and continues to adapt them in subsequent pictures. This cumulative synthesis, refinement and innovation are central to what Hunt called the 'power' of his pictures.[16] They contributed to a growing maturity in the way he treats his themes. *The Hireling Shepherd* takes us to the heart of the matter hinted at in *The Eve of St Agnes*, the moment of seduction. Questions of love or lust, innocence or corruption, are distilled in the form of the responsibility of the man and the choice of the woman. They are no longer neatly divided between protagonists and society, but rather internalized within a far more ambiguous interaction between the couple themselves. The family/society is here metaphorized as the shepherd's strayed flock. The synthesis in one figure of lover and shepherd, private and public, complicates the relationship between personal responsibility and collective well-being. In the following year, flirtation progresses into a *fait accompli*, a picture of a man with his half-dressed mistress called *The Awakening Conscience*. The changed relationship is expressed by a com-position in which the figures overlap completely. As the title of the picture makes clear, however, the trope of female choice has also been developed. The man lolls, somewhat like the shepherd, but the mistress stands. Hunt now enquires not into the choice itself, but into whether it is final: might the 'fallen' woman rise?

These examples illustrate the way Hunt's considered returns and revi-sions lead him beyond standard psychological narratives and formulaic compositions, but also the way they contribute to a fundamental ambi-guity in his work. Hunt created some of the most innovative motifs of the century, but this absence of convention made his pictures unstable. Issues of misreading and misunderstanding, or multiple readings, bedevil his work. At least one Royal Academy critic assumed that the audaciously intimate pair in *The Awakening Conscience* must be sister and brother, for example.[17] This phenomenon is, paradoxically, compounded by the care with which Hunt elaborated compositional, iconographic and gestural nuance. Although these complement the immediacy provided by the detailed style, helping to draw the viewer in, the two tend to split the painting's effect. Each was a product of the artist's characteristic enthusiasm for investigation, but they derived from very different origins. The sophisticated selection and arrangement of motifs and figures was, unlike likenesses and light-effects, engendered from texts, pictures, thoughts, doodles and sketches, rather than nature, worked out and finalized in line rather than colour well before painting was begun. Only *after* the lines had been designed and transferred to the white canvas was appropriate natural detail selected, observed and copied into the outlines. Hunt's writings about his pictures only stress this second stage. They emphasize mimesis, the transcription of appearances of particular locations and people, to confer an apparently objective authenticity.

Design and mimesis can be elided in print, but their discontinuities are evident in the pictures and in responses to them. *The Hireling Shepherd* was executed at the height of Hunt's mimetic powers. The figures were modelled from life in a brilliant Surrey setting, right down to the ticks of blue shadow that trace the stitching of their clothing, the dilated pupils of their eyes and the tell-tale stems of bent and broken grass. For all its sensual immediacy, however, commentaries on this picture rarely dwell on sex. The painting is instead perceived as an allegory of rural or national negligence. The sheep evoke a 'flock' in the sense of a congregation or a populace, the apples suggest temptation and 'fall'; the halo-like yellow scarf of the shepherdess and her red dress are linked to Marian imagery and anxieties (political and doctrinal) about the restoration of the Catholic church in 1850, or the debates between Low and High within the Anglican church itself.[18] Hunt, having friends in both camps, did take an interest in these issues; readings of the picture are reflections of readings conducted by the artist himself. His research during its conception was typically wide, ranging from John Milton's pastoral poem *Lycidas* (1637) and Richard Hooker's post-Reformation treatise *Of the Laws of Ecclesiastical Polity* (1593–7) to contemporary considerations of sectarianism such as John Ruskin's pamphlet *On the Construction of Sheepfolds* and Charles Kingsley's novel *Yeast* (both 1851). Typically, this complex of ideas influenced the choice and arrangement of motifs. No matter how vividly the components of the picture have been painted from life, their original role as a network of signs is preserved, and they demand to be read.

Figure 9 William Holman Hunt, *The Shadow of Death*, 1869–73, oil on canvas, 214.2 × 168.2 cm, City of Manchester Art Galleries.

In a popular introduction of 1981 to the Pre-Raphaelites, Christopher Wood spoke for many when he described *The Hireling Shepherd* as a kind of narrative/mimetic hybrid: 'another elaborate moral fable, but also a brilliant piece of painting'.[19] This sense of fragmentation is nearly universal in accounts of Hunt's pictures. In practice, though, his experimental ambition to elaborate extremes of two kinds of truth – design (the imaginative truth of ideas) *and* mimesis (the imitative truth of material things) – caused difficulties for the artist as well as the viewer. Hunt's rare private journals, such as those made while working on *The Shadow of Death* (Figure 9), record a vivid sense of mismatch between transcribed appearances and imaginative concept, instigating repeated repaintings and, more importantly, anguished anxieties about the validity of the ideas depicted. Despite Hunt's exceptional technical expertise, his output was severely limited by these doubts. Hunt's testing of elaborate ideas and ideals against the 'claylike and finite' during mimetic painting produced a compelling, complex and unresolved aesthetic. Extracts from his diary represent three months of the four years he spent on the work:

8 *February* 'I am bothered much about the head ... I draw it rightly from Isaac but ... when I begin to refine upon this and succeed in getting the proportion of the face to suit the character, lo! The head has got out of place again ... I work on in a fever.'

3 *March* 'correct my face'.

16 *March* changes head although friends consider it perfect.

30 *March* redesigns the head.

7 *April* 'head is right for finishing'.

12 *April* alters head.

17 *April* scrapes and renews the white ground on the head.

22 *April* repaints the head.

26 *April* 'Touch a little ... on the head bringing the line of the left cheek a little further out'.

2 *May* 'To get it ready for my final days painting make several changes in drawing in little parts'.

3 *May* 'shocked to find' this 'too extreme and too partial ... quite bewildered about the head which looks right close but at a distance looks wrong I am quite in despair'.[20]

From here to eternity

Of all the themes and ideas that cascade through Hunt's career, those drawn from the Bible were perhaps the most important. In 1848 Hunt and Rossetti placed Jesus Christ at the top of a 'list of Immortals'. Jesus was a purely practical hero, however; the document proclaimed their atheistic disbelief in 'any spiritual principles but the development of talent ... Shelley and Lord Byron with Keats were my best modern heroes – all read by the light of materialism or sensualism.'[21] A few years later, *The Light of the World*

(Figure 5) softened this line, but it was intended as a personal exploration of spirituality. Its odd collection of religious tropes within a portrait format and romantic night setting eludes religious boundaries. Its intimacy and ambiguity have made it Hunt's most adaptable and famous image.

The list's juxtaposition of contemporary men and women – Elizabeth Barrett Browning and Coventry Patmore are sandwiched between Joan of Arc and Raphael, for example – underlines the importance of historical heroes to the Brotherhood's understanding of modern times. An understanding of the contemporary age as history-in-the-making was fundamental to Victorian culture. The perception of continuity between past and present provided Hunt with a basis for a new kind of history painting: past events pregnant with implications for the present and modern scenes resonating with the past. While ancient stories like *Rienzi* dignify modern predicaments, *The Hireling Shepherd* does the opposite, bringing Arcadia up to date. Like Gustave Courbet's pictures, which Hunt had seen in Paris, it replaces the idyllic balance of leisure and toil in generic images of peasantry with an interrogation of the tension between them. Hunt signals this with the intrusion of the word 'hireling' into his title, stressing commercial motivation, the disruption of long-standing relationships between the land and those who work it brought about by capitalism and rural industrialization. Like Courbet, Hunt offers an assemblage of material facts: the distorted anatomies of sheep demonstrate the illness they suffer if allowed to eat clover. The shepherd's blazing cheeks and the keg at his hip may allude to his irresponsibly inebriated state, or the higher irresponsibility of landowners paying workers with alcohol. As we have seen, however, these immediate meanings are augmented by an array of non-material associations going back as far as Eden. Hunt felt Courbet's brand of realism was limited, acknowledging only concrete truth; his concrete present resonates with a literary and historical past. The interchangeability of past and present is most conspicuous in the pairing, the following year, of *The Light of the World* with *The Awakening Conscience*, a synthesis of tradition and worldliness that looks forward to Edouard Manet's exhibition of a similar partnership of prostitute and Christ, *Olympia* (1863, Musée d'Orsay) and *Christ Scourged* (1865, The Art Institute of Chicago), for the Paris Salon a decade later.

The Bible had an advantage over Renaissance and Romantic subjects in that it was a trace of an ancient history, an apparent insight into older principles and more universal truths. Its fascination was that it suggested history on an epic scale and, crucially, encompassed the future as well as the past. Hunt's first voyage to Egypt and the Middle East in 1854 was a swashbuckling exercise in creating fame in emulation of heroes such as Sir

Richard Burton, but it was also a search for a closer synthesis of spiritual narratives and historical and archaeological fact. Nearly thirty years later, when world travel had expanded Hunt's vision further, he imagined how our history would have looked to occupants of other planets and whether men might meet these strangers and see photographs they had taken of events on Earth.[22] This epic vision is fundamental to Hunt's thought and to our understanding of his changing fascination with the Bible's predictions, and with the East, where its past and future were meant to take place. Jerusalem's centrality to several revealed religions, especially its biblical status as the prophesied site of a 'New Jerusalem', was in the mid-nineteenth century complemented by an acceleration of practical debates about its role in the world. A more global understanding of politics catalysed both fears of conflict and fantasies of utopia, and with Ottoman power faltering, the city seemed, to Hunt, on the verge of playing a pivotal role.

Edward Said's *Orientalism* (1978) prompted late twentieth-century reassessments of Hunt's response to the East and much was made of his criticism or incomprehension of the cultures he came across, and his ready adoption of a beard and patriarchal British persona to deal with these.[23] Some recent research has uncovered a more reciprocal relationship, however. Most critics agree that Hunt had a particularly well-informed interest in Jewish communities and beliefs.[24] When Hunt arrived in Jerusalem, an Anglican campaign of religious and political appropriation was focused on the conversion of Muslims and Jews. The sequence of rabbis regarding Christ in *The Finding of the Saviour in the Temple* can be read as a wishful metaphor for Jewish recognition of Christian authority and a commandeering of a Muslim shrine (biblical archaeologists were claiming that the setting of the picture, *Haram al-Sharif*, was the legendary Golden Temple). Hunt was, however, unsympathetic to the conversion programme. He came to believe that the solution to the absence of any strong governmental presence in Jerusalem was to turn the city into a Jewish state to provide a neutral and multicultural arbiter in the region as a whole and harbour the dispossessed. *The Finding of the Saviour* can be read as a coincidence of three faiths rather than an eclipsing of two, a literal meeting of Judaism and Christianity in a space also sacred to Islam, an image of historical commonality expressing political ideals of present and practical cooperation. As Hunt grew older he developed a prescient concern for measures that might prevent a more general world war. When the third *Light of the World* was painted as a peace token for South Africa in the aftermath of the Boer War, he added an Islamic crescent moon to the stars on Christ's lantern. Hunt thought of it as an ambassador, like the torch-carrying Statue of Liberty in New York (1870–86), that could dissolve denominational differences.

Hunt's biblical subjects are tools for modern living, therefore, and change with time. Just as *The Finding of the Saviour* reflects circumstances very different from those of *The Light of the World*, so *The Shadow of Death*, begun in 1868 on Hunt's second visit to Jerusalem, is a Christ for a post-Darwinian age. It revisits the enquiry into the spirit that marked out the first image, but where *The Light of the World* searched hesitantly in the dark, this assemblage of pristine visual data exposed a naked Jesus of extraordinary physical presence, countering doubts raised by archaeology, geology and science on their own materialist terms. Hunt wrote at the time: 'my picture is strictly ... *historic* with not a single fact of any kind in it of a supernatural nature'.[25] Where the insubstantial anatomy of *The Light of the World* and *The Finding of the Saviour* accorded with the Romantic and monastic types that complemented the name of the original Brotherhood, *The Shadow* appealed to notions of Muscular Christianity pioneered by Charles Kingsley and Madox Brown's *Work*. The figure of Christ again reflects leadership and the artist's role, but here it glorifies labour, the self-evident toil of the mimetic painter in the hot sun of Palestine.

This was more than myth-making. Hunt spent five years on the picture and his journal and letters blur his exhaustion, and his hopes for reward, with those of his subject. As I have already suggested, the role of images such as *The Shadow of Death* in verifying the ideas contained within them was a matter of intense importance. The loss of Hunt's wife in 1866, and fears for their child, had prompted him to embrace religion in a new way and letters of the time dwell on eschatological hope. They express doubt, however, and are preoccupied with trying to reconcile faith with science. Could the ascension of Jesus have something in common with the physical transition of solids into gas, for example? While this uncompromisingly Middle Eastern, empirical Jesus asserted the Saviour as reality at a time of general doubt, the gleaming resurrected specimen responded to very particular, personal anxieties about mortality. The Virgin's unprecedented iconoclastic pose, exotic dress and jewellery dramatically disassociate her from conventional depictions of the nurturing Madonna, expressing the alienation and bitter disillusion with domestic comfort which followed the tragic curtailment of Hunt's marriage.

The Shadow of Death is, like all Hunt's work, intricately bound up with its times: an era when death in childbirth was common and when the consolation of faith was fragile and threatened; when travel and technology made the strange familiar and the familiar strange; when the work of art began to address the masses but struggled to be all things to all men, while at the same time becoming the expression of highly personal crises of identity and belief. It is typical of the striking focus on the domestic in

Pre-Raphaelite art, in which great events of literature, history and faith are played out between lovers, children and parents. Hunt's preoccupation with subjectivity and its exploration through the family drama reflects a renegotiation of relationships which paralleled broader social change. Just as Hunt's psychological reconfigurations of Shakespearean and biblical plots look forward to Freudian models of the twentieth century, so his engagement with religion as a means of understanding modern circumstance has found resonance in the twenty-first. It no longer seems anachronistic in the aftermath of global reactions to 9/11. Continuity can also be found in the diverse and elaborate critical reactions to Hunt. The ambivalent and unresolved passion of his writings is echoed in the reactions of others to the present day. This phenomenon is not so much a measure of a failure to pin down the meaning of his paintings as it is a symptom of the restless ambition and complexity of his meaning-making.

NOTES

1 G B-J [Georgiana Burne-Jones], *Memorials of Edward Burne-Jones* (London: Macmillan, 1904), vol. I, p. 139.

2 Jeremy Maas, *Gambart: Prince of the Victorian Art World* (London: Barrie & Jenkins, 1975), chapters 12 and 13.

3 Jeremy Maas, *Holman Hunt and The Light of the World* (Aldershot: Wildwood House, 1987).

4 Hunt, fragment, letter to F. G. Stephens, 25 May 1860?, Bodleian Library MS. Don. e. 66, p. 48v.

5 William Holman Hunt, 'The Present System of Obtaining Materials in Use by Artist Painters as Compared with that of the Old Masters', *Journal of the Society of Arts*, 28 (23 April 1880), pp. 485–99.

6 Carol Jacobi, *William Holman Hunt: Painter, Painting, Paint* (Manchester and New York: Manchester University Press, 2006), pp. 17–40.

7 The best source is the letters themselves, particularly those to F. G. Stephens in the Bodleian Library; see also Carol Jacobi, 'Women: Portraits and Passion', in Katharine Lochnan and Carol Jacobi (eds.), *Holman Hunt and the Pre-Raphaelite Vision*, exhibition catalogue (Toronto: Art Gallery of Ontario, 2008), pp. 84–94. (Catalogue cited hereafter as Lochnan and Jacobi.)

8 Laura Marcus, 'Brothers in Their Anecdotage: Holman Hunt's "Pre-Raphaelitism and the Pre-Raphaelite Brotherhood"', in Marcia Pointon (ed.), *Pre-Raphaelites Re-viewed* (Manchester and New York: Manchester University Press, 1989), pp. 11–21.

9 Judith Bronkhurst, *William Holman Hunt: A Catalogue Raisonné*, 2 vols. (New Haven and London: Yale University Press, 2006); Allen Staley and Christopher Newall, *Pre-Raphaelite Vision: Truth to Nature*, exhibition catalogue (London: Tate, 2004); Nicholas Tromans (ed.), *The Lure of the East: British Orientalist Painting*, exhibition catalogue (London: Tate, 2008); Lochnan and Jacobi.

10 Jacobi, *William Holman Hunt*, pp. 117–36; Joyce H. Townsend and Jennifer Poulin, 'Painting: Materials and Methods', in Lochnan and Jacobi, pp. 161–8.

11 George P. Landow, *William Holman Hunt and Typological Symbolism* (New Haven and London: Yale University Press, 1979); Albert Boime, 'William Holman Hunt's *The Scapegoat*: Rite of Forgiveness/Transference of Blame', *Art Bulletin*, 84 (March 2002), pp. 94–114.

12 Jacobi, *William Holman Hunt*, pp. 89–116.

13 The most detailed biography is Anne Clark Amor, *William Holman Hunt: The True Pre-Raphaelite* (London: Constable, 1989); see also Parry, 'Textile Background', in Lochnan and Jacobi, pp. 57–75.

14 Ruskin, vol. III, p. 624.

15 Eugène Delacroix, *The Journal of Eugène Delacroix*, ed. H. Wellington (Ithaca: Cornell University Press, 1980), p. 280 (30 June 1855).

16 Hunt, vol. I, pp. 348–9.

17 Kate Flint, 'Reading *The Awakening Conscience* Rightly', in Pointon (ed.), *Pre-Raphaelites Re-viewed*, p. 60.

18 Bronkhurst, *William Holman Hunt*, vol. I, pp. 147–50.

19 Christopher Wood, *The Pre-Raphaelites* (London: Weidenfeld & Nicolson, 1994), p. 46.

20 William Holman Hunt, Journal, 8 February–3 May 1872, John Rylands Library, MS 1212.

21 William Holman Hunt to John Ruskin, 6 November 1880, quoted in M. Allentuck, 'William Holman Hunt, Monk, and Ruskin: An Unpublished Letter', *Apollo*, 97 (1973), p. 156; paraphrased in Hunt, vol. I, p. 159.

22 William Holman Hunt to John Lucas Tupper, 21 April 1879, *A Pre-Raphaelite Friendship: The Correspondence of William Holman Hunt and John Lucas Tupper*, ed. J. H. Coombs and others (Ann Arbor, Michigan: UMI Research Press, 1986), p. 275.

23 Marcia Pointon, 'The Artist as Ethnographer', in Pointon (ed.), *Pre-Raphaelites Re-viewed*, pp. 11–21.

24 Boime, 'William Holman Hunt's *The Scapegoat*', pp. 94–114; Nicholas Tromans, 'Palestine: Picture of Prophecy', in Lochnan and Jacobi, pp. 135–60.

25 Letter fragment, Bodleian Library, quoted by Judith Bronkhurst, in Leslie Parris (ed.), *The Pre-Raphaelites*, exhibition catalogue (London: Tate Gallery, 1984), p. 221; see also George Landow, 'The Exhibition Pamphlet for W. Holman Hunt's *The Shadow of Death*', *Journal of Pre-Raphaelite Studies*, 16 (2007), pp. 9–29.

9

PAUL BARLOW

John Everett Millais (1829–1896)

John Everett Millais's position within Pre-Raphaelitism is unusual. For most early commentators he was its undoubted leader. His painting *Christ in the House of His Parents* (Figure 4) brought the PRB to public notice in 1850. His later paintings, beginning with *A Huguenot, on St Bartholomew's Day* of 1852 (Figure 11), were the first to find popular favour, and his was the style that was taken up by the earliest imitators of the movement. However, for later writers, Millais's position has seemed less secure. His two colleagues, Hunt and Rossetti, both had partisans who claimed for them the decisive role in the creation of Pre-Raphaelitism. Rossetti became the model for later artists such as Burne-Jones, to the extent that the term 'Pre-Raphaelite' in the public imagination often refers to his style. For others, it is Hunt who is the 'true Pre-Raphaelite'. He created its distinctive blend of realism and artifice, and remained consistent throughout his career.

Hunt's reputation follows his own account of the PRB, while Rossetti's was sanctified by his brother William. Their importance is thus enshrined in the founding literature of Pre-Raphaelitism. Millais wrote almost nothing. His biography was written by his son John, who believed that his father's later paintings, created after he had abandoned Pre-Raphaelitism, were his best. Later critics condemned these works as 'sentimental' or 'academic'. Millais was seen almost as a Pre-Raphaelite fellow-traveller. Once he moved beyond his friends' influence, following his marriage to Effie (Ruskin's former wife, born Euphemia Gray), he lost both his Pre-Raphaelitism and his claim to be an artist worth our attention.

This view has been challenged in recent years.[1] Nevertheless, whether we see his changes of style as decline or not, they present us with difficulties in writing about Millais as a Pre-Raphaelite. Firstly, we have to contend with the complex transformations in Millais's art during the 1850s and 1860s. By 1870 it is clear that it is no longer 'Pre-Raphaelite'. But when and how does Millais *stop* being one? This problem leads us back to the central question of what it means to be 'Pre-Raphaelite'.

Figure 10 John Everett Millais, *Isabella*, 1848–9, oil on canvas, 102.9 × 142.9 cm, © Walker
Art Gallery, National Museums Liverpool/The Bridgeman Art Library.

Millais's early Pre-Raphaelite paintings are strikingly similar to Hunt's,
though it is very difficult to know which artist can claim precedence. Millais's
relationship to Rossetti is less clear at this time. Indeed he seems to be clos-
est to Rossetti in the years when his art begins to move *away* from 'pure'
Pre-Raphaelitism towards his later manner.

The first painting that Millais produced after the formation of the
Brotherhood was entitled *Isabella* (Figure 10). It was part of a collaboration with Hunt towards illustrations to Keats's poem 'Isabella; or, the Pot
of Basil'. Hunt had drawn a scene in which Lorenzo, the dreamy medieval clerk who loves the sister of his employers, is contrasted with the latter's brutish behaviour towards their underlings.[2] Millais's scene is close to
Hunt's in style and theme. The family is depicted at home rather than at
work, but their brutishness is displayed by their vulgar table manners, while
the delicate Lorenzo offers a sliced orange to the slightly flushed and awkward figure of Isabella.

This painting is almost a manifesto of Pre-Raphaelitism in the literal
meaning of the term, since its style is as pointedly medieval as its subject.
The perspective is deliberately, if subtly, distorted so that twice as many
figures manage to be seated at one side of the table as at the other. The
minimizing of modelling and deliberate juxtaposition of dramatically

contrasting blocks of intense colour mimic the decorative effects of late Gothic art. Though Millais knew engravings of art from this period, the only painting with which with which he is certain to have been familiar is Jan van Eyck's *Arnolfini Portrait*, recently acquired by the National Gallery. Early guidebooks repeatedly emphasize the purity of colour and precision of detail in this painting, as compared to the later paintings in the collection, of which the most famous was Sebastiano del Piombo's *The Raising of Lazarus* (c.1517–19) painted as a companion-piece to Raphael's last major work, the *Transfiguration* (1516–20, Vatican Museums, Rome). In this respect, the contrast between the two paintings defines the difference between 'Raphaelite' and 'Pre-Raphaelite' art.[3]

This contrast is also one between recognizable visual rhetoric and mysterious, perhaps even unknowable forms of intimacy in art. Sebastiano's painting was constructed from dramatic postures and simplified forms, the kind that had given rise to the so-called Mannerist style and, more broadly, to the later tradition of history painting, a tradition that was promoted by that early Victorian attempt to improve British art, the 1843 competition for commissions to decorate the Houses of Parliament. The three principal winners had all depicted heroic, muscular figures in dramatic scenes of conflict. This was imitated by the young Millais in his own student works. In contrast, the *Arnolfini Portrait* is a small painting depicting a scene bristling with strange details, evident but obscure symbolism, and instinct with the specificity of life lived at the time that it was painted. It is both intensely real and a kaleidoscope of vividly distinct motifs.

In these respects *Isabella* clearly mimics van Eyck's painting rather than Sebastiano's. Just as the wooden carvings in the background of the *Arnolfini Portrait* seem to press against the couple's conjoined hands, so Millais too compresses the space of his painting so that objects seem to intrude themselves onto the bodies of the figures. Unpredictable juxtapositions of motifs constantly suggest potential meaning. However, secrecy is also clearly one of the principal themes of this painting. The story itself is made deliberately difficult to interpret.

This will become a distinctive feature of Pre-Raphaelitism. In Hunt's work the difficulty of interpreting what we see assumes a moral dimension. This does not seem to be so with Millais, but it is clear that making the image difficult – unpredictable and disconcerting – comes to define his early art. In *Isabella* the main 'action' is the dramatic kick of the brutish figure at the left. Though visually startling, this kick has no direct narrative function. It is an intrusion on a scene in which everyone is, to all appearance, dining politely. The narrative is in the tiny details of the body language between Lorenzo and Isabella. Here Millais reduces the rhetoric of gesture to a slight turning of a head and an overly intense gaze. As we look at these barely readable signs we must attend more closely to the individuality of each figure. The servant at the right is as precisely characterized as the 'main' characters and can occupy our attention as fully. Each action – raising glasses, holding napkins and other seemingly trivial gestures – can be read as 'innocently' polite or as concealing hidden threats. The brother at the left who looks at his wine glass, genteelly extending his little finger, seems to gaze past the glass to the lovers, his other hand held up to his mouth, fingers pressing his lips, as if to conceal his expression.

Here, then, secrets unite the form and content of the image. While every detail seems preternaturally clear, the meaning of each of these little moments and motifs is bound up with the attempts of each character to repress the bodily expression of their emotions, to maintain a decorum that is continually threatening to break. The painting sets neat, rationally repeating patterns against bizarre violations of expected norms. It is concerned with the oddities of human experience. In this respect it creates a new form of art from the fascination which the Pre-Raphaelites felt with the sheer strangeness of such paintings as the *Arnolfini Portrait*. This is not to say that recent precedents did not exist. Similar historical precisionism and oddity of posture is apparent in some works by William Dyce, and the combination of complex detail, satire and ambiguous body language dates back to Hogarth. Millais has merged these diverse traditions to create a wholly new way of expressing the relationship between human and pictorial artifices.

Can we call this innovation Millais's alone, or is it a common Pre-Raphaelite project? Millais's fascination with human self-repression is mirrored by Rossetti's early paintings of the Virgin Mary as an almost anorexic teenager. His later work also stressed the forced containment of figures. Hunt, likewise, was preoccupied by the tension between bodily self-control and liberation, as epitomized by his versions of *The Lady of Shalott*, hair flying free, as she jerks round convulsively and twists herself into a spider's-web of her own making (Figure 1). Millais's concerns, however, are different. He is far more fully occupied by the ways in which people interact with each other, with the difficulties and conflicts of communal life. This concern will last throughout his career. It is also evident in the exhibit that was to make him famous, *Christ in the House of His Parents* (Figure 4).

Hunt's and Millais's paintings for the 1850 Royal Academy exhibition were hung together as companion-pieces. Both recreated early Christian experience, as had Rossetti's two Virgin Mary paintings. Hunt's *A Converted British Family Sheltering a Christian Missionary from the Persecution of the Druids* (Ashmolean Museum, Oxford) envisaged primal Christian culture in Britain, while Millais portrayed the Holy Family itself at work. Both paintings depicted crude, seemingly incomplete, wooden buildings within which primitive labours were interrupted by physical injury. There were precedents for both subjects, but their compositions were radical. Millais's painting proved the more provocative. Some depictions of Jesus at carpentry work had been condemned as unbecoming. The 'vulgarity' of the idea that Jesus would have worked at carpentry was linked to the claim that excessive detail betrayed the mentality of an artisan rather than an artist. Charles Eastlake, newly appointed President of the Royal Academy, declared this in his 1851 lecture. He asserted that 'uniform hardness, or universal distinctness, tends to indistinctness', and suggests the 'inactivity of mind' of 'mere manual labour'. He added that 'violent exaggeration' arises 'from an inability to make the truth interesting'.[4] This dual accusation of excess – detail tending to both confusion and caricature – epitomized the negative critical response to Millais.

Millais's scene is indeed characterized by 'manual labour'. It is built from the mechanics of carpentry. The structure of the building is open to the viewer and the technical details of *making* objects are vividly visualized, including the tools and the wood shavings among which the bare-footed figures walk. The clothing is difficult to locate in time or space. Animal skins are worn, but so are rolled-up sleeves and trousers. It's as if the scene seeks to present itself as simultaneously modern and prehistoric. Of course this strange primitive contemporaneity is linked to Millais's aspiration to depict communal experience. The watching figure at the left stands for the viewer, detached but fascinated by the drama. Like Isabella's brother, he ponders indecipherable details.

Many of these elements are also found in Hunt's painting, which is also structured by a crude wooden building, open to the elements, within which a family help an injured person. Beyond the barely contained privacy of the hut, more severe violence is threatened as a priest is restrained by a pagan mob. Both paintings imply future acts of sacrifice. Hunt's work hints at the likely fate of a captured priest. Millais's uses the tradition that Jesus's carpentry prefigures his crucifixion. Both paintings portray incomplete constructions to imply the primitive building of Christian morality, which is exposed, tentative and threatened. In both pictures lack of refinement is linked to intrusive detail, but it is Millais who is more fully focused on intimate body-language. Joseph pushes back the young Jesus's hand with awkward delicacy. Mary kneels and bends her head with furrowed brow, seeming both pained and concerned.

It was the intensity and ambiguity of these postures that seemed most to distress critics, who described the central characters as deformed. Dickens notoriously vilified Millais for portraying Mary as an emaciated alcoholic.

All the figures seemed to be suffering from forms of bodily stress. Again, it is the 'medieval' angularity that makes this scene and its companion Pre-Raphaelite in the literal meaning of the term, but it is the close observation of human interaction that gives it its power and which uncomfortably reminded critics of contemporary social realities. Millais creates a form of alienated intimacy within the family.

Such flirtations with the grotesque were most likely the strongest cause of the distaste with which critics greeted the painting. Millais was to continue in this vein in *Ferdinand Lured by Ariel* (1849–50, The Makins Collection) which is built around extreme contrasts of contradictory experiences figured by dramatic visual conflict.

In *Ferdinand* the hero strains to listen to the voice of Ariel, whom he can't see. The viewer, in contrast, sees the grass-green sprite's face shoved up against Ferdinand's. Ferdinand himself seems to be both cupping his ears to listen and holding the thread of his cap to keep it on. The image is built from bizarre disjunctions: the uncomfortable proximity of Ariel to the intense gaze of Ferdinand, staring through him. Ariel's semi-transparent body merges with the undergrowth, while grotesque Gothic bats surround him. This intense emphasis on grotesquery, merging detailed natural observation with medievalism, would seem to imply the influence of Ruskin. Ruskin had argued that the grotesque represented the creative play of the imagination, transforming nature into emblems. Certainly Millais plays on the idea that both the natural and supernatural worlds display harmonious integration of colour and form, while also erupting into 'something rich and strange' as Shakespeare put it in Ariel's song. Just as Ariel hides from Ferdinand, so the lizards at the bottom left merge with the grass, while the robin at the right stands out against the green like Ferdinand's primary-coloured clothing. Throughout, Millais's play with visibility is linked to the act of descriptive painting itself, as colours and forms mutate and merge. Ariel's body slides between greens and pinks, while its outlines shift between clarification and dissolution.

This interest in the way that pure, flat colour and pattern work in relation to the ceaseless formal complexities of nature was to preoccupy Millais in the next few years. In *Mariana* (1850–1, Tate) he depicts a frustrated and confined woman, endlessly awaiting the arrival of her absent lover. Mariana is depicted stretching her stiff back in a moment of relief from her labours at embroidery. The theme represents the transformation of nature into art as an act of labour. It is also closely related to other Pre-Raphaelite works in which embroidery plays a significant role, such as Charles Allston Collins's *Berengaria's Alarm for the Safety of her Husband, Richard Coeur de Lion* (1850, City of Manchester Art Galleries), which is built around overlaid geometrical patterns, and Rossetti's *The Girlhood of Mary Virgin* (Figure 6). These paintings pre-dated *Mariana*, but neither is so fully defined by the process of describing the detailed relationship between pure pattern and the mysterious atmospheric effect of light in confined space. Mariana stretches before a rigidly geometrical window containing an image of the Virgin Mary. She is making embroidery with leaves from the garden, seen *through* the decorated window. This emblem of natural forms mediated by human ideologies makes sense of the portrayal of her strained body, forced into painfully restricted experiences. Behind her is a mysterious space in which a small devotional image sits on a table, above which hangs a lantern. The lantern creates strange pools of light which are difficult clearly to locate in space. Here Millais is moving even further away from rigid precisionism towards a fascination with the dissolution of material objects into kaleido-scopic experiences of colour.

This once more raises the question of Millais's distinctive take on 'Pre-Raphaelitism'. The theme of embroidery was to persist in Hunt and Rossetti, and was to preoccupy later artists who have been labelled as Pre-Raphaelites. Burne-Jones's work repeatedly deploys such imagery. John William Waterhouse, an artist whose loose brushwork resembles Millais's own late work, along with that of the French realist Jules Bastien-Lepage, has been defined as a Pre-Raphaelite in part because his works retain the imagery of multi-layered embroidered patterns that characterize Hunt and Rossetti. Millais was to abandon this completely after the 1860s. Is this what stops him being a Pre-Raphaelite? Certainly in *Mariana* we can see the beginnings of this abandonment of pattern in favour of uncertain moments of visual sensation. And yet, this is exactly what Ruskin, who is so often portrayed as the intellectual mentor of the Pre-Raphaelites, so repeatedly stressed in his writings. As an admirer of Turner, he hoped that Pre-Raphaelitism could evolve into an art of atmospheric effect. *Mariana* showed that such a development was possible – that a medievalist obsession with elaboration could include within it the broken, shimmering light that informed Turner's landscapes.

This leads us to the painting that is typically proffered as the epitome of Millais's Pre-Raphaelitism – and even of the movement itself – *Ophelia* (Tate). It was first exhibited in 1851 alongside *A Huguenot* (Figure 11). The latter painting was better received at the time, and was quickly engraved. It proved popular throughout the nineteenth century. However it is *Ophelia* that has come to define Millais's art in our own time. It began to acquire this stature in the later nineteenth century, and was clearly established as the perfection of the Pre-Raphaelite when Salvador Dalí wrote an essay extol-ling the work as an image of ecstatic death prefiguring the Surrealist ideal

Figure 11 John Everett Millais, *A Huguenot, on St Bartholomew's Day, Refusing to Shield Himself from Danger by Wearing the Roman Catholic Badge*, 1851–2, oil on canvas, 92.7 × 62.2 cm (arched), © The Makins Collection/The Bridgeman Art Library.

of 'convulsive beauty'. This was a painting poised between hysterical documentation and imminent disintegration.

How important is this insight and what does it tell us about the fact that *A Huguenot* had such power in the nineteenth century and that *Ophelia* had it in the twentieth? Victorian writers were impressed by *A Huguenot*'s intense intimacy. The lessons Millais learned working on the convoluted compositions of *Isabella* and *Christ in the House of his Parents* had led him to develop a means to express subtleties of human intimacies and tensions. These developments were shared with Hunt. The two artists were still working on similar subjects and were no longer mimicking pictorial primitivism.

Hunt, nevertheless, was still interested in *crudity*, as reviewers of *The Hireling Shepherd* (Figure 8) noted, one of whom spoke of the 'romp and rubicundity' of his cider-flushed peasant couple. The clutching fingers of Hunt's shepherdess are groping the grass between the lad's splayed legs. In contrast, Millais's characters are locked in a relationship defined by a struggle so subtle that it barely seems to register. They are embracing and pulling away from one another at the same time. Millais's paintwork also differs subtly from Hunt's, and with similar significance. While Hunt juxtaposes clashing colours, creating an acidic sharpness, Millais always retains a pre-occupation with underlying tonal transitions, while allowing his colours to appear in spots of intense purity. Throughout the painting colours continu-ally slide in and out of prominence.

This is even more fully evident in *Ophelia*, a painting built from a dense network of interlinking lines, tones and hues which are constantly describ-ing motifs, while emerging from and dissolving into one another. Millais depicts Ophelia floating, at her last moment of lucidity, before her saturated dress, 'heavy with its drink', as Shakespeare says, pulls her to 'muddy death'. Millais's choice of this moment allows him to play several visual games with the viewer, presenting us with concentrated detail at some points, and almost abstract and amorphous shapes at others, most notably the great green smear in the foreground, representing submerged flora. Ophelia's head stands out sharply from the water. It is painted with fascinated dedication to the individual features of the model, Elizabeth Siddall. This dedication is equally devoted to the wayside plants that compete to occupy the riverbank behind. Indeed vegetation almost overwhelms the composition, as though no part of the painting is free from nature's capacity to colonize space. The whole surface is suffused with competing signs of life, pushing themselves upon our gaze. Millais has created an aesthetic of overwhelming competi-tive demand for visual niches within a constricted space.

What makes this painting unique is the fact that this power-struggle within the composition takes the form of visual patterns of transition between abstract shapes and natural forms. This is a development of the techniques initiated in *Mariana*, but it is more fully realized. Ophelia's hair floats into swirls which merge with the movements of the water. Her dress mirrors the swatch of green before it, a blur of grey in which spots of light partly form fluid embroidered flowers while fragments of real petals and stems float over it.

Here begins Millais's distinctively ecological vision of nature, in which the human presence merely forms part of an ever growing, decaying and regenerating system. This theme was to persist throughout his life, long after critics ceased to call him a Pre-Raphaelite. Is this, then, a feature of 'Millais' that cannot be reduced to the movement itself? It is difficult to say, since devotion to nature's complexity has always been thought to be distinct-ively Pre-Raphaelite. It seems appropriate to say that Millais took up a Pre-Raphaelite 'idea' but developed it in a way that became distinctive to him.

This problem certainly characterizes Millais's relationship to Pre-Raphaelitism in the next few years, since it is difficult to separate from his relationship to Ruskin and to his future wife Effie. The complexities of these personal traumas certainly inform both Millais's art and Ruskin's response to it, but it is difficult to say exactly *how*. For our purposes what is important is that new developments are fully visible in 1856, the year after his marriage. In that year he exhibited five paintings at the Royal Academy. Together they represent an emerging new model for Millais's art.

All Millais's major paintings of 1856 communicate this same vision. Along with a portrait of a child he exhibited *Autumn Leaves* (City of Manchester Art Galleries), *Peace Concluded* (The Minneapolis Institute of Arts), *L'Enfant du Régiment* (Yale Center for British Art, New Haven) and *The Blind Girl* (Birmingham Museums & Art Gallery). Ruskin's review of this collection was ecstatic. He insisted that *Peace Concluded* would in future be counted among 'the world's best masterpieces' and that of all artists only Titian was now superior to Millais.[5] The paintings do display a new confidence with massing of colour and ambiguities of form. They are all preoccupied with the pictorial complexities of visual pleasure. Taken as a whole they also display a Dickensian interest in the full range of social experience, from the beggars in *The Blind Girl* to the gentry in *Peace Concluded*. Millais also shows his emerging fascination with generational differences. In *L'Enfant du Régiment* we see a sleeping, wounded girl nestling in a tomb's notch, her head intimate with the cold marble. The colours with which the stone is described are fluid. Pinks blush from the spatially uncertain surface and patches of green seem to grow from the interstices. The mutating stone is like the foliage in *Ophelia*, presenting a dangerous pictorial intimacy between life and decay.

The same motifs occur in *Peace Concluded* and *The Blind Girl*. In the former a wounded officer recovers at home with his family as he reads the news that the Crimean War is over. His pose, twisted across a divan, mirrors that of the statue on which the girl in *L'Enfant du Régiment* lies, including the sleeping dog at his feet. Here it implies comfort rather than threat. His wife, modelled by Effie, sits on his lap in the centre of the composition, an icon of fertility from behind whose head a myrtle bush sprouts. Millais deploys the ambiguities of the shallow space to create a convoluted interlinking of forms in which the couple's bodies and the space they occupy visually merge into one another, setting up a contrast with the foreground in which children play with sharply defined toys symbolizing the war's combatants.

The confrontational gaze of one of the children is replicated in *Autumn Leaves*, depicting four children at different ages. The two older ones gaze out at us, while the younger, and apparently poorer, pair stare at the products of the natural world: a ripe apple and the smouldering pile of leaves. The suggestion of sacrificial ritual mirrors the imagery in the other paintings.

The merging of colours and forms is here represented by the kaleidoscope of muted hues unleashed by autumnal decay. Behind the girls objects become blurred in twilight. The leaves become a jumble of lines and varied tones. The composition is dominated by this extraordinary mass of confused materials which becomes a sign of the struggle between the merging and differentiation of motifs, a struggle that had been central to Millais's art since *Isabella*. *Autumn Leaves*, then, displays the same concern with the loving delineation of difference that had characterized Millais's earliest works. Each leaf is sharply distinguished, as much as is its chromatic conflation with the others in the pile. The same is true of the class difference between the girls. It is defined by pose and clothing but is also diminished by the commonality of their experience. This is also much more broadly painted than Millais's earlier works. Ruskin clearly imagined that Millais was moving in the direction of Turner. We see blocks of colour representing that twilight radiance in which definition breaks up into what Ruskin described as the 'glow within darkness'. These big slashes of pigment are a new development, most notable in the red scarf of the youngest girl and the bright flash of yellow leaf that hovers on the edge of the basket.

While *Autumn Leaves*, like *Peace Concluded*, implies a safe environment in which diverse social classes work in harmony, *The Blind Girl*, like *L'Enfant*, depicts an alienated space in which two destitute sisters are excluded from the middle-class town behind them, holding tightly to each other in a scrubby wasteland. In this case the alienation that defines the situation is epitomized by the central motif, as the blind girl lifts her face to the sun, while her sister gazes at the double rainbow that seems to irradiate the town from which they are excluded.

These paintings develop *Ophelia*'s exploration of the natural dynamic of eco-systems, but display a new concern with *painterly* drama. This is the moment when Millais's position as a Pre-Raphaelite begins to be questioned, since Ruskin was famously to condemn his exhibits of the following year as a catastrophe. Millais himself believed he was striking out on his own, linking this in his mind to a new sensuality. As he wrote to Holman Hunt, 'Marriage is the best cure for that wretched *lingering* over one's work, which seldom betters it, and racks the brain and makes miserable.'[6] Millais seems to connect Pre-Raphaelitism with emotional frustration, almost as though obsession with detail is a form of neurotic inhibition: a view that is by no means inappropriate to describe Hunt's work, so filled with scenarios of forcibly restrained physical desire within obsessively elaborated visual networks.

If Hunt's paintings enact the relationship between painting and self-control, Millais's work is increasingly about the unleashing of visual pleasure itself. In this, though he is moving away from Hunt, he may be said to be coming closer to Rossetti. Indeed one of Millais's early works, *The Bridesmaid* (1851, Fitzwilliam Museum, Cambridge), seems to anticipate the later works of Rossetti, at a time when Rossetti himself was still portraying repressed Virgins. An image of a woman with overwhelmingly abundant golden hair, it is an exercise in the free-flow of liquid colour, far more radically sensuous than anything painted by Rossetti for many years. The image is a visual assault of gold against blue, linked to an erotic scenario in which the bride fantasizes her future husband.

So again we find ourselves asking whether Millais is becoming more or less 'Pre-Raphaelite' at this time. His paintings of 1857 certainly begin to display characteristics of his later work. This is most obvious in the least known of them, *News from Home* (Walters Art Museum, Baltimore), depicting a Scots soldier of the Crimean war reading a letter. He is placed before a barricade which is painted in tonally varied browns, while the modelling of the central figure is structured to define his body against the space. Certainly, were it not for Millais's monogram, it is difficult to imagine that this would ever have been thought of as Pre-Raphaelite. Nevertheless, it resembles in subject and form his earlier image of a Scots soldier, *The Order of Release* (1852–3, Tate). What it lacks is the unresolved complexity of the poses and expressions of the figures.

Banal though this may seem, the other paintings of 1857 were considered bizarre, and not only by Ruskin. *The Escape of the Heretic* (Museo de Arte de Ponce, Puerto Rico) included an almost pornographic caricature of dancing demons, on the female figure's costume for the auto-da-fé, while the figures were modelled in dramatically contrasting slashes of lurid pigment. And yet ... such blocks of colour can be traced to *Isabella*, and the girl's outstretched, exposed neck seems, once again, to anticipate Rossetti's late work. Most of all, the eccentricities of the image betray the influence of Ford Madox Brown, an artist Ruskin deeply disliked, but whose work has always been included within the Pre-Raphaelite fold. Lastly, Millais's major work of the year, *Sir Isumbras (A Dream of the Past)* (Lady Lever Art Gallery, National Museums Liverpool), develops his tendency to contrast potential violence and delicate vulnerability. It is as pointedly medieval and as full of pictorial and psychological complexities as his earliest works.

Nevertheless, it is not difficult to appreciate Ruskin's rejection of these works. Millais is clearly introducing elements of caricature in order to dramatize psychological and ideological clashes more vividly. There is less loving interest in observation, whether of detail or of Turneresque atmosphere. Instead, in these paintings, he seems entranced by the idea that art can portray the subtleties of body-language such that form is at one with human feeling. Like many earlier works, they describe endangered intimacy. The way the frightened children in *Sir Isumbras* hold tightly to the knight who carries them mirrors the desperate intensity with which the sisters grasp each other's hands in *The Blind Girl*.

What is initiated in the paintings of 1856–7 was to be the model for Millais's future art: a meditation on the palpable rhythms of human life: generational cycles, innocence, experience and old age. The paired paintings *Spring* (Lady Lever Art Gallery) and *The Vale of Rest* (Tate), exhibited in 1859, mark this. They are constructed as friezes, creating a hieratic quality with a flattened space comparable to the early work of Frederic Leighton and James McNeill Whistler. The former depicts fertile young women in springtime, circulating milky substances in a garden. They are abandoned to pleasure, as rich expanses of colour glow from their gowns. In the latter, two nuns prepare to bury a deceased sister. The mystery of death is mirrored by the oddities of evening light. Strange radiances emerge behind clouds and from unseen sources within the foliage.

Millais's uncertainty about his future direction is evident at this time, since in the following year he exhibited *The Black Brunswicker* (Lady Lever Art Gallery), which was essentially a reprise of *A Huguenot*, also depicting a man departing to almost certain death while his beloved haplessly restrains him. The painting is as detailed as his earliest Pre-Raphaelite works, but with a difference. While *A Huguenot* depicted natural fecundity, here we see threatened domesticity. The emotional conflict is visualized in the dramatic contrast of black broadcloth and white satin. Details reveal the vulnerability through artefacts rather than nature, but these commodities incarnate human needs. The girl's ball-gown is heavily creased from its long sojourn folded unused. The wallpaper bubbles up, betraying damp, and, most poignantly, a puzzling object lies draped in deep purple cloth, betraying beneath its fold the form of an empty cradle.

The Black Brunswicker is a painting about the death of domestic dreams. It uses Pre-Raphaelite techniques to describe human difficulties different from the romantic yearnings of the earlier works. Here detail is mediated by chiaroscuro. Millais's later 'Pre-Raphaelite' works would all be defined by this balance of detail with mastery of colour and form. *The Black Brunswicker* is an extraordinary example of Millais's ability to adapt his methods while remaining true to his principles.

Over the next few years Millais experimented with loosely painted Whistlerian images in which bodily pleasure is defined through visual sensation rather than detail. However he always retains his very un-Whistlerian emphasis on human weakness, interacting with aesthetic pleasure, as in *Esther* (1865, private collection), which depicts a moment of dangerous self-display in which the heroine creates glamorous spectacle to mask fear for her life. This and other images are characterized by the fact that they minimize the earlier preoccupation with circumstantial detail by concentrating instead on human expressivity in a way that avoids rhetoric, but which retain the idea that people are trapped in conventions.

In this regard Millais continues the themes of the earliest of his Pre-Raphaelite works, *Isabella*, but unlike the later paintings, *Isabella* was still engaged with the rhetoric it rejected, through those complex and eccentric postures suggesting half-hidden meanings and motivations. As the 1860s drew to a close, Millais became interested in the ways in which the paint surface itself, built from powerful and even conflicting brushstrokes, could express the uncertainties that were so important to his earlier work. In *Victory O Lord!* (1870, City of Manchester Art Galleries), narrative and paint combine to express a chaotic struggle against the void. It depicts Moses holding up his arms to help the battling Israelites by force of will. This is a painting about both power and impotence, about the experience of stress as one concentrates emotional and bodily strength, a struggle expressed in the knotted surface of the paint itself.

These late paintings use paint itself as the source of vitality. The earlier works are preoccupied by pattern-making as the essential power of art; they are about the relationship between visual order and insubordinate humanity. The link between the two worlds of his art is clearest in the last paintings of Millais's that can truly be said to be Pre-Raphaelite: *Waking* (Perth Museums & Art Gallery) and *Sleeping* (private collection), exhibited in 1867. They are child pictures, typical of his later work, but painted with all the precision of *Isabella*. In one, a wide-eyed newly woken young girl looks intently at a singing bird in a cage hanging above her bed. In the other a child sleeps, while a nurse sits beside her bed, concentrating on embroidery. We do not see her work. Instead, the power of pattern is made visible in the elaborate surface of the quilt, but, like Ophelia's dress, its silvery-grey expanse breaks up into tonal variations against which sudden vivid spots of red and blue fabric are set. In *Waking* the unseen bird stands for this same vision of intensity constrained by comfort.

Both these paintings draw on the aestheticism of the 1860s, but also look back to among the earliest instances of Pre-Raphaelitism. *Sleeping*, in particular, is greatly indebted to Rossetti's *Ecce Ancilla Domini!* (1849–50, Tate), which also concentrates on a vulnerable girl, swathed in white, with flat blocks of blue and red fabric beside her. Millais is a far more skilful artist than Rossetti, and he manages the transitions of tone and space with almost miraculous ease. This mastery of technique is what seems to motivate his later desire to paint with the freedom of Velázquez and Rembrandt.

These later works are wholly preoccupied by humanity itself, on the model of Rembrandt. They try to show that detail is less important than the struggle to express experience – that paint destabilizes the conflict of flesh and power. The paintings that defined Millais's early career minimized both flesh and energy by creating abstract but palpable patterns to overlay or repress the human body. This brings us back to the difficult question of how we can know when a painting is Pre-Raphaelite and when it is not. The term is applied very loosely in much popular literature on the movement. Millais's apparent abandonment of the style may lead us to question what the term actually means. What we can say is that his art always contained a distinct and personal vision that persists throughout his life. It is the interaction of that vision with Rossetti's and Hunt's work that makes Millais's Pre-Raphaelitism a unique resource for understanding its complexities.

NOTES

1 Paul Barlow, *Time Present and Time Past: The Art of John Everett Millais* (Aldershot, Hants. and Burlington, Vermont: Ashgate, 2005); Peter Funnell, Malcolm Warner and others, *Millais: Portraits*, exhibition catalogue (London: National Portrait Gallery, 1999); Jason Rosenfeld and Alison Smith, *Millais*, exhibition catalogue (London: Tate Publishing, 2007).

2 *Lorenzo at his Desk in the Warehouse*, 1848–50, pen and brush and grey ink, Musée du Louvre, Département des Arts Graphiques, Paris.

3 *The Raising of Lazarus* was typically praised as the most important painting in the National Gallery's early collection. It was officially catalogued as NG1.

4 Charles Lock Eastlake, *Discourse Delivered to the Students of the Royal Academy*, 10 December 1851 (London: Clowes, 1852), p. 20.

5 Ruskin, vol. XIV, pp. 56–7.

6 Diana Holman-Hunt, *My Grandfather, His Wives and Loves* (London: Hamish Hamilton, 1969), p. 168.

10

TIM BARRINGER

Ford Madox Brown (1821–1893)

A resoundingly paradoxical figure, Ford Madox Brown was never a member of the Pre-Raphaelite Brotherhood, yet his works stand at the heart of the Pre-Raphaelite corpus. He contributed to *The Germ*, taught Rossetti, and his work of the late 1840s seems to prefigure many of the most radical achievements of the PRB. Despite his avowed focus on history painting, it was left to Brown to perfect Pre-Raphaelite modern-life painting and to create in *Work* (1852–65, City of Manchester Art Galleries) and *The Last of England* (1852–5, Birmingham Museums & Art Gallery) its greatest monuments. Brown's landscapes, moreover, are among the finest painted explorations of 'truth to nature'. In 1865 he published a lengthy descriptive catalogue to a retrospective exhibition of his major works which stands as a key text for the history of the Pre-Raphaelite movement. In the 1860s Brown became a leading figure in the Aesthetic Movement and a pioneering designer in the 'Firm' of Morris, Marshall, Faulkner & Co., and in later years he espoused an idiosyncratic form of socialism. Brown embodied, in other words, all the major currents of Pre-Raphaelitism.

And yet he was nonetheless perpetually the outsider during his lifetime, outside even of the 'avant-garde' grouping of the Pre-Raphaelite Brotherhood itself. He systematically alienated himself from the main streams of patronage and critical approbation, consistently placing himself in antagonistic relations with the establishment. Undoubtedly this was in part the result of the artist's personality – querulous; hasty in his judgements; easily wounded. But in Brown's seemingly self-defeating professional conduct we can see the same refusal to compromise, or to accommodate the status quo, which is the essence of his art. Brown's work is notable for its frequent recourse to the grotesque; its frequent obscurity of subject and meaning; and its refusal to conform to the requirements of any tendency – including those of Pre-Raphaelitism. The combination of a harsh, even truculent, verisimilitude with unrestrained inventiveness places Brown's finest works among the key visual productions of the mid-nineteenth century.

Brown's status as an outsider, already clear from the critical reception of his work during his lifetime, has been carried through into the historiography. This is largely due to Holman Hunt's ubiquitous text *Pre-Raphaelitism and the Pre-Raphaelite Brotherhood*, first published in 1905. Conceived as a riposte to the account of the movement proposed by what he called the 'Brown–Rossetti circle', Hunt's self-aggrandizing volumes miss no opportunity to belittle Brown's achievements, and to cast him as a follower rather than a leader of the Pre-Raphaelite movement.[1] Obituaries following Brown's death on 6 October 1893 were polite rather than enthusiastic in their appreciation of his oeuvre. A memoir published in 1896 by his grandson Ford Madox Hueffer (who later became well known as a novelist under the name Ford Madox Ford) offers an eloquently affecting family tribute, but unsurprisingly fails to provide a definitive critical perspective.[2] Brown was thereafter virtually ignored until a major retrospective exhibition in Liverpool in 1964 curated by Mary Bennett rescued his work from neglect.[3] Her fundamental research on the artist, which has now reached its culmination in a complete catalogue raisonné, has been the cornerstone of all that followed.[4] Bennett contributed entries on Brown to the Tate Gallery's revelatory exhibition *The Pre-Raphaelites* of 1984, which rightly emphasized Brown's central contribution to the movement. Despite the publication of a biography by Ray Watkinson and Teresa Newman, and an insightful scholarly monograph by Kenneth Bendiner, Brown still sits awkwardly in surveys of Pre-Raphaelitism, with the central question unanswered: was Brown a prophet and innovator, whose radical ideas found a warm reception from his younger Pre-Raphaelite contemporaries; or was he (as Hunt suggests) an unsuccessful if noble eccentric whose work took a decisive turn only when he responded to the true innovations of the Pre-Raphaelites?[5] Whether Brown can indeed figure as Pre-Raphaelitism's John the Baptist, or whether he is a mere belated apostle of a faith created by others, certainly remains a matter for debate.[6] This chapter argues for a central place for Brown, not only in our assessment of Pre-Raphaelitism, but more generally in the history of nineteenth-century art.

Proto-Pre-Raphaelitism: *Harold, Wycliffe* and *Chaucer*

Brown's artistic formation was radically different from that of the Pre-Raphaelites, and indeed from that of virtually any other British painter of the period. The best tuition available in London was that provided by the haphazard system of 'Visitors' at the Royal Academy Schools. Brown, however, grew up in France, and began his studies under Aelbert Gregorius (1774–1853), a student of Jacques-Louis David, at the Bruges Academy. A year later in 1836 he transferred to the Academy at Ghent, where he studied under another David pupil, Pierre Van Hanselaer (1786–1862). These early masters offered Brown a rather hard-edged neoclassicism with which he never seems to have been entirely at ease; but it was here, too, that he first mastered 'the mechanism of a historical picture', a subject of which he would offer an incomplete exegesis in *The Germ* in 1850. However, it was from Gustaf, Baron Wappers (1803–74), with whom he trained in Antwerp from 1837, that Brown acquired his central belief that history painting should engage with contemporary moral and political issues. It was to the genre of history painting – in his own characteristically eccentric definition – that Brown would devote himself for the next five decades.

In 1843, the announcement of an annual competition to select designs for frescoes to decorate the new Palace of Westminster indicated a rare source of patronage for history painting in England. The teenage future Pre-Raphaelites were well aware of the stakes in the Westminster competitions, and Millais himself submitted a specimen of fresco painting in 1847. In 1844, seeing the rare potential for a major commission, Madox Brown had submitted a large cartoon of *The Body of Harold Brought before William*, which survives in fragments (South London Art Gallery), a work which, as Hunt records, occasioned from Rossetti 'expressions of unbounded enthusiasm'. Hunt's very full account of this work is instructive:

> the drawing was robust and nervous, and the costume was treated with manly taste, giving actuality to the historic scene ... but Brown had adopted a glaringly unreasonable reading of the fact that William went into battle with the bones of the saints round his neck, over which relics Harold had made his renunciation of the crown. Instead of painting a reliquary, he had hung femur, tibia, humerus, and other large bones dangling loose on the hero's breast, surely a formidable encumbrance both to riding and fighting. In the lower corner of the picture were a Norman and Saxon engaged in a final struggle, the uppermost biting the throat of the lower, while the latter, with both arms stretched around his foe, was drawing with all his force the blade of a huge dagger deep into the enemy's back. These grotesque incidents in the first of his works seen by me somewhat counterbalanced the merits I saw in conception, and tended to puzzle spectators by no means narrow in taste.[7]

Though this vivid description reveals the great power of this image, Brown was too extreme, too uncompromising, for Hunt's taste. The work's visual rhetoric, though 'manly', is 'glaringly unreasonable'. Needless to say, this, like all Brown's other competition entries, failed to please the jury. Perhaps they jibbed at its sardonic portrayal of the Normans – implying a critique of their descendants, the present-day aristocracy (an abiding theme in Brown's works). A more likely cause for its failure, however, was Brown's refusal to conform to pictorial orthodoxy.

A journey to Rome in 1845 exposed Brown to two key influences: the collection of works of Hans Holbein at Basle and, in Rome itself, contemporary work by the German 'Nazarenes', a group of German artists who had formed a 'Guild of St Luke' in Rome in 1809. The Nazarenes provided a significant precedent both for the Pre-Raphaelites' reforming, historicist project, and for their choice of a group identity. Their work was well known to a number of English painters, including Daniel Maclise and William Dyce, but Brown seems to have been the most significant conduit between the Nazarenes and the young Pre-Raphaelites.[8] In 1845, possibly on the advice of his friend William Cave Thomas, Brown had sought out the leading Nazarene painters, Johann Friedrich Overbeck and Peter Cornelius, who became key influences in his subsequent works such as *Wycliffe Reading his Translation of the New Testament to his Protector, John of Gaunt, Duke of Lancaster, in Presence of Chaucer and Gower* (1847–8, Cartwright Memorial Hall, Bradford).

Wycliffe appeared at the 'Free' Exhibition of 1848, where, the following year, Rossetti's *Girlhood of Mary Virgin* (Figure 6) became the first Pre-Raphaelite painting to be exhibited in public. Was *Wycliffe* a fully fledged Pre-Raphaelite painting made before the PRB was formed? This must remain an unanswered question, particularly since Brown characteristically retouched the work in 1859–61 and its original appearance is not recorded. As it stands today, *Wycliffe* bears many of the same hallmarks that identify *The Girlhood of Mary Virgin* as a new and radical departure. Facial features, notably those of the craggy Wycliffe, are carefully painted from life, a departure from the ideal Raphaelesque types of the Nazarenes and of the painters of the parliamentary frescoes. While the spacious composition of *Wycliffe* remains decorously symmetrical, in contrast to the strangely congested and crowded planes of Rossetti's *Girlhood*, the sharpness of detail in the depiction of the wooden furnishings, and in the distant representation of Sompting Church, in Sussex, clearly prefigures in 1847–8 (or does it replicate in 1859–61?) Pre-Raphaelite practice. The van Eyckian glimpse of a street through an arrow slit in the fictive palace walls pays homage to one of the key sources of Brown's proto-Pre-Raphaelite fusion of archaism and hyper-realism – the early Netherlandish painting that he, alone among the Pre-Raphaelite circle, knew from an extensive knowledge of collections in the Low Countries.

One significant remnant of Brown's involvement in the Westminster competitions is a small study for *The Seeds and Fruits of English Poetry* (1845–53, Ashmolean Museum, Oxford) initially conceived as a competition entry.

Figure 12 Ford Madox Brown, *Geoffrey Chaucer Reading the 'Legend of Custance' to
Edward III and his Court, at the Palace of Sheen, on the Anniversary of the Black Prince's
Forty-Fifth Birthday*, 1845–51, oil on canvas, 372 × 296 cm (arched), Art Gallery
of New South Wales, Sydney/The Bridgeman Art Library.

Only the large central panel was taken up and completed on a monumental
scale as an independent painting (1846–51, Figure 12). This elaborate multi-
figure composition was displayed at the Royal Academy six years after its
conception, in 1851, when its Pre-Raphaelite affiliations were immediately
recognized. Brown's massive painting was given the full – and somewhat
pedantic – title *Geoffrey Chaucer Reading the 'Legend of Custance' to
Edward III and his Court, at the Palace of Sheen, on the Anniversary of
the Black Prince's Forty-Fifth Birthday*. It might seem to constitute an antiquarian's complete rejection of modernity. Brown derived the subject from
Sir James Mackintosh's *History of England* (published serially from 1830),
which he studied in the library of the British Museum. As he recalled in his
diary in 1847, a passage on Geoffrey Chaucer 'at once fixed me, I immediately saw visions of Chaucer reading his poems to knights & Ladyes fair,
to the king & court amid air & sun shine'.[9] But the painting's Gothicism
was no reactionary rejection of the present. Chaucer, for Brown, represented
not merely a figure of redoubtable academic worthiness, but a remarkably

vibrant and accessible figure, a paradigm of the modern artist: 'Spelling, and a few of the minor proprieties apart, after a lapse of five hundred years, his delicate sense of naturalistic beauty and his practical turn of thought ... comes home to us as naturally as the last volume we hail with delight from the press.'[10] *Chaucer at the Court of Edward III* is a highly original composition, bathed in real sunlight ('air & sun shine'), and set against a precisely rendered naturalistic landscape. The clarity, individual definition and local colour of each object gives the painting's surface a kaleidoscopic dizziness as fabrics and features compete for the viewer's attention. The careful individualization of each face confirms that every figure was painted from an individual model.

Once again, the question must be raised: was it Brown who conceived the 'Pre-Raphaelite' rejection of the doctrine of Sir Joshua Reynolds, and of the practices of his own Davidian tutors in Belgium, by throwing out the orthodoxy under which figures must be idealized and generalized, and compositions should pay homage to the great works of the old masters? There is no doubt that, sharp and scientific, painted in a style wholly modern, *Chaucer* is an image of history entirely in keeping with the spirit of the Great Exhibition. It could, then, be taken as the first paradigmatic statement of a new kind of history painting. But, on the other hand, was Brown by 1851 crucially influenced by seeing Pre-Raphaelite works in 1849 and 1850, such as Millais's *Isabella* (Figure 10) or Hunt's *A Converted British Family Sheltering a Christian Missionary from the Persecution of the Druids* (1849–50, Ashmolean Museum, Oxford)? As if defending himself from the by then familiar accusation that he was a mere follower of the Pre-Raphaelites, Brown insisted in his 1865 exhibition catalogue that *Chaucer* had been 'the first [painting] in which I endeavoured to carry out the notion, long before conceived, of treating the light and shade absolutely, as it exists at any one moment, instead of approximately, or in generalised style. Sunlight not too bright, such as is pleasant to sit in out of doors, is here depicted.'[11] He worked on a historical composition as if it were painted from life. Holman Hunt, however, insisted in 1905 that when he first saw *Chaucer* the painting 'failed to represent the unaffected art of past time, and it stood before me as a recent mark of academic ingenuity which Pre-Raphaelitism in its larger power of enfranchisement was framed to overthrow'.[12] Brown, for Hunt, had contravened the 'first principle of Pre-Raphaelitism [which] was to eschew all that was conventional in contemporary art'.[13] But this rather disingenuous criticism is transparently intended to bolster Hunt's self-proclaimed position as the central innovator of the group. Because the work, begun in 1845, was not completed until 1851, we have no way of judging for ourselves whether Brown was the true source (as he himself

implies) of the central Pre-Raphaelite claim (expressed here in Ruskin's brilliant summary) to 'draw either what they see, or what they suppose might
have been the actual facts of the scene they desire to represent, irrespective
of any conventional rules of picture-making'.[14] Nonetheless, the diary entry
of 1847, referring to the 'king & court amid air & sun shine', adds crucial
support to Brown's assertion of his intentions to paint the work in this style
from the beginning, and thus identifies him as the author of central Pre-
Raphaelite innovations; and *Chaucer* stands as a founding monument of
Pre-Raphaelitism.

Brown and *The Germ*

By 1851, Brown had known the artists of the Pre-Raphaelite Brotherhood
for more than three years. Rossetti had approached Brown for lessons in
1848, in a letter whose extravagance the touchy Brown took as satirical,
setting off with a 'stout stick' to rebuke the perpetrator.[15] The tutorial relationship was of short duration. Rossetti was directed by Brown to complete a still life of bottles (now in the Delaware Art Museum), a discipline
he 'found so abhorrent that it ... tormented his soul beyond the power of
endurance'.[16] Although he soon turned to Hunt for lessons, Rossetti became
a lifelong friend of Brown, and his early works markedly show the older
artist's influence.

Brown's role in the early years of Pre-Raphaelitism does indeed seem
to have been that of a mentor, despite Holman Hunt's retrospective construction of him as a follower. Brown's pedagogical voice in this period can
be heard in his article for *The Germ* 'On the Mechanism of a Historical
Picture', which appeared in the second issue in February 1850. Opening
with sentiments of (perhaps false) modesty, he addresses himself to 'numbers who at the onset of their career have not the least knowledge of any
one of these methods', and more specifically to all 'about to paint their first
picture'. The Pre-Raphaelites themselves had only very recently passed this
point; Rossetti's *Girlhood of Mary Virgin* might well qualify as his 'first
picture', for example.

Brown's article (the first and only completed text of a planned series) is
an artful combination of academic orthodoxy and radical avant-gardism.
Brown lays out a conventional procedure with sketches, compositional
studies and cartoons, in preparation for a final exhibition painting as con-
doned by academic practice (adhered to by his former masters in Belgium).
Yet he also insists on rigorous historical accuracy in matters of detail:
'The first care of the painter, after having selected his subject, should be

to make himself thoroughly acquainted with the character of the times, and habits of the people, which he is about to represent; and next, to consult the proper authorities for his costume, and such objects as may fill his canvass; as the architecture, furniture, vegetation or landscape, or accessories, necessary to the elucidation of the subject.'[17] This advice ran directly counter to that of the holy text of the Royal Academy Schools, Sir Joshua Reynolds's *Discourses*, which held that generalization rather than specificity, overall form rather than specific detail, were the key to successful history painting. The greatest achievements of Pre-Raphaelite history painting, from Brown's own *Chaucer* to Millais's *Christ in the House of His Parents* (underway as Brown was writing at the beginning of 1850, Figure 4), and Holman Hunt's *The Finding of the Saviour in the Temple* (1860, Birmingham Museums & Art Gallery), would all place the highest emphasis on local detail. Once again, however, it is an open question as to whether Brown's theoretical position had been influenced by seeing the very earliest Pre-Raphaelite paintings. The course Brown proposed in February 1850 had already been mapped out by Millais's *Isabella* (Figure 10) exhibited at the Royal Academy in 1849. Moreover, Brown expressed concern that the artist should carefully plan the chiaroscuro of the work: 'He must also consider the color, and disposition of light and dark masses in his design, so as to call attention to the principal objects.'[18] This seems to contradict the early Pre-Raphaelite principle of allowing light and local colour to appear as they would in nature irrespective of an overall plan. Brown does not advocate painting directly from the model, minutely inch-by-inch, but he does strike a distinctively Pre-Raphaelite note by advocating a detailed sketch of each figure in the composition, made not from professional models but 'any friend he may have of an artistic or poetic temperament' (D. G. Rossetti was sitting at this time for Brown's figure of Chaucer).[19] Entirely typical of Brown is the invocation that follows:

> let the artist spare neither time nor labor, but exert himself beyond his natural energies, seeking to enter into the character of each actor, studying them one after the other, limb for limb, hand for hand, finger for finger, noting each inflection of joint, or tension of sinew, searching for dramatic truth internally in himself, and in all external nature, shunning affectation and exaggeration and striving after pathos, and purity of feeling, with patient endeavor and utter simplicity of heart.[20]

The assertion that the sincere expenditure of labour on a painting would ensure its aesthetic and moral worth, as well as its psychological acuity, would emerge as the underlying claim of Brown's masterpiece, *Work*

(1852–65, City of Manchester Art Galleries). But in this passage, Brown also seems to echo something of Ruskin's renowned insistence, published in *Modern Painters* vol. I (1843), that young artists should:

> go to Nature in all singleness of heart, and walk with her laboriously and trustingly, having no other thoughts but how best to penetrate her meaning, and remember her instruction; rejecting nothing, selecting nothing, and scorning nothing; ... and rejoicing always in the truth.[21]

While echoing his terms, Brown seems to offer a riposte to Ruskin, and perhaps to his Pre-Raphaelite co-authors of *The Germ*, when he describes 'constructive beauty in art' as 'being rather the slow growth of experience than the spontaneous impulse of the artistic temperament'. This, he continues, 'is a feature in art rather apt to savor of conventionality to such as would look on nature as the only school of art'. Art, Brown cautions, 'has beauties of its own, which neither impair nor contradict the beauties of nature'.[22]

'Out of a back window'

While his article in *The Germ* seems to imply a sceptical attitude to naturalistic landscape painting, Brown's exercises in the observation of nature, made during the subsequent decade, are consummate examples of that genre. Brown had created some experimental landscapes in the 1840s, such as *Southend* (1846–58, retouched 1861, collection Lord Lloyd Webber) and *Windermere* (1848, cut down and retouched in 1854–5, Lady Lever Art Gallery, National Museums Liverpool) in which unorthodox formats and the vivid representation of detail yield striking results. The hyper-clarity of painting in the grassy foreground of *The Pretty Baa-Lambs* (1851, retouched 1852–3 and 1859, Birmingham Museums & Art Gallery) was an augury of a series of views which are still startling, so flagrantly do they abandon the picturesque and sublime subject matter typical of English Romantic landscape painters. In these works, Brown meticulously chronicled nondescript stretches of land, found within walking distance of his various residences in North London, at Hendon, Finchley and Hampstead.

He scrutinized the urban hinterland, revealing its strange beauty in one of the masterpieces of nineteenth-century painting, *An English Autumn Afternoon*, begun in a period of extraordinary creative energy in 1852 (Figure 13). The painting was intended as an experiment in seeing, its oval shape drawing attention to the optical process, perhaps even alluding to the shape of the eye. The artist here is all-seeing: on the one hand a scientific apparatus conveying empirical truth, and on the other a poetic visionary

Figure 13 Ford Madox Brown, *An English Autumn Afternoon*, 1852–4, oil on canvas, 71.8 × 134.6 cm (oval), © Birmingham Museums and Art Gallery/The Bridgeman Art Library.

seeing in the quotidian world value and pathos which others would miss. Madox Brown wrote in his 1865 exhibition catalogue:

> The smoke is seen rising half way above the fantastic shaped, small distant cumuli, which accompany particularly fine weather ... The time is 3 P.M., when late in October the shadows already lie long, and the sun's rays (coming from behind us in this work) are preternaturally glowing, as in rivalry of the foliage.[23]

The artist (unlike the camera) can record both the natural and the preternatural, the optical and the spiritual, effect and affect. The landscape is not merely one of botanical, climatic and topographical facts: it is a social landscape, full of human life, and replete, also, with personal associations for Brown. The view is from the back window of an upper floor of a house in which Brown lodged in Hampstead High Street.

The painting is a striking example of Brown's refusal to adopt the familiar compositional devices which artists such as Constable and Turner had employed to maintain order and structure. The only work of comparable radicalism in the canon of Pre-Raphaelite landscape is Holman Hunt's *Our English Coasts, 1852* (Tate) which likewise adopts an unusual viewpoint, but nonetheless depicts a famous picturesque site. *An English Autumn Afternoon* completely eschews inherited conventions such as *repoussoir* trees at one side of the composition which so often frame a central vista with a low horizon. Madox Brown's high, flat horizon is bereft of vertical elements.

An English Autumn Afternoon was too much for Ruskin, who, it is clear, disliked Brown's gruff manner and his refusal to court favour with the critic.

A vivid (and characteristically mis-spelled) passage in Brown's diary from 13 July 1855 describing a tea party at Rossetti's house reveals the personal animosity between Brown and Ruskin, whom the artist observed

> [talking] divers nonsense about art, hurriedly in shrill flippant tones – I answer him civilly – then resume my coat & prepare to leave. Suddenly, upon this he sais 'Mr Brown will you tell me why you chose such a very ugly subject for your last picture [*An English Autumn Afternoon*] ... it was a pitty for there was some *nice* painting in it.['] I ... being satisfied that he meant impertinence, replied contemptuously 'Because it lay out of a back window' & turning on my heel took my hat & wished Gabriel goodbuy.[24]

This mutual personal animosity was to cost Brown dear: Ruskin turned his back on Brown and directed patrons to support Rossetti and others instead. The true source of Ruskin's rage, however, was Brown's rejection of the picturesque, which Ruskin's idol Turner, for all his radicalism, had ultimately embraced. Though Ruskin had advised young artists to 'go to Nature ... rejecting nothing, selecting nothing', he was horrified when Ford Madox Brown did exactly that.

'In the strictest sense historical'

Never abandoning the role, or the methods, of the history painter, for a decade from 1852 Brown turned his attention to modern society. While genre painting had been prominent throughout the preceding decades in the hands of masterly narrative painters such as David Wilkie, William Mulready and Richard Redgrave, Brown was unique in his attempt to merge close observation of modern life with the larger theoretical and intellectual ambitions previously reserved for history painting. His iconic roundel, *The Last of England* (1852–3, Birmingham Museums & Art Gallery), was, as the artist explained, 'in the strictest sense historical. It treats of the great emigration movement which attained its culminating point in 1852.'[25] The immediate stimulus was the departure of Thomas Woolner, the sculptor among the Pre-Raphaelite Brothers, for the gold-fields of Australia. Brown signalled the seriousness of his intentions by grouping the figures into an oval, almost circular shape, referencing the tondo forms of the Renaissance. These frequently portrayed the Holy Family or the Virgin and Child, as in Michelangelo's celebrated Taddei tondo in the collection of the Royal Academy in London, which would have been known to Brown. The image of the wife and mother here clearly alludes to the iconography of the Virgin Mary, her bonnet suggesting a halo and her gaze turned heavenward, although in anguish rather than ecstasy. This pointed allusion to a highly esteemed iconographic precedent raised the status of the subject to one of global significance. Meanwhile, subsidiary figures form a Hogarthian – or perhaps Dickensian – sideshow revealing the seedier side of modern life.

Also begun in Hampstead in 1852, but completed only in 1863 and not exhibited until 1865, *Work* can lay claim to being the most complex and sophisticated Pre-Raphaelite modern-life painting. More systematically than *The Last of England*, if less emblematically, it applies the methods of the history painter to labour, one of the great themes of the modern, industrial world. *Work* self-consciously presents itself as an intellectual statement, and includes portraits of two contemporary authorities on social questions, the Rev. F. D. Maurice and Thomas Carlyle, with whose ideas the artist was deeply engaged. Brown admired Maurice's Christian Socialist theology and taught a class of artisans at the Working Men's College, of which the churchman was Principal, from 1858 to 1860. *Work*, moreover, makes many references to Carlyle's texts such as *Past and Present* (1843). Although it ostensibly records an everyday scene in which navvies are installing a new water main in Heath Street, Hampstead, the numerous dramatis personae, subtle social analysis and elaborate visual language of *Work* required an extensive written explanation in the catalogue of Brown's 1865 exhibition. The image has spawned numerous subsequent interpretations.[26] Critical of the idle, rich and poor, it lauds the manual labourer 'in the pride of manly health and beauty', while acknowledging also the influence of intellectual work. [27] A perceptive critic of the day noted that the fantastic elaboration of the painting itself 'may be admitted as one accepted example of the dignity of labour'.[28] Brown failed to persuade the dealer Ernest Gambart to commission an engraving of *Work*, preventing the hoped-for spreading of its gospel into homes and institutions across the country, and only in the twentieth century did it achieve its true status as one of the great icons of the industrial era. For sympathetic viewers, however, the painting seemed 'originally and powerfully treated ... Brilliant, solid, sound, studied with extraordinary earnestness, elaborate and masterly'.[29] Seeing the painting in November 1859, Edward Lear was moved to note in his diary of Brown: 'after all he is the real first P. R. B.'[30]

Pre-Raphaelite patrons and publics

Brown was never financially successful, but in the late 1850s he found a number of patrons in the North of England, all of them also purchasers of work from the Pre-Raphaelites. Thomas E. Plint, an Evangelical stockbroker from Leeds, commissioned *Work*, demanding some changes in the composition, but died before its completion. Had the painting been delivered to Leeds, it would have hung alongside Millais's *Christ in the House of His Parents* and Hunt's *Finding of the Saviour in the Temple* as well as key works of Rossetti, Arthur Hughes and others of the Pre-Raphaelite circle. Other Pre-Raphaelite supporters, such as George Rae of Birkenhead, John Miller of Liverpool and James Leathart, a lead manufacturer from Newcastle, also commissioned and purchased important canvases from Brown. But his work was less successful with the critics and the general public. Angered by the refusal of some of his works and the poor hanging of others, Brown abandoned the Royal Academy after 1853, and rebuffed Millais's offer to support his candidacy for Associate membership. Brown continued, however, to exhibit in Liverpool, where he won prizes in 1856 and 1858. Brown himself organized a Pre-Raphaelite exhibition at Russell Place in 1857 and his work featured in a similar show in New York and Philadelphia in 1857. Brown's enthusiasm for the art of William Hogarth – like himself, fiercely independent and committed to the representation of modern life – led to one more avant-garde gambit: the founding in 1858 of the Hogarth Club, intended as an alternative to the Royal Academy, an exhibiting forum where artists and patrons could meet informally. Key figures in the Club were Rossetti and two young followers of his who first met Brown in 1856. They were William Morris, who immediately purchased Brown's *The Hayfield* (1855–6, Tate), and Edward Burne-Jones, for whom Brown was 'wisest and kindest of friends'.[31] The Club began well, but collapsed amid controversy in 1861. Brown's sudden resignation, another example of his notable touchiness, came when the hanging committee refused to include his designs for furniture in the 1860 exhibition. Characteristically, Brown was anticipating the move towards greater integration of fine and decorative arts which characterized the Aesthetic Movement of the later 1860s. Ironically, whereas Brown's paintings are virtually invisible in collections outside Britain, his work as a designer is on permanent display at the Museum of Modern Art in New York, where a Sussex Chair, made by Morris & Co to Brown's design (c.1865) is the oldest object on display.

The culmination of Brown's Pre-Raphaelite decades came in the form of his 1865 one-man show, at 191 Piccadilly. The publication of his exhibition catalogue *The Exhibition of WORK, and Other Paintings* amounted to an artistic credo, or perhaps an apologia. Written in Brown's eccentrically self-referential, Carlylean prose, and packed with puns and enigmas, the catalogue remains among the most important primary texts of Pre-Raphaelitism even though the term 'Pre-Raphaelite' is never used. Its description of *Work* alone runs to three densely set pages. Unlike Hunt's single-painting exhibition of *The Finding of the Saviour in the Temple*, of 1860, which also boasted an accompanying publication by Frederic George Stephens, Brown's exhibition was sparsely attended. Rossetti jokingly suggested sending men with sandwich boards around London, like those Brown represented in the background of *Work*. While most of Brown's oeuvre left critics baffled, the critic of the *Athenaeum* – the same F. G. Stephens, a founding member of the PRB and highly sympathetic to Brown – spelled out clearly the merits of this masterpiece:

> Brilliant, solid, sound, studied with extraordinary earnestness, elaborate and masterly, the vigour of *Work* will astonish those who do not know what the artist has done before. Undoubtedly many will challenge parts of these pictures, but no one will deny honour to the painter who produced them.[32]

Conclusion

Although he enjoyed a decade of prosperity and relative celebrity in the 1870s, Brown's later career was marked, like his early years, by a studious and strategic positioning of himself beyond the pale of mainstream critical acceptability. His final works, the series of twelve mural paintings for Manchester Town Hall, which occupied him until his death, remain undervalued despite their outlandish inventiveness and originality. By turns grotesque and decorative, playful and confrontational, these late works reveal a very different style from the hyper-clarity of Brown's Pre-Raphaelite realism of the 1850s. *Work*, *An English Autumn Afternoon* and *The Last of England* alone are achievements significant enough to command for Brown a central position in Pre-Raphaelitism and, indeed, in nineteenth-century painting internationally. A full reconsideration of his entire oeuvre, long overdue, would reveal even greater riches.[33]

NOTES

1   Hunt, vol. I, p. 151.
2   Ford Madox Hueffer, *Ford Madox Brown: A Record of his Life and Work* (London: Longmans, Green and Co., 1896).
3   Mary Bennett, *Ford Madox Brown, 1821–1893*, exhibition catalogue (Liverpool: Walker Art Gallery, 1964).
4   Mary Bennett, *Ford Madox Brown: A Catalogue Raisonné*, 2 vols. (New Haven and London: Yale University Press, 2010).
5   Teresa Newman and Ray Watkinson, *Ford Madox Brown and the Pre-Raphaelite Circle* (London: Chatto & Windus, 1991); Kenneth Bendiner, *The Art of Ford Madox Brown* (University Park, PA: Pennsylvania State University Press, 1997).

6 I owe this image to Michaela Giebelhausen. See 'Introduction', Michaela Giebelhausen and Tim Barringer (eds.), *Writing the Pre-Raphaelites: Text, Context, Subtext* (Farnham, Surrey and Burlington, Vermont: Ashgate, 2009), p. 13. My thanks to Tony Raban for this reference.

7 Hunt, vol. I, p. 120.

8 See Jason Rosenfeld, 'The Pre-Raphaelite "Otherhood"', and Mitchell B. Frank, 'The Nazarene Gemeinschaft: Overbeck and Cornelius', in Laura Morowitz and William Vaughan (eds.), *Artistic Brotherhoods in the Nineteenth Century* (Aldershot, Hants.: Ashgate, 2000), pp. 67–81 and 48–66.

9 Ford Madox Brown, *The Diary of Ford Madox Brown*, ed. Virginia Surtees (New Haven and London: Yale University Press, 1981), pp. 1–2, hereafter *Diary*. The diary entry was written retrospectively on 4 September 1847.

10 Ford Madox Brown, *The Exhibition of WORK, and Other Paintings, by Ford Madox Brown*, exhibition catalogue (London: McCorquodale & Co., 1865), p. 3, hereafter *Work*. Brown's catalogue is also reprinted in Bendiner, *Art of Ford Madox Brown*, pp. 131–56.

11 *Work*, p. 4.

12 Hunt, vol. I, p. 126.

13 Hunt, vol. I, p. 125.

14 'To the Editor of the "Times", 13 May 1851', Ruskin, vol. XII, p. 322.

15 Newman and Watkinson, *Ford Madox Brown*, p. 39.

16 Hunt, vol. I, p. 108.

17 *Germ*, p. 70.

18 *Germ*, p. 71.

19 *Germ*, p. 71. See Elizabeth Prettejohn, 'The Pre-Raphaelite Model', in Jane Desmarais, Martin Postle and William Vaughan (eds.), *Model and Supermodel: The Artist's Model in British Art and Culture* (Manchester and New York: Manchester University Press, 2006), pp. 26–46 (pp. 30–3 on *Chaucer*).

20 *Germ*, p. 71.

21 Ruskin, vol. III, p. 624.

22 *Germ*, pp. 72–3.

23 *Work*, pp. 7–8.

24 *Diary*, p. 144.

25 *Work*, p. 8.

26 See for example Albert Boime, 'Ford Madox Brown: Meaning and Mystification of Work in the Nineteenth Century', *Arts Magazine*, 56 (1981), pp. 116–25; Gerard Curtis, 'Ford Madox Brown's *Work*: An Iconographic Analysis', *Art Bulletin*, 74 (December 1992), pp. 623–36; Tim Barringer, *Men at Work: Art and Labour in Victorian Britain* (New Haven and London: Yale University Press, 2005), chapter 1.

27 *Work*, p. 27.

28 *The Builder*, 18 March 1865.

29 *Athenaeum*, 11 March 1865, p. 353.

30 Edward Lear, Diary, Houghton Library, Harvard University, MS Eng. 797.3., transcribed by Marco Graziosi. www.nonsenselit.org/diaries/2009/11/13/sunday-13-november-1859 (accessed 5 January 2009).

31 Newman and Watkinson, *Ford Madox Brown*, p. 115.

32 *Athenaeum*, 11 March 1865, p. 353.

33 A start has been made, however, in the exhibition curated for Manchester Art Gallery and The Museum of Fine Arts, Ghent, by Julian Treuherz, *Ford Madox Brown: Pre-Raphaelite Pioneer*, exhibition catalogue (Manchester: Manchester Art Gallery/ Philip Wilson Publishers, 2011).

I I

LORRAINE JANZEN KOOISTRA

Christina Rossetti (1830–1894)

In 1847, when Christina Rossetti was sixteen, her grandfather Polidori published her first book of poetry, *Verses: Dedicated to my Mother*, on his private press. Her oldest brother, Dante Gabriel, drew illustrations for selected poems on special art paper; these were then inserted between appropriate leaves and bound into one of her personal copies. Themes of love and death, with Gothic moods, medieval settings, dream visions and Christian symbolism, pervade both poems and pictures. This small extra-illustrated volume bears witness to the siblings' shared 'Pre-Raphaelite' aesthetic before the formation of the Brotherhood the following year. Fundamentally collaborative in methodology and expression, this aesthetic brings into communion the visual and the verbal, the past and the present, the spiritual and the material, the reader/viewer and the maker. For the devout Christina this intensely symbolic, precisely realized methodology was especially directed towards reading ephemeral signs for the eternal truths they could disclose. She was, in every way, a woman of the book. If Pre-Raphaelite art schools its viewers in 'close looking',[1] the Pre-Raphaelite poetry of Christina Rossetti seeks to instruct its readers in close reading and interpretation.

As this illustrated copy of *Verses* suggests, Christina Rossetti had a central, if understated, role in Pre-Raphaelitism as it emerged in 1848. Excluded by her gender from meetings of the Brotherhood, she was, nevertheless, far more than an interested bystander. An influential force and early practitioner of the visual-verbal aesthetic that distinguished the movement, Christina was involved in collaborative projects with many of its members. She modelled as the mother of God for Dante Gabriel Rossetti's first two oil paintings, *The Girlhood of Mary Virgin* (1848–9, Figure 6) and *Ecce Ancilla Domini!* (1849–50, Tate). She also sat for William Holman Hunt's *The Light of the World* (1851–3, Figure 5), as he wished to catch her expression in his representation of Christ's face[2]; in the collaborative spirit that characterized the movement Christina took up the same subject in her contemporary poem, 'Behold, I stand at the door and knock'.[3] The only female participant in the PRB's magazine of art and poetry, she was prominently featured in *The Germ* with a total of seven titles over three of its four numbers. Later, she published her poetry in books and periodicals illustrated by Pre-Raphaelite artists Dante Gabriel Rossetti, John Everett Millais, Frederick Sandys and Arthur Hughes, as well as the fin-de-siècle revivalists Laurence Housman and Charles Ricketts. Just as Christina made the earliest extant reference to the PRB in a sly reference to her 'double sisterhood' in a letter to William in 1849,[4] so too she was the first to acknowledge its demise in 1853, this time in verse:

> The two Rossettis (brothers they)
> And Holman Hunt and John Millais,
> With Stephens chivalrous and bland,
> And Woolner in a distant land –
> In these six men I awestruck see
> Embodied the great P. R. B.
> D. G. Rossetti offered two
> Good pictures to the public view;
> Unnumbered ones great John Millais,
> And Holman more than I can say.
>
> William Rossetti, calm and solemn,
> Cuts up his brethren by the column.[5]

In the same letter as this self-styled piece of 'remarkable doggerel' playfully mocking her Pre-Raphaelite brethren, Christina thanked William for sending her the brushes she urgently required for the portraits she was then painting.[6] Perhaps the poetic teasing masked a quiet wish to make her own mark in the world of art as a painterly sister. Teaching with her mother in Frome at the time, Christina was also working hard to develop her skills in drawing and watercolour. In London she had taken evening classes with Ford Madox Brown at the North London School of Drawing and Modelling and with this rudimentary instruction she was, as Dante Gabriel observed, 'energetic in her pursuit of Art'. Although he teasingly reminded her to 'keep within respectful limits' of his beloved Elizabeth Siddall's artistic aspirations, cautioning her not 'to rival the Sid',[7] Dante Gabriel was supportive of Christina's efforts and always believed she had the talent to become an artist if she applied herself with perseverance.[8] While Dante Gabriel may well have seen promise in work no longer extant, there is little suggestion of a lost artist in Christina's remaining portraits, sketches of animals and flowers and rudimentary illustrations in manuscripts and books. She was not gifted in the 'double art' of Dante Gabriel and their admired predecessor, William Blake, whose *Life* the Rossetti brothers completed after biographer

Alexander Gilchrist's sudden death. Christina did, however, share with Blake and Dante Gabriel a visual imagination realized in the dynamic relationships of word, image, page and book. When, in the mid-1850s, Christina decided to abandon painting and focus her career ambitions exclusively on poetic achievement, she had already established the basis for the verbal-visual aesthetic that would inform both her writing and her publication process henceforth. Christina Rossetti's Pre-Raphaelite legacy is not to be found in inchoate graphic lines, but rather in the physical forms of her verses and books.

A verbal-visual aesthetic

Christina Rossetti's visual imagination was formed in the chrysalis of her Anglican faith, nourished by her devout reading of Scripture and Tractarian devotional writing and confirmed by the Pre-Raphaelite movement in which she participated. Perceiving phenomenal nature with a Pre-Raphaelite sensuousness, she also saw it spiritually, with 'the mind of Christ', apprehending 'two worlds, visible and invisible ... double against each other'.[9] This 'double vision' accorded with what Ruskin perceived to be the 'Tractarian tendencies'[10] of early Pre-Raphaelitism and Dante Gabriel termed 'the Art Catholic'. Defined by Jerome McGann as 'a discipline for studying faithful images, in every sense', 'the Art Catholic' also describes the siblings' shared approach to poetic art as aspiring 'to the condition of the devotional image'.[11] 'All the world over', Christina wrote, 'visible things typify things invisible' because of the divine authorship of the world, God's Book.[12] The analogous creation of poet or artist who was an earthly type of God thus came with a strict discipline. In the material form of the printed book, in the illustration that accompanied a verse and in the iconic page itself, the word took flesh and lived in the midst of human endeavour, ready to be consumed. As a way to realize the full possibilities of this hermeneutic, Christina drew on the emblem form. A mode of verbal-visual representation and interpretation stretching back to the Renaissance and revived in the nineteenth century, emblems were a devotional form dependent on the interrelation of body (image) and spirit (word).[13] Appealing equally to the typological propensities of Tractarians and Pre-Raphaelites, emblems encouraged the double reading of material details, so that physical or literal facts revealed spiritual or symbolic meanings.

As a poet, Christina Rossetti sought to inspire this emblematic way of looking, reading and interpreting in her readers. For her, poetry's task (like painting's) was not only to represent truthfully the natural world's forms, colours and actions, but also to point to the immaterial, ineffable, eternal meaning of that temporal, mutating beauty. Her poems use a vivid imagery that overlays the literal with the symbolic and a pattern of allusion (chiefly biblical) that invites an understanding of physical forms and historical events as spiritual types. Often, the underlying theme has to do with looking and reading, or interpreting, material signs. But she also recognized that the art of reading is built into the art of the book. When she began to publish collections of her verses in the 1860s, she worked closely with visual artists to ensure that the physical language of each book, including its binding, sequence, layout and illustrative matter, reinforced the subject and purpose of her verses. Whether she first began to develop this verbal-visual aesthetic when the teenaged Dante Gabriel illustrated her juvenile *Verses*, or even earlier, when the four Rossetti siblings produced an illustrated family magazine, *Hodge-Podge*, the linking of image and word became an artistic practice because it expressed her double vision of the world and her hermeneutics of correspondence.

From the age of twelve Christina attended services at Christ Church Albany Street, the principal centre for the Oxford Movement in London.[14] Establishing a new Anglo-Catholic emphasis on ritual, communion, prayers and pre-Reformation liturgy, the Oxford Movement expressed its theology in *Tracts for the Times* and devotional poetry that, by association, became known as 'Tractarian'. Christina was profoundly influenced by the Tractarian poetry of John Keble's *The Christian Year* (1827) and Isaac Williams's *The Altar, or Meditations in Verse on the Great Christian Sacrifice* (1849). Simply written but intensely symbolic, Tractarian poetry aimed to educate its readers in the deepest mysteries of the Christian faith through the indirect method of 'reserve', in imitation of God's example of concealment and gradual revelation in Scripture and nature through figures, types and analogies.[15] Such poetry required its readers to meditate on the literal and symbolic meanings contained in the words, their scriptural allusions, anagogic or spiritual import and hidden truths. Christina left vestiges of her own responses as a faithful reader of Tractarian poetry in personal copies of Keble's *Christian Year* and Williams's *The Altar*, which she annotated with carefully conceived pencil illustrations. While they have slight artistic value, these tiny sketches are significant indicators of her emblematic methodology at work.

In her marginal illustration for Keble's 'Second Sunday in Advent', for example, Christina drew a mother holding an infant in her arms as a type for Christ's loving watch over the church on earth.[16] This image is implicit, but not developed, in Keble's verses; Christina's illustration thus figures forth a meaning latent but concealed in the words. In her drawing, she emphasized the literal actuality of mother and baby by positioning them in a nursery decorated with wallpaper and furnished with dressing table, toys, basin and pitcher. At the same time, poem and picture work together emblematically to encourage a symbolic reading of the quotidian scene. In the Christian year the Advent Season – the four weeks before Christmas – is both a time of waiting for the arrival of the Christ child and a reminder that the believer's entire sojourn on earth should be considered a waiting period for his Second Coming. Just as the annual Advent symbolizes the final Advent, so too the infant in Christina's drawing is a type for the devout Christian who, like a child, sees and understands things imperfectly but will see 'face to face' and know completely when Christ returns.[17]

This small textual decoration speaks volumes about the poet's emblematic method: while her illustration of Keble's poem pictures the literal scene it describes, its symbolic meaning emerges through its dialogic interaction with both the poet's immediate verses and the scriptural allusions they suggest. Throughout her illustrations for Keble's *Christian Year*, she used the image/text dialogue to expound her understanding of the meaning held 'in reserve'. In her own works, Christina Rossetti used visual imagery (both linguistic and iconic) to encourage her readers to read emblematically and anagogically, as her meaning would only emerge gradually. Explaining her symbolic method to Dante Gabriel, she wrote: 'Of course I don't expect the general public to catch these refined clues; but there they are for such minds as mine.'[18]

Perhaps because she herself was born in this significant season of the liturgical year (5 December 1830), Advent occupied a central place in Christina's imagination and pervaded the themes and tropes of her poetry. Like Keble, she wrote many verses celebrating Anglican feasts and fasts; an extraordinary number focus on Advent and the symbols associated with it. One of these ('This Advent moon shines cold and clear') might be considered her signature work, as it appeared in both her first (*Goblin Market and Other Poems*, 1862) and last (*Verses*, 1893) commercial publications; Swinburne considered it 'perhaps the noblest of all her poems'.[19] Drawing on a rich variety of sensuous images and scriptural allusions, Rossetti develops one of her favourite themes: watching and waiting for Christ's promised return. The central parable is that of 'The patient virgins wise' whose 'lamps have burned year after year' as they wait for the Bridegroom, whose arrival initiates a sensuous and emotional perfection never experienced on earth:

> Eye hath not seen, ear hath not heard,
>   Nor heart conceived that rest,
> With them our good things long deferred,
>   With Jesus Christ our Best. (lines 37–40)

In this description of future fulfilment, Rossetti stresses the insufficiency of the material world, the physical senses and the human imagination. Like the forms of nature, the visual art of the eye and the poetic art of the ear are not valuable or sufficient in themselves, but as types shadowing forth the deferred 'Best' to come. Rossetti's 'Advent' concludes with a vision of consummated union with the Bridegroom that draws on the biblical Song of Songs to express spiritual desire through the physically erotic:

> Then figs shall bud, and dove with dove
>   Shall coo the livelong day;
> Then He shall say, 'Arise, my love,
>   My fair one, come away.' (lines 52–6)[20]

This 'long deferred' union comes only after a prolonged and peaceful 'rest'. Fascinated by 'the world of twilight dreaming' experienced by the soul in the 'intermediate state' between death and resurrection,[21] Rossetti explored the trope of sleeping or resting before a final joyous awakening in many of her poems, even those not overtly religious or devotional. One of her first published lyrics, 'Dream Land', which appeared in issue one of *The Germ* (Figure 14), exemplifies her use of the secular fairytale form to express this sacred theme:

> Where sunless rivers weep
> Their waves into the deep,
> She sleeps a charmed sleep;
>   Awake her not.
> Led by a single star,
> She came from very far,
> To seek where shadows are
>   Her pleasant lot.
>
> She left the rosy morn,
> She left the fields of corn,
> For twilight cold and lorn,
>   And water-springs.
> Thro' sleep, as thro' a veil,
> She sees the sky look pale,
> And hears the nightingale,
>   That sadly sings.
>
> Rest, rest, a perfect rest,
> Shed over brow and breast;
> Her face is toward the west,
>   The purple land.

> She cannot see the grain
> Ripening on hill and plain;
> She cannot feel the rain
> Upon her hand.
>
> Rest, rest, for evermore
> Upon a mossy shore,
> Rest, rest, that shall endure,
> Till time shall cease; –
> Sleep that no pain shall wake,
> Night that no morn shall break,
> Till joy shall overtake
> Her perfect peace.

In this romantic lyric replete with the sensuousness of natural details we can see Tractarian revelation through concealment merge with the characteristic Pre-Raphaelite combination of 'visual abundance' and indefinite meaning, a method that deliberately encourages ongoing looking, thinking and interpretation in the reader/viewer.[22] On a first reading of 'Dream Land' we know with some clarity what we see, but we do not know what it means. With simple diction of primarily one- and two-syllable words one might come across in everyday conversation or children's stories, and a dreamy rhythm whose music is enhanced by anaphora (repetition of beginning phrases) and alliteration, the poem reads like a soporific spell that involves its reader in the experience it describes. The nature of this experience, however, seems as vague and indistinct as dreams themselves. Where does it take place, when and to whom? These interpretive questions are invited, but not directly answered, by the poem, which requires the reader to be, like its shadowy protagonist, an active seeker after meaning.

As in many of Rossetti's poems, this lyric's deceptively simple surface overlays a complex symbolism that works by the accretion of detail and allusion within a form that is itself symbolic. 'Dream Land' asks us to think about three times and three places, and it does so in tercets made up of three-stress lines punctuated by a two-stress line. The poem opens in present tense and an immediate locale. As if pointing with an index finger, the first word of the poem, 'Where', directs our attention with an emphatic place marker. We learn, as we read the first tercet, that the nameless 'she' of the poem 'sleeps a charmed sleep' in what appears to be an underground cavern, a dark place bereft of the warming sun, where buried rivers 'weep' into the sea. The word 'weep' introduces the melancholy tone that pervades the lyric, even as it recalls the opening of Coleridge's 'Kubla Khan', describing 'Where Alph, the sacred river ran /Through caverns measureless to man / Down to a sunless sea' (lines 3–5). The buried allusion suggests that Dream Land's river is sacred in some way, but reveals nothing about the sleeper. What kind of charmed sleep are we looking at, in this shadowy underground place? In fairy tales, the princess sleeps until awakened by the prince. If the sleeper of 'Dream Land' is awaiting a prince, however, he is nowhere in sight. The interdict is clear: 'Awake her not'.

The second part of the first stanza shifts to past tense to provide a brief flashback to the time before the poem's subject begins. In this interlude we discover that the protagonist is a seeker who, 'led by a single star', travelled a long distance to embrace the shadows that are now 'Her pleasant lot'. In a scant eighteen words, Rossetti characterizes her protagonist as someone who has deliberately chosen 'Dream Land' and its charmed sleep – someone who has not only gone out of her way to find this 'pleasant' place but has also benefited from celestial guidance. Suddenly, this mysterious 'she' seems less like the fairy-tale princess, whose sleep is always triggered by a mishap that puts into motion a malevolent charm, and more like one of the wise men who followed the star to find the Messiah. But why is the seeker also a sleeper?

The next two stanzas develop our understanding of the present time and place of the poem by introducing diurnal and seasonal markers. This central section is characterized by images of rejection, negation and cessation. The sleeper has 'left the rosy morn' behind in exchange for 'twilight cold and lorn'; in her 'perfect rest' she faces 'the west, / The purple land', while ripening grain grows in the teeming world above her. The darkening sky and autumnal fields indicate both the end of a single day and the close of the year's cycle; symbolically, these temporal signs also suggest the death of the individual. The verses are tinged with regret for these earthly endings, but this regret does not seem to touch the sleeper and her 'perfect rest' which, we learn in the final verse, 'shall endure, / Till time shall cease'. Thus the endings foreshadowed in the two middle stanzas are confirmed by the final stanza's indication of a coming third time and third place, another ending and harvest, which are outside the experience of the poem itself. Now, the charmed sleep begins to look like the pleasurable state of rest between death and resurrection. Nothing shall rouse the sleeper from her charmed sleep (death) until the end of time, when 'joy shall overtake / Her perfect peace'. Suddenly, the colour word in this hushed twilight poem begins to resonate with new meaning. 'The purple land' the sleeper faces assumes the royal robes of the heavenly kingdom in light of the poem's final, veiled promise. Closing with the end of a day, the end of the year, and the end of time, the lyric invites its readers to meditate on endings, including their own. If there is a prince to awaken the charmed sleeper of this poem, the imagery suggests he may be the same Bridegroom who closes 'Advent' with '"Arise, My love, / My fair one, come away"'.

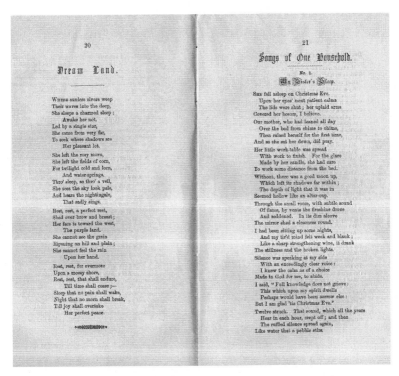

Figure 14 Double-page spread from *The Germ*, no. 1, showing Christina Rossetti's 'Dream Land' opposite Dante Gabriel Rossetti's 'My Sister's Sleep'. Courtesy of Toronto Public Library.

This apocalyptic reading seems far removed from the dreamy impression the poem leaves on first reading. Part of Christina Rossetti's strategy is to reveal meaning gradually, using verse form, diction, allusion, imagery and analogy to inculcate a hermeneutic practice in her readers. But a poem's meanings are not only generated by the images and music the verses evoke; they are also realized in its vehicular, or bibliographic, form. I have quoted 'Dream Land' as it was first printed in *The Germ* and would like to suggest that it is in this specific location that the poem develops the reading I have given. In *The Germ*, the entire poem is printed on the verso of a double-page opening. Facing it is 'My Sister's Sleep', the first poem in a projected collection by Dante Gabriel Rossetti, 'Songs of One Household'. This is the only double-page opening in the entire volume of *The Germ* in which two distinct works face each other with lined-up headers (Figure 14). Like all titles in *The Germ*, 'Songs of One Household' is printed in the same large black-letter font as 'Dream Land', while as a subtitle 'My Sister's Sleep' is distinguished in a smaller black-letter font with decorative initials. This

Gothic typography suggestive of religious publishing casts an appropriately Anglo-Catholic illumination on the poems lined up under each title. Moreover, Dante Gabriel's 'Songs of One Household' seems to connect the bibliographic with the biographic by acting as a super-title for both 'Dream Land' and 'My Sister's Sleep'. Indeed, *The Germ*'s double-page opening bears material witness to the Pre-Raphaelite collaborative practices of the Rossetti siblings – including William Michael. As editor, William seems to have deliberately paired these poems as the centrepiece to *The Germ*'s first number, just as he wittily devoted its final page to Christina's 'An End'. The double-page opening allows the paired poems to comment on each other through a shared subject matter and symbolism that might otherwise go unnoticed. Like 'Dream Land', 'My Sister's Sleep' meditates on a woman's death that looks like sleep, and blurs this physical death with an implied life after death. Furthermore, 'My Sister's Sleep' makes explicit what is concealed in 'Dream Land': the Advent season as a time of waiting prefiguring the anticipated Second Coming. The poem ends with the family acknowledging the sister's death, 'A little after twelve o'clock' on 'Christmas morn', by invoking '"Christ's blessing on the newly born!"'[23]

The art of the book

The first of the original Pre-Raphaelite circle to publish a collection of poetry, Christina Rossetti also led the way in demonstrating how the movement's collaborative practices and verbal-visual aesthetic could be realized in the material form in which it reached its public: the commercial book. For her the art of the book was also an exercise in the art of reading; as in the emblem tradition, the ideal vehicular form invited the mutual elucidation of image and text and the engagement of the reader. Despite the contemporary publishing industry's preference for issuing proven poetic sellers with a mishmash of artists and styles, encasing them in ornate covers and advertising them for the Christmas gift market, Rossetti ensured her first three volumes came out with Pre-Raphaelite illustrations and elegant bindings designed by a single artist. The long narrative poems that gave her first books their titles, *Goblin Market and Other Poems* (Macmillan, 1862) and *The Prince's Progress and Other Poems* (Macmillan, 1866), inspired the subjects for Dante Gabriel Rossetti's full-page frontispieces and title-page vignettes; in keeping with their settings, he also designed stylized medieval covers for each.[24] Following the poet's own manuscript sketches as his guide, Arthur Hughes illustrated each of the 121 lyrics in *Sing-Song: A Nursery Rhyme Book* (Routledge, 1872) and brought forward some of the dominant pictorial motifs into the ornamental binding. These volumes occupy a unique place in the history of Victorian publishing and book design. Prior to the revival of fine printing at the fin de siècle, no other first-edition trade books achieve such a unity of design and purpose.[25] No wonder Swinburne hailed Christina Rossetti on the publication of *Goblin Market* as 'the Jael who led their [Pre-Raphaelite] hosts to victory':[26] she was indeed an avant-garde leader in the art of the book.

Perhaps the best-known poem in all of Christina Rossetti's oeuvre, *Goblin Market* is also considered one of her most characteristically Pre-Raphaelite works because of the pictorial richness of its sensuous details. Certainly it has inspired more visual responses than any other of her works, in illustrations for gift books, children's literature, magazines and comics, as well as stained glass, paintings, film, ballet and theatre. Even Christina herself participated in the poem's visualization by ornamenting her own copy of *Goblin Market* with marginal illustrations in watercolour. But when Laurence Housman requested her permission to illustrate *Goblin Market* in 1892, she did not direct him to her own 'slim, agile figures in a close-fitting garb of blue',[27] but rather 'to her brother's original frontispiece' to see what the goblins looked like.[28] For the poet, the first artist's pictorial work was definitive. Even today, implicitly recognizing the significance of the collaborative aesthetic behind the first edition, publishers often reprint D. G. Rossetti's illustrations with C. G. Rossetti's poem.[29]

It seems critically important, then, that any reading of *Goblin Market* take into account the material form of its first publication, as the hermeneutic framework for Christina Rossetti's most famous poem was built into the architecture of the book. Dante Gabriel's two introductory illustrations form pictorial front matter that operates paratextually, not only to *present* Christina's text, 'but also in the strongest sense', as Gérard Genette reminds us, 'to *make present*' the text's own physicality in a world of objects. As pictorial thresholds the reader must cross before entering the verses, the frontispiece and title-page vignette introduce, direct and mediate the subsequent reading experience.[30] As a result, the linguistic text is always in implicit dialogue with the iconic paratext. To underscore this dialogic interaction, Dante Gabriel provided handwritten captions for his illustrations with distinct quotation marks to indicate their direct relationship to the ensuing poem. Functioning like *motto* and *pictura* in traditional emblem literature, these captioned illustrations direct the reader in the practice of moving back and forth between picture and poem to seek correspondences and illuminating divergences. This 'doubling' method was integral to Christina Rossetti's project of encouraging her readers to discern in material signs – words, pictures, physical forms – figural representation of invisible truths.

Written in the short, skipping lines of a nursery rhyme, *Goblin Market*[31] is a fairy tale that tells of two golden-haired sisters, Lizzie and Laura, and their encounter with mysterious goblin men, who entice them with mouth-watering cries:

'Come buy our orchard fruits,
Come buy, come buy:
Apples and quinces,
Lemons and oranges,
Plump unpecked cherries,
Melons and raspberries,
Bloom-down-cheeked peaches,
Swart-headed mulberries,
Wild free-born cranberries,
Crab-apples, dewberries,
Pine-apples, blackberries,
Apricots, strawberries; –
All ripe together
In summer weather, – (lines 3–16)

This confused cornucopia of fruit from every corner of the globe, 'all ripe together' in one place and time, is clearly not natural and seems potentially dangerous. However, one sister interprets these material signs correctly; one does not.[32] Lizzie resists temptation and runs home. 'But sweet-tooth Laura' stays to negotiate, ultimately trading 'a precious golden lock' for the goblin fruit. This is the scene Dante Gabriel depicts in his frontispiece, with the caption, 'Buy from us with a golden curl'.

Despite the differences in the girls' responses, however, the detailed physical description of their reunion after the goblin encounter makes no moral distinction between the one who succumbed to temptation and the one who resisted. As if nothing momentous had occurred, the sisters retire as always:

Golden head by golden head,
Like two pigeons in one nest
Folded in each other's wings,
They lay down in their curtained bed:
Like two blossoms on one stem,
Like two flakes of new-fall'n snow,
Like two wands of ivory
Tipped with gold for awful kings.
Moon and stars gazed in at them,
Wind sang to them lullaby,
Lumbering owls forbore to fly,

> Not a bat flapped to and fro
> Round their rest:
> Cheek to cheek and breast to breast
> Locked together in one nest. (Lines 184–98)

Taken from this remarkably lush passage describing the sisters' sleep, the title-page vignette's caption, 'Golden head by golden head', deliberately repeats the dominant physical image of the frontispiece caption, the 'golden curl'. The pictorial movement from frontispiece to title page, like the movement of the ensuing narrative, emphasizes that despite different choices and experiences, each sister's moral worth (symbolically measured in seemingly identical golden heads) remains the same. Golden hair, always a potent signifier of feminine beauty in Pre-Raphaelite art, is a symbol, in *Goblin Market*, of a 'natural', and apparently renewable, innocence and purity likened to blossoms and snow.

This hushed scene showing the sisters' undisturbed and peaceful rest offers a critical pictorial touchstone for the unfolding and resolution of the narrative. When Laura is no longer able to eat or drink 'for balked desire', Lizzie reads her sister's death sentence in the diminished wealth of what should be her body's crowning glory: 'Her hair grew thin and grey'. In order to procure some restorative juices for Laura, Lizzie endures a vicious attack by the goblins, who squeeze their fruits against her lips and face in an attempt 'to make her eat'. When Laura, in kissing her sister, tastes the juices that streak Lizzie's face, what was once 'poison in the blood' becomes 'the fiery antidote'. Laura falls down in a fit that looks like death, but rises next morning as her 'innocent old' self: 'Her gleaming locks showed not one thread of grey'. *Goblin Market* ends with Lizzie and Laura, now 'wives / With children of their own', telling 'the little ones' the story of their goblin market experience and reminding them 'there is no friend like a sister'.

Thus the end of the poem, with its focus on sisterly sameness, returns to the innocent idyll captured in the title-page vignette, 'Golden head by golden head'. Strategically placed at the front of the volume, Dante Gabriel's two paratextual illustrations mediate the reading experience by directing readers at the outset to the narrative's movement from temptation and fall to renewal. With their many pictorial details visualizing key aspects of the poem's events, characters and themes, these introductory images also signal that *Goblin Market* is fundamentally a poem about looking and interpreting. Indeed, as Mary Arseneau has demonstrated, the title poem 'enacts the process of education in moral reading that is likewise the project of the entire volume', whose poetic sequence and arrangement are designed to reveal spiritual truths gradually, and to encourage rereading of the first, secular group of poems in light of the concluding devotional section.[33] Proleptically involving her first readers in the experience of the title poem and volume before the first page was turned, frontispiece and vignette helped establish the hermeneutic framework for reading with the end in view, a practice available for 'those with such minds' as the author's.

Four years after the publication of *Goblin Market and Other Poems*, the Rossetti siblings collaborated again with the same format for *The Prince's Progress and Other Poems*. Despite lengthy delays to publication occasioned by Dante Gabriel's slow production of his frontispiece and title-page vignette, Christina refused to go to press without his designs. Insisting 'Your woodcuts are so essential to my contentment that I will wait a year for them if need is', Christina remarked: 'My *Prince*, having dawdled so long on his own account cannot grumble at awaiting your pleasure; and mine, too, for your protecting woodcuts help me to face my small public.'[34] Christina's reference to her laggard Prince alludes to both the protracted composition of this long narrative poem, which she developed, with her brother's encouragement, out of an earlier work,[35] and the slow 'progress' of the eponymous hero himself. The Prince's delayed start and dilatory quest ultimately result in his reaching the Princess after she had been taken by 'Bridegroom Death'. As the song of the 'Veiled figures carrying her' informs him, he has arrived

> Too late for love, too late for joy,
> Too late, too late!
> You loitered on the road too long,
> You trifled at the gate:
> The enchanted dove upon her branch
> Died without a mate;
> The enchanted princess in her tower
> Slept, died, behind the grate;
> Her heart was starving all this while
> You made it wait. (Lines 481–90)[36]

The woodcuts 'so essential' to Christina for *The Prince's Progress* are also Dante Gabriel's last refinement of the paratextual format first developed for *Goblin Market*; he was to do no more illustrations for printed books after 1866. Fittingly, he designed the compositions for both frontispiece and title-page vignette around distinct apertures, thus making their liminal position function as literal as well as symbolic entrances into the world of the poem.[37] The full-page frontispiece depicts the Prince, overcome with grief, standing on the threshold of the dead Princess's room, barred from entry by one of her women. The handwritten caption, drawn from the dirge sung at the end, reads 'You should have wept her yesterday' – a bitter reminder that the Prince has only himself to blame for this unhappily-ever-after ending. Across the double-page opening, the title-page vignette shifts back to an earlier moment in the poem to show the Princess sitting at her open window, patiently awaiting the arrival of her tardy Prince. Captioned 'The long hours go and come and go', this design emphasizes the Princess's hopeful watch while underscoring, as did the frontispiece, the inexorable passage of time. As thresholds the first readers of *The Prince's Progress* had to cross before reading poem and volume, these introductory illustrations directed readers to read with the end in mind, and to judge the Prince from the sure knowledge of his own fatal failure to do so.

Although it has been relatively overlooked by critics until recent years, *Sing-Song: A Nursery Rhyme Book* is undoubtedly one of Christina Rossetti's major achievements in the art of the book. Conceived, designed and finally published as a series of 121 small emblems in the tradition of William Blake's *Songs of Innocence and of Experience*, *Sing-Song* nearly perished for want of a publisher. Unlike Blake, Christina was not able to illustrate, etch, print, bind and distribute her own work; she had to realize her intentions in the vehicular forms possible through commercial trade publishing. After several false starts and considerable effort, she located an enterprising American publisher, Roberts Brothers of Boston, willing to take on a copiously illustrated book with the Dalziel Bros engraving firm, who brought it out in England under the Routledge imprint.[38] As indicated in her illustrated fair-copy manuscript, each lyric was to be headed by an image that worked dialogically with its accompanying lyric; both were to be simple in appearance and expression. Her selected illustrator, Arthur Hughes, used the layout and pictorial suggestions of this fair-copy guide to develop images that worked with the verses to illuminate and expand their multivalent meanings. He was so successful in this that Christina wrote the Dalziels asking that Hughes's name be printed larger on the title page in recognition of his collaboration, remarking 'his cuts deserve to sell the volume'.[39] Dante Gabriel, who admired the 'Blakish wisdom' of his sister's verses, called Hughes 'a true poet in painting' and averred: 'There is no man living who would have done my sister's book so divinely well.'[40] In *Sing-Song* we have a final realization of the Pre-Raphaelite verbal-visual aesthetic and collaborative practice.

As Sharon Smulders comments, *Sing-Song* shares with Christina Rossetti's other poetry a concern for temporality, change and sequence. 'Unfolding a narrative from cradle to grave, from winter to fall, from sunrise to sunset', Smulders writes, '*Sing-Song* invites readers to understand life as an ordered totality.'[41] As in all her work, Rossetti develops this understanding by establishing an interpretive apparatus that encourages both literal and symbolic readings; deeper truths are revealed gradually, as readers are able to receive them. One of her most frequently anthologized poems, 'Who has seen the wind?', schools the young reader or listener in this art of reading physical signs:

> Who has seen the wind?
>   Neither I nor you:
> But when the leaves hang trembling
>   The wind is passing thro'.
>
> Who has seen the wind?
>   Neither you nor I:
> But when the trees bow down their heads
>   The wind is passing by.[42]

Like many of Rossetti's nursery rhymes, this two-quatrain lyric is a dialogue poem that advances its subject through incremental repetition within a question-and-answer format. Each stanza begins with the same question, 'Who has seen the wind?', followed by a negative reply. The third line of each quatrain introduces a qualification to that negation with the conjunction 'But' and goes on to describe physical signs that demonstrate the visible presence of the invisible wind such as trembling leaves and bowing branches. Following the poet's manuscript sketch, Hughes illustrates the lyric literally by picturing a windy outdoor scene with trees bending and leaves blowing from the evident gusts. The child reader/viewer can see, in the picture as in the world, that the invisible wind has material effects – a simple enough lesson in reading and interpreting visible signs.

Also implied in the paired picture and poem, however, is the indirect revelation of a spiritual presence in the phenomenal world, the wind that moved upon the waters at the beginning of biblical story and which, for Rossetti, thereafter moved all things, including her own poetic creation. This is, both literally and figuratively, an inspired reading. Christina Rossetti used the art of the book to give physical expression to spiritual insight. From *Verses* of 1847 to *Verses* of 1893, not only linguistic and iconic texts, but also bibliographic forms, were to inspire readers to interpret physical signs as emblems expressive of divine meaning.

In an Introduction to a new edition of *The Germ* published in 1901 at the height of the Pre-Raphaelite revival, William Michael Rossetti observed that 'one of the influences which guided' the movement was 'the intimate intertexture of a spiritual sense with a material form'.[43] It was this 'intimate intertexture' that made Christina Rossetti's poetry central to Pre-Raphaelitism from its mid-century beginning to its fin-de-siècle renaissance. The foremost designers of the 1890s – Charles Ricketts, Laurence Housman and Lucien

Pissarro – were all inspired by the example of Christina Rossetti's verbal-visual aesthetic. In a tribute to her collaborations with Dante Gabriel, Ricketts illustrated her sonnet, 'An Echo from Willowwood', for the *Magazine of Art* in 1890.[44] Laurence Housman, whom Ricketts trained in the art of illustration by having him make facsimile drawings of Dante Gabriel's illustrations for Christina's poetry, designed a stand-alone, lavishly illustrated *Goblin Market* for Macmillan in 1893.[45] The son of Impressionist artist Camille Pissarro, Lucien, who came into Ricketts's sphere when he immigrated to England,[46] published a beautiful decorated edition of Christina Rossetti's first book – the small, privately printed *Verses* of 1847 – at his Eragny Press in 1906.[47] Inspired by Christina Rossetti's verses and their bibliographic forms, this new generation of designers reaffirmed Pre-Raphaelitism's commitment to visual/verbal collaboration and the art of the book, continuing its legacy of art and poetry into the twentieth century.

NOTES

1 Elizabeth Prettejohn, *The Art of the Pre-Raphaelites* (London: Tate Publishing, 2000), p. 11.
2 Ibid., p. 73.
3 Christina Rossetti, 'Behold, I stand at the door and knock', *The Complete Poems of Christina Rossetti*, ed. R. W. Crump, 3 vols. (Baton Rouge and London: Louisiana State University Press, 1979–1990), vol. III, pp. 27–8.
4 *The Letters of Christina Rossetti*, ed. Antony H. Harrison, 4 vols. (Charlottesville: University of Virginia Press, 1997–2004), vol. I, p. 17.
5 'The P. R. B.: I', *The Poetical Works of Christina Georgina Rossetti, with Memoir and Notes &c by William Michael Rossetti* (London: Macmillan and Co., 1904), p. 424, hereafter *Poetical Works*.
6 *Letters of Christina Rossetti*, vol. I, p. 78.
7 DGR *Correspondence*, vol. I, p. 268 (letter 53.38); vol. I, p. 197 (letter 52.8).
8 William Michael Rossetti, Notes, *Poetical Works*, p. 464.
9 Christina G. Rossetti, *Letter and Spirit: Notes on the Commandments* (London: SPCK, 1883), p. 131.
10 Ruskin, vol. XII, p. 320.
11 Jerome McGann, *Dante Gabriel Rossetti and the Game That Must Be Lost* (New Haven and London: Yale University Press, 2000), p. 5.
12 Christina G. Rossetti, *Seek and Find: A Double Series of Short Studies of the Benedicite* (London: SPCK, 1879).
13 Jean H. Hagstrum, *The Sister Arts: The Tradition of Literary Pictorialism and English Poetry from Dryden to Gray* (Chicago: University of Chicago Press, 1987), pp. 96–7.
14 Jan Marsh, *Christina Rossetti: A Literary Biography* (London: Jonathan Cape, 1994), pp. 55–8.
15 G. B. Tennyson, *Victorian Devotional Poetry: The Tractarian Mode* (Cambridge, MA: Harvard University Press, 1981), pp. 44–56.

16 John Keble, *The Christian Year*, autograph extra-illustrated copy of Christina G. Rossetti, British Library Prints and Drawings Department, Permanent loan no. 113.

17 I Corinthians 13:11–12.

18 *Letters of Christina Rossetti*, vol. I, p. 228.

19 Mackenzie Bell, *Christina Rossetti: A Biographical and Critical Study*, facsimile of 4th edn. (New York: Haskell House, 1971), p. 244.

20 'Advent', *Poetical Works*, pp. 202–3.

21 Diane D'Amico, *Christina Rossetti: Faith, Gender, and Time* (Baton Rouge: Louisiana State University Press, 1999), p. 35.

22 Prettejohn, *Art of the Pre-Raphaelites*, p. 259.

23 *Germ*, p. 22.

24 Alastair Grieve, 'Rossetti's Applied Art Designs: 2. Book Bindings', *Burlington Magazine*, 115 (February 1973), pp. 79–81.

25 Paul Goldman, *Victorian Illustration: The Pre-Raphaelites, the Idyllic School and the High Victorians* (Aldershot, Hants.: Scolar Press, 1996), p. 3.

26 Edmund Gosse, *The Life of Algernon Charles Swinburne*, in *The Complete Works of Algernon Charles Swinburne*, vol. XIX (London: Heinemann, 1927), p. 127.

27 William Michael Rossetti, Notes, *Poetical Works*, p. 460.

28 Simon Nowell-Smith (ed.), *Letters to Macmillan* (London: Macmillan, 1967), p. 239.

29 For reproductions see 'Goblin Market: Various Designs', in *The Rossetti Archive*.

30 Gérard Genette, *Paratexts: Thresholds of Interpretation*, trans. Jane E. Lewin (Cambridge University Press, 1997), pp. 1–2.

31 *Poetical Works*, pp. 1–8.

32 Mary Arseneau, *Recovering Christina Rossetti: Female Community and Incarnational Poetics* (Basingstoke: Palgrave Macmillan, 2004), pp. 122–9.

33 Ibid., p. 121.

34 *Letters of Christina Rossetti*, vol. I, pp. 239, 246.

35 Jan Marsh, *Christina Rossetti*, p. 321.

36 *Poetical Works*, p. 34.

37 For reproductions see 'Prince's Progress', in *The Rossetti Archive*.

38 William Michael Rossetti, *The Diary of William Michael Rossetti, 1870–1873*, ed. Odette Bornand (Oxford: Clarendon Press, 1977), pp. 51, 56, 72; George and Edward Dalziel, *The Brothers Dalziel: A Record of Fifty Years' Work, 1840–1890* (London: Methuen, 1901), p. 92.

39 *Letters of Christina Rossetti*, vol. I, p. 375.

40 DGR *Correspondence*, vol. IV, p. 376 (letter 70.31); vol. V, p. 201 (letter 71.203).

41 Sharon Smulders, 'Sound, Sense and Structure in Christina Rossetti's *Sing-Song*', *Children's Literature*, 22 (1994), p. 3.

42 Christina G. Rossetti, 'Who has seen the wind?', *Sing-Song: A Nursery Rhyme Book* (London: George Routledge and Sons, 1872), p. 93. For reproductions of Arthur Hughes's illustrations see the facsimile of this edition (New York: Dover, 1968).

43 *Germ*, 'Introduction by William Michael Rossetti', p. 18.

44 Christina G. Rossetti, 'An Echo From Willowwood', illustrated by Charles Ricketts, *Magazine of Art*, 13 (September 1890), p. 385.
45 Christina G. Rossetti, *Goblin Market*, illustrated by Laurence Housman (London: Macmillan & Co., 1893); for reproductions see the facsimile of this edition (New York: Dover, 1983).
46 Lora Urbanelli, *The Wood Engravings of Lucien Pissarro and a Bibliographical List of Eragny Books* (Oxford: Silent Books and the Ashmolean Museum, 1994), pp. 19–24.
47 *Verses by Christina G. Rossetti*, decorated by Lucien Pissarro (Hammersmith: Eragny Press, 1906).

12

DEBORAH CHERRY

Elizabeth Eleanor Siddall (1829–1862)

In 1857, in a period of intense productive creativity, Elizabeth Siddall[1] completed several watercolours.[2] One of these, *Clerk Saunders* (Figure 15), portrays a scene recounted in an old Scottish ballad in which May Margaret meets the ghost of her murdered lover, the Clerk Saunders of the title. As May Margaret kisses the 'chrystal wand' to pledge of her fidelity, Clerk Saunders reaches out to receive it. In the dim light of the chamber, both figures appear ghostly and pale. Dawn breaks over the medieval city glimpsed through the aperture; on Margaret's prie-dieu, an hour-glass stands empty. It is a dramatic moment in which the dead confronts the living. With its literary inspiration, glowing textured watercolour and themes of love and desire, the image is exemplary of a major new direction of Pre-Raphaelite art. It is also exemplary of Pre-Raphaelite art in taking its inspiration from art before the High Renaissance, less the early Italian painters than Gothic art and medieval illumination. By the mid-1850s Siddall had developed a distinctive artistic style characterized by compositional layering, enclosed space, attenuated figures and jewel-like colours in which the furniture, dress and bulky folds of the drapery, as well as the execution in watercolour, all consciously rework pre-modern visual languages.

Clerk Saunders was one of a number of finished art works that the artist contributed to the exhibition of Pre-Raphaelite art, held at Russell Place in central London in the summer of 1857. This was one of several independent alternative shows to showcase Pre-Raphaelite art to a largely invited audience.[3] By now Siddall had established a strong portfolio, working consistently in watercolour, as well as in pen and ink and pencil, and occasionally in oils, and her art was substantially represented. In the history of Pre-Raphaelitism, Siddall's art, produced between 1852 and 1861, has three principal points of significance. Her major watercolours, such as *Clerk Saunders*, *Lady Clare* or *Lady Affixing a Pennant*, anticipated and contributed to a significant medievalizing redirection of Pre-Raphaelitism in the second half of the 1850s. Her untutored practice of art exemplified, and

Figure 15 Elizabeth Siddall, *Clerk Saunders*, 1857, watercolour, bodycolour
and coloured chalks on paper, 28.4 × 18.1 cm, The Syndics of the Fitzwilliam
Museum, Cambridge/The Bridgeman Art Library.

some of her works give visual form to, Pre-Raphaelite concepts of poetic
invention and theories of expressive genius. And her images of women intervened in and challenged the emerging visual cultures of modernity.

The past in the present

From the evidence of her work Siddall was an avid reader, finding inspiration
in the romantic poetry of John Keats and William Wordsworth as well as
more recent poems by Alfred Tennyson and Dante Gabriel Rossetti. Siddall
was fascinated by the Border ballads and she quickly exploited their artistic potential in a series of watercolours and drawings undertaken between
1854 and 1857. The artist owned two volumes of the 1802 edition of the
Minstrelsy of the Scottish Border, compiled by Walter Scott, according to
whom the 'romantic ballad' of Clerk Saunders was 'uncommonly wild and
beautiful, and apparently very ancient'.[4] She marked up the ballads that
appealed to her, attracted by their evocation of a distant era of daring deeds,

supernatural appearances and star-crossed lovers. With their archaic forms and language, the ballads exerted a strong literary appeal, notably for D. G. Rossetti, William Allingham and Siddall herself. Several of her poems have survived, and she uses a simple ballad form in those that explore love, betrayal and death in a remote chivalric period.[5] In spring 1854 she embarked on an illustrated edition of ballads, to be edited by Allingham, working up several ideas and transferring her first design for *Clerk Saunders* to a woodblock. The artist's predilection for dramatic encounter, sorcery and the supernatural were all to be found in the Border ballads: the ghost of Clerk Saunders finds a counterpart in the heroine of 'The Gay Goshawk' who feigns death by taking a sleeping draught. Siddall's sketches for 'The Lass of Lochroyan' portray the heroine as an outcast, following the enchantment of her lover and her branding as a 'witch'. One of the first to portray ghosts and hauntings, Siddall was at the forefront in developing one of the most distinctive Pre-Raphaelite themes – sorcery, enchantment and spell-casting. Her 'witch' drawing (1854) was prompted by D. G. Rossetti's modern ballad, 'Sister Helen'; it portrays the seduced and abandoned protagonist, Helen, melting a waxen image of her faithless lover who subsequently sickens and dies; Helen's own death is anticipated in her hands clutching her throat. In *The Haunted Wood* (dated 1856, also known as *The Haunted Tree* when shown in 1857) a woman encounters a ghost or spectre in the woods.

In the mid-1850s Siddall's archaicizing art placed her at the forefront of Pre-Raphaelitism's new medievializing. Medieval subjects could be developed by reading Sir Thomas Malory's *Le Morte d'Arthur* or Froissart's chronicles of the wars of the fourteenth century as well as Alfred Tennyson's *Poems* (1842). Scenes of chivalry, the knight's quest and courtly love were executed in watercolour or pen and ink on vellum in emulation of medieval illumination. *Sir Galahad and the Holy Grail* (undated watercolour), as its inscription 'EES inv EES & DGR del' indicated,[6] was devised by Siddall and undertaken jointly with Rossetti. Her only contribution to a theme remarkably enduring in Pre-Raphaelite art, it shows the knight at the end of his lengthy travails receiving the Holy Grail in a ruined chapel, accompanied by two angels. *Lady Affixing a Pennant to a Knight's Spear* (c.1856–8, Tate) is one of a group of Pre-Raphaelite drawings and watercolours portraying medieval knights at tournament or going into battle. Siddall's watercolour partakes of, and perhaps anticipates, a common theme of leave-takings and preparations for battle such as Burne-Jones's *The Knight's Farewell* (1858, Ashmolean Museum, Oxford) or *Going to the Battle* (1858, Fitzwilliam Museum, Cambridge) and Rossetti's *Before the Battle* (1858–62, Museum of Fine Arts, Boston). Works by Rossetti, Siddall, William Morris and Edward Burne-Jones echoed and cross-referenced each other, and Rossetti considered his own 'ultra-mediaeval' *Before the Battle* to be a pendant to Siddall's *Clerk Saunders*.[7] *Lady Affixing a Pennant*, however, offers not the tumult of departures, but, akin to Burne-Jones's *The Knight's Farewell*, portrays a quiet, private moment, a gesture of affectionate companionship as the lady rests her arm on her knight's shoulder while he nails her colours to his spear. The entwined figures of Siddall's *Lady Clare* may well be reprised in the intimate embrace of the couple in Burne-Jones's drawing, while Siddall's *Clerk Saunders* and Morris's *La Belle Iseult* (c.1857, Tate) both share the enclosed setting of a chamber with a bed with rumpled sheets. Parallels can also be found in archaizing details and dress, as well as secluded locations. Within this shared endeavour, each artist developed a distinctive approach. Against the melee of figures, horses, waving pennants and departing knights, in *Before the Battle* Rossetti highlights a singular stylized female figure, a form that was becoming increasingly marked in his art. Equally conspicuous in many of these collaborative works, notably in Burne-Jones's early drawings, is an intricate patterning and decoration. As narrative slips away or becomes undecidable, the viewer's attention is held by an elaborate surface that intrigues and enmeshes the gaze.

Lady Affixing a Pennant seems to have no explicit story. But narrative and dramatic encounters remained significant for Siddall, unlike her male counterparts. This is particularly evident in her watercolour *Lady Clare* (1857), based on Tennyson's poem in which the protagonist discovers on her wedding day that her servant, Alice, is her mother. The two women wear contrasting colours of blue and red. The telling detail of the coronet on her golden cuff indicates Lady Clare's supposedly aristocratic status, and the poignant theme is underscored by the stained-glass vignettes depicting the judgement of Solomon. But Siddall's watercolours and drawings have neither intricate detail nor surface decoration. She uses vivid blocks of strong colour. The artist enriched their textures with coloured chalks and bodycolour (where watercolour is mixed with white to render it opaque, as in *Clerk Saunders*) and sometimes she used metallic paint. The intense emotional charge of her work comes from bold colour fields, striking colour contrasts and an alertness to colour's emotional and symbolic resonance, also evident in her poetry where, for example, she visualizes love's fickleness in shifts 'from blue to red/From brightest red to blue'.[8] While *Lady Clare* makes effective use of the primaries, the sombre scene of *Clerk Saunders* is envisaged in darker hues, deploying a wide tonal range of blues and greens. The *Holy Family* (c.1856, Delaware Art Museum) is sumptuous and bold: Mary's resplendent (and traditional) blue cloak is set off against her deep crimson dress, the angel's vivid green robe and the brilliant gold of her hair and the angel's wings.

Knights and ladies, chivalry and courtly love offered models of gendered social roles that differentiated between the outdoor world of men and the interior world of women. The medieval 'lady' suggested an ideal of feminine virtue, gentleness and domesticity, and the knight one of masculine heroic endeavour, which with its Christian and crusading overtones had considerable resonance with the aggressive colonial wars and imperial expansion of the period. The Arthurian court like the Border ballads also provided examples of adultery and 'fallen women'. While Siddall sketched the body of Arthur carried downriver accompanied by weeping queens (*The Passing of Arthur*, c.1855–6), she never depicted Queen Guinevere or the adultery, rivalry and conflicts of the Arthurian court that so preoccupied Rossetti and Morris. Like many others she was, however, fascinated by the visual differentiation of feminine purity and impurity. In *Clerk Saunders* the crucifix, prayer table with a Bible and winged angel bearing a lily all suggest Margaret's purity, whereas the disordered linen suggests that she is no longer a virgin. Such modern concerns are explored in other works with literary inspiration. *Pippa Passes* (1854, Ashmolean Museum, Oxford) draws on Robert Browning's poem of the same name to portray a silkwinder with a day's holiday encountering a group of 'women of loose life'. Pippa's modest downcast gaze, her quiet attire and composure are strongly differentiated from the flashy clothes, bold gestures and direct stares of the prostitutes. At one level, the scene elaborates different kinds of paid work for women: in the textile trades, in prostitution. Siddall's *Pippa Passes* coincides with Rossetti's drawing of *Found* (1853, British Museum) and Anna Mary Howitt's now lost picture of *The Castaway* (1854–5). It also addresses a question of abiding interest in the visual cultures of the mid-century, and explored in *Lady Clare* as well: what visible distinctions, legible on the feminine body, demarcated different social classes of women?

The palace of art

Pre-Raphaelite medievalizing brought about redefinitions of the artist and of the locus of artistic activity. Unlike Pre-Raphaelite drawings and paintings that directly engaged with contemporary life, this medievalizing favoured a turning inwards, an emotional intensity and the exercise of creative imagination. In retreat from 'counties overhung with smoke … the spreading of the hideous town', as William Morris would write in *The Earthly Paradise*, artistic creativity withdrew into a 'palace of art', an interior space entirely devoted to art's execution and in which the world beyond is only glimpsed through small apertures. Several of Siddall's drawings set forth these new concepts, especially those inspired by Tennyson's poem 'The Palace of Art'. Siddall's drawings show the patron saint of music, *Saint Cecilia*, sleeping or swooning, accompanied by an angel playing a small organ, in a sequestered space at the top of a tower. *The Lady of Shalott*, dated 'Dec. 15/[18]53', the artist's first known finished work, offers a sustained visual elaboration of art and artist. *The Lady of Shalott* is held by a mysterious curse in which she may not observe the outside world, but only regard it in the mirror and, depicting scenes reflected there, she is to weave 'a magic web of colours gay'. When Sir Launcelot 'flash'd into the crystal mirror', the Lady is distracted, the web unravels and the Lady takes a boat downriver to Camelot, singing as she dies. In drawings for Moxon's illustrated edition of Tennyson's *Poems*, Holman Hunt imagines a woman entangled in a frenzy of unravelling (compare Figure 1), and Rossetti pictures Lancelot gazing at the Lady in death. Siddall's image seems at odds with the prevailing imagery of the Lady of Shalott and with a central icon of nineteenth-century femininity, one distilled in Millais's image of the deranged, dying Ophelia, for which Siddall so famously modelled. Siddall refutes the poem's narrative drive, providing instead a vision of artistic activity. In a simple, unstructured robe, the Lady inhabits an airy, spacious workroom complete with little touches added by the artist, such as the bird atop the weaving frame (rather than a horizontal embroidery frame) on which the threads are just beginning to unravel. A crucifix suggests her piety, another detail added by the artist. This drawing finds comparison with Rossetti's images of *Dante Drawing an Angel on the First Anniversary of the Death of Beatrice* (1849 (Figure 2); watercolour, 1853, Ashmolean Museum, Oxford) in which Dante, declining to communicate with the visitors who seek to interrupt and disturb his artistic concentration, retreats to an enclosed space to depict not a living figure but an angel, his drawing inspired by memory and imagination. Like Dante, the Lady of Shalott works at a remove, her art inspired by reflection. But whereas Dante can successfully shield his art from outside intrusions, the Lady's contemplative weaving is interrupted. Siddall's vision of the 'palace of art' is one more deeply marked by risk and danger: direct engagement with the world can be destructive to art and fatal for the artist.

These new theories of Pre-Raphaelite art and artist entailed rethinking concepts of artistic expression. Pre-Raphaelite theories of expressive genius proposed that the practice of art depended not on professional guidance in composition, perspective or figure drawing, nor on compliance with convention, all of which were seen as limiting creative expression. Instead the practice of art was equated with inner genius, and construed as the outpouring of an innate poetic imagination. Such views undoubtedly encouraged those with no artistic training or background, like Siddall or Burne-Jones, to become artists. A woman on the borders of the working class and lower-middle class, Elizabeth Siddall was the daughter of a Sheffield cutler who ran an ironmongery business in South London. Coming into contact with Pre-Raphaelite circles in the later 1840s, she worked as an artist from 1852–3 onward. Although she attended a ladies' art class at Sheffield Art School in 1857, she embarked on her artistic career with little or no formal instruction, a predicament she shared with many nineteenth-century women artists whose access to art education and especially figure study was severely limited.[9] Siddall may have taken some lessons from Rossetti. And Rossetti, who turned to his own tutor when he needed assistance, prompted Siddall in the same direction. In January 1854 Ford Madox Brown advised her about her oil *Self-portrait* (1853–4, Figure 16) and the following spring he accompanied her to buy oil paints.[10] Her technical deficiencies and her profound lack of anatomical knowledge are evident in works such as *Clerk Saunders*. Nevertheless, Siddall and her art embodied – and were encouraged by – Pre-Raphaelite beliefs in expressive artistic genius unfettered by established ideas or professional training. Avant-garde beliefs about the freedom of the artist only strengthened during the nineteenth century.

The practice of art

Most of Siddall's works are in pen and ink or in watercolour, usually on a small scale. She also essayed oils, working in this more exacting medium in her *Self-portrait* in 1853–4, and in December 1856 beginning an oil version of *Clerk Saunders*.[11] One or two of Rossetti's drawings show her seated at an easel, working in oil and balancing her painting hand on a mahl stick (a stick or rod often used by painters to steady their hands).

In *Clerk Saunders*, as in her other finished watercolours, the angularity and awkwardness of the figures, along with the complicated arrangements of architectural space and unsettling shifts of perspective, are at odds with the laws of anatomy, perspective and composition. Siddall derived her pictorial language, as well as archaizing details, from careful study of Gothic art and medieval manuscripts (probably seen at the house of John Ruskin and the British Library). At times there are pronounced parallels. A small casket in the form of a Gothic reliquary, perhaps given to Jane Burden Morris as a wedding present (c.1860–1, Society of Antiquaries), features decorative panels of courtly, chivalric subjects painted by Siddall and Rossetti, one of which is closely based on a miniature in a fifteenth-century manuscript volume of the poems of Christine de Pisan (British Library London, MS Harley, 4431).[12]

Siddall's drawing style is varied, and it includes an angular linearity (also in evidence in the more technically proficient studies by Millais and others) as well as a supple fluidity of line. Across all her oeuvre, the artist demonstrated a tendency for repeatedly working out her subjects through several compositional drawings, for working in series with a predilection for variation and modification and for working between drawing and watercolour. Comparison between the drawing in reverse (presumably for the woodblock) and the finished watercolour of *Clerk Saunders* shows how Siddall revised the watercolour's composition, making the space more complex with alcoves, apertures and built-in furniture which not only accentuates the disparity between inside and outside, but intensifies the gulf between the living and the dead. Clerk Saunders, who appears in a green robe with contrasting sleeves, more akin to his daily wear than the tightly bound shroud of the drawing, is spatially separated from May Margaret by the curtain and the bed-rail. When working on *Lady Clare*, the main lines of the intertwined figures were established in the drawing while the introduction of zigzagging stairs in the watercolour almost flattens the space, throwing the viewer's attention forward onto the encounter between the two women.

Siddall's practice of variation can be demonstrated in a number of depictions of the Madonna and Child. Subjects from the life of the Virgin began to appear in Siddall's work in the first half of the 1850s. In July 1854 D. G. Rossetti informed William Allingham that Siddall has 'made a design which is practicable for her to paint quietly at my rooms … She will begin it now at once … The subject is the Nativity, designed in a most lovely & original way.'[13] Commenting on a number of other works underway, Rossetti may also be referring to nativity scenes in which Mary kneels beside a crib. Siddall also made a small highly worked pen-and-ink study of a *Madonna and Child with an Angel* and a finished watercolour now (erroneously) entitled *Holy Family* (Delaware Art Museum). Here Mary cradles a tiny Christ child in the crook of her arm; beside her an angel holds a portable organ. A third watercolour (undated, Ashmolean Museum, Oxford) shows an older child standing on his mother's knee, reaching out for a flower.

The presentation of sacred figures in simple surroundings was a hallmark of early Pre-Raphaelite art, and the artist was well acquainted with a visual language that has been linked to the Anglo-Catholic movement. The dove drinking from a basin in *Madonna and Child with an Angel* may signal the presence of the Holy Spirit, while the sheep glimpsed through the window in the *Holy Family* may foretell Christ's future ministry. The theme of music finds comparison to Rossetti's watercolours of the period, but the angel's playing suggests not a secular worldliness but devotional masses offered to the Virgin. Siddall's Christian subjects are deeply felt, reverential, contemplative and calm. Echoing the hymns and prayers of her youth, Siddall's poems are full of Christian feeling, although it is Christ, rather than the Virgin, who is invoked.

Patrons and exhibitions

Elizabeth Siddall's works were exhibited on a number of occasions, and plans were made to send to London shows. Her work attracted the notice of a number of Pre-Raphaelite patrons. In 1855 she struck a deal with John Ruskin who had a penchant for assisting artists, male and female. Rossetti reported that the critic and patron 'saw & bought on the spot every scrap of designs hitherto produced by Miss Siddal'.[14] He acquired several works including a version of *Pippa Passes*, along with a drawing of *Lovers Listening to Music* (1854, Ashmolean Museum, Oxford) in which two women of colour play music for a white man and woman. As *Lovers Listening to Music* had already been promised to William Allingham, the artist may have produced a second version (Wightwick Manor) as a replacement for him. This is one of a number of instances when she completed another version of a finished work for competing patrons, an approach much favoured by Rossetti. Aspirations for a professional practice of art are indicated by plans in 1853 to send her *Self-portrait* to one of London's winter exhibitions and 'to begin a picture at once for the R. A. [Royal Academy]',[15] and by her contribution to the 1857 exhibition. Remarking on her works here, the poet Coventry Patmore considered that although her drawings demonstrated 'an admiring adoption of all the most startling peculiarities of Mr. Rossetti's style … they have nevertheless qualities which entitle them to high praise'. *Study of a Head* (perhaps her oil *Self-portrait*) showed 'great care, considerable technical power, and a high, pure, and independent feeling for that much misunderstood object, the human face divine'.[16] *Clerk Saunders*, bought by the American collector Charles Eliot Norton for 40 guineas, was included in the New York showing of the American Exhibition of British Art. Whatever the outcome of her arrangements with Ruskin, who had also offered an annual stipend of £150 for everything she produced,[17] in November 1860 she had sufficient work in her own possession to contribute to a new decorative scheme at her marital home. She had married Rossetti in spring 1860 and the couple lived in Rossetti's old rooms at no. 14 Chatham Place, Blackfriars, with additional space on the second floor of no. 13. Rossetti reported that '[w]e have got one of our rooms completely hung round with Lizzie's drawings'.[18]

Imagining herself

Siddall was at work on her *Self-portrait* by summer 1853. She portrays herself directly facing her beholder, her deep-lidded eyes wide open. Copper-coloured hair and a dark dress with green and brown tints are set against a deep green ground. William Michael Rossetti, writing long after Siddall's death, declared this *Self-portrait* to be 'an absolute likeness', 'an excellent and graceful likeness'.[19] Long considered the aim of portraiture, likeness signifies not replication but resemblance; the portrait is not a copy of a person but a representation. Siddall's face appears three-quarter view; like so many others this self-portrait was painted using a mirror. The mirror gives back a seemingly whole, complete image of the self, one which like the artistic endeavour of the portrait is transformed by imagination, desire, projection and (mis)recognition. Watching herself drawing (herself in the mirror) the artist remakes her own image from the mental work of (self-)reflection and the conventions of art. The simplified format of figure against a coloured ground is by no means unstudied but based on a portrait format adopted from Northern Renaissance art.

Siddall wears a simple dress with pleats falling from the shoulder-line and a high neckline, worn with a chemise. As early as 1852, Rossetti wrote that Siddall had 'lately made herself a grey dress, also a black silk one'.[20] Given the innovative cut and varied construction of the dresses that she wears in Rossetti's drawings, it seems likely that, with her possible experience in the millinery/dressmaking trades, she was an inventive dress designer. Siddall's dresses departed from the tightly fitted corseted bodice, dropped shoulder, many petticoats, crinolines and flounces of contemporary wear in the 1850s, while retaining a basic fashionable line in an artistic form of dress with softly flowing lines, a looser cut, higher set shoulders, sleeves that permitted free movement and a skirt that was relatively lightly supported and fell in deep folds from a natural waistline, or on occasion from a dropped line sitting at the hip. Her hair was loosely pinned at the nape of the neck, not pulled back with side curls. Her style was, to some extent, based on observation of medieval, especially fourteenth-century, dress; she attired the figures in her art in similarly inspired garments. Artistic dress became popular in the following decade, and a more elaborate version is worn by Jane Burden Morris in John R. Parsons's famous photographs of her (1865, London, Victoria and Albert Museum).

Siddall's self-portrait contributes and responds to a dense archive of images of her in circulation in Pre-Raphaelite circles. If she was the 'one face [that] looks out from all his canvases' as Christina Rossetti wrote of her brother in 'In an Artist's Studio', Siddall could find her unlike double

Figure 16 Elizabeth Siddall, *Self-portrait*, c. 1853–4, oil on canvas,
20.3 cm (diameter), whereabouts unknown.

on many other occasions: in Deverell's *Twelfth Night* (exhibited in 1850, private collection), Holman Hunt's *A Converted British Family Sheltering a Christian Missionary from the Persecution of the Druids* (1850, Ashmolean Museum, Oxford) and his *Valentine Rescuing Sylvia from Proteus* (1851, Birmingham Museums & Art Gallery), and Millais's *Ophelia* (1852, Tate). From 1852 she sat to Rossetti, often for Dante's Beatrice, a figure with whom she would become closely identified. Whereas the oil paintings by his Pre-Raphaelite peers were all publicly exhibited, Rossetti's many studies, like the drawings made of Siddall in 1854 by two women artists, Anna Mary Howitt and Barbara Bodichon, circulated to a closed circle of acquaintances, critics and buyers. Rossetti's many studies of Elizabeth Siddall remain tantaliz-ingly puzzling. They have been variously perceived as testimony to his love and her frailty, as records of her appearance or insights into her character. Conversely, with their repeated portrayals of the model reclining, sleeping, reading, looking down or away, they have also been identified less as por-trayals of a distinctive individual than as highly stylized visual encodings of 'woman as sign' that are characteristic of the visual cultures of modernity. In this account, these images distil the model's appearance into visual signs of masculine creativity.[21] At the same time, the studies may also be interpreted as counterpoints to this same visual regime. By looking elsewhere, dropping or closing her eyelids, this sitter may well be disregarding and eluding a gaze that persistently and intimately regarded her.

Siddall's image was made and remade in the rapidly developing visual cultures of the 1850s, becoming a visual icon in a process which found its epiphany in Rossetti's *Beata Beatrix* (1864–70, Tate) painted after her untimely death in 1862, perhaps from an accidental overdose of an opium derivative. Siddall's early death, Rossetti's responses – in *Beata Beatrix*, and in burying his poems with her and later exhuming them – and their sensational retellings have fuelled mythologies about an artistic genius and his tragic muse which in turn underline the ways in which Siddall has come to represent woman as a sign of masculine creativity.

She left no written record of her response to one of the central manoeuvres of modernity, the development of a visual culture marked by and productive of cultural and sexual difference. In this new visual economy woman's look came to signify not only woman looking, but an emphasis on appearance in which woman is transformed into a visual sign, the screen or target of the gaze. It is, after all, at this critical moment in the visual cultures of the mid-nineteenth century that woman is encoded as a visual sign and simultaneously present as the active agent of cultural production. Women artists emerge in considerable and conspicuous numbers in the 1850s.[22] This double movement of woman as sign and woman as artist comes together in Elizabeth Siddall, who was at once a working artist and the model for a remarkable series of paintings and drawings. Her *Self-portrait* marks her intervention into modern visual culture. Poised and composed, Elizabeth Siddall regards her beholders with a steady, unwavering regard, meeting and challenging those who are looking at her.

NOTES

1 The artist's family name was 'Siddall'. She signed at least one letter 'Siddal' (to William Allingham, [1856], Troxell Collection, Princeton University Library). This spelling, also used by D. G. and W. M. Rossetti, prevails in modern literature. On the significance of the spelling of her name see Deborah Cherry and Griselda Pollock, 'Woman as Sign in Pre-Raphaelite Literature: A Study of the Representation of Elizabeth Siddall', *Art History*, 7.2 (June 1984), pp. 206–27.

2 Many of Siddall's art works (and her poems) are reproduced in the exhibition catalogue by Jan Marsh, *Elizabeth Siddal 1829–1862: Pre-Raphaelite Artist* (Sheffield: The Ruskin Gallery, 1991). Works mentioned in the text are in private collections unless locations are given.

3 See Deborah Cherry, 'The Hogarth Club: 1858–61', *Burlington Magazine*, 122 (April 1980), pp. 237–44.

4 Sir Walter Scott, *Minstrelsy of the Scottish Border* (1802) (London: Thomas Tegg, 1869), p. 376. Siddall's copy is at the Fitzwilliam Museum, Cambridge.

5 Roger C. Lewis and Mark Samuels Lasner (eds.), *Poems and Drawings of Elizabeth Siddal* (Wolfville, Nova Scotia: Wombat Press, 1978).

6 'Elizabeth Eleanor Siddall invented, Elizabeth Eleanor Siddall and Dante Gabriel Rossetti painted'.

7 DGR *Correspondence*, vol. II, p. 439 (letter 62.3).

8 Elizabeth Siddall, 'Dead Love', in Lewis and Lasner (eds.), *Poems and Drawings*, p. 10.

9 Deborah Cherry, *Painting Women: Victorian Women Artists* (London and New York: Routledge, 1993), chapter 3.

10 DGR *Correspondence*, vol. I, p. 305 (letter 54.1); vol. II, p. 31 (letter 55.19).

11 DGR *Correspondence*, vol. II, p. 147 (letter 56.59), p. 127 (letter 56.40).

12 Jennifer Harris, 'Jane Morris's Jewel Casket', *Antique Collector*, 55 (December 1984), pp. 69–70.

13 DGR *Correspondence*, vol. I, p. 363 (letter 54.55).

14 DGR *Correspondence*, vol. II, p. 25 (letter 55.14), according to which Ruskin paid £30.

15 DGR *Correspondence*, vol. I, p. 281 (letter 53.48); Rossetti continues 'from Tennyson I believe'.

16 Coventry Patmore, 'A Pre-Raphaelite Exhibition', *Saturday Review*, 4 July 1857, p. 12.

17 DGR *Correspondence*, vol. II, p. 31 (letter 55.18); see also pp. 31–2 (letter 55.19) in which Rossetti says that he prefers this arrangement to Ruskin's purchase of her works as she produces them.

18 DGR *Correspondence*, vol. II, p. 329 (letter 60.49); they were still there early in 1862, *Correspondence*, vol. II, pp. 440–1 (letter 62.3).

19 William Michael Rossetti (ed.), *Dante Gabriel Rossetti: His Family-Letters with a Memoir*, 2 vols. (London: Ellis and Elvey, 1895), vol. I, p. 175; W. M. Rossetti, 'Dante Rossetti and Elizabeth Siddal', *Burlington Magazine*, 1 (May 1903), p. 277.

20 DGR *Correspondence*, vol. I, p. 197 (letter 52.8). Warmest thanks to Jennifer Harris for discussions on Siddall's dress.

21 Cherry and Pollock, 'Woman as Sign'.

22 Cherry, *Painting Woman*.

13

JEFFREY SKOBLOW

The writings of William Morris (1834–1896)

The most important thing to remember and the easiest to forget when considering William Morris's varied writings is that all of his writing, like all of his other multifarious work, is part of a radical project: that is, the renovation of art for contemporary and future purposes. This project ultimately encompasses an even broader renovation of society as a whole along politically revolutionary lines – when I say 'radical' I mean primarily that Morris aims to reconsider matters from the ground up, inquiring into root causes and essential functions, but he is radical in this other sense, too, that is, socialist, in the end essentially Marxist, an advocate of revolutionary overthrow of the current economic and political order. This renovation of art and its relation to that broader project is explicitly the subject of the lectures and essays he produced in the last twenty years of his life, and is a central concern in his socialist utopian romance of that period, *News from Nowhere* (1890). But at the same time, in the last decade of his life he was also writing a series of extended prose romances typically referred to as 'quasi-medieval', which, especially in the case of the later ones like *The Well at the World's End* (1896) or *The Water of the Wondrous Isles* (1897, published posthumously), would seem as far from having a revolutionary thought in their heads as they could possibly be – and these works too are ultimately part of that same project. The great antiquarian fantasies he produced earlier, by which his poetic reputation was largely made – *The Earthly Paradise* (1868–70), which avowedly *denies* any possible radical (or even remotely, faintly agitating) intent, and *The Story of Sigurd the Volsung and the Fall of the Niblungs* (1877) – these too are part of it. From the beginning – even in the stories he published, or the essay on 'The Churches of North France', in the *Oxford and Cambridge Magazine* (1856) when he was twenty-two and a student at Oxford – the reconsideration and renovation of art and what artists do is at the centre of Morris's thought and work.

The point is easy to forget because (leaving aside the socialist essays and lectures) so much of Morris's work is so relentlessly antique in surface appearance, and so often so very mild-mannered, tuned in the key of some honeyed lethargy, that the struggles of any contemporary world and the imagination of any future one seem far from under consideration at all, let alone under radical critique. But so it is: the critique underlies and frames it all. This is one way, at any rate, to appreciate the peculiar power of Morris's work: to see it as a matter of these fundamental tensions, always about the past as a way of addressing the present, always radical even when it appears, perhaps, purely ornamental.

Morris himself frames the matter retrospectively in these terms in 'How I Became a Socialist' (1894): 'Apart from the desire to produce beautiful things, the leading passion of my life has been and is hatred of modern civilization', which he characterizes not only in terms of its 'eyeless vulgarity which has destroyed art, the one certain solace of labour', but also its vast 'mechanical power ... [and] stupendous organization – for the misery of life!' 'All this I felt then as now', he says, referring to his early days, though 'I did not know why it was so'.[1] Socialism, in other words, will give him a way of explaining what he knows, and will give him a hope of change, which will motivate him to articulate that explanation in explicit terms, but the vision is in place from the start, at least implicitly. In most reduced terms, the tension between 'beauty' and 'modern' drives the whole enterprise; the pressure that the latter brings to bear on the former is always part of the frame.

Among other things this means that the forms in which 'beautiful things' might still be produced in the nineteenth century – by Morris & Co., for instance, or by Morris himself as a poet or a printer – serve not only as matters of aesthetic delight, but also as critique, as a response to and in some measure commentary on contemporary conditions governing the production of art. One way to dramatize the extremity of those conditions is to place 'the contemporary' out of reach of 'the beautiful', as it were; in Morris's poetry and narrative prose, at any rate, the contemporary world hardly makes an appearance, as if its stink would make any consideration of beauty – and thus all art – inconceivable. A further or corollary element of this dramatization is the sense of utter distance between 'the (mostly medieval) past' and Morris's present moment: so great is the magnitude of our losses, he seems to say, that if we are going to learn anything from an earlier way of making art, we are going to have to make a strenuous act of historical imagination (or dislocation) to conjure it – a leap across a great divide.

We can see this already in the opening lines of 'The Story of the Unknown Church', Morris's first publication in the *Oxford and Cambridge Magazine*, written when he was twenty-one years old:

> I was the master-mason of a church that was built more than six hundred years ago; it is now two hundred years since this church vanished from the face of the earth; it was destroyed utterly, – no fragment of it was left … No one knows now even where it stood. (Vol. I, p. 149)

The story goes on to tell of the narrator's life as a stone-carver, and of his death 'with my chisel in my hand' – a portrait of the artist and his work, pre-modern style, presented as a kind of 'dream' in which 'I could see even very far off things much clearer than we see real material things on the earth' (vol. I, pp. 158, 154–5). What is stressed here as throughout Morris's work is the 'very far off' – in this case vanished, destroyed utterly, no fragment left, no longer even remembered – and the clarity of vision that can be sustained nevertheless. We also observe from the start the dream of absolute access to that lost world: to say 'I was the master-mason' is to express (or embody) that dream, and the imaginative claim that is thus made can only be a modern one.

All of which is to say, too, that Morris is essentially a Romantic writer, his point of departure a conception of profound cultural loss, and his project the discovery and elaboration of a plan of 'recompense' (in Wordsworth's terminology), or strategies, even dream-strategies, of survival in the face of that loss. One could say that Morris is distinguished from earlier Romantic generations (from Blake or Wordsworth, Byron or Shelley, or for that matter Tennyson) by the relative degree of his alienation, which leads on the one hand to a revolutionary politics and activism (beyond the dreams, perhaps, even of Byron), and on the other to an imaginative literature (in poetry and prose romance/fantasy fiction) that makes no claim whatsoever to speak to contemporary concerns in contemporary language, let alone to sort anything out. There is an air of despair in this dimension of Morris's poetry and imaginative prose, as if he is in exile from his own time and place, as if poetry itself were a reduced thing – and that despair is always half of the story; the other half is what possibilities (even heroic possibilities) nevertheless remain.

The *Oxford and Cambridge Magazine* was a student venture (an early collaboration with Burne-Jones and Rossetti, funded by Morris himself) which ran for only a year, but Morris's work in it sets the tone and establishes the vision for a literary career that, for all its considerable diversity, holds unswervingly to certain key principles over the course of the next four decades, its fundamental commitments remarkably unchanged. In his poetry and imaginative prose narratives, with rare exceptions Morris's work throughout will be set in a medieval (or classical) world, or a medieval-ized imaginary world; and the poet himself will typically not appear in his own contemporary voice (another measure of his alienation), presenting us instead with lyrics, dramatic monologues and dialogues, early on, and later long narratives out of the mouths of others. This is two absences in one, really: the absence of the contemporary world entails the absence of the contemporary poet. In any case, whether his sources are classical Greek, medieval British or French, Germanic, Scandinavian or Persian, this doubled absence informs his poetry and prose narrative throughout, as if by vow or fundamental principle.

What are we to make of such steadfast purity of approach, such rigorous exclusions? The exceptions are rare: 'Frank's Sealed Letter', a contempor-ary love story, in the *Oxford and Cambridge Magazine*; *The Novel on Blue Paper*, an autobiographical meditation in novel form, concerning questions of marriage and betrayal, which Morris abandoned in 1872, and never titled, and which was not published until 1982; 'The Pilgrims of Hope' (1885–6), a long poem in rhyming hexameter couplets, on the Paris Commune of 1871; *News from Nowhere*, set in the future and, fleetingly but crucially, in the present; scattered short poems. Paradoxically again, the principled absence or exclusion of the contemporary world from Morris's work is itself a deep mark of its contemporaneity, a kind of present (or continuously felt) absence that frames the experience of reading him.

Certainly this seems to be the case with *The Defence of Guenevere and Other Poems* (1858), Morris's fully public poetic debut. Nowhere in the volume is a single reference made to the contemporary world, its land-scapes or objects, personages or events. (Even in the high Gothic Revival climate of the mid-nineteenth century, this stands out.) Of the book's thirty poems all but the final three are unmistakably medieval in their settings; and of those three, 'Praise of My Lady', evidently a contemporary portrait of Jane Burden (Morris's future wife), is medievalized through the conceit of 'my lady' and the passing reference to 'a knight's pennon', and by the Latin prayer of the refrain that rings throughout, *'Beata mea Domina!'*, and 'In Prison', which closes the volume, leans towards the medieval as well, with its 'great banners' and 'banner-poles', as if some forlorn knight were singing from a dungeon, 'Feet tether'd, hands fetter'd / Fast to the stone'. This leaves really only one poem, 'Summer Dawn', unequivocally ambiguous in setting, equally imaginable in modern or antique dress. ('In Prison' itself is an interesting poem, considered in contemporary terms: the imprisoned singer of the lyric is 'all alone', his 'life all dark', but still, almost inexplicably, hears the straining of the banners in 'the wind's song' outside – an image of utter alienation and persistent possibilities of resistance; vol. I, pp. 143, 145.) The remaining poems fall into three main categories, relying for their incident, characters, landscapes and themes mostly on Malory's *Morte d'Arthur* (1485), Froissart's *Chronicles* (1369–c.1400) of the Hundred Years War between France and England or Morris's own (medievalizing) invention, with a few pieces drawn from other sources of old tales, like the Brothers Grimm.

Yet clearly these are all contemporary poems – how could they be otherwise? In fact this first volume of Morris's might be seen as the first exposition of a contemporary poetry conceived under the sign of that 'desire to produce beautiful things' and that 'hatred of modern civilization' he will speak of later in life, just as the work of Morris, Marshall, Faulkner & Co., another radical enterprise, only three years later (in 1861) will first exhibit contemporary stained glass, furniture and textile arts conceived under the same double sign. After all, nobody was writing poems like 'The Defence of Guenevere' in the fourteenth century – an account in terza rima of the Queen's speech to King Arthur's knights, who are accusing her of infidelity to the King. Nobody was writing poems like 'The Haystack in the Floods', a stark, image-driven narrative of romantic love and brutal violence, or like 'The Blue Closet', a kind of masque performed by 'Lady Louise', 'Lady Alice' and 'The Damozels', a dream of some safely cloistered place of 'dream on dream / … in a happy stream', dreamt in spite of the fact that 'the sea-salt oozes through / The chinks of the tiles of the Closet Blue', that the sanctuary in other words is no safeguard, and that the singers themselves are apparently dead (vol. I, p. 112).

One aspect of this contemporary poetry is, again, the apparent absence (or exclusion) of the contemporary world from it, but it would be more apt to say, putting the matter in pictorial terms, that the modern frame has been cropped out of the picture. This technique is itself a 'modern' one, exemplified in Morris's time by Browning's monologues, which typically achieve their dramatic effects in part by dispensing with all (or most) framing or mediating context. In Browning's monologues, however, unlike in Morris's poetry, the speaker sometimes is a contemporary figure, and not all of Browning's poems are cast in the voice of others. In Morris's poetry, where virtually all of the voices are the voices of others, and where all are marked by an unrelenting historical distance, the 'missing' frame functions in a different way, signalling in part the alienated status of art and beauty in the contemporary world, the impossibility, so to speak, of a contemporary art, or contemporary poetry. The apparent framelessness of Morris's work – its presentation of itself as essentially pre-modern – argues the disconnection between two worlds, the recognition of sharp historical (even historic) realignments in the advent and establishment of the modern world.

All of these features of the contemporary are features of the Pre-Raphaelite too; in fact *The Defence of Guenevere* volume could well be the Pre-Raphaelite book of verse par excellence. These poems' decorative visuality and stylistic roughness – a kind of cross between crudeness of technique and high refinement – not to mention their fascination/obsession with medieval garb and lore, come as close as any effort in words to approximating or translating Pre-Raphaelite graphic arts (as if the poems were an illustration of the illustration); indeed three poems, 'The Blue Closet', 'The Tune of Seven Towers' and 'King Arthur's Tomb', bear direct relation to watercolours of Rossetti's (now in the Tate and British Museum, London).

Two central poems show the matter plainly. 'The Defence of Guenevere' (which opens the volume) begins:

> But, knowing now that they would have her speak,
> She threw her wet hair backward from her brow,
> Her hand close to her mouth touching her cheek,
> As though she had had there a shameful blow (lines 1–4)

The hair, the brow, the mime show of hands and mouth and cheek (we can virtually see the exposed neck, with the long hair thrown back), as well as the emotional charge, the shame or rather the refusal of shame in this case – Guenevere might well be a woman in a Rossetti portrait too (perhaps Jane Burden). The (Browningesque) jagged opening evokes a different aspect of the Pre-Raphaelite project, too, less visible in the Rossetti portraits than in, for instance, Ford Madox Brown's *An English Autumn Afternoon* (1852, Figure 13): a tendency towards deformation, towards a breaking down of formal assumptions, and a re-naturalizing of aesthetic practice.

The 'Defence' has Browning's modern sense of moral ambiguity, too, telling a tale of moral systems in conflict – itself a feature of the Pre-Raphaelite posture. (From the beginning Pre-Raphaelitism is a moral crusade, waged on a battlefield of art and history, with the weapons of aesthetic politics.) The Queen (with her loyal subject Launcelot) is accused by Gauwaine and various other knights of infidelity to the King, and in the course of the poem she seems at once to confess and refuse the charge, repeating as a refrain: 'Nevertheless you, O Sir Gauwaine, lie, / Whatever may have happened'. Indeed, as that 'nevertheless' suggests, much of Guenevere's own testimony would seem to support Gauwaine's charge, as when she says of Launcelot,

> this is true, the kiss
> Wherewith we kissed in meeting that spring day,
> I scarce dare talk of the remember'd bliss,

When both our mouths went wandering in one way,
And aching sorely, met among the leaves;
Our hands being left behind strained far away. (Lines 133–8)

The conflict between Guenevere and Gauwaine, with the other 'knights and lords' behind him, is a conflict between incompatible views of justice, love and duty – ideas about sin and bliss, wrong and right, heaven and hell – which the poem drives to a kind of stalemate, with Launcelot, in the closing lines, riding 'at good need' to the rescue.

'The Haystack in the Floods', in which the rescue does not arrive in time, indeed in which there is no imaginable escape, may be more in keeping with the mood of the volume as a whole. Here, instead of heroic claims, like Guenevere's, and heroic rescues like her knight's, we have flight, terror and primitive grasping need (for survival or sexual domination as the case may be), the mute ironies and cold brutalities of defeat, this latter a signature in particular of Morris's Froissart material. In this case it is an English soldier and his French lover, Jehane, fleeing enemy territory on horseback, being captured by Godmar and his troops and faced with an impossible moral and emotional choice between the woman's rape and her lover's murder; 'For in such wise they hem me in', she reflects, 'I cannot choose but sin and sin, / Whatever happens' (lines 95–7). In the end Jehane refuses Godmar's offer, and wins her own imprisonment and likely execution along with her lover's immediate death. She sees

The long bright blade without a flaw
Glide out from Godmar's sheath, his hand
In Robert's hair; she saw him bend
Back Robert's head; she saw him send
The thin steel down; the blow told well,
Right backward the knight Robert fell,
And moan'd as dogs do (lines 141–7)

The soldiers then beat Robert's 'head to pieces at their feet.'

Jehane and Guenevere are both great refusers, but if Guenevere's refusal buys her time and the promise of a way out, Jehane's is almost a helpless impulse that only buys her own destruction, as she 'sigh'd quietly, / And strangely childlike came, and said: / "I will not"' (lines 124–6). In any case throughout the volume, the crushing forces of history will have their victory, as Godmar does here, but the dream of resistance does not die, however helpless and hopeless it might appear.

'The Defence of Guenevere' and 'The Haystack in the Floods' are among Morris's most anthologized texts, and the lyrics and fragmentary narratives of the volume as a whole are probably most closely in line, among

Morris's poetic works, with modern, at least twentieth-century, tastes; but this work is in fact not typical. With his next project Morris establishes what will become the dominant line in his work, his own particular poetic signature: the extended narrative. *The Life and Death of Jason* (1867), the enormous cycle of poems *The Earthly Paradise* (3 vols., 1868–70) and *The Story of Sigurd the Volsung and the Fall of the Niblungs* (1876) form the bulk of Morris's poetic output (beyond this there only remain 'Love Is Enough' (1873), another, more extended masque, 'The Pilgrims of Hope', itself an extended narrative, and the miscellaneous collection of *Poems by the Way* (1891)).

Walter Pater in an important 1868 consideration of *Jason* and the first volume of the *Paradise* is at pains to distinguish between *Guenevere* and these later works – and there are distinctions to be made – the first a 'thing tormented and awry with passion' and 'convulsed intensity', its imagery 'intricate and delirious', the work which followed a matter of 'simple elementary passions', and 'a tranquil level of perfection', a movement 'from dreamlight to daylight'; but to our twenty-first-century eyes and ears the similarities may be more striking than the differences.[2] After *Guenevere* certainly Morris's materials are consistently drawn from further back in time, embodying the 'grace of Hellenism relieved against the sorrow of the middle age' in Pater's lovely phrase, or with regard to *Sigurd* the spirit and force of ancient Teutonic and Icelandic lore relieved against that same, later sorrow – and on these grounds alone, perhaps, by virtue of this deepened historical perspective, these later works merit less fully the designation 'Pre-Raphaelite', although certainly too they are consistent with the core principles of Pre-Raphaelite imagination in their apparent purging of post-Renaissance forms and subject matter, and their interest in the cultural politics of great leaps backward.[3] Again, throughout, 'No single idea about it seems to have even the slightest reference to any modern thought or feeling', as is observed in the *Sunday Times* with regard to *Jason*, even as the same review hails the poem as 'profoundly original', and thus, one would think, the very fruit of modern thought and feeling (as Pater himself points out).[4]

Jason is conceived initially as one of the tales composing *The Earthly Paradise*, but growing too big for that purpose (it is a poem in seventeen books) and being published separately, first, becomes a sort of vast antechamber to the main work which follows. Both *The Earthly Paradise* and *Sigurd the Volsung* are poems that aspire to a high degree of comprehensiveness. In *Sigurd* this means a gathering of Icelandic, Scandinavian and Germanic lore surrounding a foundational chain or collection of stories, a kind of multi-generational primal family saga, the 'Great Story of the North, which should be to all our race [i.e. the British] what the Tale of Troy was to the Greeks' (vol. VII, p. 286). (Morris also published his own translations of *The Odyssey* (1887), and *The Aeneids of Vergil* (1876), but after the *Paradise* his literary gaze tends more to the north.) In the *Paradise* the net is cast even more widely, and the scale of the work is even more colossal, taking in virtually all of European story culture, from the Mediterranean to the Scandinavian. This is work that is hard to appreciate by excerpts – it demands an immersion that anthologies, by their nature, and our own modern and post-modern reading habits militate against – which is another dimension of Morris's insistence that the modern and the beautiful live in two different worlds.

The Earthly Paradise is also where Morris makes his most explicit and extended engagement with the question of – the relation between – past and present in his work. The poem's three volumes comprise twenty-four sizeable tales drawn mostly from classical Greek and northern European (Gothic or Scandinavian) mythologies, with a few other sources (for example French and Persian) represented as well, all framed by a twenty-fifth tale, a story of Morris's invention involving fourteenth-century Norwegian mariners fleeing the Black Death then decimating Europe – a framing story framed in turn by the poet's direct reflections on his own work, and in particular on the fraught relation between his own time and the medieval or classical ages from which his tales, and the spirit of their telling, are drawn. This is a relation, again, of utter distances and inextinguishable, if almost imperceptible, persistences – the past, in other words, is gone, but with a sufficient degree of alienation we will be able to catch its faint strains sounding still – a situation of feeble hope, but hope nonetheless. In the case of *The Earthly Paradise*, this is a hope extended over a year's worth of tales, the poem as a whole structured in pairs of tales for each month of the year, and so not an inconsiderable achievement, however feeble or 'empty' the result.

'The idle singer of an empty day' is how the poet of the *Paradise* identifies himself; the line, which repeats throughout the poem's framing apparatus, comes in effect to represent Morris's essential being as a poet – it becomes his reputation. The singer is idle in the sense that he effects no change, and does not even claim to address in the least way anything real at all. As he puts it in the opening lines of 'An Apology', with which the poem begins:

> Of Heaven or Hell I have no power to sing,
> I cannot ease the burden of your fears,
> Or make quick-coming death a little thing,
> Or bring again the pleasure of past years,
> Nor for my words shall ye forget your tears,
> Or hope again for aught that I can say,
> The idle singer of an empty day. (Lines 1–7)

'The heavy trouble, the bewildering care / That weighs us down who live and earn our bread, / These idle verses have no power to bear' (lines 15–17). The idle singer, a 'Dreamer of dreams, born out of my due time', will not 'strive to set the crooked straight' (lines 22–3). All of which frames the Paradise as a kind of escape – a 'murmuring rhyme' of 'names remembered' – or at least a refuge,

> a shadowy isle of bliss
> Midmost the beating of the steely sea,
> Where tossed about all hearts of men must be;
> Whose ravening monsters mighty men shall slay,
> Not the poor singer of an empty day. (Lines 38–42)

The day is empty for precisely the reason that the singer can only be idle: because there is nothing to be done, no hope of any action, in the modern world, no tale of it fit for telling – all steely sea and ravening monsters, fears and tears, death and loss.

Even so, it is the modern world so resolutely shoved aside here that frames the whole enterprise. When the long 'Prologue' about the Norwegian mariners begins 'Forget six counties overhung with smoke, / Forget the snorting steam and piston stroke, / Forget the spreading of the hideous town' (lines 1–3), the matter could not be clearer: the modern world is reduced to three bold strokes, chosen for their exemplary quality of being impossible to forget – unless one is blind, or deaf, or numb unto insensibility (which, it seems, we 'latter day' people by and large are, in Morris's view). The idle singer 'dream[s]' of London, small, and white, and clean' instead, and spins the medievalisms of his twenty-five tales as a kind of spell to keep his own trance going. The only possible response to the modern world here is to get out of it – Baudelaire, around the same time, is coming to similar conclusions – and the only possibility of escape is in the form of an enveloping dream. This is critique in the form of surrender.

Sigurd the Volsung, which follows *The Earthly Paradise*, is the most prominent example of Morris's deep, abiding interest in Northern literatures and cultures, which produced as well a prose translation of *Grettis Saga* (1869) among other pieces, in addition to two *Journals of Travel to Iceland* (1871, 1873), and strong echoes in the landscapes and cultural formations of the late full-length prose romances, especially in the first two, *A Tale of the House of the Wolfings* (1889) and *The Roots of the Mountains* (1890). *Sigurd* itself is epic in scope, linking several key stories from various Northern traditions in a multi-generational, multi-cultural saga of virtually continuous betrayal and destruction – of people and peoples – over the course of some five thousand rolling (or hammering) hexameter couplets. The North as a cultural reference point is something Morris shares, of course, with many Victorian writers and artists – the Gothic Revival in architecture, with which Morris was closely concerned, had broad cultural resonance – but for Morris, again, the North functions specifically, in *Sigurd* and these other works, as an alternative conception of society. The past in these works speaks to the English present as at once its foundation and negative space, its anti-world. In *Sigurd*, the story of gold-lust, and the curse of the Rheingold, not to mention the supernatural and highly stylized eroticism in the wooing and tragic demise of Sigurd and Brynhild, is readily subject to various nineteenth- and twentieth-century readings, whether (for shorthand) Marxist or Freudian to begin with; but the understanding of gold, and of personal and societal doom, in *Sigurd* is essentially medieval, a sort of storehouse (or crystal ball) of obsolete values and knowledge, and for Morris therein lies its indispensable value.

Sigurd the Volsung marks a kind of turning point in Morris's literary career, virtually at the midpoint of its forty-year span. From this point forward poetry ceases to be his primary mode of literary expression. The same year in which *Sigurd* is published, 1877, Morris delivers the first of an extensive series of lectures on the arts, their crucial importance to human life and society, and their grievous, nigh terminal contemporary condition – this first one called 'The Decorative Arts', later published as 'The Lesser Arts'. These lectures, and the essays in many cases based on them, form one critical core of his literary activity through to the end of his career. (The key collections are *Hopes and Fears for Art* (1882) and *Signs of Change* (1888).) His other central work in this period, in addition to these explicitly didactic works, is also in prose, although more or less all under the heading of prose fantasy, some of it explicitly socialist in nature (most importantly *News from Nowhere* (1890) and 'A Dream of John Ball' (1888)), and much of it, as mentioned previously, framed with no apparent reference to politics of any kind, a type of return to the vaguely medieval magical world of the *Oxford and Cambridge Magazine* stories, conceived at something more like epic scale.

The lectures and essays are where the critique underlying Morris's work from the start becomes explicit. Already in 'The Decorative Arts' we have passages like:

> Is money to be gathered? cut down the pleasant trees among the houses, pull down ancient and venerable buildings for the money that a few square yards of London dirt will fetch; blacken rivers, hide the sun and poison the air with smoke and worse, and it's nobody's business to see to it or mend it: that is all that modern commerce, the counting-house forgetful of the workshop, will do for us herein. (Vol. XXII, p. 24)

Later in the talk he characterizes commerce as 'war commercial' and speaks of 'the Curse of labour', when men are either 'servants' or 'masters', all in the course of pursuing his argument regarding the ugliness of the world (pre-eminently in London and other large cities), and in particular the decay of quality in the decorative or ornamental arts in modern times, and the very distinction between decorative and fine, or higher art that is part – both cause and effect – of that decay (vol. XXII, p. 26). By 1879 in 'The Art of the People' he is speaking of the necessity 'to the further progress of civilization that men should turn their thoughts to means of limiting, and in the end doing away with, degrading labour' (vol. XXII, p. 45). By 1883 – when Morris joins the Social Democratic Federation, one of the first social-ist organizations to take shape upon Marx's death, and in part under the aegis of Engels's presence in London in the early 1880s – in lectures like 'Art, Wealth, and Riches' and 'Art Under Plutocracy' the analysis becomes expli-citly socialist and remains so until the end. 'Art: A Serious Thing' in 1882 ends with a vision of 'the track of waste and squalor which the misnamed monster Commerce leaves behind him now', and a call to 'join me I beg of you in hastening forward the day when the motto of our country and of all countries shall be "one for all, and all for one"'[5] and in 'Art Under Plutocracy' he announces his membership in 'a Socialist propaganda' and begs 'those of you who agree with me to help us actively, with your time and your talents if you can, but if not, at least with your money as you can' (vol. XXIII, pp. 190–1). In 'How We Live and How We Might Live' (1884), 'Useful Work vs. Useless Toil' (1886) and many other pieces, Morris's ana-lysis of the arts and their impact on human society and life is framed not only by the native British socialist tradition of Ruskin and Carlyle, which has been a crucial frame of reference for him from the beginning, but by Marx as well, and the revitalization of art is linked to full-scale economic and political revolution.

The arts, in the end, in Morris's view, consist of virtually everything that is not Nature: all the works of human hands, from transformations of the landscape and environment, to architecture and its attendant design handi-crafts, including textiles and furnishings of all kinds – not to mention paint-ing, poetry and so on. When considering the process by which any of these transformations or objects come to be – from fields to factories ('A Factory as It Might Be' is one of his lectures) to chairs and books, wallpaper and spoons – Morris starts from a number of simple principles drawn from his own lifelong practice as an artist, designer, craftsman and businessman, as much as from his study of 'Art and Industry in the Fourteenth Century' (lecture title from 1887) or his reading of *Capital*. The formula he presents in 'The Beauty of Life' (1880) comes as close as any one statement to the fundamental principle: art once was and should be, he argues, *made by the people and for the people as a joy for the maker and the user* (vol. XXII, p. 58, Morris's italics). From this fount flows all the rest, from approaches to design and craft and manufacture concerns, to labour conditions, questions of ownership and the profit motive, all of which latter considerations threaten that 'joy', the 'compound pleasure in handiwork I claim as the birthright of all workmen' (vol. XXIII, pp. 174–5). '[T]he aim of art [is] to destroy the curse of labour by making work the pleasurable satisfaction of our impulse towards energy, and giving to that energy hope of producing something worth its exercise' (vol. XXIII, p. 91); when such is the case, or to the extent that such is the case, the result is beautiful, and when the case is otherwise – largely through constraints on the freedom of the individual workman, imposed by economic arrangements given over to radical inequalities of wealth and the enslavement, in economic terms, of the many by the few – the result is, in Morris's term, 'a makeshift' at best, an eyesore or horror at worst.

News from Nowhere: Or, an Epoch of Rest, Being Some Chapters from a Utopian Romance is essentially a picture of the world run according to such principles. Socialist thought provides the framework, and an explanation of how we get there – the book begins in contemporary Victorian London with arguments at a meeting of the Socialist League, then enters a 'dream' of twenty-first-century English life following a socialist revolution – but the world this revolution creates is a world in which all labour is transformed into art as Morris conceives it: a matter first of pleasure, and compensation in itself. The book links this essential transformation in the relation of a worker to his or her labour, the transformation in some sense of all workers into artists, to a wide range of other social transformations, from the ways people dress and shop to the relations between genders, religion and the entire apparatus of governance – and of course to the beauty of the man-made world. The view from the river Thames, for instance, just 'last night' dominated by 'the soap-works with their smoke-vomiting chimneys', 'engineer's works', 'lead-works' and 'riveting and hammering [coming] down the west wind', now is dominated by an extraordinary bridge:

> I had perhaps dreamed of such a bridge, but never seen such an one out of an illuminated manuscript; for not even the Ponte Vecchio at Florence came anywhere near it. It was of stone arches, splendidly solid, and as graceful as they were strong; high enough also to let ordinary river traffic through easily. Over the parapet showed quaint and fanciful little buildings, which I supposed to be booths or shops, beset with painted and gilded vanes and spirelets. The stone was a little weathered, but showed no marks of the grimy sootiness which I was used to on every London building more than a year old. (Vol. XVI, p. 8)

Somewhere between a novel and a treatise, or a systematic dream explanation, *News from Nowhere* is perhaps where Morris most fully synthesizes his multifarious preoccupations with art, history and radical politics; certainly it is the most nakedly modern of his works, although even here, in the future, the world feels decidedly pre-industrial.

The other prose romances of this late period depict worlds markedly pre-industrial, too, but lack the utopian socialist framework of *News from Nowhere*. If these late works have a political dimension at all, it is only on the most generalized level; they do not engage with current debates and contemporary struggle. Even *The House of the Wolfings*, which tells the tale of a Gothic people (identified significantly as a strongly communal people) heroically resisting imperial Roman conquest, and thus is fully open to a political reading, nevertheless functions more as a mythic tale of loss and transcendence, a tale of archetypes, an 'ancient glimmer' seen 'across the waste that hath no way' (vol. XIV, p. 1), the waste, that is, of time; and in the later works, where time and place and peoples are altogether more indeterminate, this mythic dimension is even plainer. *The Glittering Plain* (1890), the first of these, is paradigmatic: a love tale and a quest tale like all of them, involving (in this case) a journey to a land where people gain immortality – at a price – this is a narrative that seems to want to cast a spell rather than to identify any contemporary problem or propose any solution. That the language of these books is relentlessly (if unostentatiously) archaic adds to the effect: the modern world is willed away as fully as in 'The Story of the Unknown Church'.

In a letter of 1856 to a friend Morris writes:

> I can't enter into politico-social subjects with any interest, for on the whole I see that things are in a muddle, and I have no power or vocation to set things right in ever so little a degree. My work is the embodiment of dreams in one form or another.[6]

Certainly socialism gives Morris a way to imagine setting things right that is not available to him in 1856, and he will come to 'enter into politico-social subjects' with a vengeance; but 'the embodiment of dreams', if we lay equal weight on both 'embodiment' and 'dreams', remains an apt characterization of Morris's entire career. These might be dreams of revolutionary transformation of society, embodied by his work for the Socialist League and other organizations, or dreams of a pre-modern (which is to say pre-industrial, pre-capitalist) world, long gone yet still seen clearly, in the form of poems and prose narratives (not to mention tables and tapestries), the germ of hope in either case (revolutionary or antiquarian) that the modern world itself – this 'counting-house on the top of a cinder-heap' – is only a spell after all, and that spells can be broken.[7]

NOTES

1 William Morris, *The Collected Works of William Morris, with Introductions by his Daughter May Morris*, 24 vols. (London: Longmans, Green & Co., 1910–15), vol. XXIII, pp. 279–80 (volume and page references hereafter in text).
2 Peter Faulkner (ed.), *William Morris: The Critical Heritage* (London and Boston: Routledge & Kegan Paul, 1973), pp. 80, 82, 84, 86.
3 Ibid., p. 88.
4 Ibid., p. 52.
5 William Morris, *The Unpublished Lectures of William Morris*, ed. Eugene LeMire (Detroit, MI: Wayne State University Press, 1969), p. 53.
6 William Morris, *The Collected Letters of William Morris*, ed. Norman Kelvin, 4 vols. (Princeton, NJ: Princeton University Press, 1984–96), vol. I, p. 8.
7 Vol. XXII, p. 280.

14

IMOGEN HART

The designs of William Morris

Morris the Pre-Raphaelite

William Morris was determined to make the world a more beautiful place. The previous chapter cited one of Morris's most famous sayings: 'Apart from the desire to produce beautiful things, the leading passion of my life has been and is hatred of modern civilization.'[1] In that context, the second half of this quotation was of highest importance. Here, however, the first half deserves attention. Most of Morris's life was spent responding to his 'desire to produce beautiful things'. The 'things' Morris made were usually what we would categorize as 'decorative art', but Morris's work also challenged the divisions previously drawn between the 'fine' and the 'decorative'. Working as a visual artist with his Pre-Raphaelite friends from his student days in the 1850s, Morris not only found an outlet for his urge to create beauty, but also developed another principle that would define his career: the ideal of collaboration. Through collaboration, Morris furthered his goal of combining the arts, not only the 'fine' and the 'decorative', but also the visual and the literary.

Whether we understand Pre-Raphaelitism as a historical phenomenon or as a state of mind it is a helpful concept when dealing with Morris. His work fits the bill if we define Pre-Raphaelitism as characterized by a disillusionment with contemporary artistic practice that manifests itself in the evocation of an imagined medieval period, specifically pre-Renaissance, when art was freely expressive and lacked the homogenizing polish perceived to characterize the prevailing style ever since Raphael. Historically speaking, Morris was also a member of the Pre-Raphaelite 'circle'. While studying at Oxford, Morris came into contact with Dante Gabriel Rossetti through his friend Edward Burne-Jones. With Rossetti and Burne-Jones Morris was involved in a broad range of artistic projects, from minor experiments to major commissions. For example, joined by other painters, the three took on the task of painting murals in the Oxford Union in the summer of 1857, despite Morris's lack of experience as a painter. Fiona MacCarthy, Morris's most recent biographer, suggests that Rossetti perceived his association with Morris and Burne-Jones as 'a Pre-Raphaelite Brotherhood of the second phase'.[2]

It was thanks to Rossetti's encouragement that, from 1856, Morris had briefly taken up painting as a new vocation in place of architecture. The influences that surrounded Morris the painter, in addition to Rossetti and Burne-Jones, included Arthur Hughes, one of whose pictures, *April Love* (1855–6, Tate), Morris bought in 1856, and who also contributed to the Oxford Union murals. In the same year Morris moved from Oxford to London, where he lived with Burne-Jones first on Upper Gordon Street and then at Red Lion Square. Morris's only extant painting, *La Belle Iseult* (1858, Tate), a portrait of Jane Burden (whom he would marry the following year), was produced during his time at Red Lion Square, and in it Pre-Raphaelite qualities are clearly visible. Its subject – an Arthurian legend – as well as its style – characterized by flat surfaces, constricted space and bright colours – combine with the depiction of a loose, uncorseted dress and abundant flowing hair to stamp this image as a homage to a time when painting and society were unconstrained by the rules that, in the eyes of the Pre-Raphaelites, suffocated Academic art and Victorian life.

Having abandoned architecture and painting, Morris found his calling in the decorative arts. In 1861 he co-founded a decorating firm, Morris, Marshall, Faulkner & Co. with six partners: Burne-Jones, Rossetti, Ford Madox Brown, Philip Webb, Charles Faulkner and Peter Paul Marshall. Hughes, who was originally an eighth partner, withdrew at an early stage. In 1875 Morris took over the firm on his own, changing the name to Morris & Co. Having been immersed in Pre-Raphaelitism at the beginning of his career, Morris continued to uphold many of the ideals developed during this early period, particularly in his commitment to beauty and to a collaborative model of production, in his work for the firm and beyond.

'The desire to produce beautiful things'

Morris imagined – and to some extent realized – a world in which people did not have to go to museums and galleries to find beauty. His ideal system, which he came less close to achieving, did not encourage individuals to amass beautiful things in private homes either. Instead, beauty would be a public matter. 'If we were all socialists', Morris explained, beautifully printed, decorated and bound books, for example, would be found in public libraries 'at each street corner'.[3] While this scenario was, Morris admitted, dependent upon a social revolution some time in the future, he was able, in the Victorian present, to take some small steps towards making beauty an aspect of everyday life.

In Morris's early career as a decorator, the focus was mainly on objects on a rather grand scale. Monumental painted furniture and stained glass were the forte of the fledgling Morris, Marshall, Faulkner & Co. Consequently, many of the firm's first commissions were for churches or public spaces such as the South Kensington Museum (ancestor of the Victoria and Albert Museum). The firm's output grew, however, to incorporate objects more easily accommodated by a domestic interior, such as wallpapers and textiles. Whether produced for churches, palaces or houses, Morris's objects rarely set themselves aside as things to be contemplated as 'art'. Even in the case of the South Kensington Museum, the commission was for a refreshment room – the Green Dining Room – and thus a space conceptually different from the galleries in which visitors would encounter 'art'. The fact that the press enthusiastically promoted the Green Dining Room (1867) as a worthwhile destination in itself bears witness to the firm's success in bringing beauty to unexpected places.[4]

For Morris, two things were beautiful above all: nature and medieval art. These two sources of inspiration manifest themselves in most of his work in the visual arts. In the tasks he undertook alone, such as the designing of wallpaper patterns, nature took centre stage, while in the collaborative projects in which he participated, Morris brought his love of nature to the 'decorative' aspects of the design: the grasses under the feet of Burne-Jones's figures, the flowers through which Philip Webb's woodland creatures frolicked or the vine weaving itself along the margins of a Kelmscott Press volume. Morris consistently returned to natural forms as the basis of decoration. The influence of the medieval is similarly ubiquitous in Morris's artistic life. On Upper Gordon Street he had lived, in Burne-Jones's words, 'in the quaintest room in all London, hung with brasses of old knights and the drawings of Albert [sic] Dürer'.[5] Together with Rossetti and Burne-Jones he painted the substantial, heavy furniture that he himself had designed and commissioned for Red Lion Square. These pieces were described by Rossetti and by the cabinet-maker who executed the designs as 'medieval'.[6] At the same time, this furniture, Morris's first experiment with domestic decoration, has the simplicity of form that would later become associated with the proto-modern aspects of the Arts and Crafts movement, of which Morris is usually considered a founder. The Oxford Union murals, meanwhile, to which he contributed during the same period, were based on Thomas Malory's *Le Morte d'Arthur* (1485). Later, the work of Morris's firm would be labelled – sometimes enthusiastically, sometimes scornfully – as 'medieval', and even towards the end of his career, Morris's art was still perceived as evoking a bygone era. While we might expect that the ongoing influence of nature and the medieval would make Morris's work monotonous, a subtly different interpretation of those sources is offered in each of Morris's designs, as we shall see.

In Morris's visual art, nature and the medieval are often inseparable. One of his earliest designs was *Daisy*, a simple repeating pattern featuring alternating clumps of flowers, which appeared first in red and yellow on blue serge, embroidered by his wife, Jane, and others in the early 1860s, and shortly afterwards in a wallpaper for the firm (1864). Along with other early works, including the first embroidery he designed and worked himself, *If I Can* (1856–7), the *Daisy* pattern was based on a fifteenth-century illuminated manuscript, Froissart's *Chronicles*.[7] Appearing frequently in Morris's work, the motto 'If I Can', or, in its French translation, 'Si je puis', was his tribute to medieval artist Jan van Eyck (c.1390?–1441), who famously employed the Flemish phrase 'Als Ich Kan' (see p. 40 above). Morris often approached nature via the medieval by employing the stylistic treatment of natural forms he found in medieval sources.

Nature and the medieval, of course, are also two of the hallmarks of Pre-Raphaelitism. We could see the dominant swirling acanthus leaves in Morris & Co.'s *The Forest* tapestry (1887) as the 'decorative' equivalent of Millais's meticulous undergrowth in *Ophelia* (1851–2, Tate). In each work, the leaves, as carefully rendered as the figures, refuse to take a subordinate role in the composition. These verdant plants seem animated and mobile, surrounding and even beginning to obscure each scene's supposed protagonists. Morris's shallow, unshaded patterns, meanwhile, including his *Kennet* furnishing textile (1883), echo the scandalously flat forms of an early Rossetti. In both cases, Renaissance modelling and chiaroscuro are shunned. In place of perspective and illusion we find simple outlines and intense colours: the startling brightness of Holman Hunt's *The Hireling Shepherd* (Figure 8), for example, mirrors the richness of the natural dyes developed by Morris for his firm.

What was it about nature and the medieval that Morris so admired? There was certainly an important political dimension to his preferences. Nature was honest (unlike deceptive veneers, for example), freely available to all (at least in an ideal world), and timeless (and so could be accommodated to utopian visions). The medieval period, meanwhile, witnessed the flourishing of the guilds, which Morris, along with John Ruskin, perceived as models of cooperative craftsmanship. Whether it was independent of, or because of, these political advantages, Morris's admiration for nature and the medieval seems also to have been a matter of taste. Morris enjoyed being surrounded by nature and medieval forms, and he enjoyed making art that reminded him of those things. As sources of inspiration, they were also preferable to 'modern civilization', which, as we have seen, Morris detested.

Figure 17 Morris, Marshall, Faulkner & Co., *Jasmine* wallpaper, designed by William Morris and printed by Jeffrey & Co. from 1872. Photo © Victoria and Albert Museum, London.

'What is there in modern life for the man who seeks beauty?' Morris asked, rhetorically. 'Nothing – you know it quite well.'[8]

In his designs Morris found ways of evoking nature without direct imitation. Decorative patterns that created an illusion of three-dimensionality through excessive detail and shading were attacked by mid-century design reformers, who offered disciplined, flat, geometric designs in their place. Morris found a middle ground between these two extremes. His *Jasmine* wallpaper (c.1872), for example, is based on a strict overall composition (Figure 17). Circular clusters of seven blossoms appear at regular intervals, the recurring scroll keeps the jasmine under control and the darker shoots on the surface spread themselves evenly over the background to provide a sense of balance. At the same time, the complexity of the design, which consists of at least three layers, evokes the unpredictability and organicism of nature. The jasmine is interwoven with the underlying hawthorn, its leaves sometimes obliterating the hawthorn blossoms, and sometimes disappearing behind them. The composition suggests the wildness of natural growth while maintaining a sense of logic and unity.

Morris's treatment of flowers is consistent with A. W. N. Pugin's interpretation of medieval ornament. Pugin's comparisons of medieval and modern art inspired both Ruskin and Morris. In 1849, Pugin wrote that medieval artists 'disposed the leaves and flowers of which their design was composed into geometrical forms and figures, carefully arranging the component parts so as to fill up the space they were intended to enrich', whereas a modern artist 'would endeavour to give a fictitious idea of relief, as if bunches of flowers were laid on', employing 'shadow and foreshortening'.[9] By arranging the *Jasmine* pattern evenly across the surface of the wallpaper, as discussed above, Morris again follows the medieval precedent. Morris's love of the medieval may have been partly due to the fact that, in Pugin's words, 'Nature supplied the medieval artists with all their forms and ideas.'

Though his admiration for nature was serious, Morris was not oblivious to nature's capacity for humour. This is clear from one of his most popular furnishing textiles, *Strawberry Thief* (1883), in which wide-eyed birds pause, as though freshly apprehended, with the fruit clasped firmly in their beaks. Morris was evidently alert to the diversity of nature and his designs embrace its different sides. There is a tendency to treat Morris's patterns as though they are interchangeable, or as though their variety lies only in stylistic disparities arising from Morris's interest in different visual influences over the course of his career. When we look closely, however, it becomes clear that each of Morris's designs is unique, communicating a distinctive meaning and atmosphere. In contrast to the light-hearted *Strawberry Thief*, or the calm *Jasmine*, *Pimpernel* is an example of a much more sombre and dramatic wallpaper. Morris used this pattern in his dining room at Kelmscott House, his London home from 1878 until his death in 1896. The thick stem, long, slippery leaves and large limp flowers of a poppy are arranged in a dominant scrolling formation. The design attests to the power of nature, just suggesting its terror, but balancing that suggestion with the reassurance of the more cheerful pimpernel flowers that fill the spaces in between the surging poppy stems. Beauty, for Morris, was not restricted to pleasant peacefulness. It could be found, his designs declared, in all the colours and moods of nature: the bright, the playful and the dark.

In exploring the bizarre, humorous and disquieting aspects of nature, Morris follows a medieval precedent. Morris's birds, for example, evoke the grotesque. The splayed legs, protruding claws and contorted necks of the peacocks in *Peacock and Dragon* (1878) emphasize the oddness and clumsiness of creatures usually endowed with grace and elegance, particularly by Morris's contemporaries in the Aesthetic Movement, including James McNeill Whistler in his famous Peacock Room (1876–7, Freer Gallery of Art, Washington, DC). The open-beaked birds in *Peacock and Dragon* and other designs, such as *Strawberry Thief*, *Bird and Vine* (1879) and *Bird and Anemone* (1882), for example, also call to mind Gothic gargoyles. Although Philip Webb designed the birds and animals in many of Morris & Co.'s products, Morris wrote in 1877, 'I am studying birds now to see if I can't get some of them into my next design.'[10] While Webb is credited with designing the birds and animals in *Trellis* (1864) and *Brother Rabbit* (1880–1), for example, Morris incorporated birds into a number of his own designs, including *Bird* (1877–8), *Strawberry Thief* and *Peacock and Dragon*.[11]

Like the fauna that adorn the margins of medieval illuminated manuscripts, Morris's birds are full of character and entangled with twisting shoots, stems and flowers. A Morris wallpaper or textile design could be seen as ornament that has detached itself from an illuminated capital letter and taken on a life of its own, growing to fill the entire visual field. A glance at Morris's experiments with calligraphy illumination, in the *Odes of Horace* (1874), for example, reveals how easily a pattern could have flowed off the page to become a freestanding design.[12] Even an animal-free design, such as *Jasmine*, echoes medieval precedents in its interweaving, structured quality, as though originating from an ordered manuscript. Indeed, there is something allusively textual about a design like this. *Jasmine*'s visual rhythm combines with the curling effect of the thin, snaking jasmine stem to evoke writing. It is as though the design has been written across the paper, following an underlying logic but also expressing vitality and freedom, like creative yet controlled handwriting. We might therefore see Morris's patterns as an evolved form of manuscript illumination in which the text itself, though absent, is just under the surface.

'A work of art is always a matter of co-operation'

One of Morris's most important early collaborative projects was Red House (1860). Together with his architect friend Philip Webb, Morris planned and designed a home in Bexleyheath, Kent, for himself and his new bride, Jane Burden. The building itself was just the beginning. The task of furnishing and decorating the house formed part of the household's daily life. Embroideries, wall hangings, painted furniture, stained glass and tiles were among the objects created for Red House by Morris, Jane and their friends.

In many ways, Red House evoked a small medieval castle. The massive furniture designed for the house contributed to this impression. For example, the dresser in the dining room had three pitched roofs while the drawing room settle tripled as a means of access to the loft and a minstrels' gallery. On the settle-cupboard in the hall – another massive item with a peaked roof – was an unfinished painting depicting *Sir Lancelot Bringing*

Sir Tristram and the Belle Iseult to Joyous Gard. The medieval themes, the abundance of natural forms, especially flowers and leaves, the strong colours and the flatness of much of the decoration at Red House all relate visually to Pre-Raphaelitism.

We do not know how much of the decoration of Red House is of Morris's hand or design. To Morris such questions might well have seemed irrelevant. The advantages of teamwork were as obvious to Morris as was the need for beauty. In 1888 the Arts and Crafts Exhibition Society held its first exhibition, providing a forum for work in 'all kinds of very different materials' to be judged by the public 'upon strictly artistic grounds in the same sense as the pictorial artist'.[13] Morris is often credited with inspiring the Society's policy of naming everyone involved in the creation of an exhibit, including both designer and executant, but in fact Morris was ambivalent on this subject. As he explained in 1893, 'The object of the Arts and Crafts is to give people an opportunity of showing what they could do apart from the mere names of firms ... The executant generally gets in. It is impossible, besides, to give the name of everybody concerned in the production ... A work of art is always a matter of co-operation. After all, the name is not the important matter. If I had my way there should be no names at all.'[14]

Morris's work ethic was fundamentally collaborative, an ideal embodied in the medieval guilds. For Morris individual genius was less important than cooperation to produce the best possible result. Tapestry was one of the fields that required a collaborative approach. Morris was eager to emphasize the opportunities tapestry making offered for creativity on the part of his team: 'it is really freehand work, remember, not slavishly copying a pattern'. Being 'both by nature and training, artists, not merely animated machines', the weavers were allowed 'a considerable latitude in the choice and arrangement of tints'.[15] Of course, there was a tension between Morris's ideal and the reality of the market. The names of famous designers (particularly Morris and Burne-Jones) had, in fact, won customers for the firm.

Morris, Marshall, Faulkner & Co.'s first high-profile commission was very much a team effort. The Green Dining Room, although it incorporated painting, was entirely 'decorative' in Ruskin's sense, in that the paintings were 'fitted for a fixed place'.[16] They did not, however, simply evoke pre-Renaissance murals by artists such as Giotto (c.1267–1337), as the Oxford Union paintings had. Instead, the Green Dining Room was a complex interior scheme that wove together a number of components to create a harmonious whole. Different members of the firm were responsible for various parts of the decoration, but it was essential that these elements worked together. Collaboration was thus essential to the Green Dining Room's success.

Reconciling difference is a crucial aspect of Morris's practice in the visual arts. It is difficult enough to achieve a harmonious effect when one artist has complete control over a project. Indeed, Whistler sought praise for doing just that, arguing in his famous trial against Ruskin (1878) that a *Nocturne in Black and Gold* should be valued for its aesthetic wholeness independent of its content or lack thereof.[17] The challenge faced by Morris, Marshall, Faulkner & Co. was to achieve harmony despite not only accommodating more than one artist, but also blending a variety of media. From the beginning the firm marketed itself as unique in bringing together artists specializing in different techniques, thus achieving a rare unity of the arts.

This practice of combining objects, often in different media, was one of the most significant aspects of Morris's collaborative projects. The firm regularly undertook extensive interior decoration commissions. One of the most high-profile of these was 1 Holland Park, on which Morris & Co. worked between 1880 and 1888. Alongside the possessions of the Ionides family, who occupied the house, were displayed carpets, furniture, silks, wallpaper and other decorations. *The Forest* tapestry, for example, hung in the morning room, whose walls were covered with *Vine* wallpaper (1874). *Vine*'s bold scrolling formation echoes the emphatic, twisting acanthus leaves in *The Forest*, providing a sense of unity throughout the room. A wallpaper pattern that Morris & Co. advertised in 1883 as 'more decided' than, for example, the 'quiet' *Jasmine*, *Vine* stands up to, and maintains, the powerful tone of the space.[18] Its verticality also balances the pronounced horizontality of *The Forest*.

Collaborative projects did not cease, therefore, after the reconstitution of the firm in 1875, even though some members were no longer involved. For a variety of reasons, the ideal of collaborative craftsmanship had proved less compelling for his colleagues than it had for Morris himself. His co-founders seemed less inspired, too, by the range of media embraced by the firm at its outset. As far as some of the firm's partners, particularly Rossetti and Ford Madox Brown, were concerned, painting was always their number one priority. Yet Burne-Jones remained committed to the firm, continuing to provide designs for Morris & Co. after 1875, and interweaving his 'fine' and 'decorative' work. Many of the Merton Abbey tapestries feature his distinctive figures and the firm produced large-scale stained glass windows of his design. As we have seen, Webb remained an important collaborator in these years, designing birds and animals for some of the later textiles. John Henry Dearle, who joined the firm as an assistant in 1878, also made significant contributions to many of the firm's products. *The Forest* and *Adoration* (1888) tapestries, for example, are each credited to three artists: Morris, Webb and Dearle in the first case, and Morris, Burne-Jones and Dearle in the second. The *Adoration* design was so popular that ten versions were woven, despite the expense (£525). One critic's verdict bears witness to the success of the collaboration: 'The outlines of the design only are Mr Burne-Jones's, the colouring and the ornamentation being Mr Morris's, and very beautiful are all three – so perfect, indeed, in every detail, that there is nothing left to desire.'[19]

Two of Morris's most important collaborators were his wife Jane and their younger daughter May Morris, their older daughter Jenny having been effectively incapacitated by epilepsy since her teens. When newly married, Jane and William Morris worked together on a number of experimental projects. For instance, the *Daisy* curtains made for the bedroom at Red House in the early 1860s were a team effort. Jane found the indigo-dyed blue serge; Morris designed the flowers; and Jane, along with others including her sister, Bessie Burden, carried out the embroidery. Later, Morris's designs for embroidery were often worked by May, who herself produced many designs, and she took over the embroidery section of the firm in 1885.

Morris developed a new forum for teamwork when he founded the Kelmscott Press in 1891. He worked with illustrators and binders, and consulted friends in the printing industry, to produce the sixty-six books published by the Kelmscott Press, of which the most famous is the monumental *Works of Geoffrey Chaucer* (1896). Morris's aim in founding the Kelmscott Press was to produce beautiful books, and he did so by bringing together, as usual, nature and the medieval. Twenty-two of the titles printed were medieval works, including of course the *Chaucer*, as well as Jacobus de Voragine's *The Golden Legend* and Raoul Lefevre's *The Recuyell of the Histories of Troye* (both issued in 1892). Morris also printed as a separate publication Ruskin's chapter, 'On the Nature of Gothic', from *The Stones of Venice* (1851–3), which famously discusses the superiority of medieval craftsmanship. Not only the content, but also the books' visual features, were medieval in inspiration. For example, Morris developed his own types based on medieval models. Many pages had decorative borders filled with botanical patterns similar to Morris & Co.'s wallpaper and textile designs. The last book published by the Press before Morris's death was the Kelmscott *Chaucer*, a fitting finale for Morris, with its medieval subject matter and Gothic-inspired 'Troy' type, its origin in a collaborative working process, represented especially by Burne-Jones's integrated illustrations, and its Morris-designed borders based on interweaving natural forms.

The Pre-Raphaelites presented a number of challenges to contemporary artistic practice and one of these challenges was taken further by Morris than by the other figures discussed in this volume. More than any of his colleagues, Morris was interested in how Pre-Raphaelite ideals, particularly a renewed interest in nature and the medieval and a commitment to collaboration, could be extended beyond the fine arts. Morris pursued the idea of Pre-Raphaelitism as a way of life, by allowing it to inform the environment in which he lived and worked. In continuing to foreground nature and the lessons learned alongside his Pre-Raphaelite friends from medieval models, Morris took Pre-Raphaelitism forward with him into his new ventures, from the tiniest daisy, closely observed from nature, in a humble chintz or wallpaper, to the most elaborately illuminated manuscript book.

NOTES

1 William Morris, *The Collected Works of William Morris, with Introductions by his Daughter May Morris*, 24 vols. (London: Longmans, Green, & Co., 1910–15), vol. XXIII, p. 279.
2 Fiona MacCarthy, *William Morris: A Life for Our Time* (London: Faber & Faber, 1994), p. 115.
3 'The Poet as Printer: An Interview with Mr William Morris', *Pall Mall Gazette*, 12 November 1891, pp. 1–2 (reprinted in Tony Pinkney [ed.], *We Met Morris: Interviews with William Morris, 1885–96* [Reading: Spire Books, 2005], p. 56).
4 See, for example, *Building News*, 29 July 1870, p. 74; Sally-Anne Huxtable, 'Re-reading the Green Dining Room', in Jason Edwards and Imogen Hart (eds.), *Rethinking the Interior, c.1867–1896: Aestheticism and Arts and Crafts* (Aldershot, Hants.: Ashgate, 2010), chapter 1.
5 Quoted in MacCarthy, *William Morris*, p. 110.
6 Ibid., p. 118.
7 Caroline Arscott, *William Morris and Edward Burne-Jones: Interlacings* (New Haven and London: Yale University Press, 2008), pp. 87–9.
8 'Art, Craft and Life: A Chat with William Morris', *Daily News Chronicle*, 9 October 1893. London, Hammersmith and Fulham Archives, ref. DD/341/319 a–c.
9 A. W. N. Pugin, *Floriated Ornament: A Series of Thirty-One Designs* (London: Henry G. Bohn, 1849), unpaginated. See Derek W. Baker, *The Flowers of William Morris* (London: Barn Elms, 1996), p. 70.
10 William Morris to Thomas Wardle, 25 March 1877, in *The Collected Letters of William Morris*, ed. Norman Kelvin, 4 vols. (Princeton, NJ: Princeton University Press, 1984–96), vol. I, p. 358.
11 For attributions see Linda Parry (ed.), *William Morris*, exhibition catalogue (London: The Victoria and Albert Museum, 1996), pp. 206–23 ('Wallpapers').
12 William Morris, Edward Burne-Jones and Charles Fairfax Murray, *Odes of Horace* (Bodleian Library, MS. Lat. class e.38), illustrated in Parry (ed.), *William Morris*, p. 308.
13 Walter Crane, 'Introduction' to Arts and Crafts Exhibition Society, *Catalogue of the First Arts and Crafts Exhibition* (London, 1888), pp. 7, 5.
14 'Art, Craft and Life: A Chat with William Morris', *Daily News Chronicle*, 9 October 1893. Hammersmith and Fulham Archives, London, DD/341/319 a–c.
15 Quoted in Aymer Vallance, 'The Revival of Tapestry-weaving: An Interview with William Morris', *The Studio*, 3 (1894), p. 101.

16 'Modern Manufacture and Design' (1859), Ruskin, vol. XVI, p. 320.

17 Linda Merrill, *A Pot of Paint: Aesthetics on Trial in Whistler v. Ruskin* (Washington and London: Smithsonian Institution Press in association with the Freer Gallery of Art, 1992), pp. 143–4, 153–4.

18 Morris & Co., 'The Morris Exhibit at the Boston Foreign Fair' (Boston, 1883), London, National Art Library, ref. 276.C Box I, p. 19.

19 *The Queen*, 26 April 1890, cited in Parry (ed.), *William Morris*, p. 293.

15

CAROLINE ARSCOTT

Edward Burne-Jones (1833–1898)

Edward Burne-Jones was drawn into the Pre-Raphaelite circle in the latter half of the 1850s. He and William Morris, his close friend from Exeter College, Oxford, were in awe of the charismatic Dante Gabriel Rossetti and from letters and reminiscences we gain a vivid sense of the spell cast by the attractive Rossetti with his sonorous, rolling speech patterns, intensity and urgency of manner and visionary projects. Rossetti, whose work had caught their attention, responded to the young enthusiastic Burne-Jones who tracked him down in London at a meeting of the Working Men's College. Later Burne-Jones was to describe himself in the following period as 'clinging tight to Gabriel whom I loved, and would have been chopped up for'.[1] The earnest valuation of friendship, the jokingly hyperbolic statement and the startling image of a wounded and dispersed self are all characteristic of Burne-Jones.

Burne-Jones started to work in pen and ink, and embarked on a painting on the theme of *The Blessed Damozel*, deriving from Dante Gabriel Rossetti's poem, for the Leeds-based collector Thomas Plint. He also began to design church windows for the stained-glass company Powell and Son. Along with Morris he was in 1857 invited by Rossetti to participate in a decorative scheme for the Oxford Union debating chamber and established strong bonds with the array of young artists aiming to beautify the whitewashed walls with scenes in glowing colour based on stories from a book they loved, Malory's *Morte d'Arthur* (1485). With the establishment of Morris, Marshall, Faulkner & Co. in 1861, Burne-Jones continued his stained-glass work, undertook tile and embroidery design and painted furniture. He was also producing graphic work in the 1860s for periodicals and for the Dalziel Brothers' projected *Illustrated Bible*.

His career as a painter was decisively established when he was elected to the Old Water-Colour Society in 1864 and in the exhibition of that year he showed his large composition in the opaque water-based medium gouache, highlighting the picture with gold; this was *The Merciful Knight* (1863,

Birmingham Museums & Art Gallery), a somewhat controversial picture, the theme of which was the miraculous animation of a statue of Christ at a medieval shrine. The gloomy forest setting was offset by a blaze of brilliant marigolds below the shrine, and gleams of gold or brass on the dark armour of the praying knight. The knight is a solemn figure, constrained and hemmed in by the structures and accessories round about him. His moment of rapturous contact with God seems to be experienced in ascetic mode, modulated by pain or deprivation, and his prayerful stance signals submission. Operating in a largely Anglican environment Burne-Jones provoked the critics with this picture that had an emotional intensity which seemed suspiciously Roman Catholic, linking as it did piety, pain and magic.[2] His own religious beliefs were somewhat unorthodox, aligned neither with the Methodism of his wife's background nor with the Church of Rome, nor with the high church faction of the Church of England. A conviction of the importance of the divine remained with him throughout his life, though. The terrors and joys of experience that are conveyed in his work and the fascinating mystery that colours his scenarios have a spiritual aspect that is fundamental to his outlook.

Burne-Jones continued to work in a variety of media, developing his technique from the mid-1860s in oil paint as well as gouache. In all media his execution was meticulous, his attention to detail painstaking and his control over the total composition or design carefully judged. The tightness produced by the well-wrought surfaces and the busy, visually stimulating effects of detail in the closely studied material objects of the environment might have stultified or over-filled his work were it not for the strong sense of design that pulls the compositions into balanced decorative ensembles. Drawing from nature was a central principle of Pre-Raphaelite practice that shaped Burne-Jones's art. John Ruskin's views on beauty in actuality allowed Burne-Jones to find beauty in the quaint, the crabbed and the encrusted even more than in the regular, the flawless or the smooth. Typically he worked very slowly, having a number of projects on the go at any one time, and revisiting subjects that he had elaborated at an earlier date. Consequently his work on a project such as the *Briar Rose* series (1870–90, Faringdon Collection, Buscot Park), based on the Sleeping Beauty story, spanned several decades starting with a tile series in 1864.[3] He drew his subjects from literature, folklore and mythology, attending to the retelling of tales in poetry by Tennyson and his friend William Morris and presenting scenes that mixed classical and medieval elements.

The turreted buildings and richly ornamented woodwork and metalwork of his scenes, the marble surfaces, the patterned textiles and costumes that he elaborates, the gnarled trunks, twisting stems and abundant blossom of his plants, the jagged striated rocks of his uncanny landscapes all contribute to the intricate realization of a fairy-tale or horror-fiction world. The specificity of setting and accoutrements is essential for his project which depends upon the eloquence of circumstance in place of speaking gestures and explicit interaction between characters. We gain an insight into his attitude to the objective world when we hear of him sending back the work of an aspirant painter exclaiming that it was essential that the ground on which the figure stands be specified. 'Is it earth or bricks or stone or carpet?' he asked.[4] Burne-Jones cared above all for story and for the conflicts, heartache and joys of human adventure and love. However, paradoxically, he adopted a mode in which human action is subdued, sometimes stilled altogether. In his pictures figures stand or sit, their poses limp and enervated, their expressions wistful or vacant and dreamy. Their bodily experience and their personal beauty are emphasized at the cost of indications of psychological coherence and moral standing. The minimal indications of will or motivation make the compositions hard to read in narrative terms, indeed it is difficult to imagine his figures as the suave or doughty heroes and passionate heroines of myth, or the complicated, scheming individuals of the realist novel. In a form of displacement the story is invested in the setting. I would contend that the unique quality of Burne-Jones's work lies in this summoning up of a hyperbolically storiated landscape that buoys up the perplexingly vacant characters.

Stories and objects were in many ways interchangeable in Burne-Jones's imagination. This is why he described the Bible's Book of Kings to his son Philip as 'a glorious heap of antiquity', visualizing it as a three-dimensional accumulation of items.[5] The jumble of disconnected episodes, the proliferation of personnel and circumstances, the quaintness of incidental detail are piled up just as robes, crowns, ritual vessels and masonry might be. Equally landscape itself could be imbued with meaning through historical circumstance and the more moving and dramatic the events the more beautiful the landscape. Therefore tranquil landscape free of significant reference points could not be beautiful to him. The soft landscape of Surrey was anathema to him; his verdict on it was that it was 'too soft … like a silly heaven'. He went on to say 'Now and then I want to see Hell in a landscape … at such a point was such a battle … by that tower was such a combat … in that tower such a tragedy'.[6] In the repetition of 'such' the continuum of the scene is broken. Specific events are linked to specific landscape elements. Effectively the material forms of landscape become the keys to diverse meaningful actions and to the extremes of human experience. In the real world the passing of time concentrates historic episodes into a single location and in Burne-Jones's compositions there is an equivalent concentration of meaning, a condensation of the gamut of emotions and the chronicles of bloody deeds or selfless actions in the objects that crowd the visual field.

Architectural and sartorial elements fulfil this function even more insistently than natural forms. The artist draws attention to the forms and stuffs by detailing the structure. The way in which Burne-Jones specified the settings and the outfits of his figures, usually imagined in some pre-industrial era, involved him in virtual fabrication; he envisaged and showed the locking together of blocks in construction and the fixing together of fabrics in clothing and furnishing. Everywhere in his work he shows the conjoined edges of marble, the ridged settings for jewels, the torsion and welding of metal structures, the jointing of woodwork or interweave of twigs. In his work we can count the studs, the links and the laces. To achieve this literal presentation of the environment he studied from historical examples, evidenced by the pages of his sketchbooks, and sometimes went so far as to create models, for instance of armour, in cardboard, brass or tin. His involvement with the practical projects of Morris & Co., where decorative items were actually made for domestic or church use, can be said to govern his attitude to the material environment. He was exercising his imagination in a world of fabrication. We can recognize a second stage of piecing together, beyond the individual costumes, props or models, as the individual crafted elements of the environment are conjoined in the tightly managed space of the picture, producing an integrated composition which has the character of an artefact.

We can differentiate the investment in physical objects characteristic of Burne-Jones's art from the symbolic investment in items that is found in the work of his fellow Pre-Raphaelite William Holman Hunt. For both artists the irreducible physicality, the sheer material presence, of the thing was accompanied by a sense of the thing's potential to unlock meaning. The symbolic potential of the dying goat in Hunt's *The Scapegoat* (1856, Lady Lever Art Gallery, National Museums Liverpool), for instance, standing as it does for the crucified Christ and his assumption of the sins of mankind, is very different from the resonant meaningfulness of the material environment in Burne-Jones where the intimations of story, of love or of terror are never fully explicable. Suggestive mystery is produced by the speaking objects of Burne-Jones's pictured worlds. The complex, puzzle-world is cryptic but defies decryption. He was fond of an Irish legend about the poignant story of two separated lovers who left a record of their tragic love in inscriptions on two planks of wood. Years later a king ordered the two planks to be brought together from the far extremes of his kingdom so that he could view them in his hall. In the hall the two planks magically clamped together, the two inscribed surfaces meeting each other in an embrace never to be separated.[7] The objects and structures of Burne-Jones's pictures bear their narratives in an analogous way. Sometimes the indications of story are available on the surface, though the viewer may not have access to the whole of the story. At other times the crafted object seems to have enclosed the story in the inaccessible inner recesses of the thing. The object that bears a hidden message does not lose its narrative potential; it retains the possibility of being a declarative or speaking object but the story, message or declaration is occluded. In this way Burne-Jones achieves a kind of occult materialism, where mystery rather than purposeful didacticism is produced.

The Pre-Raphaelite commitment to the faithful transcription of existent forms derived from Ruskin's writings is maintained but transformed in Burne-Jones's art. There is a fidelity in his art, fidelity to the material substantiality of things which he depicts with scrupulous care. The truth-telling that he undertakes is not truth-telling about the random appearances of nature, its pattern and its thwarting, however. His descriptive powers are concentrated on the social environment, chambers, courtyards, gardens with their books, looms and musical instruments, or else their hangings, doorways and trellises. Where he moves beyond the garden or river meadow it is to explore the mythic equivalent of the social setting: a nature worked upon by deities or magicians. The objects depicted by Burne-Jones are therefore always liable to be worked, to be wrought upon by artisanal or magic skill and to fold in upon themselves to bar our access to the full story or to spring apart to reveal the secret soul.

We can take the example of the oil painting *The Beguiling of Merlin* (Figure 18), exhibited at the Grosvenor Gallery in 1877, as a work in which the folding in of nature under the spells of Nimuë threatens to capture the body of Merlin in the hawthorn bush. We see in that work a book of spells held open by Nimuë that can be snapped shut. Offered as a point of comparison, the semi-recumbent Merlin on the spreading limbs of the hawthorn tree is subject to the same potential enclosure. Indeed the pallor of his face seems already to have taken its place among the tightly clustered pale blossoms and the turn of his neck and shoulders, and especially the twist produced by the crossing of his dark-stockinged legs seems to participate in the dry twisting of the hawthorn trunk and branches. Burne-Jones in a letter about this picture imagines his own fate enchanted by a lover as akin to that of Merlin: 'I was being turned into a hawthorn bush in the forest of Broceliande – every year when the hawthorn buds it is the soul of Merlin trying to live again in the world and speak – for he left so much unsaid' (his reference is to his love affair with Maria Zambaco who sat for the figure of Nimuë).[8] We can conceive of many of the flowers that bud and bloom or are

Figure 18 Edward Burne-Jones, *The Beguiling of Merlin*, 1873–4, oil on canvas, 186 × 111 cm,
© Lady Lever Art Gallery, National Museums Liverpool/The Bridgeman Art Library.

gathered and strewn in the compositions of Burne-Jones as corresponding
to an effort at locution.

One example of flowering elements that are allied to an effort to speak
is the profuse almond blossom of another scene of metamorphosis, the
watercolour *Phyllis and Demophoön* (1870, Birmingham Museums & Art
Gallery). In this picture the flowering almond tree splits apart to release the
princess Phyllis who on her suicide, despairing of Demophoön's love, had
been turned into a tree. We can also point to the burgeoning flowers and
stems of the rose briar in all the pictures of the *Briar Rose* series, which
seem to correspond to the mental processes and physiological presence of
the princess sleeping an enchanted sleep within the castle.[9]

Burne-Jones worked with and against the conventional language of flowers, choosing to include a pansy and a book showing heartsease in the oil
portrait of his wife *Georgiana Burne-Jones* (commenced 1883, unfinished,
private collection) which drew on the conventional association of heartsease
(and the cultivated pansy) with loving thoughts and memory, along with the
legend of the change of colour brought about by the wounding of the heart

by Cupid's arrow. However Burne-Jones transformed the language of flowers in a curious form of reverse cypher in his album of watercolours, *The Flower Book* (1882–98, British Museum), where the poetic implications of flower names were realized by imagining the literal presence of the element referred to in the name. This led him to depict Danaë closely enclosed in the brazen tower for the plant known as Golden Shower (no. XVIII in the album), and the figures from his painting *The Beguiling of Merlin* for the plant known as Witches' Tree (perhaps elder, no. XV in the album). It is characteristic of Burne-Jones's imagination that the language of flowers can be made to work in two ways. The plant carries with it the code built up from legend and association. The motif of pansy, lily or rose gives access to that code. But the lexicon of floral names gives access to another set of legends and associations; the actual flower becomes the secret to be discovered. Burne-Jones therefore puts the flower in a double perspective. The cryptic is not just a matter of concealment and revelation: Merlin concealed, trapped inside a hawthorn bush struggling to speak through the opening blossoms, and Merlin in view, visibly fascinated by Nimuë. The flower, or indeed any element of the environment, is overdetermined; Burne-Jones's picture-craft is one that involves the layering or torquing of multiple elements.

Burne-Jones was hugely enthusiastic about historic and modern literature and his love of the stirring stories in Malory's *Morte d'Arthur* is well known. In the episodes recounted by Malory bodily battle and spiritual peril were conjoined. Equally important for him were the rousing and sentimental narratives of the modern novelist Charles Kingsley (1819–75).[10] In terms of the material environment that he recreates in his painting there are two less discussed literary sources, one historic and one modern, to which I wish to draw attention. I will be arguing that they each, in different ways, shed light on the inscrutable and yet speaking view of nature that he presents. These literary sources help us to recognize the Burne-Jones environment that snaps shut to trap its multiple secrets and yet seems as if it could be cranked open to expose the emotional core. The first of these is a book that has been identified as a source of fascination for him from the mid-1860s, the Renaissance text *Hypnerotomachia Poliphili* (authorship disputed, written in 1467, published in Venice by Aldus Manutius, 1499). He had a copy, probably given to him by William Morris and sourced in the shop of Frederick Ellis in Covent Garden.[11] The second literary reference point that can be seen as significant for his mode of engagement with the material environment is the fiction of Edgar Allan Poe (1809–49).

Hypnerotomachia Poliphili is an illustrated text telling of the dream experiences of the narrator as he makes his way through strange courtly environments where elaborate doorways, enclosures, monuments and ornamental structures appear in bewildering succession as he seeks his love, eventually embracing her in a secret garden before the dissipation of the dream.[12] The architectural specificity of the text and the illustrations allows the reader to imagine these constructions and spaces in a particularly material way: this is not hazy evocation, but a careful description of an enigmatic series of objects and spaces. Inscriptions in decipherable and indecipherable form are cut into the stonework, and transcribed or illustrated. Only a fraction of the powers and histories that are indicated are graspable by the narrator. The curious assemblages of items and symbols that constitute the monuments produce wonder – the speaking environment is produced by a grafting together of incommensurable items and by the piecing together of materials into novel architectural or sculptural form. The strange conjunctions are not experienced primarily as bizarre or uncanny, though, because it is fully recognized as an architecture and pageantry of power.

The degree to which Burne-Jones drew upon the illustrations of this work has not been fully recognized. Many of his compositions represent a reworking of visual formulae presented in *Hypnerotomachia Poliphili*. For instance his design of Chaucer sleeping (1862, for tiles on the theme of Chaucer's *Legend of Good Women*, and reworked in a number of different contexts) relates to the illustration of Poliphilio dreaming in chapter 3 of the book; *The Baleful Head* (1886–7, Staatsgalerie, Stuttgart), in *The Perseus Series* relates to the illustration of the hexagonal fountain in chapter 24 of the book; and the composition of *The Car of Love* (Victoria and Albert Museum, London) relates to the scene of Eros with bound nymphs drawing his chariot in chapter 27 of the book. These instances could be multiplied since many of Burne-Jones's compositions are reminiscent of scenes in *Hypnerotomachia Poliphili*; for instance *Danaë and the Brazen Tower* (1887–8, Glasgow Art Gallery and Museum, Kelvingrove) seems to owe something to the illustration that starts chapter 14. Penelope Fitzgerald points out the reliance on the book for Burne-Jones's work in 1866 on the compositions relating to the story of Pygmalion for the projected illustrated version of William Morris's *Earthly Paradise*.[13] I would suggest that Burne-Jones gained more than ideas for compositions, though, because the object world of the book spoke so strongly to his literalizing imagination. It offered him the possibility of a form of fiction in which the wonderful could be found without any loss of the literal.

As a modern and debased corollary I would draw attention to Burne-Jones's half-apologetic interest in the short stories of Poe in which Georgiana his wife reports that he maintained an interest throughout his life. He shared his enthusiasm for Poe with other members of the Pre-Raphaelite circle such as Dante Gabriel Rossetti. Burne-Jones wrote that they were 'marvellously startling' in their combination of the grand, the beautiful and the horrific. He said that there was 'a delicate refinement in all that hideousness' and expressed an interest in the way Poe offered an analysis of and identification with another's thinking.[14] In a story such as 'The Gold-Bug', which Burne-Jones admired, a search for treasure takes place with the aid of a document and a beetle. The alarming actions of the treasure hunter William Legrand seem delusional to his friend, and to be driven by magic from the point of view of his servant. The reader is allowed to shuttle between these possibilities; if the gold is revealed surely there is some very disturbing magic, or if none is found surely this is just psychotic behaviour. In fact the actions are driven by Legrand's ability to reveal a message in invisible ink on the document and to interpret the cryptogram (coded message) as a treasure map, correlating the features mentioned to the island's geographical features. The solution depends not on knowing more but on repeatedly, physically repositioning the subject to see differently. The outcome is the discovery of a stash of gold and jewels and a macabre group of skeletons thought to be Captain Kidd's labourers executed to ensure their silence. The rational is therefore no guarantor of an escape from horror.

Poe described a world in which banal and material parameters are inescapable, but one in which sudden shifts in perspective could swing the everyday into the supernatural and vice versa. Mystery is not a realm that is separated from the everyday. Looking differently at the everyday takes us straight to the magical or the sinister with the plunging emotional effects of wonder and fear. For Poe the shift in perspective is very often not so much a matter of insight into a person as a reorientation in terms of spatial coordinates. This extraordinary firmness with respect to space and materials is something that Burne-Jones is able to take from these widely divergent literary sources. From them he found a way of producing a chivalric-real where crowns, armour, ledges and lances could be crowded together in bewildering multiplicity, where the evidence of story and circumstance was inescapable and yet fully enigmatic.

One of Burne-Jones's most celebrated pictures instantiates this overdetermined, encrypted mode of composition in which information appears to be hidden by means of a secret system. *King Cophetua and the Beggar Maid* (Figure 19) was exhibited to considerable acclaim at the Grosvenor Gallery in 1884 and in Paris at the Exposition Universelle in 1889. The picture is based on a ballad telling the story of King Cophetua who spies a grey-garbed beggar maid from his window and is enamoured, suffering agonies of love and contemplating suicide. He proposes marriage to the trembling and astonished beggar maid. She accepts his proposal. When it comes to their wedding she behaves regally; their married life is happy,

Figure 19 Edward Burne-Jones, *King Cophetua and the Beggar Maid*, 1880–4, oil on canvas, 290 × 136 cm, Tate, London. © Tate, London, 2011.

both are dear to the courtiers and in death they are buried together in a single tomb.[15] Burne-Jones's composition relates loosely to an episode highlighted by Tennyson in his poem on the theme, 'The Beggar Maid' (1842). When the beggar maid comes to the court her beauty strikes all observers, shining out from her rags like the moon in clouded skies. The King comes down 'in robe and crown' to greet her and declares that he will make her his queen.

Nothing in either version exactly corresponds to the elevated position of the blankly staring beggar and the subordinate position of the patiently attentive, armoured King, shield and lance set aside and jewelled crown in hands. A viewer who is unfamiliar with the story might think that this is a depiction of unrequited love, supposing that the King is doomed to petition unsuccessfully and has been driven to renounce action and wealth for his love. In the gloomy bronze-clad interior the colour range is limited to steely greys and brownish copper and bronze tones and maroon. The pale body of the maid appears as an unearthly and luminous presence, perhaps in response to Tennyson's idea of the moon. The maid clutches a drooping bunch of anemones and some of the flowers lie isolated on the bronze-covered steps. These barely tinted, black-centred flowers are linked to her pale face with its dark-rimmed, lustrous eyes. Anemones were associated with modesty appropriately enough for the shrinking maid, but in classical mythology they were associated with the tears of Venus; they do not strike a joyous note in the picture.[16]

The enigma of the picture is set up by the non-interaction of the two main figures. The action is hard to read; fear, bewilderment, indecision, misery, wonder or steady resolve are equally credible interpretations for the figure of the maid. The King could be set in faithful adoration or be paralyzed by despair. The palace to which the King has brought the maid is suggestive of the tomb mentioned in the conclusion of the original ballad. The stepped and balustraded environment makes a metallic cage for both figures, equivalent to the cage-like structure of the crown which captures the King's fingers and making of the crown a cage within a cage. Particularly in the foreground the space is complex and puzzle-like as ground level is not established; moreover horizontal, burnished surfaces that serve for footholds show barely legible reflections of the violent scenes of battle and hunting that are embossed on the vertical portions of the enclosure. All these features make the picture one in which the material environment loses nothing of its objective existence and yet seems deeply mysterious.

The picture as a whole offers a cryptogram like the document in 'The Gold-Bug'. There is not one single method of interpretation that is made available but multiple frames that enclose the actors. The embossed ornament is Assyrian in derivation in many portions where vultures attack lions and lions attack winged beasts. The bronze-clad walls may owe something to the Assyrian Barawat Gates with embossed bronze friezes that came into the British Museum in 1878. The imagery picks up motifs from the carved reliefs (880–612 BC) that came to Britain from the excavations in the 1840s and 1850s at Nimrud. Burne-Jones is recorded as having the archaeologist Austen Henry Layard's account of the excavations, *Nineveh and Its Remains* (1848–9), at the age of eighteen in 1851.[17]

Elsewhere the ornament is Byzantine in reference, as in the textile hanging over the gallery. Paired peacocks stand as royal insignia on the bronze pillars at the level of the maid's head and are woven into textiles, for instance the King's cloak. On the pillars there are square portions of a script that resembles meroitic script (closely related to Egyptian hieroglyphs) at the level of the maid's upper arms. In a letter Burne-Jones mentions the 'thin, cheap books published by Samuel Bagster & Co., called "Records of the Past." Two numbers are out, one more due soon – they are translations of cuneiform and hieroglyph, and make one happy.'[18]

The space as a whole has clear references to Renaissance altarpieces; references to Mantegna, Crivelli and Pontormo have been pointed out.[19] The metallic environment was understood by some viewers in 1889 as a commentary on the high tech modern-day materialism of the Exposition Universelle which was dominated by the machine hall and the Eiffel Tower.[20] The embossed figures on the metal-clad walls might also be taken as referring to the horrific pictures of devils, 'pictured horrors of blood', which eventually glow red-hot on the ever-approaching walls of the prison cell in Poe's story 'The Pit and the Pendulum' (1842). Indeed King Cophetua can be thought of as caught between the pit that opens at his feet and the pendulum of the beggar maid's choice which swings lethally but without deliberate agency above him. The eclectic contexts are crowded together, indeed pinned together with hundreds of meticulously depicted little nails, in a method of construction which displays many speaking surfaces. Most of the ornament is very hard to see, though, and what can be seen is deliberately obscure. The viewer is left with the possibility that some elements are entirely hidden or fully enclosed so that the possibilities of decryption are lost for ever.

This one example gives us an insight into the way that Burne-Jones set up his fictive worlds and helps to explain the curious blend of the literal and the mystical that characterizes his work. He traced back a habit of mind to his schooldays. One master taught map drawing so that Burne-Jones could place all locations within the overview of the earth as if seen from a great height. This master encouraged the boys to expand from any single flat or banal sentence picked at random to cosmic associations by working on every separate word. In the 1890s Burne-Jones recalled 'with the flattest sentence in the world he would take us to ocean waters and the marches of Babylon and hills of Caucasus and wilds of Tartary and the constellations and abysses of space'.[21] The thrill of Burne-Jones's work is the finding of story in objects and environments by delving into all the individual elements. The poignancy of his work is the loss of locution as the objects close over the speaking surfaces.

NOTES

1 Penelope Fitzgerald, *Edward Burne-Jones* (1975) (London: Hamish Hamilton/ Penguin, 1989), p. 51.

2 Caroline Arscott, *William Morris and Edward Burne-Jones: Interlacings* (New Haven and London: Yale University Press, 2008), pp. 53–5.

3 Stephen Wildman and John Christian, *Edward Burne-Jones: Victorian Artist-Dreamer*, exhibition catalogue (New York: The Metropolitan Museum of Art, 1998), pp. 156–62.

4 G B-J [Georgiana Burne-Jones], *Memorials of Edward Burne-Jones*, 2 vols. (London: Macmillan, 1904), vol. I, p. 91, hereafter *Memorials*.

5 *Memorials*, vol. II, p. 89.
6 *Memorials*, vol. II, p. 95.
7 *Memorials*, vol. II, pp. 53–5 ('The Story of Aileen and Basille').
8 Fitzgerald, *Edward Burne-Jones*, p. 150.
9 See Arscott, *William Morris and Edward Burne-Jones*, pp. 105–25.
10 Caroline Arscott, 'Mutability and Deformity: Models of the Body and the Art of Edward Burne-Jones', *Nineteen: Interdisciplinary Studies in the Long Nineteenth Century*, no. 7 (2008), unpaginated, www.19.bbk.ac.uk/index.php/19/article/viewFile/482/342
11 Fitzgerald, *Edward Burne-Jones*, p. 107.
12 Liane Lefaivre, *Leon Battista Alberti's Hypnerotomachia Poliphili: Re-Cognizing the Architectural Body in the Early Italian Renaissance* (Cambridge, MA: MIT Press, 2005), electronic facsimile at http://mitpress.mit.edu/e-books/HP/index.htm
13 Fitzgerald, *Edward Burne-Jones*, p. 107.
14 *Memorials*, vol. I, p. 88.
15 'King Cophetua and the Beggar Maid', *A Book of Old English Ballads*, available at www.sacred-texts.com/neu/eng/boeb/boeb04.htm
16 John Lindley, *Edwards' Botanical Register, or Ornamental Flower Garden* (London: Ridway, 1830), vol. XVI, p. 1385.
17 *Memorials*, vol. I, p. 58.
18 *Memorials*, vol. II, p. 53.
19 W. S. Taylor, 'King Cophetua and the Beggar Maid', *Apollo*, 97 (February 1973), pp. 148–55; Duncan Robinson, 'Letter to the Editor: Burne-Jones's *King Cophetua and the Beggar Maid*', *Apollo*, 97 (June 1973), p. 626.
20 *Memorials*, vol. II, p. 139.
21 *Memorials*, vol. I, p. 30.

16

CATHERINE MAXWELL

Algernon Charles Swinburne
(1837–1909)

Algernon Charles Swinburne was the dominant literary influence on many of the best-known writers of the late Victorian period, his verse still representing an apparently unsurpassable model to the aspirant young poets of the early twentieth century. Swinburne's own development as a writer was the product of many diverse influences including British Romanticism, modern French literature, Elizabethan and Jacobean drama and Italian revolutionary politics, but his contact with the Pre-Raphaelites, William Morris and Dante Gabriel Rossetti in particular, was undoubtedly one of the major shaping forces. This chapter briefly sketches Swinburne's links with the Pre-Raphaelite circle before assessing the impact of Pre-Raphaelitism on his writing and, most importantly, his poetry.

It is usual to think of Swinburne's first contact with Pre-Raphaelitism as his meeting with Morris on 1 November 1857 and subsequent introduction to Burne-Jones and Rossetti during the period when all three artists, along with others such as Arthur Hughes and Val Prinsep, were engaged in the famous enterprise of painting Arthurian frescoes on the walls of the Oxford Union. However, Swinburne would already have been familiar with Pre-Raphaelite art through his close friend and 'good angel' Lady Trevelyan. Pauline Trevelyan, wife of Sir Walter Calverley Trevelyan, was chatelaine of Wallington, a large house near Capheaton, the Northumberland home of Sir John Swinburne, Swinburne's grandfather. She is best known as a patron of the arts and for her cultivation of a circle which included her close friend and mentor John Ruskin, the sculptor Thomas Woolner, one of the original Pre-Raphaelites, and the painter and Pre-Raphaelite associate William Bell Scott, all of whom contributed artworks to decorate the hall at Wallington. Through Pauline, Swinburne had already met Bell Scott, probably in 1855 before he went up to Balliol in January 1856, and possibly Ruskin.[1] He would also have been able to see at least two of Scott's fine Wallington paintings by the end of the summer vacation of 1857.[2] Pauline Trevelyan had herself met Morris and Burne-Jones in December 1856, and, visiting

Rossetti's studio earlier that year, declared him 'fascinating' and herself 'quite enchanted' with him.³ Swinburne is thus likely to have heard her impressions of the trio some time before he actually met them, impressions matched by those of his undergraduate friends George Birkbeck Hill, who had also met them previously, and Edwin Hatch, who was responsible for the introductions. Swinburne's admiration for Tennyson meant that, like Birkbeck Hill, he would have relished the designs of Millais, Hunt and Rossetti in Moxon's edition of Tennyson, published earlier in 1857. Thus by November, he was already primed to respond enthusiastically to Pre-Raphaelitism, and the arrival early that month of Pauline Trevelyan and Ruskin to view the Union paintings must also have underlined their significance.

Dazzled by the artists' imaginative energy and delighted by their easy camaraderie, Swinburne became fast friends with Burne-Jones, Rossetti and Morris – Burne-Jones famously commenting 'Now we were four in company and not three.'⁴ Rossetti and Morris in particular made a huge impression on him, with Scott commenting in 1859 that 'only those books or things they admire or appropriate will he entertain'.⁵ Swinburne made a start on his first Morris-inspired poem, *Queen Iseult*, within days of meeting his new idol and hearing him recite his work, while Pre-Raphaelite medievalism, visible in the frescoes and in Morris's first book of poems, *The Defence of Guenevere*, which Swinburne read admiringly in February 1858, was to be an abiding influence.⁶ The Union project had more or less petered out by Easter 1858, but Swinburne remained in close contact with his new friends, much to the disapproval of his Oxford tutor Benjamin Jowett, who thought them a bad influence in encouraging the poetry that distracted him from his studies.

After he left Oxford in 1860 without taking his final degree examinations, he was given an allowance of £400 per annum by his father, and began his career as a writer. His residence in London allowed him to deepen his relationships with his friends, especially Rossetti, to whose wife Elizabeth Siddall he was chivalrously devoted. Greatly moved by her death in February 1862, he agreed to keep Rossetti company as a fellow lodger at a new address, Tudor House, Cheyne Walk, with both moving in on 24 October. He had also by this time formed important and enduring relationships with William Michael and Christina Rossetti and was a regular (if often inebriated) visitor at the home of Ford Madox Brown. Besides being an enthusiastic advocate of Pre-Raphaelite painting, Swinburne was himself the subject of sketches and painted portraits by Rossetti (Fitzwilliam Museum, Cambridge) and Scott (Balliol College, Oxford), was posed kissing a female model for Rossetti's planned frontispiece for *The Early Italian Poets* (1861) and appears as a shepherd in Burne-Jones's *Adoration of the Kings and Shepherds* (1861,

Tate). His poem 'Laus Veneris', based on the Tannhäuser myth, is most likely an influence on Burne-Jones's painting of that name (1873–8), now in the Laing Art Gallery, Newcastle.

During his intermittent occupancy of Tudor House, which lasted until the summer of 1864, Swinburne composed much of the verse that would make him famous in *Poems and Ballads* (1866) and most of his pioneering study *William Blake* (1868). He left, somewhat irked, after Rossetti indicated that he would like the house to himself, although they remained close with Rossetti trying unsuccessfully to persuade Alexander Macmillan to publish Swinburne's poetry. Rossetti designed the book covers for *Atalanta in Calydon* (1865) and *Songs before Sunrise* (1871) and nursed Swinburne at Tudor House when he was recovering from a drunken episode in June 1870. He tried, again not very successfully, to moderate Swinburne's riotous behaviour and unguarded speech, but did persuade him to omit some of his more outrageous poems from *Songs before Sunrise*. Although Swinburne's shift to a more politicized poetry in the late 1860s meant that he began to modify the aestheticism he initially shared with Rossetti – he claimed that it 'was only Gabriel and his following (l'art pour l'art) who for a time frightened me from speaking out' (*Letters*, vol. I, p. 195) – the two remained best friends until Rossetti's breakdown and the onset of his increasingly reclusive lifestyle. After 1872 Rossetti never saw Swinburne again,[7] finding his wild behaviour intolerable and perhaps blaming him for intensifying the dispute with Robert Buchanan, the reviewer whose attacks on the Pre-Raphaelite 'Fleshly School of Poetry' precipitated Rossetti's mental breakdown. However, the two had regular news of each other through William Michael Rossetti and through their mutual friend and Swinburne's latter-day guardian, Theodore Watts-Dunton, who visited Rossetti weekly up to the time of his death in 1882. Although Swinburne was mystified by Rossetti's withdrawal, he continued on the whole to remember him fondly and Rossetti still seems to have enjoyed recounting anecdotes of Swinburne. Swinburne's warm relationships with Scott, Morris and Burne-Jones continued unabated till their deaths in 1890, 1896 and 1898, although he turned against Scott after reading unflattering remarks about himself in the posthumously published *Autobiographical Notes* (1892). Burne-Jones dedicated one of his last paintings, *Love Leading the Pilgrim* (1896–7, Tate), to Swinburne, citing the opening two lines of Swinburne's 1882 epic *Tristram of Lyonesse* – 'Love, that is first and last of all things made, / The light that moving has man's life for shade'[8] – in the catalogue when the painting was exhibited.[9]

The dominant aspect of Pre-Raphaelitism that attracted Swinburne was its medievalism, although Antony Harrison suggests that his ever-expanding knowledge of medieval literature, invigorated by his contact with the

Pre-Raphaelites and his studies at Oxford, was in sum much deeper and wider than that of either Morris or Rossetti 'whom he always regarded as expert medievalists'.[10] Specialist knowledge, in his case derived from his Northumbrian background, informs his fascination with the native British ballad, a passion he shared with Rossetti and Elizabeth Siddall, which made his imitations of Border ballads arguably more authentic than Rossetti's evidently more hybridized forms. He was delighted to have one of his ballads thought 'a genuine Border specimen, and of the earliest mediaeval build' by some knowledgeable fellow Northumbrians (*Letters*, vol. I, p. 22).

However, Swinburne's medievalism, like mainstream Pre-Raphaelite medievalism, is strongly mediated by Romanticism. Walter Pater would influentially identify the poetry of Morris and Rossetti as a second wave of Romanticism, and certainly for Rossetti and Swinburne their shared passion for Keats, and, in particular, Shelley and Coleridge, forged an enduring bond. The later Romantic medievalism of Tennyson, an important source text for Pre-Raphaelite art, was also important though Swinburne would express dissatisfaction with Tennyson's sanitized and moralistic treatment of Arthurian myth. Rossetti introduced Swinburne to Blake, then scarcely known, allowing him to read the prized manuscript notebook of Blake's prose, verses and sketches that he and William Michael had acquired in 1847. He thus fired an interest that would eventually result in Swinburne's *William Blake*, the first critical monograph on the poet. Famously this book also contains the English expression 'art for art's sake' as used for the first time in relation to contemporary art. It occurs in an important reiteration of Swinburne's aesthetic values, previously expressed in his earlier published assessments of George Meredith's *Modern Love* and Baudelaire's *Les Fleurs du mal*.[11] Such values derive from Théophile Gautier and Rossetti, with Rossetti possibly introducing Swinburne to Gautier's novel *Mademoiselle de Maupin* (1835) with its important aestheticist Preface. Certainly Swinburne came to regard the two writers as indivisible, referring in 1887 to his young self as 'too much under the morally identical influence of Gabriel Gautier and of Théophile Rossetti' (*Letters*, vol. V, p. 207).[12]

Many of Swinburne's essays up to 1871, mostly collected in his *Essays and Studies* (1875), were written in a nuanced impressionistic descriptive style with a strong synaesthetic element, which, while it sounded an authentically new note in English prose, owes a certain debt to Shelley and Gautier. The essays chiefly praise and celebrate the authors and artists they treat, aiming to evoke for readers Swinburne's own sense of the effects and impressions aroused by the texts and artworks. In style and motivation they are a major influence on Walter Pater's aesthetic prose and thus all the late nineteenth-century writers who followed him. The essays of this period can also be seen directly or indirectly as promoting both the shared and immediate interests of Swinburne's Pre-Raphaelite circle. He produced essays on the Romantic poets Shelley, Coleridge and Byron, but also wrote important review essays (1867, 1870) lauding verse collections by Morris and Rossetti. His 'Notes on Some Pictures of 1868' (1868) concludes with eloquent descriptions of several of Rossetti's paintings, including *Lady Lilith* and *La Pia de' Tolomei*, while 'Notes on the Text of Shelley' (1869) is a careful consideration of William Michael's suggested emendations and subsequent edition of Shelley. Even when writing about Renaissance art in 'Notes on Designs of the Old Masters at Florence' (1868), Swinburne makes direct complimentary reference to Burne-Jones and Rossetti; he includes a gracious footnote to Morris in 'Byron' (1866), whilst other notes in 'Matthew Arnold's New Poems' (1867) celebrate poems by William Bell Scott and Christina Rossetti.[13] Swinburne's review of a prose poem and pictures by his friend, the Jewish homosexual painter Simeon Solomon, a figure on the edge of the Pre-Raphaelite circle, is also notable for its provocative treatment of complex emotion and sensation stemming from transgressive sexual desire, and would also have considerable impact on Pater.[14]

Swinburne's letters provide an invaluable record of his relations with his Pre-Raphaelite circle, particularly in his formative years. Of particular interest are his meticulous, perceptive responses to Rossetti's poetic drafts – responses that include frequent judicious comments on specific lines or word choices. Such critiques are example of a larger collaborative practice of mutual evaluation in the Pre-Raphaelite circle, and clearly Swinburne appreciated Rossetti's assessments of his own works. Swinburne's lively and engaging letters are also a key source for his views on his circle, containing such gems as his famous summation of Rossetti's sensuous painting of Fanny Cornforth as *Bocca Baciata* (1859, Museum of Fine Arts, Boston) – 'more stunning than can decently be expressed' (*Letters*, vol. I, p. 27) – his many admiring remarks about Christina Rossetti's poetry and children's stories and his affectionate and appreciative recollections of Elizabeth Siddall, which, emphasizing her wit and vivacity, helpfully counterpoint the somewhat wispy Romantic stereotype. Swinburne praised Siddall's poetry and would often pause to examine her painting *Sir Patrick Spens*, hung in the dining room at The Pines, the Putney house he shared with Theodore Watts-Dunton.[15] Swinburne's loyalty to his Pre-Raphaelite circle can also be seen in his book dedications, with the early *The Queen Mother* and *Rosamond* (1860) dedicated to Rossetti; *Poems and Ballads 1* (1866) to Burne-Jones; *William Blake* (1868) to William Rossetti; *A Century of Roundels* (1883) to Christina Rossetti; *Poems and Ballads 3* (1889) to Scott; *Astrophel and Other Poems* (1894) to Morris; and his last volume, *A Channel Passage and*

Other Poems (1904), commemorating Morris and Burne-Jones. In addition individual poems are dedicated to or commemorate all of these figures.

One of the keynotes of the Romantic medievalism that Swinburne took from the poetry and painting of Morris and Rosssetti was female grace and beauty, typified by damsels notable for their luxuriant – usually golden – hair, pale skin, curved or parted lips, and absorbed or absorbing gaze, a gaze sometimes withheld and thus made more tantalizing by shut or half-closed eyelids. William Morris's 'Praise of My Lady', from *The Defence of Guenevere* (1858), a collection already under consideration for publication by the time he met Swinburne, is a litany of the cherished attributes of the beloved woman, coupled with their enchanting, even enervating effect on the admiring male lover. Here, for instance, are the exaggerated lips familiar to viewers of Rossetti's female portraits:

> Her full lips being made to kiss,
> Curl'd up and pensive each one is;
> This makes me faint to stand and see.
> *Beata mea domina!* (Lines 41–4)

Swinburne will echo such detail in *Poems and Ballads* 1, for example, in 'The Leper', where the 'poor scribe' admires his lady's 'curled-up lips and amorous hair' (lines 10, 12), the 'Curled lips' of 'Faustine' (line 167), or the 'large pale lips of strong Semiramis, / Curled like a tiger's that curl back to feed' in 'Laus Veneris' (lines 200–1), although the added note of aggression is a specific trait of the Swinburneian woman. In Swinburne's poetry, the woman's graces are typically hymned with a fetishistic intensity. In the unfinished *Queen Iseult*, an early poem of some charm inspired and praised by Morris, Iseult's 'golden corn-ripe hair', obsessively admired and kissed by Tristram, clearly owes a debt to Rossetti's 'Blessed Damozel' and many of Morris's fair ladies; yet that obsessive note is Swinburne's own, as are other identifiable motifs such as the sexual submission of the male to female power visible in Tristram's desire on first seeing Iseult:

> And he thought it well and meet,
> Lain before that lady sweet
> To be trodden by her feet.[16]

The enervation felt by the Morrisian male lover in the presence of his beloved turns into full surrender in Swinburne's poetry, as underlined in another incident when Iseult comes to Tristram by night and tenderly bears him to her chamber on her back.

A more aggressive version of female power, indicating Swinburne's emergent interest in the *femme fatale*, can be seen in his early verse drama *Rosamond*, published with *The Queen Mother* in 1860. *Rosamond*, which

Swinburne began in 1858 and which was read approvingly by both Morris and Rossetti, contains an important adumbration of this type in its portrayal of Rosamond Clifford, King Henry's mistress, forcibly poisoned by his wife, Queen Eleanor of Aquitaine. In the first scene, which dwells on Rosamond's captivating loveliness, she describes her hair

> as a strong staked net
> To take the hunters and the hunt, and bind
> Faces and feet and hands; a golden gin
> Wherein the tawny-lidded lions fell,
> Broken at ankle.[17]

Later in a speech that anticipates Pater's Mona Lisa as the archetype of feminine archetypes, she characterizes herself as the eternal *femme fatale*:

> Yea, I am found the woman in all tales,
> The face caught always in the story's face;
> I Helen, holding Paris by the lips,
> Smote Hector through the head; I Cressida
> So kissed men's mouths that they went sick or mad,
> Stung right at brain with me; I Guenevere
> Made my queen's eyes so precious and my hair
> Delicate with such gold in its soft ways
> And my mouth honied so for Launcelot,
> Out of good things he chose his golden soul
> To be the pearlwork of my treasuring hands,
> And so our love foiled God.[18]

Rosamond's lover, Henry II, experiences her beauty as a source of physical pain:

> God help! your hair burns me to see like gold
> Burnt to pure heat; your colour seen turns in me
> To pain and plague upon the temple-vein
> That aches as if the sun's heat snapt the blood
> In hot mid measure....
> Your beauty makes me blind and hot, I am
> Stabbed in the brows with it.[19]

This note will recur in later poems such as 'Anactoria' in which Sappho tells her lover that 'thine eyes / Blind me, thy tresses burn me, thy sharp sighs / Divide my flesh and spirit with soft sound' (lines 1–3).

Most likely part-inspired by Swinburne, Rossetti and Burne-Jones would produce their own compelling images of Rosamond from 1861 onwards.[20] But Rossetti's own preoccupation with the *femme fatale*, prominent in female images following *Bocca Baciata*, along with the general interest among the

Pre-Raphaelites in figures such as Lucrezia Borgia and Wilhelm Meinhold's eponymous heroine Sidonia von Bork, painted respectively by Rossetti (1860–1, Tate) and Burne-Jones (1860–1, Tate), doubtless helped increase Swinburne's growing fascination with the figure of the sexually dominant woman. Lucrezia informs the figure of the beautiful woman in 'A Ballad of Life' and 'A Ballad of Death', which open *Poems and Ballads*, as well as an unpublished prose romance, *The Chronicle of Tebaldeo Tebaldei*.[21] In the first of the two poems, written in the Italian *canzone* form that Swinburne would have encountered in Rossetti's *The Early Italian Poets*, the speaker declares that 'My lady is perfect and transfigureth / All sin and sorrow and death, / Making them fair as her own eyelids be' (lines 62–4). In contrast to the treatment of 'fallen women' we find in Morris or Rossetti, Swinburne's sexually assured heroines evince no guilt themselves nor rouse it in their male admirers.

Rossetti's experimentation with older poetic forms such as sestinas and *canzoni*, along with his skill as a translator, fulsomely praised by Swinburne in his essay of 1870, would have stimulated the younger poet's efforts in these directions. As *Poems and Ballads* I shows, Swinburne would prove himself a consummate craftsman. He was the first in his circle to have tried his hand at the roundel (a short poem with stanzas based on two rhymes, developed from a medieval French verse form). There are two fine examples in *Poems and Ballads* (both entitled 'Rondel'), and Swinburne later composed an entire volume in this form, two of which under the title 'On an Old Roundel' pay tribute to Rossetti's own moving translation of the roundel 'To Death, of his Lady', by François Villon, the medieval French poet admired and translated by both of them. Christina Rossetti, the dedicatee of *A Century of Roundels*, seems to have learnt her own use of the form from Swinburne's example, while some of her early poems, in particular 'Dream Land' (see Figure 14), rubbed off on him. In his essay '*Poems and Ballads*: A Criticism' (1866), William Michael Rossetti suggested that his sister's influence could be traced in the rhythms of Swinburne's 'Rococo', the lyrical tone of 'The Garden of Proserpine' and the structure of 'Madonna Mia'.[22]

However, in terms of their medieval subject matter and stylistic echoes, it is Morris who is the most palpable influence on Swinburne's early poems including those unpublished in his lifetime,[23] in addition to others that found their way into *Poems and Ballads* such as 'Madonna Mia', 'St Dorothy', and 'A Christmas Carol' – this last, according to Swinburne's appended note, 'Suggested by a drawing of Mr. D. G. Rossetti's'.[24] There are evident superficial echoes of Morris's 'Golden Wings' with its glowing medieval colour scheme in 'August', a poem that unusually for Swinburne has a strong palette, although the atmospheric blurriness is already identifiably his own, and the poem as a whole owes as much to the synaesthesia of Baudelaire's 'Correspondances'.[25] As an apprentice-poet Swinburne was concerned that he might be '*Eglamor* to Morris as *Sordello*' (that is, the lesser poet to a greater), and was aware of the dangers of 'Topsification' or imitating Morris too heavily (*Letters*, vol. I, p. 16; Morris was nicknamed 'Topsy' because his unruly hair reminded friends of the slave girl of that name in Harriet Beecher Stowe's *Uncle Tom's Cabin* of 1852). But Swinburne was already bringing his own individual creative energies to the models provided by his older, more experienced friend. After 1862 his poems have far fewer evident Pre-Raphaelite echoes, and Hellenic subject matter begins to compete with and even outstrip medieval topics. He would, however, return to the story of Tristram and Iseult, a tale that exerted a powerful attraction for all the Pre-Raphaelite painters who loved to illustrate it. Swinburne's epic *Tristram of Lyonesse* (1882), started in earnest in 1869, is often said to be his masterpiece, while the long ballad-like Arthurian poem *The Tale of Balen* (1896), with its Northumbrian hero, has been called 'the last truly important Victorian medievalist poem'.[26]

Once Swinburne had come into his own with his Greek epic drama *Atalanta in Calydon* (1865) and the later verses included in *Poems and Ballads*, the obvious signs of indebtedness to his peers begin to diminish. However, his work may be deemed to share some general traits with the poetry of Morris and Rossetti. The wistful melancholy of the poems in Morris's *The Defence of Guenevere* with their nostalgia for bygone days is common to many of Swinburne's compositions, while *Poems and Ballads 2* (1878) is a volume pervaded by elegiac reminiscence. As Jerome McGann points out, Swinburne, like Morris and Rossetti, eschewed the progressivist, perfectibilian beliefs of other mainstream Victorian poets such as Tennyson and Browning, and broke from 'the poetry of quest, effort, and personal advancement' to focus on passion and sensation.[27] Nonetheless many of Swinburne's poems, although they treat the passage of time and what is lost to the past, refuse to remain fixed on that loss but urge acceptance, while some, having rehearsed a romantic scenario, challenge convention by boldly refusing the burden of regretful sentiment:

> Let this be said between us here,
>   One love turns green when one turns grey;
> This year knows nothing of last year;
>   To-morrow has no more to say
>   To yesterday.
>
> Live and let live, as I will do,
>   Love and let love, and so will I.

But sweet, for me no more with you:
　Not while I live, not though I die.
　Goodnight, goodbye. ('Félise', lines 286–95, *Poems and Ballads* 1)

The three leading male Pre-Raphaelite poets Morris, Rossetti and Swinburne, although each had his own distinctive style, were all admirers of Browning. Browning's demanding elliptical style, his experiments with voice and dramatic characterization that require the reader's interpretative energies, undoubtedly affect those elements in the works of his successors that make their poems seem 'modernist' ahead of their time. Thus Elizabeth Helsinger writing of the strangeness and enigma of *The Defence of Guenevere* notes how 'Morris's techniques of abrupt transition' render some of his compositions 'like later modernist poems ... demanding of readers: we must leap narrative gaps, connect what remains unconnected'.[28] Swinburne also makes a considerable demand on his readers who are denied easily legible meaning but have to create meaning from a complex web of metre, rhyme, imagery and allusion.

To appreciate Swinburne's poem 'The Leper' (*Poems and Ballads* 1), for example, one needs to understand its ironic relation to its late French medieval epigraph, to know what that epigraph means, but also to know that it is one of Swinburne's brilliant forgeries, allowing him to treat a scandalous topic under guise of glossing a long-ago historical incident. The poem is greatly enhanced if one reads it in the context of Swinburne's review of Baudelaire and his comments on the French poet's 'Une Charogne': 'even of the loathsomest bodily putrescence and decay he can make some noble use; pluck out its meaning and secret, even its beauty, in a certain way, from actual carrion'.[29] The word 'sweet', repeated endlessly by the scribe who narrates the poem, seems curious in that it is uttered over his mistress's decaying corpse, but his very insistence is part of Swinburne's challenge to his readers' values as he forces them to consider if the scribe, mixed though his motives are, is not nobler than the courtly society that expelled his lady once she became ill. Its former toleration of her 'sin' while it remained invisible mimics the Victorian hypocrisy that allowed middle- and upper-class men to have extra-marital sexual interests so long as these were not evident in polite society. Swinburne's use of the word 'leper', which picks up on the Victorian discursive language of moral health and morbidity, undoubtedly plays with the idea of those who, becoming 'moral lepers', are thrust beyond the pale of society, as well as perhaps hinting obliquely at the contemporary 'plague' of syphilis, which made sexual 'sin' visible.

While D. G. Rossetti was a less evident immediate influence on Swinburne's style, Swinburne's mischievous take on Rossetti's 'Sonnets for Pictures' in the

Heptalogia (1880), his collection of contemporary poetic parodies, shows that he had observed with a wicked accuracy the sometimes stagey, mannered mode of these earlier ecphrastic sonnets with their dramatic pauses, rhetorical exclamations, recondite vocabulary, and identifiable Rossetti keywords ('monochord') and mannerisms such as hyphenation ('wild-eyed woes'). Rossetti, one assumes, would not have thanked Swinburne for exaggerating the 'fleshiness' that had made him the principal target of Robert Buchanan's attack:

> That nose is out of drawing. With a gasp,
>> She pants upon the passionate lips that ache
>> With the red drain of her own mouth, and make
> A monochord of colour. Like an asp,
> One lithe lock wriggles in his rutilant grasp. ('Sonnet for a Picture', lines 1–5)

Interestingly this poem also recalls Swinburne's own early sonnet 'Love and Sleep' (*Poems and Ballads* 1), which in its opening evokes one of Rossetti's dreamy poems or paintings:

>> Lying asleep between the strokes of night
>> I saw my love lean over my sad bed,
>> Pale as the duskiest lily's leaf or head, (lines 1–3)

but escalates swiftly into something altogether more fleshly and fervid, more markedly Swinburneian than Rossettian:

>> The quivering flanks, hair smelling of the south,
>> The bright light feet, the splendid supple thighs
>> And glittering eyelids of my soul's desire. (Lines 12–14)

The young Swinburne here, perhaps inadvertently, parodies not just Rossetti but his own need to be a sexual provocateur and go one further. This element of self-parody seems to me to become wholly conscious in the exaggerations of 'Sonnet for a Picture'.

Parody aside, Rossetti's predilection for poetic dream visions and waking trance states arguably has a profounder effect on Swinburne than do other more obvious features of his style such as his particularity, his preoccupation with small significant detail. (Swinburne could do particularity perfectly well, as a poem such as 'The Sundew' shows (*Poems and Ballads* 1), but it is not his preferred descriptive mode.) Many of the poems in *Poems and Ballads* 1 adopt the form of the dream vision or an entranced visionary state somewhere between sleep and waking. The atmospheric dim twilight of these poems may also owe something to Rossetti's own fondness for poetic dimness, dusk and crepuscular light which will eventually pervade *The House of Life* (1870, 1881), a work which, as James Richardson observes, mainly eschews particularity and is marked by haunting dissolutions, something more readily associated with Swinburne's verse.[30] While the rhythmic effect of other Swinburne poems is to rouse and enliven, the meditative hypnotic rhythms of his visionary verse enact Yeats's claim that the purpose of rhythm is 'to prolong the moment of contemplation … that state of perhaps real trance, in which the mind … is unfolded in symbols'.[31] Swinburne's disarming metres mesmerize and pulse through his readers' sensibilities, attuning them to states in which they allow themselves to open to or be absorbed by the complex, often challenging matter of the verse.

It is this contemplative state of mind which Rossetti portrays in his poems that feature trance. For Rossetti, the visionary experience, though touching the soul, is accessed through the senses and is experienced simultaneously as an indivisible bodily and spiritual knowledge. Pater famously remarked of Rossetti, that for him, as for his precursor Dante, 'the material and the spiritual are fused and blent'; Swinburne too, always interested in the point where apparent opposites meet and cross over, saw no division between soul and body, repeatedly voicing his belief in what he called, after Shakespeare, 'the spirit of sense' or 'spirit within the sense'.[32] While Swinburne's visual faculty tends to be less vividly pictorial than Rossetti's, both poets employ a range of sensuous reference – touch, taste, smell, hearing – as well as the mixing of sense impressions that occurs in synaesthesia. However, both do so as part of a concerted attempt to heighten perception, or raise consciousness to another, higher level. Swinburne's blending of material and spiritual properties, often overlooked but already present in *Poems and Ballads* 1, and doubtless reinforced by Rossetti's like practice, would emerge most fully in *Tristram of Lyonesse* and his later poems, where synthesis heightens awareness of the natural energies of nature.

In sum, then, Swinburne's Pre-Raphaelite credentials stem primarily from his active involvement in the intellectual and social relations of the group surrounding Rossetti, Morris and Burne-Jones, associated with the second phase of Pre-Raphaelitism. Swinburne formed strong and, in many cases, lifelong friendships with men and women in the group and participated energetically in the exchange of ideas and the development of shared intellectual and aesthetic enthusiasms, sometimes introducing new topics of interest and stimulus. His early poetic style and subject matter is more evidently 'Pre-Raphaelite' but, in evolving his own mature style, he learnt and assimilated much, especially from Rossetti. Although his later poetry is generally identified as Hellenist, he retained an interest in medievalism, which informs some of his best work.

Swinburne spent the years 1879 to his death in 1909 living with the novelist and man of letters, Theodore Watts-Dunton, another stalwart of the

Pre-Raphaelite circle and one of Rossetti's most loyal and devoted friends. Their Putney residence, The Pines, filled with books and paintings by the Pre-Raphaelites and furniture donated by Rossetti from his own house, 16 Cheyne Walk, bore witness to the fact that Swinburne remained temperamentally 'at home' with Pre-Raphaelitism throughout his life.

NOTES

1 William Bell Scott, *Autobiographical Notes of the Life of William Bell Scott, and Notices of his Artistic and Poetic Circle of Friends 1830 to 1882*, ed. W. Minto, 2 vols. (London: James R. Osgood, McIlvaine, 1892), vol. II, pp. 14–15.

2 *Building the Roman Wall* (painted January–June 1857) and *King Egfrid and St Cuthbert* (painted June–December 1856). Raleigh Trevelyan, *Wallington* (Swindon: Acorn Press for National Trust (Enterprises) Ltd, 2007), pp. 18–19.

3 John Batchelor, *Lady Trevelyan and the Pre-Raphaelite Brotherhood* (London: Chatto & Windus, 2006), p. 115.

4 G B-J [Georgiana Burne-Jones], *Memorials of Edward Burne-Jones*, 2 vols. (London: Macmillan & Co., 1904), vol. I, p. 163.

5 Cited in Algernon Charles Swinburne, *The Swinburne Letters*, ed. Cecil Y. Lang, 6 vols. (New Haven: Yale University Press, 1959–62), vol. I, p. 25 (hereafter *Letters*, with volume and page numbers, in text).

6 Georges Lafourcade, *Swinburne: A Literary Biography* (London: G. Bell & Sons, 1932), p. 67.

7 Although they possibly may have met on 12 November 1874 at the funeral of Oliver Madox Brown, the son of Ford Madox Brown.

8 Algernon Charles Swinburne, *The Collected Poetical Works of Algernon Charles Swinburne*, 6 vols. (London: Chatto & Windus, 1904), vol. IV, p. 5.

9 Stephen Wildman and John Christian, *Edward Burne-Jones: Victorian Artist-Dreamer*, exhibition catalogue (New York: The Metropolitan Museum of Art, 1998), pp. 168–9.

10 Antony H. Harrison, *Swinburne's Medievalism: A Study in Victorian Love Poetry* (Baton Rouge, Louisiana and London: Louisiana State University Press, 1988), p. 6.

11 Elizabeth Prettejohn, *Art for Art's Sake: Aestheticism in Victorian Painting* (New Haven and London: Yale University Press, 2007), p. 33. For Swinburne's letter to the editor of *The Spectator* on Meredith see *Letters*, vol. I, pp. 51–3; 'Charles Baudelaire: *Les Fleurs du mal*', *Spectator*, 6 September 1862 (not reprinted in Swinburne's lifetime), repr. in *Swinburne as Critic*, ed. C. K. Hyder (London and Boston: Routledge & Kegan Paul, 1972), pp. 27–36.

12 See Thomas E. Connolly, 'Swinburne's Theory of the End of Art', *English Literary History*, 19 (1952), p. 279.

13 Algernon Charles Swinburne, *Essays and Studies* (London: Chatto & Windus, 1875), pp. 330, 340 ('Notes on Designs of the Old Masters at Florence'); p. 252 ('Byron'); pp. 159, 175 ('Matthew Arnold's New Poems').

14 Algernon Charles Swinburne, 'Simeon Solomon: Notes on his "Vision of Love" and Other Studies', *The Dark Blue*, 1 (July 1871), pp. 568–77, not reprinted in Swinburne's lifetime but subsequently included in *The Complete Works of*

Algernon Charles Swinburne, ed. Edmund Gosse and T. J. Wise, 20 vols. (The Bonchurch Edition; London and New York: William Heinemann and Gabriel Wells, 1925–7), vol. XV, pp. 443–58.

15 Clara Watts-Dunton, *The Home Life of Swinburne* (London: A. M. Philpot, 1922), p. 208.

16 'Queen Iseult', in *A. C. Swinburne*, Arthurian Poets, ed. James P. Carley (Woodbridge: Boydell & Brewer, 1990), p. 255. On Morris's admiration for Swinburne's poem see *Letters*, vol. I, p. 17.

17 *The Tragedies of Algernon Charles Swinburne*, 6 vols. (London: Chatto & Windus, 1905), vol. I, p. 234.

18 Ibid., pp. 238–9.

19 Ibid., p. 261.

20 Prettejohn, *Art for Art's Sake*, p. 38 and note 8, p. 288.

21 *Lucretia Borgia: The Chronicle of Tebaldeo Tebaldei*, ed. Randolph Hughes (London: Golden Cockerel Press, 1942).

22 William Michael Rossetti, *Swinburne's Poems and Ballads* (1866), in *Swinburne: The Critical Heritage*, ed. Clyde K. Hyder (London: Routledge & Kegan Paul, 1970), p. 80.

23 See the Arthurian 'Joyeuse Garde', 'Lancelot' and 'The Day before the Trial', in *A. C. Swinburne*, Arthurian Poets, ed. James P. Carley, pp. 291–3, 301–11, 299–300.

24 Swinburne, *Collected Poetical Works*, vol. I, p. 218.

25 Catherine Maxwell, *The Female Sublime from Milton to Swinburne: Bearing Blindness* (Manchester: Manchester University Press, 2001), pp. 196–9.

26 Harrison, *Swinburne's Medievalism*, p. 134.

27 Jerome McGann, *Swinburne: An Experiment in Criticism* (Chicago and London: University of Chicago Press, 1972), p. 35.

28 Elizabeth Helsinger, *Poetry and the Pre-Raphaelite Arts: Dante Gabriel Rossetti and William Morris* (New Haven and London: Yale University Press, 2008), p. 74.

29 'Charles Baudelaire', *Swinburne as Critic*, p. 30.

30 James Richardson, *Vanishing Lives: Style and Self in Tennyson, D. G. Rossetti, Swinburne and Yeats* (Charlottesville: University Press of Virginia, 1988), pp. 106–13.

31 W. B. Yeats, 'The Symbolism of Poetry', *Essays and Introductions* (London: Macmillan, 1961), p. 159.

32 Walter Pater, 'Dante Gabriel Rossetti', *Appreciations* (London: Macmillan, 1910), p. 212; Shakespeare, *Troilus and Cressida* 1.i. 58 and 3.iii. 106.

17

ANGELA THIRLWELL

William Michael Rossetti (1829–1919)

William Michael Rossetti was twice a brother. As a Rossetti he was sibling to the more famous Dante Gabriel and Christina, not to mention the practically unknown but seriously clever Maria. As a PRB he was one of the magical number of seven men who formed the original Brotherhood in 1848. If William Michael Rossetti was not a professional artist, he was, nevertheless, crucial to the whole construction of the Pre-Raphaelite movement. He promoted it, activated it, understood it, explained it, contextualized and memorialized it in a whole range of editorial, journalistic, critical, entrepreneurial and biographical enterprises. William E. Fredeman, pioneer of modern Pre-Raphaelite studies, estimated that in contrast with all the more flamboyantly glamorous figures associated with the Brotherhood, William 'was almost the only man of action, and without him there would have been no Brotherhood, no *Germ*, no *P. R. B. Journal*, and no movement to leave its mark on the history of English art'.[1]

William Michael Rossetti invented his contemporary and our still enduring view of the PRB. He was its advocate, secretary and historian – and these functions made him a key player. Although he was a taxman by day, rising to senior ranks within the Inland Revenue, he was a critic of art and literature by night. Pre-Raphaelitism was above all a literary art movement, inspired by Dante, Chaucer, Shakespeare and the Romantic poets, and William's role put him at the crossover between image and words. His dark Italian good looks meant he was actually incorporated into Pre-Raphaelite pictures. He modelled, among other paintings, for Adrian Colonna in Holman Hunt's *Rienzi* (1848–9, private collection), Lorenzo in Millais's *Isabella* (Figure 10) and the angel in Dante Gabriel Rossetti's radically white composition, *Ecce Ancilla Domini!* (1849–50, Tate).

With his professional expertise in taking minutes of meetings, and his private taste for lifelong diary keeping, it was natural for William to keep a *PRB Journal*. As Secretary to the PRB and its 'catalytic agent',[2] it was his special function to log their informal meetings and day-to-day doings. William's

PRB Journal 1849–1853, in the version restored by Fredeman in 1975, gives us the only first-hand insight, apart from surviving letters, into the early days of the progressive young art movement. At their most vivacious, William's *PRB Journal* entries are concise, informative and amusing:

> Millais said that he had thoughts of painting a hedge (as a subject) to the closest point of imitation, with a bird's nest, – a thing which has never been attempted. Another subject he has in his eye is a river-sparrow's nest, built, as he says they are, between three reeds; the bird he describes as with its head always on one side, 'a body like a ball, and thin legs like needles'.[3]

It was a time of concerted creativity among the Pre-Raphaelite Brothers, captured by William as both participant and observer. At this early date he was experimenting with both writing and art. Although it is little known, he made some striking sketches which survive in private collections.[4] In May 1849, a Pre-Raphaelite Brother, sculptor Thomas Woolner, 'recommended me to follow out one of the designs I had begun, and laid aside, for "Maud's madness" [a scene from Coventry Patmore's poem, 'The Woodman's Daughter']'.[5] Later, 'Gabriel and I were engaged, the greater part of the day, on our respective designs.'[6] The following week William arranged a first sitting for Miss Saunders, a new model. Late on a May evening in 1849, William and Holman Hunt, and probably Gabriel, 'talked and did portraits'.[7] The next day William complained about a middle-aged, overweight model at the life class that he and his brother regularly attended.[8]

While it is little known that William drew and sketched at this period, perhaps it is even less known that he produced a remarkable, extended poem in 1849, 'Mrs. Holmes Grey'. In a daring experiment he decided to apply to poetry the principles his Pre-Raphaelite 'Brothers' were pioneering in art. An essential part of the Pre-Raphaelite credo was to see the world with rigorous naturalism, in the spirit of Wordsworth and Coleridge's manifesto in their 1798 Preface to the *Lyrical Ballads*. Like these Romantic poets who wanted to describe 'the essential passions of the heart' in a 'language really used by men', William excluded any elaborate, conscious poetic tropes from 'Mrs. Holmes Grey'. Instead, he aimed to reproduce 'speech uttered in ordinary real life'.[9] And just as some of the most revolutionary subjects of Pre-Raphaelite pictures would focus on what Wordsworth had called 'subjects from common life' – such as the fallen women in Dante Gabriel Rossetti's *Found* (1854–82, unfinished, Delaware Art Museum) or Holman Hunt's *The Awakening Conscience* (1853–4, Tate) – so William's poem possibly alluded to an actual crime of passion reported in the press. It concerned the 'death of a lady, a surgeon's wife, who had died suddenly in the house of another medical man for whom she had conceived a vehement and unreciprocated passion'.[10] William cast the sensational material in the form of newspaper reports of the coroner's inquest. Even though his medium was blank verse, he tried to convey the tone and language of authentic journalistic reportage:

> 'A Juror to the witness: "Did no acts
> Of familiarity occur between
> Deceased and you?"
>
>   'Here Mr. Grey addressed
> The Coroner, demurring to a reply.
>
> 'The Coroner: "It grieves me very much
> To pain your feelings; but I feel compelled
> To say the question is a proper one.
> It is the Jury's duty to gain light
> On this exceedingly distressing case;
> I owe a duty to the public. Let
> The witness answer."
>
>   'Witness: "She would clasp
> Her arms around me in speaking tenderly,
> And kiss me. She has often kissed my hands.
> Not beyond that."
>
>   'The Juror: "And did you
> Respond – " The Coroner: "The witness should,
> I think, be pressed no further. He has given
> His painful evidence most creditably." (lines 600–17)[11]

It was an ambitious attempt to write a genuinely Pre-Raphaelite poem and both Dante Gabriel Rossetti and Swinburne praised the stark result that culminated in a final night scene and a line reminiscent of Dante's *Inferno*: 'Equal, unknown, and desolate of stars.' However, 'Mrs. Holmes Grey' remained unpublished until it appeared in February 1868 in a monthly magazine, *The Broadway*. Swinburne was enthralled by William's daring project to transfer criminal court proceedings into poetry. 'I *can't* get that blessed poem of yours out of my head. It's all very well, but you beginning in that way ought to have knocked us all out of sight ... I'm not writing "chaff" – but I have today re-read your poem – and I *can't* hold my tongue, or my fingers. That idea of yours in "Mrs. Holmes Grey" beats everything but Balzac.'[12]

Like the *PRB Journal*, William's poetry was originally intended for private consumption only. But he undertook the first of many public literary acts when he became editor of the Brotherhood's avant-garde arts magazine, *The Germ* (four issues, 1850) which offered the public a stimulating mix of poems, short stories, illustrations and reviews by their members and associates. William wrote its cover sonnet, so convoluted that Bell Scott grumbled 'it would almost need a Browning Society's united intellects' to unpack its meaning[13] – though Arthur Hughes found it inspiring. William included some of his own poems in *The Germ* (see Appendix One), but more importantly, the first of his perceptive reviews of modern poetry: Arthur Clough's *Bothie*, Matthew Arnold's *Strayed Reveller* and Robert Browning's *Christmas Eve and Easter Day*. William's critical radar was alert to the new, both in literature and art. In August 1850 *The Guardian* commented that some of the best pieces in the by then defunct *Germ* were 'by two brothers named Rossetti'.[14]

A Pre-Raphaelite critic

It was *The Germ* that launched William's career as a critic. From that spring-board he became art critic in 1850 for a weekly called *The Critic* which gave him complete freedom to express his views. This led directly to art reviewing at a more visible level, for the influential *Spectator* within whose pages he published a seminal article on 'Præraphaelitism' (4 October 1851), asserting the modernity and democracy of the new art of his Pre-Raphaelite Brothers. They were in protest against the dry rules of the Victorian academy. Instead, 'what they saw, that they would paint – all of it, and all fully'. Rejecting 'all meretricious embellishment', their aim was 'truth' through 'exactitude of study from nature'. Challenging the controversy stirred up by their paintings, in his *Spectator* article William acclaimed the bravery of the English Pre-Raphaelites whose art was 'specially needed at the present moment'.

Through his art journalism William continually promoted the work and ideas of the radical young Pre-Raphaelite artists, William Holman Hunt, John Everett Millais and Dante Gabriel Rossetti, in whose pictures he posed. In addition, he drew the public's attention to the movement's associates such as Arthur Hughes and John Brett. His prolific and influential reviews of Victorian art and literature made him a cultural barometer, an innovator and arbiter of contemporary taste.

Criticism is underestimated as a creative process. William's contribution to Pre-Raphaelitism was essentially critical and interpretative. His virtuosity in dealing with both art and literature parallels his brother's more celebrated dual skills in poetry and painting. This extract from a handwritten document by William reveals his views on the methodology of an art critic:

> The moment I see a picture I receive a first impression from it, wh. is very
> generally the abiding impression: I know in an instant whether it is to my

judgment good, bad, or indifferent – &, if good, whether it is good in a great way or in a small one.

Lay great stress upon your first impressions, & don't readily fritter them away.

Form a sincere opinion whether you like a picture or not ... in total disregard of the question whether other people share it or the contrary.[15]

The advice reads as if offered to a young critic just starting a career in art journalism. William's instructions are practical, encouraging a direct approach expressed in accessible language. First impressions are often best impressions, but you must support these with technical analysis of 'composition, design, draughtsmanship, chiaroscuro, texture, colour, execution'. Beyond the purely technical, dare to voice an opinion about 'imagination, conception, style, expression, beauty'.[16] His practical guide to art criticism is in the authentic, autobiographical language of William Michael Rossetti, liberal pragmatist, autodidact, professional reviewer, critic, connoisseur, man of letters, who became a popularizer and demystifier of contemporary art for Victorian gallery-goers.

Over more than a quarter of a century, from his appointment to the *Spectator* in 1850 until 1878, he produced nearly 400 art 'critiques' for English and American periodicals.[17] He studied works of art and poetry intently, always taking notes as he read, or on gallery visits. William's critical attention to detail matched the way Pre-Raphaelite artists looked at the natural world 'stamen by stamen'.[18] He won and deserved the admiration of artistic contemporaries including Thomas Woolner, George du Maurier, John Brett and John Ruskin. Thomas Woolner praised his unpretentious tone to poet William Allingham: 'I am glad to hear from W. Rossetti that you liked his review on your poems; he bids fair to be one of our best in the review line – he takes more pains to discover the author's intention and less to display his own learning than most journalists.'[19]

William practised criticism with attitude but avoided cruel destructiveness. Aiming at 'unbiassed opinion', he also confessed to some only human 'smoothing down of edges' when evaluating works by friends, and 'a little tartness' when reviewing those outside his charmed circle.[20] The illustrator and later the author of *Trilby* George du Maurier appreciated William's unusual impartiality as well as his critical insight in a letter to artist Thomas Armstrong:

You mention William Rossetti's critique in *Fraser* of this month. Have you read it? I think he's the *only* critic who's not a hack and whose opinion[s] are genuine & felt – and strange to say he appears to me to have wonderfully little party feeling considering his bringing up & associations. His article on Millais' Moonlight is enough to stamp him as a genuine critic to my mind.[21]

Other practising artists trusted William's critical acumen. John Brett wrote to his sister Rosa about the reception of his picture *The Hedger*, that 'W. Rossetti thinks satisfactorily of it and he is the best judge I know after JR [John Ruskin].'[22] When Ruskin recommended him to W. J. Stillman, editor of the New York art magazine, *The Crayon*, he said that William possessed a 'peculiar power of arriving at *just* critical opinions; and I hardly know anyone else who I could – in his default – recommend to you'.[23]

William's articles appeared in a variety of London and regional papers, ranging from the *Spectator* to the *Liverpool Post*, and in specialist art publications such as the *Fine Arts Quarterly Review*. In their pages he responded to key exhibitions of the day: the Royal Academy exhibitions that marked each London summer season; Crystal Palace displays; international exhibitions in Paris (1855) and London (1862); exhibitions by individual artists and illustrators, including Ford Madox Brown, George Cruikshank and John Leech. He discussed Turner, British sculpture – which was unfashionable at the time – and esoteric Japanese woodcuts.

Although William wrote copious notices of works by Pre-Raphaelite artists, he specifically excluded discussion of his brother's pictures, mainly because Gabriel preferred not to show in public galleries. Nevertheless, William always maintained that Gabriel had been the 'brains' behind the Pre-Raphaelite movement, 'its intellectual impulse and originating *vis*'.[24] One correlative of William's ideal of impartiality in criticism was his dislike of the Victorian convention of anonymous reviews. This position was praised by Henry James who considered William, jointly with F. T. Palgrave and P. G. Hamerton, one of 'the three principal art-critics now writing in England – the only three, we believe, who from time to time lay aside the anonymous, and republish their contributions to the newspapers'.[25] William said critics should 'stand up openly and stoutly' for their opinions, and the reading public had a right to know where those opinions came from.[26]

Reviewing the Royal Academy's annual exhibitions gave William scope to expound his views on contemporary art – always his area of special interest. His aesthetic position by the late 1860s prioritized style above subject matter. He attributed advances in style by modern British artists to 'the stern and true discipline of Præraphaelitism', believing that 'if you have good style, you have simply and entirely good art'. A picture's content was secondary to its 'style' because 'good style will make a good picture out of the most ignoble subject'. However, he advocated that modern artists should choose modern subjects, either drawn from life as they saw it, or from history as they interpreted it, because 'life still is life all the world over, and all the centuries through'. The artist's range of possible subjects is 'as endless as the range of life and of society' and the artist's job was to give his subjects 'real palpitating life'.[27]

William's strength as an art critic lay in his visual accuracy, the result of intense looking at pictures, such as Millais's *Mariana* (1851, Tate) where 'throughout the long day's watching, the moist leaves have drifted in, and lie unheeded on her table; a mouse, fearless of disturbance, has come out from "behind the mouldering wainscot"; and sunset lights up in the casement the emblem of the broken lily'.[28] When William compared two Pre-Raphaelite 'Brothers', Hunt and Millais, he traced Hunt's reflective art to its origins in intellectual effort, while he saw Millais's work springing more naturally out of flair and intuition. As Millais moved away from subjects that 'told a story' towards suggestive mood paintings, epitomized by *Autumn Leaves* (1856, Manchester City Galleries), William immediately noted his innovatory achievement. He praised Millais for 'power, brilliancy, suavity, ease and "go"' but was not afraid to take him to task for the increasing carelessness that came with success: 'look at the mere smear of formless umber which stands for the boy's hand', in *Sir Isumbras (A Dream of the Past)* (1857, Lady Lever Art Gallery, National Museums Liverpool).[29]

In Holman Hunt's more literal art, William noticed, with a corresponding literality of his own, the odd jarring detail. Appreciating Hunt's *Claudio and Isabella* (1853, Tate), William observed that in spite of its subtlety of expression, its moral dignity and complexity, Claudio's hair looked like a wig. Unattuned to Hunt's religious fervour and opposed to overt symbolism, William nevertheless loved the exactitude of Hunt's rendering of the details that composed the English countryside in *The Hireling Shepherd* (1852, Figure 8), 'from the marsh-mallows, elecampane-plant, and thickly-tangled grass of the foreground, to the August corn-field and pollard-willows, and above all the elms and bean-stacks of the distance'.[30] When *Our English Coasts, 1852* (Tate) by Hunt was shown in 1853, William hailed it not only as 'the most triumphant vindication yet seen of the Præraphaelite principle' but also as 'a new experience in art'. The small sheep-picture 'barren of a single human figure, and confining itself to strictly ovine expression, contains as deep a human interest as any in the gallery' and was distinguished in William's opinion by its 'absolute truth, and beauty'.[31]

True as ever to his Pre-Raphaelite aesthetic, William's terms of praise derived from realism. Criticism could be compared with the emerging new art of photography, William thought, but not merely because of photography's capacity for realism. In his view both criticism and photography were interpretative arts which, at their best, could 'well-nigh re-create a subject; place it in novel, unanticipable lights; aggrandize the fine, suppress or ignore the petty; and transfigure both the subject-matter, and the reproducing

Figure 20 Julia Margaret Cameron, *William Michael Rossetti*, 1865, albumen photographic
print from wet collodion negative, 25.5 × 20 cm, private collection. Inscribed on verso by
William Michael Rossetti: 'The hand with umbrella is Browning's'.

process itself, into something almost higher than we knew them to be'.[32] He
saw this as an aim and function of both photography and criticism. Perhaps
that's why William sympathized with Julia Margaret Cameron's dramatic
experiments in photography and allowed her to make his portrait in moody,
theatrical pose (Figure 20). 'The golden age', William conjectured mischiev-
ously, 'might include the silence of critics; but that is the golden age, and
this is the iron one.'[33] William's critical voice, if neither golden nor iron, was
nevertheless unmistakable.

International intervention

William's knowledge of international art and his annual travels to Europe
made him the most cosmopolitan of the Rossettis. He became a cultural
conduit, interpreting British art to a global audience and bringing foreign
art, especially Oriental and French, to the attention of art lovers at home.
He contributed to transatlantic dialogue with his regular column, 'Art News
from London', which appeared in the New York *Crayon* during 1855–6.

In 1857, William turned from criticism to action in the international art world. He became joint promoter of an exhibition of modern British art shown in American cities, New York, Philadelphia and Boston. Organizing the show proved a logistical nightmare. Not only did it overlap with the Art Treasures Exhibition in Manchester, but it also coincided with a crash on the New York stock exchange. However, the American exhibition was a landmark – because of the Pre-Raphaelite pictures that William, with all his contacts, was able to assemble.

The show marked a significant moment of cross-cultural fertilization. It brought mid-century British art, with its startling new subjects and techniques, to American critics, artists and gallery-goers. Most importantly, it put the tenets of Pre-Raphaelitism into the American public arena. The Pre-Raphaelite art works triggered controversy in the American press. William had anticipated a mixed reception but he could not have anticipated the venom which greeted subtle pictures such as Arthur Hughes's *April Love* (Tate) or Elizabeth Siddall's *Clerk Saunders* (Figure 15). He also showed paintings by other artists connected, however loosely, with the Pre-Raphaelite movement: Barbara Bodichon, Ford Madox Brown, William Holman Hunt, William Henry Hunt, Frederic Leighton, John Ruskin, William Bell Scott and William Lindsay Windus.

Undoubtedly the Pre-Raphaelite pictures spoke to ordinary people. Workmen hanging Holman Hunt's *Light of the World* commented: 'Never mind the gas, the picture will light us up.' Although the American press had initially found Pre-Raphaelite pictures 'childish' with their concentration on mundane details such as 'all the weeds, dandelions, bits of straw, old glass, fence-rails, and pokers that can be found in Great Britain', gradually their tone changed.[34] The American exhibition of new British art caused hilarity and admiration, scorn and praise almost equally. It stimulated debate and gave a global dimension to Pre-Raphaelitism which the *Atlantic Monthly* judged had taken 'its position in the world as the beginning of a new Art – new in motive, new in methods, and new in the forms it puts on'.[35] Pre-Raphaelitism was on the international art map.

Politics and poetry

International politics as well as culture were key areas of William's thinking. Always a socialist and a 'democratic republican' in Victoria's England, William was an agnostic, a feminist and an opponent of tyranny everywhere. He expressed his political allegiances in fifty *Democratic Sonnets*, mostly written in 1881, not published until 1907. By then they had lost their fiery topicality and his brother Dante Gabriel was no longer alive to argue against publication.

In these sonnets, William found an outlet for his political passion. He was inspired to write by events such as the American Civil War, the Irish famine, the Crimean and Boer wars, the abolition of serfdom in Russia, the unification of Italy, the Paris Commune and revolutionary movements across Europe. It was poetry as polemic, more usually found in prose. During the American Civil War, his libertarian anti-slavery principles in England made him often feel 'singular and solitary in a roomful of company'.[36] William loathed tyrants, slavery, war and starvation. His ideals were those of Shelley and Whitman. Naturally he sympathized with the 1871 uprising known as the Paris Commune. He denounced Napoleon's legacy in the festering carcass of imperialism:

> Shall the Republic be once more betrayed?
> ... shall the Corsican's
> Unlineal nephew foist again on France
> His festered carcass, or his changeling's grade
> Of empire purple-born? ('The Parisian Commune, 1871', lines 1, 6–9) [37]

Sonnets on Cavour, Mazzini and Garibaldi endorsed his special heroes, the arbiters of Italian unification. In the Austro-Hungarian section, William attacked Metternich, 'The despot's prop, the people's adversary', and contorted his lines to react to the physical impact of 'the garotte of tyranny'.[38] Writing about revolution in Hungary, William denounced the Austrian general Julius Jacob von Haynau, who implemented barbaric reprisals against insurgents:

> He bared the backs of women, and he whipped
> Their naked flesh: women, Hungarians born,
> Whose crime was thrilling with their country torn
> By dual beak of Austria's eagle. ('Haynau, 1849–50', lines 1–4)[39]

Playing on words, William conflated Haynau's very name into a ravening hyena. Using similar onomatopoeic language, he almost choked on his loathing of kings, tsars and Caesars in his sonnet marking the date when twenty-three million Russians 'the age-long-cankering collar quitted'.[40] Serfdom in Russia was finally abolished in 1861.

Bringing his sonnet sequence to a conclusion, William surveyed 'The Past' and tried to see 'A purpose in the ages'.[41] Drawn from gradations of light, his imagery and outlook were only partially optimistic. It was clear how sceptical William remained about the realization of his political ideals in 1907, when the *Democratic Sonnets* were published at last.

Historian and documenter of the PRB

Among William's most important literary works were those acts of scholarship and remembrance he undertook to establish not only the whole Rossetti family myth but also much of Pre-Raphaelite history. He outlived all the Rossettis to raise their monument in his editions, biographies and memoirs, and in published collections of their personal papers and letters. In so doing, he became literary executor not only to the Rossetti family but also to the PRB. With his appetite for collecting and archiving documents, editing poetry, memorializing and writing biographies, he was the most effective public relations officer the PRB never appointed. On the celebrated Rossetti family, William was his own and the public's best informant. Without conceit he saw his function not merely as 'keeper of the flame' of the PRB and Rossetti family history but also as their interpreter and transmitter to posterity.

Following the deaths of Dante Gabriel and Christina Rossetti, William collated and published successive editions of his siblings' major works. He edited Gabriel's collected works in 1886, 1891, 1904 and 1911, produced his own account of *Dante Gabriel Rossetti as Designer and Writer* in 1889, a major two-volume biography of his brother in 1895, an invaluable *Bibliography* of his brother's works in 1905 and in 1906 his own autobiography, *Some Reminiscences*, richly textured with Pre-Raphaelite detail.

In his monumental biography, *Dante Gabriel Rossetti: His Family-Letters with a Memoir*, published nearly half a century after the PRB had disbanded, William encapsulated what had been their fundamental aims:

> 1, To have genuine ideas to express; 2, to study Nature attentively, so as to know how to express them; 3, to sympathize with what is direct and serious and heartfelt in previous art ... and 4, and most indispensable of all, to produce thoroughly good pictures and statues.[42]

As one of the original 'Brothers', he felt a duty to the future to record the innovative objectives of the Pre-Raphaelite artists, and his account laid the basis for all later historiography of the movement. Through their peculiarity, a small metropolitan group had made English art universal or at least international. 'The pre-Raffaelites [sic] are the only English artists who cut any ice at all outside England', thought Ford Madox Brown's grandson, the writer Ford Madox Ford who considered himself their literary descendant.[43]

When presenting his biography of Dante Gabriel, William asserted his moral rights to reticence, in a statement that most biographers and autobiographers today would find alien. 'I have told what I choose to tell,' he said, but added tantalizingly, 'it does not follow that I know nothing beyond that which I write. In some cases I do know a good deal more; but to cast a slur here or violate a confidence there would make me contemptible to myself.'[44] The biographical task for William was deeply complex. Although he knew he would be accused of a brother's partiality, ultimately he turned what might seem a disadvantage into a special strength. He presented facts that only he could know. Aware of the inevitable subjectivity of his opinion of Gabriel, he juxtaposed his hind-sighted narrative with his private diary extracts written at the time, and called in evidence from other key eyewitnesses: family members, artistic associates and even the medical profession. William's account knitted autobiography with biography to achieve unique texture. His approach multiplied the angles from which Gabriel could be viewed and had an almost cinematic effect.

William justly estimated his brother's vital contribution to nineteenth-century British art, inspired by 'the pure loveliness and self-withdrawn suavity' of Elizabeth Siddall, and by Jane Morris's 'face of arcane and inexhaustible meaning'.[45] He agreed with Gabriel's own opinion that his finer achievement was in poetry rather than in painting, a debatable assessment. For William, Gabriel was a tragic and divided Hamlet figure who had 'that within which passeth show', a man 'of astonishing genius, ardent initiative, vigorous and fascinating personality, abundant loveableness, many defects, and in late years overclouded temperament and bedimmed outlook on the world, whom it was once my privilege to call brother'.[46] Although Gabriel could be 'imperative, dominant, self-sustained, and stiff-necked', William affirmed that if 'his work was great; the man was greater'.[47] His personal tragedy was that though Gabriel's work was done 'it did not prove to be its own exceeding great reward'. If Gabriel was Hamlet, then William was Horatio, left alone after the deaths of brother, mother, sisters, wife, to tell his story, 'a faithful biographer' who had 'no wish to thrust [him]self constantly forward'.[48] In writing the life-stories of both Gabriel and Christina, William had no agenda to display his own ego. He held it his familial duty to ensure the lasting reputation of siblings he considered geniuses.

Although he modestly evaluated himself as a brother 'of very minor pretensions',[49] William knew his *Family-Letters with a Memoir* of Gabriel was 'certainly the most considerable performance of my lifetime'.[50] His editions of *Family-Letters* of both Gabriel in 1895, and Christina in 1908, showed his editorial skills at their best. The letters were catalogued, dated and accompanied by contextual and biographical notes which often provided more fascinating data than the letters themselves. If William cut lines within letters, he scrupulously indicated omissions. As acts of scholarship, retrieval and re-animation, these editions could not have been produced by anyone else at the time, and have formed the basis of biographical research for over a century.

For his sister Christina, William edited *New Poems* (1896) and wrote a perceptive life for *The Poetical Works of Christina Georgina Rossetti with Memoir and Notes &c by William Michael Rossetti* (1904). Blame for this collected edition, 'cramped and crowded, poorly printed, meanly published, two columns to a small page', pursued him into the twentieth century. William was blamed for things that were not his fault. It was almost impossible to assemble a complete edition of Christina's poetry. William worked on that project from 1898, aware that 'after my death there wd. not remain any one very well qualified to undertake anything of the kind'.[51] His editorial practices may seem over-invasive by modern standards but he was motivated by the constraints of brotherly love. In his short *Memoir* of Christina, he strenuously aimed at objectivity and conveyed an accurate impression of her personality.

In all these works William tried to observe an almost impossible double loyalty – both to his famous family and its right to privacy, and to the public's right to know. William believed absolutely in both these principles and tried to resolve the inevitable conflict between them with firmness and tact. Cynics attacked him for the duplicity of observing such double standards and ignored the tension of the tightrope he was teetering on. Where he had shown an excess of conscience, they accused him of the sin of commercialism, a slur that has persisted into modern times. Long after William's death Edmund Gosse was still grumbling about 'publications, revelations, sales of objects [that] followed in a terrible succession'.[52]

Gosse misunderstood the fraternal links that had bonded the English Pre-Raphaelite Brothers and their associates and, more deeply still, the three-quarters Italian Rossetti family. That Rossetti family was expanded, anglicized and identified ever more intimately with the wider Pre-Raphaelite art world when in 1874 William Michael Rossetti married Ford Madox Brown's elder daughter, Lucy Madox Brown. From the intelligentsia, located on the borders between the Victorian middle class and artistic bohemianism, they were an unusual couple for their times, sexually frank, avowedly agnostic, politically radical and committedly feminist. An ambitious and sensitive professional artist, Lucy had trained in her father's studio like the early Florentines. Her exquisite and intelligent paintings were made according to the legacy of Pre-Raphaelite principles. Influenced partly by her father, that unofficial Pre-Raphaelite, Ford Madox Brown, and partly by her brother-in-law, Dante Gabriel Rossetti, the most visible of all the Pre-Raphaelites, Lucy's works were nevertheless characteristically her own.[53] The great literary passion she shared with William was a love of Shelley. His *Memoir* of Shelley and successive editions of his *Works* found a counterpart in Lucy's life of Mary Shelley. Their marriage was built on the intersections between art and literature; their alliance and their descendants cemented the joint Rossetti/Madox Brown inheritance. Quietly but practically, William Michael Rossetti was the linchpin of his extended Rossetti family and of the whole Pre-Raphaelite Brotherhood.

NOTES

1 William E. Fredeman, *The P. R. B. Journal: William Michael Rossetti's Diary of the Pre-Raphaelite Brotherhood 1849–1853* (Oxford: Clarendon Press, 1975), p. xxv (hereafter *PRB Journal*).
2 Ibid., p. xxv.
3 Ibid., p. 6 (23 May 1849).
4 Angela Thirlwell, *William and Lucy: The Other Rossettis* (New Haven and London: Yale University Press, 2003), pp. 105–21 (hereafter *William and Lucy*).
5 *PRB Journal*, p. 6 (24 May 1849).
6 Ibid., p. 7 (27 May 1849).
7 Ibid., p. 7 (29 May 1849).
8 Ibid., pp. 7–8 (30 May 1849).
9 William Michael Rossetti, *Some Reminiscences*, 2 vols. (London: Brown, Langham, 1906), vol. I, p. 81.
10 William Michael Rossetti (ed.), *Dante Gabriel Rossetti: His Family-Letters with a Memoir*, 2 vols. (London: Ellis and Elvey, 1895), vol. II, p. 63. Professor David Bentley has identified a possible source for 'Mrs. Holmes Grey' in the Heaviside case, one of the most sensational divorce actions of the 1840s. See D. M. R. Bentley, '"A very clever and finished piece of writing": William Michael Rossetti's "Mrs. Holmes Grey"', *The Journal of Pre-Raphaelite Studies*, 20 (Spring 2011), pp. 5–25.
11 *PRB Journal*, Appendix 7, p. 148.
12 Algernon Charles Swinburne, *The Swinburne Letters*, ed. Cecil Y. Lang, 6 vols. (New Haven: Yale University Press, 1959–62), vol. I, pp. 288–9 (letter dated 1 February [1868]).
13 William Bell Scott, *Autobiographical Notes of the Life of William Bell Scott, and Notices of his Artistic and Poetic Circle of Friends 1830 to 1882*, ed. W. Minto, 2 vols. (London: James R. Osgood, McIlvaine, 1892), vol. I, pp. 324–5.
14 *The Guardian*, 20 August 1850, cited in *Germ*, 'Introduction by William Michael Rossetti', p. 14.
15 *William and Lucy*, pp. 121–2.
16 William Michael Rossetti, *Fine Art, Chiefly Contemporary* (London: Macmillan, 1867), p. 37.
17 See Roger W. Peattie, 'William Michael Rossetti's Art Notices in the Periodicals, 1850–1878: An Annotated Checklist', *Victorian Periodicals Newsletter*, 8 (June 1975), pp. 79–92; Julie L'Enfant, *William Rossetti's Art Criticism: The Search for Truth in Victorian Art* (Lanham, MD: University Press of America, 1999).
18 Robin Ironside and John Gere, *Pre-Raphaelite Painters* (London: Phaidon Press, 1948), p. 13.
19 Amy Woolner, *Thomas Woolner, R. A. Sculptor and Poet: His Life in Letters* (New York: E. P. Dutton, 1917), p. 9 (letter dated 8 November 1850).

20 W. M. Rossetti, *Some Reminiscences*, vol. I, p. 94.
21 *The Young George du Maurier, A Selection of his Letters 1860–67*, ed. Daphne du Maurier (London: Peter Davies, 1951), p. 207 (letter of August 1863).
22 Letter in a private collection, by descent from Daisy Brett (John Brett to Rosa Brett, 22 March 1860).
23 Collection Mark Samuels Lasner (John Ruskin to W. J. Stillman, 15 February 1855).
24 W. M. Rossetti, *Fine Art*, p. xiv.
25 Henry James, *The Painter's Eye: Notes and Essays on the Pictorial Arts*, ed. John L. Sweeney (Madison, WI: University of Wisconsin Press, 1989), p. 37, 'An English Critic of French Painting, 1868', originally published (but ironically, unsigned) in the *North American Review*, April 1868.
26 W. M. Rossetti, *Fine Art*, p. xv.
27 Ibid., pp. 5, 6, 7, 10.
28 Ibid., p. 207.
29 Ibid., p. 222.
30 Ibid., p. 235.
31 Ibid., pp. 237–8.
32 Ibid., pp. 333–4.
33 Ibid., p. 330.
34 *New York Times*, 7 November 1857, p. 2.
35 *Atlantic Monthly*, 1 February 1858, pp. 505–6.
36 William Michael Rossetti, 'English Opinion on the American War', *Atlantic Monthly*, 17 February 1866, pp. 129–30.
37 William Michael Rossetti, *Democratic Sonnets*, 2 vols. (London: Alston Rivers, 1907), vol. I, p. xxxiv.
38 Ibid., vol. II, p. xxi ('Metternich, 1848', lines 2, 7).
39 Ibid., vol. II, p. xxiii.
40 Ibid., vol. II, p. xxv ('The Russian Serfs Freed, 1861', line 13).
41 Ibid., vol. II, p. xxxi ('The Past', line 1).
42 W. M. Rossetti, *DGR: His Family-Letters*, vol. I, p. 135.
43 *The Correspondence of Ford Madox Ford and Stella Bowen*, ed. Sondra J. Stang and Karen Cochran (Bloomington: Indiana University Press, 1992), p. 441.
44 W. M. Rossetti, *DGR: His Family-Letters*, vol. I, p. xii.
45 Ibid., vol. I, p. 241.
46 Ibid., vol. I, p. 331.
47 Ibid., vol. I, pp. 359, 407.
48 Ibid., vol. I, pp. 233, 278.
49 Ibid., vol. I, p. 423.
50 William Michael Rossetti's MS Diary, University of British Columbia, Rare Books and Special Collections, Angeli-Dennis Collection, and on microfilm at the Bodleian Library, University of Oxford, Modern Papers, 10 April 1895.
51 Ibid., 28 July 1898.
52 Edmund Gosse, *Sunday Times*, 6 May 1928, p. 8.
53 See *William and Lucy*, chapter 5.

18

ELIZABETH PRETTEJOHN

Envoi

But the really odd thing about the Pre-Raphaelite literature, vast though it
is, is how many of the obvious and essential books remain to be written.
Editorial, *The Burlington Magazine*, February 1973[1]

Odder still: four decades later, when the Pre-Raphaelite literature has grown
far vaster, the statement remains true. Perhaps, though, that marks not a
deficiency in Pre-Raphaelite scholarship, but rather an unquenchable vitality in Pre-Raphaelite art and literature, a continual capacity for reinvention
that keeps calling for new 'essential books'. Admittedly, there is much that
is routine, or repetitive, in Pre-Raphaelite studies. How often, for example,
have we heard the story of the initial shocked response to the PRB, followed by its rise to fame, and then its dissolution as the Brothers went their
separate ways (to D. G. Rossetti in 1853, this already read as a parallel
to the story of Arthur and his Knights of the Round Table[2])? Or the corresponding story, with its inverted curve, of the precipitous decline in the
Pre-Raphaelites' reputation at the end of the nineteenth century, followed
by a revival in more recent years? It is as though the Pre-Raphaelite defiance
of convention still needs to be tamed, through the compulsive repetition of
these familiar narrative patterns.

Much of the energy in the most recent phase of the much-vaunted revival
has been devoted to exploding the first of these conventional narratives:
to demystifying the story of the PRB's early days as it was constructed in
William Holman Hunt's autobiography, to re-evaluating and recontextual-
izing the early criticism of the group, or to questioning the story of inevitable decline that has dogged accounts of the later careers of so many of
the Pre-Raphaelites. Yet this raises importunate questions about the second
narrative that have scarcely begun to be addressed. How did the story of
Pre-Raphaelitism congeal into orthodoxy in a period when, we are told, Pre-
Raphaelite art and literature were altogether out of fashion?

For today's undergraduate students the ubiquitous stories about the Pre-
Raphaelites' twentieth-century fall from favour – the word 'nadir' is commonly found – may appear strangely defamiliarizing. How could poems
and paintings now so compulsively recognizable ever have dropped out of
view? When, indeed, was this nadir? And when was the 'revival'? A useful

collection of essays edited by James Sambrook and published in 1974, when the putative revival was well underway, includes a sequence of early writings by and about the Pre-Raphaelites, from 1850 to 1868 (together with an excerpt from Hunt's autobiography dealing with those early days). It then jumps abruptly to a second sequence of modern criticisms, in chronological order from Stephen Spender's 'The Pre-Raphaelite Literary Painters' of 1945 to John Dixon Hunt's 'A Moment's Monument: Reflections on Pre-Raphaelite Vision in Poetry and Painting' of 1974, with essays by such well-known figures as Humphry House, Graham Hough, Jerome Hamilton Buckley and Jerome McGann along the way. Spender begins with the simple statement, 'The greatest artistic movement in England during the nineteenth century was Pre-Raphaelitism', and notes that Hunt's autobiography 'made an unforgettable impression on me when I was fourteen' – that would have been about 1933, the year the Tate Gallery mounted a retrospective exhibition to celebrate the centenary of Burne-Jones's birth.[3] Spender in 1945, like the other writers in Sambrook's collection, has complete command of all of the stock stories about the Pre-Raphaelites, and he refers to paintings, poems and events in the history of the movement with obvious confidence that they will already be familiar to his readers. One begins to wonder whether the Pre-Raphaelites' fall from grace, and the inevitable nadir, are not paradoxical figures for their nagging cultural presence, rather than their disappearance from view.

This suggests that one or more of the 'essential books', still to be written, should explore the curious anxiety of influence that made it necessary to repeat, so often, the claim that the Pre-Raphaelites had gone out of fashion. As the foregoing chapters have repeatedly demonstrated, the Pre-Raphaelites and their associates were assiduous in attempting to place themselves in the histories of literature and art, from the list of Immortals of 1848 through to Hunt's autobiography of 1905 and beyond, perhaps, to the studies of Pre-Raphaelitism by such figures as Ford Madox Hueffer (later called Ford Madox Ford) in 1906 or Evelyn Waugh in 1926 (Hueffer was the grandson of Ford Madox Brown, Waugh a relation of the Waugh sisters who married Holman Hunt and Thomas Woolner).[4] That, it is easy to see, was the concomitant of the new, nineteenth-century awareness of the history of art that must have influenced the group's choice of name in the first place. Yet it can be argued that the process of finding the Pre-Raphaelites' place in history went astray, somehow, in the twentieth century, when they came to seem too singular or anomalous to be contextualized, except as an aberration or sideline.

There are two aspects to this, one geographical, the other chronological. We have seen that the essays of the 1940s to the 1970s in Sambrook's collection present the Pre-Raphaelites, for the most part, in ways that are still very familiar, but there is a notable exception: these mid-twentieth-century writers take it for granted that Pre-Raphaelitism was an insular movement, unconnected to artistic developments on the Continent, and therefore outside the mainstream development of artistic modernism. That assumption is oddly contradicted by Sambrook's own bibliography, which interestingly organizes its sources in chronological order; conspicuous among these are studies of the Pre-Raphaelites in French, from the chapter on them in Ernest Chesneau's *La peinture anglaise* of 1882 to Jacques Lethève's article in the *Gazette des Beaux-Arts* of 1959, 'La connaissance des peintres préraphaélites anglais en France, 1855–1900'. Sambrook could have added a similar number of studies in German, had he wished.[5] Clearly the Pre-Raphaelites were well connected and well known outside Britain.

In chronological terms, the Pre-Raphaelites have notably failed to gain a secure place in the standard sequence of European avant-garde movements – from Impressionism to Abstract Expressionism in painting, say, or from Romanticism to Imagism in literature. The famous chart by Alfred Barr, devised to accompany an exhibition of 1936 at the Museum of Modern Art in New York, scrupulously documents every 'ism' leading up to modernist abstraction – but not Pre-Raphaelitism.[6] Another example might be the recent *Oxford Critical and Cultural History of Modernist Magazines*, which considers *The Germ* among 'Victorian Precursors', outside the volume's 'modernist' purview (the date range deemed relevant is 1880–1955).[7] Moreover, the impact of the Pre-Raphaelites on later generations has often been confined to figures or groups seen as marginal, such as the English 'Neo-Romantics', rather than explored in relation to the modernist mainstream.[8] Statements by the early modernists themselves have seemed to confirm the Pre-Raphaelites' irrelevance; Ezra Pound, for example, tells of shaking off Rossetti's influence when he translated Guido Cavalcanti, and Yeats writes in the past tense of the youthful period when 'I was in all things Pre-Raphaelite'.[9] Yet there are fourteen page references to 'Pre-Raphaelites and Pre-Raphaelitism' in the index to Yeats's *Autobiographies*, and Pound had earlier declared that, with regard to translation, 'Rossetti is my father and my mother'.[10] The repudiations should only make the influence more interesting.

Recent studies have begun to reconsider both the geographical and the chronological isolation of the Pre-Raphaelites, but the process has had very different trajectories in literary and artistic contexts. An important project among the current generation of historians of Pre-Raphaelite art has been its reintegration into the international context in which, as a matter of the simplest historical fact, it actually operated, from the conspicuous appearance of the Pre-Raphaelites at the Paris Exposition Universelle of 1855 through the entire sequence of international exhibitions, in all the major artistic centres worldwide, up to World War One.[11] It was the twentieth century, not the nineteenth, that kept Pre-Raphaelite art in insular isolation. In England, despite the Pre-Raphaelites' putative fall from grace, their popular appeal ensured the regular appearance of exhibitions, both of individual Pre-Raphaelites and of the group, throughout the century, with a particular concentration in 1948, the centenary of the PRB's formation – but none of these travelled, and Pre-Raphaelite art was scarcely seen outside the British Isles.[12]

Suddenly, the situation has changed beyond recognition. Whereas the monographic exhibitions on the main Pre-Raphaelites from 1964 to 1975, which have often (and rightly) been credited with a major role in reviving the artists' fortunes, were shown only in England,[13] the new sequence that began in 1998 is fully international: Burne-Jones was seen in New York and Paris (1998–9), Rossetti in Amsterdam (2003–4), Simeon Solomon in Munich (2005–6), Millais in Amsterdam and Japan (2007–8), Holman Hunt in Toronto and Minneapolis (2008–9), Ford Madox Brown in Ghent (2012). Thematic or general exhibitions on Pre-Raphaelitism have appeared since 2009 in Stockholm, Stuttgart, Ravenna, Paris, Rome, Sydney and Washington, DC.[14] These exhibitions are important not only because they introduce Pre-Raphaelite art to new audiences, but also because they place it in new contexts: all of the catalogues, and in some cases a selection of exhibits, relate English Pre-Raphaelitism to the art of the country of display. This development is certain to produce a new explosion of Pre-Raphaelite studies; it is safe to predict that the view of Pre-Raphaelitism as an English insular movement will appear quaintly old-fashioned in a few years' time.

In the study of Pre-Raphaelite literature, there have been a few, more tentative attempts to widen the geographical perspective, notably from scholars in other countries who work on English literature, but the main concentration remains resolutely Anglophone. There are obvious reasons for this, yet the Pre-Raphaelites themselves were intensely interested in the literatures of other languages (as the foregoing chapters have repeatedly shown), and their works were translated into a variety of languages. Here, perhaps, the art historians have something to teach the scholars of English literature: the worldwide dissemination of Pre-Raphaelite literature, largely unresearched as yet, may prove to be as important as that of the art despite the language barrier.[15]

On the other hand, literary scholars have made much more progress than art historians in acknowledging the Pre-Raphaelites' legacy to modernism; it no longer seems strange, for example, to give Dante Gabriel Rossetti a central role in a history that includes Yeats, Pound, Joyce and Eliot.[16]

But where should we look for Rossetti's legacy, or that of the other Pre-Raphaelites, in modern art? The question is so new that art historians may have no idea where to start. There has long been a rather vague tradition of linking the Pre-Raphaelites to the continental Symbolism of the late nineteenth century, something that has begun to be explored more systematically; the Tate's exhibition, *The Age of Rossetti, Burne-Jones and Watts: Symbolism in Britain 1860–1910*, greeted gingerly by critics when it appeared in 1997, has proved surprisingly influential (several of the continental exhibitions, mentioned above, consider Pre-Raphaelite influences on the Symbolist movements in their own countries).[17] Symbolism, though, itself stands apart from the modernist mainstream in art history, and it remains an open question whether, or how, the Pre-Raphaelites can be integrated into the larger story of modern art. It took a literary scholar, Richard L. Stein in 1975, to note the compositional similarity between Rossetti's *Ecce Ancilla Domini!* of 1850 and Vincent van Gogh's *Bedroom at Arles* of 1888; the suggestion has not piqued the interest of scholars of van Gogh or Post-Impressionism.[18] The Pre-Raphaelites are known to have been admired and discussed in Picasso's Barcelona circle around 1900, but little attempt has been made to assess the significance of this to Picasso's work.[19] Salvador Dalí's article 'Le surréalisme spectral de l'Éternel Féminin préraphaélite', published in the Surrealist magazine *Minotaure* in 1936, has been mentioned once or twice in the Pre-Raphaelite literature, and one enterprising scholar of Surrealism, David Lomas, has proposed Rossetti's 'double work of art' as a point of reference for Dalí.[20] It remains to be seen, though, whether this might open up a new avenue of study for scholars either of Pre-Raphaelitism or of Surrealism.

Any of these clues, not to mention countless others still unidentified, may develop into the 'essential books' for the next generation of Pre-Raphaelite studies. If the suggestion seems eccentric, to those of us brought up on the histories of modern art and modernist literature that ruthlessly ignore the Pre-Raphaelites, it might be well to remember that Botticelli seemed an irrelevant sideline in Renaissance art before he was taken up by Rossetti and Burne-Jones in the 1860s.[21] Whereas Botticelli's art was then unfamiliar, Pre-Raphaelite paintings may have the opposite problem, so wearisomely ubiquitous are their reproductions in all manner of media. Yet some of today's artists are showing how we might see them afresh. An example is Tom Hunter, who re-staged a number of Pre-Raphaelite paintings with settings and models from a depressed area of London, to create the hauntingly beautiful, and intellectually ambitious, photographic series *Life and Death in Hackney* (1999–2001); two works from the series were included in the Stockholm exhibition, *The Pre-Raphaelites*, of 2009.[22] In that context the Pre-Raphaelite influence on contemporary art did not seem problematical; even more interesting, though, was the way the contemporary photographic works suggested new perspectives on the Pre-Raphaelite paintings they reinterpreted.

Anyone who reads a selection of discussions of Pre-Raphaelitism in chronological sequence, from the 1940s through to the present, will be struck by the frequent claim that the Pre-Raphaelites are just beginning to be revived (indeed, Roger Fry was already noting a revival of Victorian style, although not specifically of the Pre-Raphaelites, as early as 1919[23]). As the preceding reflections have hinted, there are reasonable grounds for scepticism about whether such a revival was ever required, so difficult is it to find any period when the Pre-Raphaelites were truly out of view. But if the revival is something of a fiction, it is one full of promise. If the Pre-Raphaelites were no longer in need of revival, if the 'obvious and essential books' had already been written, then Pre-Raphaelite studies would be at an end. Let us hope, then, that the Pre-Raphaelite revival is only just beginning.

NOTES

1   'Editorial: An Over-Trodden Path?', *Burlington Magazine*, 115 (February 1973), p. 73; my thanks to Richard Shone for identifying the author as Keith Roberts.
2   In a letter to Christina Rossetti of 8 November 1853, when Holman Hunt was about to depart for the Holy Land and Millais was elected A.R.A. (Associate of the Royal Academy); Rossetti quotes Tennyson: 'So now the whole Round Table is dissolved!' DGR *Correspondence*, vol. I, p. 294 (letter 53.57).
3   Stephen Spender, 'The Pre-Raphaelite Literary Painters', *New Writing and Daylight*, 6 (1945), repr. in James Sambrook (ed.), *Pre-Raphaelitism: A Collection of Critical Essays* (Chicago and London: University of Chicago Press, 1974), p. 118.
4   Ford Madox Hueffer [Ford Madox Ford], *The Pre-Raphaelite Brotherhood: A Critical Monograph* (London: Duckworth, 1906); Evelyn Waugh, *P. R. B.: An Essay on the Pre-Raphaelite Brotherhood, 1847–1854* (London: Alastair Graham, 1926). For a fuller list of early writings on the PRB see the bibliography in Sambrook, *Pre-Raphaelitism*, pp. 265–70.
5   For example, two magisterial, and influential, histories of modern art, both of which give long chapters to the Pre-Raphaelites and their later followers: Richard Muther, *Geschichte der Malerei im 19. Jahrhundert*, 3 vols. (Munich: G. Hirth, 1893–4), vol. II, pp. 480–518; vol. III, pp. 461–521 (*The History of Modern Painting*, trans. Ernest Dowson and others, 3 vols. (London: Henry, 1895–6)); Julius Meier-Graefe, *Modern Art: Being a Contribution to a New System of Aesthetics*, trans. Florence Simmonds and George W. Chrystal, 2 vols. (London: William Heinemann and New York: G. P. Putnam's Sons, 1908), vol. II, pp. 187–265 (originally published as *Entwicklungsgeschichte der modernen Kunst*, 3 vols. (Stuttgart: J. Hoffmann, 1904)). For the German reception see also Christofer Conrad and Annabel Zettel (eds.), *Edward Burne-Jones: The Earthly Paradise*, exhibition catalogue (Stuttgart: Staatsgalerie and Bern: Kunstmuseum, 2009).

6 Admittedly Barr's chart starts in 1890, but the decision to start at that date rules out Pre-Raphaelitism and places the emphasis on French origins for modernism. See Astrit Schmidt Burkhardt, 'Shaping Modernism: Alfred Barr's Genealogy of Art', *Word and Image*, 16 (October–December 2000), pp. 387–400.

7 See, however, the excellent chapter by Marysa Demoor, 'In the Beginning, There Was *The Germ*: The Pre-Raphaelites and "Little Magazines"', in Peter Brooker and Andrew Thacker (eds.), *The Oxford Critical and Cultural History of Modernist Magazines*, vol. I: *Britain and Ireland 1880–1955* (Oxford: Oxford University Press, 2009), pp. 51–65. See also the review by Stefan Collini, 'Germ and Blast', *TLS*, 9 October 2009, pp. 3–4.

8 Some of these groups were explored in an intriguing exhibition of 1989: John Christian (ed.), *The Last Romantics: The Romantic Tradition in British Art: Burne-Jones to Stanley Spencer*, exhibition catalogue (London: Barbican Art Gallery/Lund Humphries, 1989).

9 Ezra Pound, *Make It New: Essays by Ezra Pound* (London: Faber & Faber, 1934), pp. 398–400; W. B. Yeats, *Autobiographies* (1955) (London: Macmillan, 1961), p. 114.

10 'Introduction', dated 15 November 1910, to Ezra Pound, *The Sonnets and Ballate of Guido Cavalcanti* (1912), repr. in *The Translations of Ezra Pound*, intro. Hugh Kenner (London: Faber & Faber, 1953), p. 20.

11 On the Paris Exposition Universelle of 1855 see Elizabeth Prettejohn, 'Art', in Francis O'Gorman (ed.), *The Cambridge Companion to Victorian Culture* (Cambridge: Cambridge University Press, 2010), pp. 195–201. Work by doctoral students in this area is growing rapidly, though it is still too new to have been published. The catalogues of Pre-Raphaelite exhibitions shown outside Britain since 1998 also routinely include consideration of the dissemination of Pre-Raphaelite art in the relevant countries; see the 'Guide to further reading and looking' for a list.

12 Two notable, indeed pioneering, exceptions were mounted by US galleries with Pre-Raphaelite holdings: *Paintings and Drawings of the Pre-Raphaelites and their Circle* (Cambridge, MA: Fogg Art Museum, Harvard University, 1946) and *Dante Gabriel Rossetti and His Circle: A Loan Exhibition of Paintings, Drawings and Decorative Objects by the Pre-Raphaelites and Their Friends* (Lawrence, KS: University of Kansas Museum of Art, 1958). The latter was also enterprising in its inclusion of applied art; see Deborah Cherry, 'In a Word: Pre-Raphaelite, Pre-Raphaelites, Pre-Raphaelitism', in Michaela Giebelhausen and Tim Barringer (eds.), *Writing the Pre-Raphaelites; Text, Context, Subtext* (Farnham, Surrey and Burlington, Vermont: Ashgate Publishing, 2009), pp. 18–19. This volume includes a useful bibliography of Pre-Raphaelite exhibitions (pp. 250–3); see also the bibliography in Sambrook, *Pre-Raphaelitism*, pp. 265–70.

13 The series of exhibitions at the Walker Art Gallery, Liverpool, curated by Mary Bennett, initiated this sequence: *Ford Madox Brown 1821–1893* (1964, also shown at Manchester City Art Gallery and Birmingham City Museum and Art Gallery), *PRB Millais PRA* (1967, also shown in London, Royal Academy of Arts), *William Holman Hunt* (1969, also shown in London, Victoria and Albert Museum). These were followed by *Dante Gabriel Rossetti: Painter and Poet* (London: Royal Academy of Arts and Birmingham City Museum and Art Gallery, 1973, catalogue by Virginia Surtees), *Frederick Sandys 1829–1904*

(Brighton Museum and Art Gallery, 1974, catalogue by Betty O'Looney), *Burne-Jones: The Paintings, Graphic and Decorative Work of Sir Edward Burne-Jones 1833–98* (Arts Council of Great Britain, 1975, catalogue by John Christian) and *The Drawings of John Everett Millais* (Arts Council of Great Britain, 1979, catalogue by Malcolm Warner).

14   See the 'Guide to further reading and looking' for details of these exhibitions.

15   The important series edited by Elinor Shaffer, *The Reception of British and Irish Authors in Europe*, shows the way, although it has not yet covered any of the Pre-Raphaelites; there is relevant material, however, in Stephen Bann (ed.), *The Reception of Walter Pater in Europe* (London and New York: Continuum, 2004) and Stefano Evangelista (ed.), *The Reception of Oscar Wilde in Europe* (London and New York: Continuum, 2010).

16   See for example Jerome McGann, *Dante Gabriel Rossetti and the Game That Must Be Lost* (New Haven and London: Yale University Press, 2000), pp. 43–5 (McGann also hints at a trajectory from Rossetti as a 'conceptual artist' to Kandinsky, Mondrian, Klee (p. 48) and especially Duchamp (pp. 154–7), and the book consistently addresses features of Rossetti's work that can be called 'proto-Modernist'). See also, with particular reference to printing and William Morris, Jerome McGann, *Black Riders: The Visible Language of Modernism* (Princeton, NJ: Princeton University Press, 1993).

17   Andrew Wilton and Robert Upstone (eds.), *The Age of Rossetti, Burne-Jones and Watts: Symbolism in Britain 1860–1910*, exhibition catalogue (London: Tate Gallery Publishing, 1997).

18   Richard L. Stein, *The Ritual of Interpretation: The Fine Arts as Literature in Ruskin, Rossetti, and Pater* (Cambridge, MA and London: Harvard University Press, 1975), p. 184. See Elizabeth Prettejohn, 'From Aestheticism to Modernism, and Back Again', *19: Interdisciplinary Studies in the Long Nineteenth Century*, issue 2 (May 2006), http://19.bbk.ac.uk/index.php/19/article/viewFile/440/301.

19   See, however, brief comments by Richard Shone and Richard Morphet, in Richard Shone, *The Art of Bloomsbury: Roger Fry, Vanessa Bell and Duncan Grant*, exhibition catalogue (London: Tate Gallery Publishing, 1999), pp. 19, 24, and note 14 on p. 22.

20   Elizabeth Prettejohn, *The Art of the Pre-Raphaelites* (London: Tate Publishing, 2000), p. 262; David Lomas, *The Haunted Self: Surrealism, Psychoanalysis, Subjectivity* (New Haven and London: Yale University Press, 2000), p. 173.

21   See Frank Kermode, 'Botticelli Recovered', in *Forms of Attention* (Chicago and London: University of Chicago Press, 1985), pp. 3–31. Rossetti's role in the recovery of Botticelli has yet to be fully explored; see, however, Gail S. Weinberg, 'D. G. Rossetti's Ownership of Botticelli's "Smeralda Brandini"', *Burlington Magazine*, 146 (January 2004), pp. 20–6.

22   Mikael Ahlund and others, *The Pre-Raphaelites*, exhibition catalogue (Stockholm: Nationalmuseum, 2009), pp. 242–3; see also the artist's website, www.tomhunter.org.

23   Roger Fry, 'The Ottoman and the Whatnot', *Athenaeum*, 27 June 1919, repr. in Roger Fry, *Vision and Design* (1920), ed. J. B. Bullen (London and New York: Oxford University Press, 1990), pp. 28–32.

The contents of *The Germ*

A. Contents as listed on contents pages (authors' names of anonymously or pseudonymously published contributions given in square brackets)

Printed on all four covers: 'When whoso merely hath a little thought' [sonnet, William Michael Rossetti]

No. 1, January 1850 [all contributions anonymous in this issue, except the etching]

Etching by William Holman Hunt, to accompany 'My Beautiful Lady' and 'Of my Lady in Death'

My Beautiful Lady [poem, Thomas Woolner]
Of my Lady in Death [poem, Thomas Woolner]
The Love of Beauty [sonnet, Ford Madox Brown]
The Subject in Art (No. 1.) [essay, John L. Tupper (No. II in issue no. 3)]
The Seasons [poem, Coventry Patmore]
Dream Land [poem, Christina Rossetti]
Songs of One Household (My Sister's Sleep) [poem, Dante Gabriel Rossetti]
Hand and Soul [story, Dante Gabriel Rossetti]
The Bothie of Toper-na-fuosich [review, William Michael Rossetti]
Her First Season [sonnet, William Michael Rossetti]
A Sketch from Nature [poem, John L. Tupper]
An End [poem, Christina Rossetti]

No. 2, February 1850

Etching by James Collinson, to accompany 'The Child Jesus'

The Child Jesus: by James Collinson [poem]
A Pause of Thought: by Ellen Alleyn [poem, Christina Rossetti]

The Purpose and Tendency of Early Italian Art: by John Seward [essay,
F. G. Stephens]
Song: by Ellen Alleyn [poem, Christina Rossetti]
Morning Sleep: by Wm. B. Scott [poem]
Sonnet: by Calder Campbell
Stars and Moon [poem, Coventry Patmore]
On the Mechanism of a Historical Picture: by F. Madox Brown [essay]
A Testimony: by Ellen Alleyn [poem, Christina Rossetti]
O When and Where: by Thomas Woolner [poem]
Fancies at Leisure: by Wm. M. Rossetti [poem]
The Light Beyond: by Walter H. Deverell [three sonnets]
The Blessed Damozel: by Dante G. Rossetti [poem]
Reviews: 'The Strayed Reveller, and other Poems:' by Wm. M. Rossetti

No. 3, March 1850

Etching by Ford Madox Brown, to accompany 'Cordelia'

Cordelia – W. M. Rossetti [poem]
Macbeth [essay, Coventry Patmore]
Repining – Ellen Alleyn [poem, Christina Rossetti]
Sweet Death – Ellen Alleyn [poem, Christina Rossetti]
Subject in Art, No. II [essay, John L. Tupper (No. I in issue no. 1)]
Carillon – Dante G. Rossetti [poem, subtitled 'Antwerp and Bruges']
Emblems – Thomas Woolner [poem]
Sonnet – W. B. Scott [subtitled 'Early Aspirations']
From the Cliffs – Dante G. Rossetti [poem]
Fancies at Leisure – W. M. Rossetti [poem]
Papers of 'The M. S. Society,' Nos. I. II. & III. [John L., Alexander and George
Tupper, respectively, poem (no. I) and prose (Nos. II and III)]
Review, Sir Reginald Mohun – W. M. Rossetti

No. 4, May 1850

Etching by Walter Howell Deverell to accompany 'Viola and Olivia'

Viola and Olivia [poem, John L. Tupper]
A Dialogue – John Orchard [essay, with an introduction by D. G. Rossetti]
On a Whit-sunday Morn in the Month of May – John Orchard [poem]
Modern Giants – Laura Savage [essay, F. G. Stephens]
To the Castle Ramparts – W. M. Rossetti [poem]
Pax Vobis – Dante G. Rossetti [poem]
A Modern Idyl – Walter H. Deverell [poem]
'Jesus Wept' – W. M. Rossetti [sonnet]

Sonnets for Pictures – Dante G. Rossetti
Papers of 'The M. S. Society,' No. IV. Smoke [poem, John L. Tupper]
        No. V. Rain [poem, John L. Tupper]
Review: Christmas Eve and Easter Day – W. M. Rossetti
The Evil under the Sun [sonnet, W. M. Rossetti]

B. Contributions by Author (issue no. in parentheses)

Brown, Ford Madox: 'The Love of Beauty: Sonnet' (no. 1), 'On the Mechanism of a Historical Picture' (essay, no. 2), etching to accompany W. M. Rossetti's 'Cordelia' (no. 3)

Campbell, Major Calder: 'Sonnet' ('When midst the summer roses the warm bees', no. 2)

Collinson, James: 'The Child Jesus' (poem) and accompanying etching (no. 2)

Deverell, Walter Howell: 'The Light Beyond' (three sonnets, no. 2), 'A Modern Idyl' (poem, no. 4), etching to accompany John L. Tupper's 'Viola and Olivia' (no. 4)

Hunt, William Holman: etching to accompany Woolner's 'My Beautiful Lady' and 'Of my Lady in Death' (no. 1)

Orchard, John: 'A Dialogue on Art. I. In the House of Kalon' (essay, with introduction by D. G. Rossetti, no. 4), 'On a Whit-sunday Morn in the Month of May' (poem, no. 4)

Patmore, Coventry: 'The Seasons', (poem, no. 1) 'Stars and Moon', (poem, no. 2), 'Macbeth' (essay, no. 3)

Rossetti, Christina: 'Dream Land' (no. 1), 'An End' (no. 1), 'A Pause of Thought' (no. 2), 'Song' (no. 2), 'A Testimony' (no. 2), 'Repining' (no. 3), 'Sweet Death' (no. 3) (all poems; those in issues 2 and 3 signed 'Ellen Alleyn')

Rossetti, Dante Gabriel: 'Songs of One Household: No. 1: My Sister's Sleep' (poem, no. 1), 'Hand and Soul' (story, no. 1), 'The Blessed Damozel' (poem, no. 2), 'The Carillon, Antwerp and Bruges' (poem, no. 3), 'From the Cliffs: Noon' (poem, no. 3), 'Pax Vobis' (poem, no. 4), 'Sonnets for Pictures: 1. A Virgin and Child, by Hans Memmeling; in the Academy of Bruges. 2. A Marriage of St. Katharine, by the same; in the Hospital of St. John at Bruges. 3. A Dance of Nymphs, by Andrea Mantegna; in the Louvre. 4. A Venetian Pastoral, by Giorgione; in the Louvre. 5. "Angelica rescued from the Sea-monster," by Ingres; in the Luxembourg. 6. The same.' (sonnets, no. 4)

Rossetti, William Michael: Sonnet ('When whoso merely hath a little thought') printed on each issue's cover, review of Arthur Hugh Clough's *Bothie of Toper-na-fuosich* (no. 1), 'Her First Season' (sonnet, no. 1),

'Fancies at Leisure: I. Noon Rest. II. A Quiet Place. III. A Fall of Rain. IV. Sheer Waste.' (poems, no. 2), review of Matthew Arnold's *The Strayed Reveller; and other Poems* (no. 2), 'Cordelia' (poem, no. 3); 'Fancies at Leisure: I. In Spring. II. In Summer. III. The Breadth of Noon. IV. Seafreshness. V. The Fire Smouldering.' (poems, no. 3), review of George John Cayley's *Sir Reginald Mohun* (no. 3), 'To the Castle Ramparts' (poem, no. 4); 'Jesus Wept' (sonnet, no. 4); review of Robert Browning's *Christmas Eve and Easter Day* (no. 4), 'The Evil under the Sun' (sonnet, no. 4)

Scott, William Bell: 'Morning Sleep' (poem, no. 2), 'Sonnet: Early Aspirations' (no. 3)

Stephens, F. G.: 'The Purpose and Tendency of Early Italian Art' (no. 2, signed 'John Seward'), 'Modern Giants' (no. 4, signed 'Laura Savage') (essays)

Tupper, Alexander: 'Papers of "The M. S. Society": No. II: Swift's Dunces' (prose, no. 3)

Tupper, George: 'Papers of "The M. S. Society": No. III: Mental Scales' (prose, no. 3)

Tupper, John: 'The Subject in Art' (essay, in two parts, nos. 1 and 3); 'A Sketch from Nature' (poem, no. 1); 'Papers of "The M. S. Society": No. I: An Incident in the Siege of Troy' (poem, no. 3), 'Viola and Olivia' (poem, no. 4), 'Papers of "The M. S. Society": No. IV: Smoke, No. V: Rain' (no. 4)

Woolner, Thomas: 'My Beautiful Lady' (no. 1), 'Of my Lady in Death' (no. 1), 'O When and Where' (no. 2), 'Emblems' (no. 3) (all poems)

The Pre-Raphaelite 'list of Immortals'

(from William Holman Hunt, *Pre-Raphaelitism and the Pre-Raphaelite Brotherhood*, 2 vols., London and New York: Macmillan, 1905–6, vol. I, p. 159)

We, the undersigned, declare that the following list of Immortals constitutes the whole of our Creed, and that there exists no other Immortality than what is centred in their names and in the names of their contemporaries, in whom this list is reflected:–

Jesus Christ ****
The Author of Job ***
Isaiah
Homer **
Pheidias
Early Gothic Architects
Cavalier Pugliesi
Dante **
Boccaccio *
Rienzi
Ghiberti
Chaucer **
Fra Angelico *
Leonardo da Vinci **
Spenser
Hogarth
Flaxman
Hilton
Goethe **
Kosciusko
Byron
Wordsworth

Raphael *
Michael Angelo
Early English Balladists
Giovanni Bellini
Giorgioni [sic]
Titian
Tintoretto
Poussin
Alfred **
Shakespeare ***
Milton
Cromwell
Hampden
Bacon
Newton
Landor **
Thackeray **
Poe
Hood
Longfellow *
Emerson
Washington **

Keats **

Shelley **

Haydon

Cervantes

Joan of Arc

Mrs. Browning *

Patmore *

Leigh Hunt

Author of *Stories after Nature* *

[Charles JeremiahWells]

Wilkie

Columbus

Browning **

Tennyson *

GUIDE TO FURTHER READING AND LOOKING

This guide is intended to suggest avenues for further study, including ways to see Pre-Raphaelite artworks in person, in reproduction and on the internet. It includes sections on art galleries and museums with Pre-Raphaelite holdings, recent exhibition catalogues, primary texts and general studies of Pre-Raphaelitism. These are followed by sections on further reading for each of the chapters in this *Companion*.

For more extensive bibliographies, see Elizabeth Prettejohn, *The Art of the Pre-Raphaelites* (London: Tate Publishing, 2000; rev. edn., 2007, with updated bibliography); Michaela Giebelhausen and Tim Barringer (eds.), *Writing the Pre-Raphaelites: Text, Context, Subtext* (Farnham, Surrey and Burlington, Vermont: Ashgate, 2009). Still useful for older sources: William E. Fredeman, *Pre-Raphaelitism: A Bibliocritical Study* (Cambridge, MA: Harvard University Press, 1965). The bibliography in James Sambrook (ed.), *Pre-Raphaelitism: A Collection of Critical Essays* (Chicago and London: University of Chicago Press, 1974), provides an interesting list, in chronological order, of publications from 1850 through to 1973.

Art galleries and museums

Almost every art gallery in Britain holds important works of Pre-Raphaelite art, thanks largely to the first collectors of the Pre-Raphaelites, who were generous benefactors to the new, municipal art galleries formed in the later nineteenth century, as well as to the national collections. Due to the vitality of British collecting in the second half of the nineteenth century, fewer Pre-Raphaelite works made their way to collections outside Britain; although notable paintings are held in many galleries worldwide, few have larger Pre-Raphaelite collections, with some notable exceptions in the USA, listed below. Museum websites are an excellent source of information on the works they hold; these can usually be accessed by clicking on 'Collections' or 'Research' from the museum's home page. Many museums and galleries now have sections of their websites devoted to their Pre-Raphaelite collections, and the websites are constantly improving.

United Kingdom

London

Tate Britain: www.tate.org.uk (click on Tate Collection to search for Pre-Raphaelite works)

The British Museum: www.britishmuseum.org (especially Pre-Raphaelite drawings and other works on paper; click on Research for the excellent collections database)

William Morris Gallery, Walthamstow: www.walthamforest.gov.uk

Birmingham Museums & Art Gallery: www.bmag.org.uk (click on Collections for the Pre-Raphaelite Online Resource)

Cambridge: Fitzwilliam Museum: www.fitzmuseum.cam.ac.uk

Cardiff: National Museum Wales – Amgueddfa Cymru: www.museumwales.ac.uk

National Museums Liverpool: www.liverpoolmuseums.org.uk
click on the links to the two principal collections holding Pre-Raphaelite works:
Walker Art Gallery, Liverpool
Lady Lever Art Gallery, Port Sunlight

Manchester City Galleries: www.manchestergalleries.org

United States

Delaware Art Museum, Wilmington, Delaware: www.delart.org

Fogg Art Museum, Harvard University, Cambridge, MA: www.harvardartmuseums.org

Museum of Fine Arts, Boston: www.mfa.org

Yale Center for British Art, New Haven, Connecticut: www.ycba.yale.edu

Exhibitions since 1984

Much of the most important research on Pre-Raphaelite visual art appears in exhibition catalogues, which are also the best sources for good reproductions of paintings and other visual works. Exhibition catalogues are listed here in chronological order to demonstrate the growth of interest in Pre-Raphaelite art, and its increasing international dissemination, since the Tate Gallery's major survey exhibition of 1984. (For a good selection of earlier exhibition catalogues, see the bibliography in Giebelhausen and Barringer, *Writing the Pre-Raphaelites*.) All venues are listed; dates are those of opening at the first venue.

Parris, Leslie (ed.), *The Pre-Raphaelites*, London: Tate Gallery, 1984.

Christian, John (ed.), *The Last Romantics: The Romantic Tradition in British Art: Burne-Jones to Stanley Spencer*, London: Barbican Art Gallery, 1989.

Read, Benedict, and Joanna Barnes (eds.), *Pre-Raphaelite Sculpture: Nature and Imagination in British Sculpture 1848–1914*, London: The Matthiesen Gallery and Birmingham City Museum and Art Gallery, 1991.

Marsh, Jan, *Elizabeth Siddal 1829–1862: Pre-Raphaelite Artist*, Sheffield: The Ruskin Gallery, 1991.

Parry, Linda (ed.), *William Morris*, London: The Victoria and Albert Museum, 1996.

Wilton, Andrew, and Robert Upstone (eds.), *The Age of Rossetti, Burne-Jones and Watts: Symbolism in Britain 1860–1910*, London: Tate Gallery, 1997.

Marsh, Jan, and Pamela Gerrish Nunn, *Pre-Raphaelite Women Artists*, Manchester City Art Galleries, Birmingham Museum and Art Gallery, Southampton City Art Gallery, 1997.

Wildman, Stephen, and John Christian, *Edward Burne-Jones: Victorian Artist-Dreamer*, New York: The Metropolitan Museum of Art, Birmingham Museums and Art Gallery, Paris: Musée d'Orsay, 1998.

Funnell, Peter, Malcolm Warner and others, *Millais: Portraits*, London: National Portrait Gallery, 1999.

Hewison, Robert, Ian Warrell and Stephen Wildman, *Ruskin, Turner and the Pre-Raphaelites*, London: Tate Gallery, 2000.

Treuherz, Julian, Elizabeth Prettejohn and Edwin Becker, *Dante Gabriel Rossetti*, Liverpool: Walker Art Gallery and Amsterdam: Van Gogh Museum, 2003.

Dorment, Richard and others, *Pre-Raphaelite and Other Masters: The Andrew Lloyd Webber Collection*, London: Royal Academy of Arts, 2003.

Staley, Allen, and Christopher Newall, *Pre-Raphaelite Vision: Truth to Nature*, London: Tate Britain, Berlin: Altes Nationalgalerie, Madrid: Fundació 'la Caixa', 2004.

Wildman, Stephen and others, *Waking Dreams: The Art of the Pre-Raphaelites from the Delaware Art Museum*, Nottingham Castle Museum & Art Gallery and eight US venues, 2004 (Alexandria, Virginia: Art Services International).

Cruise, Colin and others, *Love Revealed: Simeon Solomon and the Pre-Raphaelites*, Birmingham Museums & Art Gallery, Munich: Museum Villa Stuck, The London Jewish Museum of Art, 2005.

Rosenfeld, Jason, and Alison Smith, *Millais*, London: Tate Britain, Amsterdam: Van Gogh Museum, Fukuoka: Kitakyushu Municipal Museum of Art, Tokyo: Bunkamura Museum of Art, 2007.

Stebbins, Theodore E., Jr., and Virginia Anderson, *The Last Ruskinians: Charles Eliot Norton, Charles Herbert Moore, and Their Circle*, Cambridge, MA: Harvard University Art Museums, 2007.

Lochnan, Katharine, and Carol Jacobi (eds.), *Holman Hunt and the Pre-Raphaelite Vision*, Toronto: Art Gallery of Ontario, Manchester Art Gallery, Minneapolis Institute of Arts, 2008.

Prettejohn, Elizabeth, Peter Trippi, Robert Upstone and Patty Wageman, *J. W. Waterhouse: The Modern Pre-Raphaelite*, Groningen: Groninger Museum, London: Royal Academy of Arts, Montreal Museum of Fine Arts, 2008.

Ahlund, Mikael and others, *The Pre-Raphaelites*, Stockholm: National Museum, 2009.

Conrad, Christofer, and Annabel Zettel (eds.), *Edward Burne-Jones: The Earthly Paradise*, Stuttgart: Staatsgalerie and Bern: Kunstmuseum, 2009.

Harrison, Colin, Christopher Newall and others, *The Pre-Raphaelites and Italy*, Oxford: Ashmolean Museum and Ravenna: MAR Museo d'Arte della Città di Ravenna, 2010.

Payne, Christiana, and Ann Sumner, *Objects of Affection: Pre-Raphaelite Portraits by John Brett*, Birmingham: The Barber Institute of Fine Arts, London: The Fine Art Society, Cambridge: The Fitzwilliam Museum, 2010.

Waggoner, Diane and others, *The Pre-Raphaelite Lens: British Photography and Painting, 1848–1875*, Washington, DC: National Gallery of Art and Paris: Musée d'Orsay, 2010.

Cruise, Colin, *The Poetry of Drawing: Pre-Raphaelite Designs, Studies and Watercolours*, Birmingham Museums & Art Gallery and Sydney: The Art Gallery of New South Wales, 2011 (catalogue entitled *Pre-Raphaelite Drawing*, London: Thames & Hudson, 2011).

Calloway, Stephen, and Lynn Federle Orr (eds.), *The Cult of Beauty: The Aesthetic Movement in Britain 1860–1900*, London: Victoria and Albert Museum, Paris: Musée d'Orsay, Fine Arts Museums of San Francisco, 2011.

Benedetti, Maria Teresa, Stefania Frezzotti and Robert Upstone, *Dante Gabriel Rossetti, Edward Burne-Jones e il mito dell'Italia nell'Inghilterra vittoriana*, Rome: Museo Nazionale d'Arte Moderna, 2011.

Treuherz, Julian and others, *Ford Madox Brown: Pre-Raphaelite Pioneer*, Manchester: Manchester Art Gallery and Ghent: The Museum of Fine Arts, 2011.

Barringer, Tim, Jason Rosenfeld and Alison Smith (eds.), *Pre-Raphaelites: Victorian Avant-Garde*, London: Tate Britain, Washington, DC: National Gallery of Art and Moscow: The Pushkin Museum, 2012.

Key primary texts

A crucial resource is *The Complete Writings and Pictures of Dante Gabriel Rossetti: A Hypermedia Archive*, ed. Jerome McGann, www.rossettiarchive.org. While this archive is based on Rossetti, it also includes abundant material on Pre-Raphaelitism in general.

Brown, Ford Madox, *The Exhibition of WORK, and Other Paintings, by Ford Madox Brown, at the Gallery, 191, Piccadilly*, London: McCorquodale & Co., 1865, repr. in Kenneth Bendiner, *The Art of Ford Madox Brown*, University Park, PA: Pennsylvania State University Press, 1998, pp. 131–56 (Bendiner also reprints other writings by Brown).

The Diary of Ford Madox Brown, ed. Virginia Surtees, New Haven and London: Yale University Press, 1981.

B-J, G [Burne-Jones, Georgiana], *Memorials of Edward Burne-Jones*, 2 vols., London: Macmillan, 1904; facsimile reprint with a new introduction by John Christian, London: Lund Humphries, 1993.

Fredeman, William E. (ed.), *The P.R.B. Journal: William Michael Rossetti's Diary of the Pre-Raphaelite Brotherhood 1849–1853: Together with Other Pre-Raphaelite Documents*, Oxford: Clarendon Press, 1975.

The Germ: Thoughts towards Nature in Poetry, Literature, and Art, 4 issues published January–May 1850 (nos. 3 and 4 retitled *Art and Poetry: Being Thoughts towards Nature: Conducted principally by Artists*); facsimile reprint with an Introduction by William Michael Rossetti, London: Elliot Stock, 1901 (this reprint also reproduced in facsimile as *The Germ: The Literary Magazine of the Pre-Raphaelites*, with a preface by Andrea Rose, Oxford: Ashmolean Museum, 1992).

Hares-Stryker, Carolyn (ed.), *An Anthology of Pre-Raphaelite Writings*, Sheffield: Sheffield Academic Press, 1997.

Hunt, William Holman, *Pre-Raphaelitism and the Pre-Raphaelite Brotherhood*, 2 vols., London and New York: Macmillan, 1905–6 (2nd edn, revised, 1913).

Rossetti, Dante Gabriel, *The Correspondence of Dante Gabriel Rossetti*, ed. William E. Fredeman and others, 9 vols., Cambridge: D. S. Brewer, 2002–10.

Ruskin, John, *The Works of John Ruskin (Library Edition)*, ed. E. T. Cook and Alexander Wedderburn, 39 vols. (London: George Allen, 1903–12).

Sambrook, James (ed.), *Pre-Raphaelitism: A Collection of Critical Essays*, Chicago and London: University of Chicago Press, 1974.

General studies of Pre-Raphaelitism, the Pre-Raphaelite Brotherhood and its Victorian context

Barringer, Tim, *Reading the Pre-Raphaelites*, New Haven and London: Yale University Press, 1999.

Bullen, J. B., *The Pre-Raphaelite Body: Fear and Desire in Painting, Poetry, and Criticism*, Oxford: Clarendon Press, 1998.

Cherry, Deborah, 'The Hogarth Club: 1858–1861', *Burlington Magazine*, 122 (April 1980), pp. 237–44.

Painting Women: Victorian Women Artists, London and New York: Routledge, 1993.

Clifford, David, and Laurence Roussillon (eds.), *Outsiders Looking In: The Rossettis Then and Now*, London: Anthem Press, 2004.

Corbett, David Peters, *The World in Paint: Modern Art and Visuality in England, 1848–1914*, Manchester and New York: Manchester University Press; University Park, PA: Pennsylvania State University Press, 2004.

Giebelhausen, Michaela, and Tim Barringer (eds.), *Writing the Pre-Raphaelites: Text, Context, Subtext*, Farnham, Surrey and Burlington, Vermont: Ashgate, 2009.

Latham, David (ed.), *Haunted Texts: Studies in Pre-Raphaelitism in Honour of William E. Fredeman*, Toronto: University of Toronto Press, 2003.

McGann, Jerome, *Black Riders: The Visible Language of Modernism*, Princeton, NJ: Princeton University Press, 1993.

Parris, Leslie (ed.), *Pre-Raphaelite Papers*, London: Tate Gallery, 1984.

Pearce, Lynne, *Woman/Image/Text: Readings in Pre-Raphaelite Art and Literature*, Toronto and Buffalo: University of Toronto Press, 1991.

Pointon, Marcia (ed.), *Pre-Raphaelites Re-viewed*, Manchester and New York: Manchester University Press, 1989.

Prettejohn, Elizabeth, *Art for Art's Sake: Aestheticism in Victorian Painting*, New Haven and London: Yale University Press, 2007.

The Art of the Pre-Raphaelites, London: Tate Publishing and Princeton, NJ: Princeton University Press, 2000, rev. edn. 2007.

'The Pre-Raphaelite Model', in Jane Desmarais, Martin Postle and William Vaughan (eds.), *Model and Supermodel: The Artist's Model in British Art and Culture*, Manchester and New York: Manchester University Press, 2006, pp. 26–46.

Prettejohn, Elizabeth (ed.), *After the Pre-Raphaelites: Art and Aestheticism in Victorian England*, Manchester: Manchester University Press and New Brunswick, NJ: Rutgers University Press, 1999.

Smith, Lindsay, *Victorian Photography, Painting and Poetry: The Enigma of Visibility in Ruskin, Morris and the Pre-Raphaelites*, Cambridge: Cambridge University Press, 1995.

Staley, Allen, *The Pre-Raphaelite Landscape*, rev. edn., New Haven and London: Yale University Press, 2001 (first published 1973).

Stein, Richard L., *The Ritual of Interpretation: The Fine Arts as Literature in Ruskin, Rossetti, and Pater*, Cambridge, MA and London: Harvard University Press, 1975.

Sussman, Herbert, *Victorian Masculinities: Manhood and Masculine Poetics in Early Victorian Literature and Art*, Cambridge: Cambridge University Press, 1995, Chapter 3: 'Artistic manhood: The Pre-Raphaelite Brotherhood'.

Townsend, Joyce H., Jacqueline Ridge and Stephen Hackney, *Pre-Raphaelite Painting Techniques: 1848–56*, London: Tate Publishing, 2004.

Vaughan, William, *German Romanticism and English Art*, New Haven and London: Yale University Press, 1979.

1. The Pre-Raphaelites and literature

Armstrong, Isobel, *Victorian Poetry: Poetry, Poetics, and Politics*, London and New York: Routledge, 1993.

Codell, Julie F., 'Painting Keats: Pre-Raphaelite Artists between Social Transgressions and Painterly Conventions', *Victorian Poetry*, 33 (Autumn–Winter 1995), pp. 341–70.

Gagnier, Regenia, *The Insatiability of Human Wants: Economics and Aesthetics in Market Society*, Chicago and London: University of Chicago Press, 2000.

Helsinger, Elizabeth K., *Poetry and the Pre-Raphaelite Arts: Dante Gabriel Rossetti and William Morris*, New Haven and London: Yale University Press, 2008.

Tucker, Herbert, *Epic*, Oxford: Oxford University Press, 2008.

2. Artistic inspirations

Christian, John, 'Early German Sources for Pre-Raphaelite Designs', *Art Quarterly*, 36 (Spring–Summer 1973), pp. 56–83.

Cooper, Robyn, 'The Popularization of Renaissance Art in Victorian England: The Arundel Society', *Art History*, 1 (September 1978), pp. 263–92.

'The Relationship between the Pre-Raphaelite Brotherhood and Painting before Raphael in English Criticism of the Late 1840s and 1850s', *Victorian Studies*, 24 (1981), pp. 405–38.

Graham, Jenny, *Inventing Van Eyck: The Remaking of an Artist for the Modern Age*, Oxford and New York: Berg, 2007.

Haskell, Francis, *Rediscoveries in Art: Some Aspects of Taste, Fashion and Collecting in England and France*, 2nd edn., Oxford: Phaidon, 1980.

Langley, Jane, 'Pre-Raphaelites or Ante-Dürerites?', *Burlington Magazine*, 137 (August 1995), pp. 501–8.

Levey, Michael, 'Botticelli and Nineteenth-Century England', *Journal of the Warburg and Courtauld Institutes*, 23 (1960), pp. 291–306.

Ormond, Leonée, 'Dante Gabriel Rossetti and the Old Masters', *Yearbook of English Studies*, 36.2 (2006), pp. 153–68.

Warner, Malcolm, 'The Pre-Raphaelites and the National Gallery', *Huntington Library Quarterly*, 55 (1992), pp. 1–11.

3. Pre-Raphaelite drawing

Cruise, Colin, *Pre-Raphaelite Drawing*, exhibition catalogue, Birmingham Museums & Art Gallery/London: Thames & Hudson, 2011.

Gere, J. A., *Pre-Raphaelite Drawings in the British Museum*, London: British Museum Press, 1994.

Grieve, Alastair, 'Style and Content in Pre-Raphaelite Drawings 1848–50', in Leslie Parris (ed.), *Pre-Raphaelite Papers*, London: Tate Gallery, 1984, pp. 23–43.

Hewison, Robert, *Ruskin and Oxford: The Art of Education*, Oxford: Clarendon Press, 1996.

Ruskin, John, *The Elements of Drawing* (1857) and *The Laws of Fésole* (1877–8), repr. in *The Works of John Ruskin (Library Edition)*, ed. E. T. Cook and Alexander Wedderburn, 39 vols., London: George Allen, 1903–12, vol. XV (1904), pp. 5–228, 337–501.

Suriano, Gregory, *The Pre-Raphaelite Illustrators*, New Castle, DE: Oak Knoll Press, 2000.

4. The religious and intellectual background

Brooks, Chris, *Signs for the Times: Symbolic Realism in the Mid-Victorian World*, London: Allen & Unwin, 1984

Errington, Lindsay, *Social and Religious Themes in English Art, 1840–1860*, New York and London: Garland Publishing, 1984

Giebelhausen, Michaela, *Painting the Bible: Representation and Belief in Mid-Victorian Britain*, Aldershot, Hants. and Brookfield, Vermont: Ashgate, 2006.

Landow, George P., *Victorian Types, Victorian Shadows: Biblical Typology in Victorian Literature, Art and Thought*, Boston, MA and London: Routledge & Kegan Paul, 1980.

Parsons, Gerald (ed.), *Religion in Victorian Britain*, 4 vols., Manchester and New York: Manchester University Press, 1988.

5. The Germ

Demoor, Marysa, 'In the Beginning, There Was *The Germ*: The Pre-Raphaelites and "Little Magazines"', in Peter Brooker and Andrew Thacker (eds.), *The Oxford Critical and Cultural History of Modernist Magazines,* vol. I: *Britain and Ireland 1880–1955*, Oxford: Oxford University Press, 2009, pp. 51–65.

Fredeman, William, review of *The Germ: A Pre-Raphaelite Little Magazine*, *Victorian Poetry*, 10 (1972), pp. 87–94.

Noble, J. Ashcroft, 'A Pre-Raphaelite Magazine', *Fraser's Magazine* (May 1882), pp. 568–80.

Propas, Sharon W., 'William Michael Rossetti and *The Germ*', *Journal of Pre-Raphaelite Studies*, 6.2 (May 1986), pp. 29–36.

Radford, Ernest, 'The Life and Death of "The Germ"', *Idler*, 13 (1898), pp. 227–33.

6. The poetry of Dante Gabriel Rossetti

Ainsworth, Maryan Wynn and others, *Dante Gabriel Rossetti and the Double Work of Art*, exhibition catalogue, New Haven: Yale University Art Gallery, 1976.

Clifford, David, and Laurence Roussillon (eds.), *Outsiders Looking In: The Rossettis Then and Now*, London: Anthem Press, 2004.

Marsh, Jan, *Dante Gabriel Rossetti: Painter and Poet*, London: Weidenfeld & Nicolson, 1999.

Marsh, Jan (ed.), *Dante Gabriel Rossetti: Collected Writings*, London: J. W. Dent, 1999.

McGann, Jerome, *Dante Gabriel Rossetti and the Game That Must Be Lost*, New Haven and London: Yale University Press, 2000.

McGann, Jerome (ed.), *The Complete Writings and Pictures of Dante Gabriel Rossetti: A Hypermedia Archive* (www.rossettiarchive.org/)

McGann, Jerome (ed.), *Dante Gabriel Rossetti: Collected Poetry and Prose*, New Haven and London: Yale University Press, 2003.

Rees, Joan, *The Poetry of Dante Gabriel Rossetti: Modes of Self-Expression*, Cambridge: Cambridge University Press, 1981.

Riede, David, *Dante Gabriel Rossetti Revisited*, New York: Twayne, 1992.

Riede, David (ed.), *Critical Essays on Dante Gabriel Rossetti*, New York: G. K. Hall, 1992.

7. The painting of Dante Gabriel Rossetti

Grieve, Alastair, *The Art of Dante Gabriel Rossetti*, 3 parts, Norwich: Real World, 1973, 1976, 1978.

· 'Rossetti and the Scandal of Art for Art's Sake in the Early 1860s', in Elizabeth Prettejohn (ed.), *After the Pre-Raphaelites: Art and Aestheticism in Victorian England*, Manchester University Press and New Brunswick, NJ: Rutgers University Press, 1999, pp. 17–35.

Pollock, Griselda, 'Woman as Sign: Psychoanalytic Readings', *Vision and Difference: Femininity, Feminism and Histories of Art*, London and New York: Routledge, 1988, pp. 120–54.

Prettejohn, Elizabeth, *Art for Art's Sake: Aestheticism in Victorian Painting*, New Haven and London: Yale University Press, 2007, chapter 7 ('Rossetti and the Fleshly School').

Rossetti and his Circle, London: Tate Gallery Publishing and New York: Stewart, Tabori & Chang, 1997.

Surtees, Virginia, *The Paintings and Drawings of Dante Gabriel Rossetti (1828–1882): A Catalogue Raisonné*, 2 vols., Oxford: Clarendon Press, 1971.

Tickner, Lisa, *Dante Gabriel Rossetti*, London: Tate Publishing, 2003.

Treuherz, Julian, Elizabeth Prettejohn and Edwin Becker, *Dante Gabriel Rossetti*, exhibition catalogue, Liverpool: Walker Art Gallery and Amsterdam: Van Gogh Museum / Zwolle: Waanders Publishers and London: Thames & Hudson, 2003.

8. William Holman Hunt

Amor, Anne Clark, *William Holman Hunt: The True Pre-Raphaelite*, London: Constable, 1989.

Bronkhurst, Judith, *William Holman Hunt: A Catalogue Raisonné*, 2 vols., New Haven and London: Yale University Press, 2006.

Hunt, William Holman, *Pre-Raphaelitism and the Pre-Raphaelite Brotherhood*, 2 vols., London and New York: Macmillan, 1905–6 (2nd edn., revised, 1913).

Jacobi, Carol, *William Holman Hunt: Painter, Painting, Paint*, Manchester and New York: Manchester University Press, 2006.

Landow, George P., *William Holman Hunt and Typological Symbolism*, New Haven and London: Yale University Press, 1979.

Lochnan, Katharine, and Carol Jacobi (eds.), *Holman Hunt and the Pre-Raphaelite Vision*, exhibition catalogue, Toronto: Art Gallery of Ontario, 2008.

Maas, Jeremy, *William Holman Hunt and The Light of the World*, Aldershot, Hants.: Wildwood House, 1987.

9. John Everett Millais

Barlow, Paul, *Time Present and Time Past: The Art of John Everett Millais*, Aldershot, Hants. and Burlington, Vermont: Ashgate, 2005.

Funnell, Peter, Malcolm Warner and others, *Millais: Portraits*, exhibition catalogue, London: National Portrait Gallery, 1999.

Mancoff, Debra N. (ed.), *John Everett Millais: Beyond the Pre-Raphaelite Brotherhood*, Studies in British Art no. 7, New Haven and London: Yale University Press, 2001.

Rosenfeld, Jason, and Alison Smith, *Millais*, exhibition catalogue, London: Tate Publishing, 2007.

10. Ford Madox Brown

Barringer, Tim, *Men at Work: Art and Labour in Victorian Britain*, New Haven and London: Yale University Press, 2005, chapter 1.

Bendiner, Kenneth, *The Art of Ford Madox Brown*, University Park, PA: Pennsylvania State University Press, 1998.

Bennett, Mary, *Ford Madox Brown: A Catalogue Raisonné*, 2 vols., New Haven and London: Yale University Press, 2010.

Brown, Ford Madox, *The Diary of Ford Madox Brown*, ed. Virginia Surtees, New Haven and London: Yale University Press, 1981.

Hueffer, Ford Madox [later called Ford Madox Ford], *Ford Madox Brown: A Record of his Life and Work*, London: Longmans, Green and Co., 1896.

Newman, Teresa, and Ray Watkinson, *Ford Madox Brown and the Pre-Raphaelite Circle*, London: Chatto & Windus, 1991.

Treuherz, Julian, and others, *Ford Madox Brown: Pre-Raphaelite Pioneer*, exhibition catalogue, Manchester: Manchester Art Gallery/London: Philip Wilson Publishers, 2011.

Vaughan, William, 'Written Out? The Case of Ford Madox Brown', in Michaela Giebelhausen and Tim Barringer (eds.), *Writing the Pre-Raphaelites: Text, Context, Subtext*, Farnham, Surrey and Burlington, Vermont: Ashgate, 2009, pp. 139–50.

11. Christina Rossetti

Arseneau, Mary, *Recovering Christina Rossetti: Female Community and Incarnational Poetics*, Basingstoke: Palgrave Macmillan, 2004.

Kooistra, Lorraine Janzen, *Christina Rossetti and Illustration: A Publishing History*, Athens, OH: Ohio University Press, 2002.

Marsh, Jan, *Christina Rossetti: A Literary Biography*, London: Jonathan Cape, 1994.

Rossetti, Christina, *The Complete Poems of Christina Rossetti*, ed. R. W. Crump, 3 vols., Baton Rouge, LA and London: Louisiana State University Press, 1979–90. *The Letters of Christina Rossetti*, ed. Antony H. Harrison, 4 vols., Charlottesville: University of Virginia Press, 1997–2004.

12. Elizabeth Eleanor Siddall

Cherry, Deborah, and Griselda Pollock, 'Woman as Sign in Pre-Raphaelite Literature: A Study of the Representation of Elizabeth Siddall', *Art History*, 7.2 (June 1984), pp. 206–27.
Lewis, Roger C., and Mark Samuels Lasner (eds.), *Poems and Drawings of Elizabeth Siddal*, Wolfville, Nova Scotia: Wombat Press, 1978.
Marsh, Jan, *Elizabeth Siddal 1869–1862: Pre-Raphaelite Artist*, exhibition catalogue, Sheffield: The Ruskin Gallery, 1991.
Marsh, Jan, and Pamela Gerrish Nunn, *Pre-Raphaelite Women Artists*, exhibition catalogue, Manchester: Manchester City Art Galleries, 1997.
Rossetti, William Michael, 'Dante Rossetti and Elizabeth Siddal', *Burlington Magazine*, 1 (May 1903), pp. 273–95.
Surtees, Virginia, *Rossetti's Portraits of Elizabeth Siddal*, exhibition catalogue, Oxford: Ashmolean Museum, 1991.

13. The writings of William Morris

Boos, Florence, and Carole Silver, *Socialism and the Literary Artistry of William Morris*, Columbia, Mo and London: University of Missouri Press, 1990.
Chesterton, G. K., 'William Morris and His School', *Twelve Types*, London: Arthur L. Humphreys, 1902, pp. 15–30.
Faulkner, Peter, *Against the Age: An Introduction to William Morris*, London: Unwin Hyman, 1980.
Faulkner, Peter (ed.), *William Morris: The Critical Heritage*, London and Boston: Routledge & Kegan Paul, 1973.
MacCarthy, Fiona, *William Morris: A Life for Our Time*, London: Faber & Faber, 1994.
Mackail, J. W., *The Life of William Morris*, 2 vols., London: Longmans, Green, & Co., 1899; facsimile reprint in one vol., Mineola, New York: Dover Publications, 1995.
McGann, Jerome J., '"Thing to Mind": The Materialist Aesthetic of William Morris', *Black Riders: The Visible Language of Modernism*, Princeton, NJ: Princeton University Press, 1993, pp. 45–75.
Morris, William, *The Collected Letters of William Morris*, ed. Norman Kelvin, 4 vols., Princeton, NJ: Princeton University Press, 1984–96.
The Collected Works of William Morris, ed. May Morris, 24 vols., London: Longmans, Green, 1910–15; facsimile reprints, New York: Russell & Russell, 1966; London: Routledge/Thoemmes Press, 1991.
The Unpublished Lectures of William Morris, ed. Eugene LeMire, Detroit: Wayne State University Press, 1969.
William Morris: Artist, Writer, Socialist, ed. May Morris, 2 vols., Oxford: Basil Blackwell, 1936.
Skoblow, Jeffrey, *Paradise Dislocated: Morris, Politics, Art*, Charlottesville, VA: University Press of Virginia, 1993.

Stansky, Peter, *Redesigning the World: William Morris, the 1880s, and the Arts and Crafts*, Princeton, NJ: Princeton University Press, 1985.

Thompson, E. P., *William Morris: Romantic to Revolutionary*, London: Lawrence & Wishart, 1955; rev. edn., London: Merlin Press, 1977.

Thompson, Paul, *The Work of William Morris*, 3rd edn., Oxford and New York: Oxford University Press, 1991.

14. The designs of William Morris

Arscott, Caroline, *William Morris and Edward Burne-Jones: Interlacings*, New Haven and London: Yale University Press, 2008.

Banham, Joanna, and Jennifer Harris (eds.), *William Morris and the Middle Ages*, exhibition catalogue, Manchester: Whitworth Art Gallery/Manchester University Press, 1984.

Edwards, Jason, and Imogen Hart (eds.), *Rethinking the Interior, c.1867–1896: Aestheticism and Arts and Crafts*, Aldershot, Hants.: Ashgate, 2010.

Hart, Imogen, *Arts and Crafts Objects*, Manchester and New York: Manchester University Press, 2010, chapters 2 ('The Homes of William Morris') and 3 ('Objects at Morris & Co.').

Harvey, Charles, and Jon Press, *William Morris: Design and Enterprise in Victorian Britain*, Manchester and New York: Manchester University Press, 1991.

Parry, Linda (ed.), *William Morris*, exhibition catalogue, London: The Victoria and Albert Museum/Philip Wilson Publishers, 1996.

15. Edward Burne-Jones

Arscott, Caroline, *William Morris and Edward Burne-Jones: Interlacings*, New Haven and London: Yale University Press, 2008.

B-J, G [Georgiana Burne-Jones], *Memorials of Edward Burne-Jones*, 2 vols., London: Macmillan, 1904; facsimile reprint, intro. John Christian, London: Lund Humphries, 1993.

Christian, John, and Stephen Wildman, *Edward Burne-Jones: Victorian Artist-Dreamer*, exhibition catalogue, New York: The Metropolitan Museum of Art, 1998.

Corbett, David Peters, *Edward Burne-Jones*, London: Tate Publishing, 2004.

Fitzgerald, Penelope, *Edward Burne-Jones*, London, Hamish Hamilton/Penguin, 1989 (first published 1975).

16. Algernon Charles Swinburne

Harrison, Antony H., *Swinburne's Medievalism: A Study in Victorian Love Poetry*, Baton Rouge, LA and London: Louisiana State University Press, 1988.

Hyder, Clyde K. (ed.), *Swinburne: The Critical Heritage*, London: Routledge & Kegan Paul, 1970.

Maxwell, Catherine, *The Female Sublime from Milton to Swinburne: Bearing Blindness*, Manchester: Manchester University Press, 2001.

Swinburne, Writers and their Work, Tavistock: Northcote House, 2006.

McGann, Jerome, *Swinburne: An Experiment in Criticism*, Chicago and London: University of Chicago Press, 1972.

Peters, Robert, *The Crowns of Apollo: Swinburne's Principles of Literature and Art*, Detroit: Wayne State University Press, 1965.

Prettejohn, Elizabeth, *Art for Art's Sake: Aestheticism in Victorian Painting*, New Haven and London: Yale University Press, 2007, chapter 2.

Rooksby, Rikky, *A. C. Swinburne: A Poet's Life*, Aldershot: Scolar Press, 1997.

Swinburne, Algernon Charles, *A. C. Swinburne*, Arthurian Poets, ed. James P. Carley, Woodbridge: Boydell & Brewer, 1990.

Algernon Charles Swinburne: Major Poems and Prose, ed. Jerome McGann and Charles Sligh, New Haven and London: Yale University Press, 2004.

The Collected Poetical Works of Algernon Charles Swinburne, 6 vols., London: Chatto & Windus, 1904.

Essays and Studies, London: Chatto & Windus, 1875.

Poems and Ballads & Atalanta in Calydon, ed. Kenneth Haynes, Harmondsworth: Penguin, 2000.

Swinburne as Critic, ed. C. K. Hyder, London and Boston: Routledge & Kegan Paul, 1972.

The Swinburne Letters, ed. Cecil Y. Lang, 6 vols., New Haven: Yale University Press, 1959–62.

17. William Michael Rossetti

See also William Michael Rossetti's writings listed under 'Key primary texts' above, and the extensive bibliography in Thirlwell, *William and Lucy* (cited below), pp. 349–51.

L'Enfant, Julie, *William Rossetti's Art Criticism: The Search for Truth in Victorian Art*, Lanham, MD: University Press of America, 1999.

Peattie, Roger W., 'William Michael Rossetti's Art Notices in the Periodicals, 1850–1878: An Annotated Checklist', *Victorian Periodicals Newsletter*, 8 (June 1975), pp. 79–92.

Rossetti, William Michael, *Fine Art, Chiefly Contemporary*, London: Macmillan, 1867.

Some Reminiscences, 2 vols., London: Brown, Langham, 1906.

Thirlwell, Angela, *William and Lucy: The Other Rossettis*, New Haven and London: Yale University Press, 2003.

'William Michael and Lucy Rossetti: Outsider Insiders – The True Cosmopolitans', in David Clifford and Laurence Roussillon (eds.), *Outsiders Looking In: The Rossettis Then and Now*, London: Anthem Press, 2004, chapter 2.

INDEX

Adam Bede (Eliot), 19
'Adieu' ('Wavering whispering trees')
    (D.G. Rossetti), 95
Adoration of the Kings and Shepherds
    (Burne-Jones), 237–8
Adoration tapestry (Morris & Co.), 219–20
Aesthetic Movement
    Brown, 148, 160
    Hunt, 42, 74
    Morris, 216
The Age of Rossetti, Burne-Jones and Watts:
    Symbolism in Britain 1860–1910 269
Aids to Reflection (Coleridge), 71
Albrecht Dürer on the Balcony of his House
    (Scott), 40
Allingham, William, 16, 19–20, 57, 191–2
The Altar, or Meditations in Verse on
    the Great Christian Sacrifice
    (Williams), 167
American exhibition of Pre-Raphaelite
    art, 258
'Anactoria' (Swinburne), 242
Angel in the House (Patmore), 17
Angiolieri, Cecco, 90
The Annunciation (Tintoretto), 22, 35
antiquarianism, 33
    Brown, 151–2
    Morris, 196
'Antwerp and Bruges' (D.G. Rossetti), 93
April Love (Hughes), 258
Architect, 117
Armstrong, Thomas, 254
Arnold, Matthew, 82, 253
Arnolfini Portrait (van Eyck), 33, 34, 35, 39,
    40, 42, 107, 135, 136
Arseneau, Mary, 176
'Art, Wealth, and Riches' (Morris), 207
'Art: A Serious Thing' (Morris), 207

'Art and Industry in the Fourteenth Century'
    (Morris), 207
Art and Poetry: Being Thoughts towards
    Nature, Conducted principally by
    Artists, 3, 83. *See also The Germ*
'The Art Catholic', 166
Art Journal, 38, 39
'Art News from London' (W.M. Rossetti),
    257
'The Art of the People' (Morris), 207
'Art Under Plutocracy' (Morris), 207
Arts and Crafts movement, 40, 213, 218
Arundel Society, 35, 39
Aspecta Medusa (D.G. Rossetti), 28
Astrophel and Other Poems (Swinburne),
    240–1
Atalanta in Calydon (Swinburne), 27, 238,
    244
The Athenaeum, 80, 161
Atlantic Monthly, 258
'August' (Swinburne), 243–4
Aurora Leigh (E.B. Browning), 17
Autobiographical Notes (Scott), 238
Autumn Leaves (Millais), 142–3, 256
'Ave' (D.G. Rossetti), 93–4
The Awakening Conscience (Hunt), 39, 121,
    124–5, 128, 251
Aylott and Jones, 83

Babylon Hath Been a Golden Cup
    (Solomon), 58, 59
Bacchus and Ariadne (Titian), 35, 120–1
The Baleful Head (Burne-Jones), 230
'A Ballad of Death' (Swinburne), 243
'A Ballad of Life' (Swinburne), 243
Barbe-Bleue (Sue), 19
Barnaby Rudge (Dickens), 19
Barr, Alfred, 267

Barringer, Tim, 8–9
Bateman, Robert, 58
Baudelaire, Charles, 27, 239, 243–4, 245
Beata Beatrix (D.G. Rossetti), 194
'The Beauty of Life' (Morris), 207–8
Bedroom at Arles (van Gogh), 269
Before the Battle (D.G. Rossetti), 185–6
'The Beggar Maid' (Tennyson), 232
The Beguiling of Merlin (Burne-Jones), 227–8, 229
Bendiner, Kenneth, 149
Bennett, Mary, 149
Berengaria's Alarm for the Safety of her Husband, Richard Coeur de Lion (Collins), 138–9
Bettall (drawing master), 48
Bible. *See also* religion
  Burne-Jones description of Book of Kings, 225
  criticism of, 69, 71–2
  influence on painting of Hunt, 127–9
Bibliography (W.M. Rossetti), 260
Bird and Anemone (Morris), 216–17
Bird and Vine (Morris), 216–17
The Birth of the Virgin (Dürer), 40
The Black Brunswicker (Millais), 145
Blake, William
  biography of, 27, 165–6
  contrasted with poetry of D.G. Rossetti, 97–8
  influence on C. Rossetti, 178
  influence on D.G. Rossetti, 27–8, 51–2, 97
  influence on Pre-Raphaelites, 58
  influence on Swinburne, 239
  literary sources, 49
  'minute particulars', 94
BLAST, 76
The Blessed Damozel (Burne-Jones), 223
'The Blessed Damozel' (D.G. Rossetti), 20, 77, 81, 93, 95–6, 98
The Blind Fiddler (Wilkie), 34
The Blind Girl (Millais), 142, 143, 145
A Blot in the Scutcheon (R. Browning), 20
'The Blue Closet' (Morris, D.G. Rossetti), 200, 201
Bocca Baciata (D.G. Rossetti), 41, 110, 240, 242
Boccaccio, Giovanni, 4, 64
Bodichon, Barbara, 17, 258
The Body of Harold Brought before William (Brown), 150–1
Border ballads, 184–5, 239
Borgia, Lucrezia, 242–3

Bothie (Clough), 253
Botticelli, Sandro
  influence on painting of D.G. Rossetti, 111
  influence on Pre-Raphaelites, 32, 41, 42, 58, 269
Boyd, Alice, 100
Brett, John, 40, 253, 254, 255
Briar Rose series (Burne-Jones), 224, 228
'A Bridal Race' (Scott), 26
'The Bride's Prelude' (D.G. Rossetti), 91–2
The Bridesmaid (Millais), 144
British Institution exhibition (1848), 32–3
The Broadway, 252
Brontë, Charlotte, Emily and Anne, 19, 83
Brother Rabbit (Morris), 217
Brown, Ford Madox, 148–61. *See also names of specific works by Brown*
  artistic formation of, 149–54
  close drawing from nature (observational drawing), 156–8
  D.G. Rossetti and, 16, 150, 154, 155, 158, 161
  formal training, 47
  furniture design, 160
  The Germ, 82–3, 154–61
  historical painting, 158–9
  Hunt and, 119–20, 123, 130, 150–1, 153
  influence of early Flemish art, 39–40
  influence of early Italian art, 37
  influence on Siddall, 189
  interest in Thackeray, 19
  Millais and, 144, 160
  Morris and, 212, 219
  observation of nature, 156–7
  oil study of bottles, 105, 106, 154
  outline drawing style, 51
  patrons and the public, 159–61
  recent exhibitions, 268
  Ruskin and, 153–4, 157–8
  sexual politics and feminism and, 17
  Swinburne and, 237
  W.M. Rossetti and, 255, 258
  Working Men's College, 54
Brown, Lucy Madox, 262–3
Browning, Elizabeth Barrett, 17
Browning, Robert
  contrasted with poetry of D.G. Rossetti, 99
  influence on D.G. Rossetti, 20, 93–4
  influence on Pre-Raphaelites, 77
  influence on Swinburne, 245
  Morris's writings and, 200, 201
  'Old Pictures in Florence', 36

review of in *The Germ*, 82, 253
Brownrigg, Elizabeth, 19
Buchanan, Robert, 238, 246
Buckley, Jerome Hamilton, 266
Burden, Bessie, 220
Burden, Jane. *See* Morris, Jane Burden
The Burlington Magazine, 265
Burne-Jones, Edward, 223. *See also names of specific works by Burne-Jones*
    D.G. Rossetti and, 57, 73, 223
    Hogarth Club, 160
    Hunt and, 116
    illustrative and narrative drawing, 49, 57–9
    influence of Botticelli, 32, 269
    influence of early Flemish art, 40
    Morris, Marshall, Faulkner & Co., 219–20
    Morris and, 211–12, 213, 219, 220, 223, 224
    obituary of, 32, 44
    Oxford and Cambridge Magazine, 5, 198
    recent exhibitions, 268
    religion and, 223–4
    Swinburne and, 236–8, 240–1, 242–3
    Working Men's College, 54
Burne-Jones, Georgiana, 228–9
Burne-Jones, Philip, 225
The Butcher's Shop (Carracci), 38
Byron, George Gordon (Lord Byron)
    Brotherhood's interest in, 20
    D.G. Rossetti's interest in, 27
    Hunt's interest in, 127
    Swinburne's interest in, 240

Cameron, Julia Margaret, 257
The Car of Love (Burne-Jones), 230
'The Card-Dealer' (D.G. Rossetti), 95
Carlyle, Thomas, 67, 159, 207
Carracci, Annibale, 38
Cary, H. F., 23–4
The Castaway (Howitt), 187
The Castle of Otranto (Walpole), 19
Catholicism
    Collinson's conversion to, 72
    perceived threat of, 65, 66
Cavalcanti, Guido, 90, 104, 105, 267
Cavour, Camillo Benso di, 259
Le Centaure, 84
A Century of Roundels (Swinburne), 240–1, 243
A Channel Passage and Other Poems (Swinburne), 240 1

'Une Charogne' (Baudelaire), 245
Chaucer, Geoffrey, 152–3, 220, 230
Chaucer at the Court of Edward III (Brown), 17–18, 151–4
Chesneau, Ernest, 267
'The Child Jesus: A Record Typical of the Five Sorrowful Mysteries' (Collinson), 24, 72, 82
'Chimes' (D.G. Rossetti), 95
Christ in the House of His Parents (Millais), 20, 37–8, 50, 64–6, 72, 133, 136–8, 140, 155
Christ Scourged (Manet), 128
'Christian and his Companions' (Wells), 26–7
The Christian Year (Keble), 167–8
'A Christmas Carol' (Swinburne), 243
Christmas Eve and Easter Day (R. Browning), 253
The Chronicle of Tebaldeo Tebaldei (Swinburne), 243
Chronicles (Froissart), 200, 214
'The Churches of North France' (Morris), 196
Claudio and Isabella (Hunt), 256
Clerk Saunders (Siddall), 183, 184, 185, 186, 187, 189, 190, 192, 258
Clifford, Rosamond, 242
Clough, Arthur, 82, 253
Cobden, Richard, 119
Coleridge, Samuel Taylor, 71, 170, 239, 240, 251–2
Collins, Charles Allston, 138–9
Collinson, James, 24, 51, 72, 82
Colonna, Vittoria, 111
Concert Champêtre (Giorgione or Titian), 35–6
La Conque, 84
Constable, John, 157
Contes de Fées (Perrault), 28
A Converted British Family Sheltering a Christian Missionary from the Persecution of the Druids (Hunt), 136–7, 153, 193
'Cordelia' (W.M. Rossetti, ill. by Brown), 82–3
Cornelius, Peter, 151
Cornforth, Fanny, 109, 240
Coronation of the Virgin (Fra Angelico), 34
The Coronation of the Virgin (Lorenzo Monaco), 37
'Correspondances' (Baudelaire), 243–4
Courbet, Gustave, 128

Crane, Walter, 58
The Crayon, 84, 255, 257
The Critic, 84, 253
Crivelli, Carlo, 233
Cruikshank, George, 255
Cyclographic Society, 50, 120
Cymon and Iphigenia (Millais), 120

Daisy curtains (Morris et al), 220
Daisy wallpaper (Morris), 214
Dalí, Salvador, 269
Dalziel illustrated Bible project (*Dalziels' Bible Gallery*), 56, 73–4, 223
Danaë and the Brazen Tower (Burne-Jones), 230
Dante
  autobiography of, 24
  Brotherhood's interest in, 23–5
  contrasted with poetry of D.G. Rossetti, 98
  depicted in *The First Anniversary of the Death of Beatrice* (D.G. Rossetti), 103–4, 105, 188
  D.G. Rossetti's interest in, 51, 72, 89–91, 93, 113
Dante Drawing an Angel on the First Anniversary of the Death of Beatrice (D.G. Rossetti), 51, 52, 103–6, 188
Dante Gabriel Rossetti as Designer and Writer (W.M. Rossetti), 260
Dante Gabriel Rossetti: His Family-Letters with a Memoir (W.M. Rossetti), 260–1
Darwin, Charles, 69
Das Leben Jesu (Strauss), 71
David, Jacques-Louis, 149
Dearle, John Henry, 219–20
'A Death-Parting' (D.G. Rossetti), 95
Decameron (Boccaccio), 4, 64
'The Decorative Arts' ('The Lesser Arts') (Morris), 206–7
The Defence of Guenevere and Other Poems (Morris), 199–203, 241, 244, 245
'The Defence of Guenevere' (Morris), 200, 201–2
Delacroix, Eugène, 123
Democratic Sonnets (W.M. Rossetti), 258–9
'Dennis Shand' (D.G. Rossetti), 93–4
Deverell, Walter Howell, 50, 51, 82, 83, 193
'A Dialogue on Art' (Orchard), 82
Dickens, Charles, 1–2, 19, 38, 64–5, 66
Dickinson and Company, 83
Discourses (Reynolds), 48, 63, 107, 155

Divine Comedy (Dante), 23–4, 111
Donatello, 42
'Dream Land' (C. Rossetti), 82, 169–73, 243
'A Dream of John Ball' (Morris), 206
'A Dream of Love' (Scott), 26
A Dream of the Past (Sir Isumbras) (Millais), 144, 145, 256
Dryden, John, 120
du Maurier, George, 254
Dudley Gallery, 58
Dürer, Albrecht, 40, 41, 57
Dyce, William, 39, 123, 151

The Early Italian Poets...Together with Dante's Vita Nuova (D.G. Rossetti), 24, 237–8, 243
The Earthly Paradise (Morris), 187, 196, 203, 204–5, 230
Eastlake, Charles, 107–8, 137
Ecce Ancilla Domini! (D.G. Rossetti), 5, 72–3, 108, 146, 164, 250, 269
Egg, Augustus, 123
The Elements of Drawing (Ruskin), 54
Eliot, George, 19, 71, 93
emblem form, 166
embroidery, theme of
  D.G. Rossetti, 106–7, 108
  Millais, 138–9
  Morris, 214
'An End' (C. Rossetti), 82
Engels, Friedrich, 207
An English Autumn Afternoon (Brown), 156–8, 201
The Escape of the Heretic (Millais), 144
Essays and Reviews, 69
Essays and Studies (Swinburne), 239
Esther (Millais), 145–6
The Eve of St Agnes (The Flight of Madeline and Porphyro during the Drunkenness Attending the Revelry) (Hunt), 36–7, 120, 121, 122, 124
'The Eve of St Agnes' (Keats), 21
The Exhibition of WORK, and Other Paintings (Brown), 160

'A Factory as It Might Be' (Morris), 207
The Fairy Mythology (Keightley), 28
Farrar, Frederic William, 70–1
Faulkner, Charles, 212
Faust (Goethe)
  illustrations by D.G. Rossetti, 51
  illustrations by Moritz Retzsch, 50

'Faustine' (Swinburne), 241

Fazio's Mistress (D.G. Rossetti), 41

'Félise' (Swinburne), 244–5

femme fatale, 241–3

Ferdinand Lured by Ariel (Millais), 3, 138

The Finding of the Saviour in the Temple
(Hunt), 69–70, 73, 117, 121, 124, 129,
130, 155, 160–1

Fine Arts Quarterly Review, 255

*The First Anniversary of the Death of
Beatrice* (D.G. Rossetti). *See Dante
Drawing an Angel on the First
Anniversary of the Death of Beatrice*

Fitzgerald, Penelope, 230

Flaxman, John, 49–50, 51–2

*The Flight of Madeline and Porphyro during
the Drunkenness Attending the Revelry
(The Eve of St Agnes)* (Hunt), 36–7,
120, 121, 122, 124

The Flower Book (Burne-Jones), 229

The Foolish Virgins (Millais), 73

'For a Venetian Pastoral' (D.G. Rossetti), 92

'For an Allegorical Dance of Women' (D.G.
Rossetti), 92, 95

'For Annie' (Poe), 81

The Forest tapestry (Morris & Co.), 214,
219–20

Found (D.G. Rossetti), 187, 251

Fra Angelico, 34–5, 36

'Fra Lippo Lippi' (R. Browning), 20

Francia, Francesco, 34, 36–7

'Frank's Sealed Letter' (Morris), 199

Fredeman, William E., 7, 250, 251

Froissart, Jean, 185, 200, 202, 214

Fry, Roger, 79, 270

Fuseli, Henry, 51–2

Gaddi, Taddeo, 37

Gambart, Ernest, 159

'The Garden of Proserpine' (Swinburne), 243

Garibaldi, Giuseppe, 259

'Gates of Paradise' (Ghiberti), 34

Gautier, Théophile, 239

'The Gay Goshawk', 185

Gazette des Beaux-Arts, 267

*Geoffrey Chaucer Reading the 'Legend
of Custance' to Edward III and his
Court, at the Palace of Sheen, on the
Anniversary of the Black Prince's Forty-
Fifth Birthday* (Brown). *See Chaucer at
the Court of Edward III* (Brown)

Georgiana Burne-Jones (Burne-Jones), 228–9

The Germ, 3, 76–85
contents of, 273–6
critics' view of, 83–4
D.G. and C. Rossetti's poetry, 172–3
etchings, 82–3
funding, 83
Masson's review of, 3–4, 5
origin and goals of, 76–7
Pre-Raphaelitism as starting afresh, 5
prose, 78–81
W.M. Rossetti and, 252–3
writing about visual art, 4–5

Ghent Altar-piece (van Eyck), 39

Ghiberti, Lorenzo, 34

Giebelhausen, Michaela, 8–9

Gilchrist, Anne, 27, 165–6

Giorgione, 35–6, 110

Giotto, 33–4, 218

The Girlhood of Mary Virgin (D.G.
Rossetti), 5, 37, 64, 65, 96, 97, 106–8,
139, 151, 154, 164

'Girlhood' sonnets (D.G. Rossetti), 96

'Gli occhi dolente per pieta del core' ('The
eyes that weep for pity of the heart')
(Dante), 91–2

The Glittering Plain (Morris), 209

Goblin Market and Other Poems (C.
Rossetti), 28, 173, 174, 180

'Goblin Market' (C. Rossetti), 22, 174–7

Goethe, Johann Wolfgang von, 50, 51

Going to the Battle (Burne-Jones), 57, 185

'The Gold-Bug' (Poe), 231, 233

The Golden Legend (Jacobus de
Voragine), 220

'Golden Wings' (Morris), 243–4

The Good Samaritan (Millais), 73

Gosse, Edmund, 262

Gothicism
Brown, 152–3
C. Rossetti, 164, 172–3
D.G. Rossetti, 19
Millais, 134–5, 138
Morris, 205–6, 216–17, 220
Ruskin, 56
Siddall, 183, 190

Gray, Euphemia (Effie Millais), 133, 141–2

Green Dining Room (Morris, Marshall,
Faulkner & Co.), 213, 218

Greenberg, Clement, 6

Gregorius, Aelbert, 149

Grettis Saga (Morris), 205

Grimm, William and Jacob, 200

The Guardian, 253
Guild of Saint George, 55

Hamerton, P.G., 255
'Hand and Soul' (D.G. Rossetti), 24–5, 27,
    78–80, 81
Harding, J.D., 54
Harrison, Antony, 238–9
Haskell, Francis, 33
Hatch, Edwin, 237
'The Haunted Palace' (Poe), 81
The Haunted Wood (The Haunted Tree)
    (Siddall), 185
'Haynau, 1849–50' (W.M. Rossetti), 259
Haynau, Julius Jacob von, 259
'The Haystack in the Floods' (Morris),
    200, 202
'He and I' (D.G. Rossetti), 99, 100
'Heart's Hope' (D.G. Rossetti), 99
Helsinger, Elizabeth, 245
Heptalogia (Swinburne), 245–6
'Her Shadow' (Woolner), 25–6
Hero. A Metamorphosis (C. Rossetti), 28
Hill, George Birkbeck, 237
'The Hill Summit' (D.G. Rossetti), 99
The Hireling Shepherd (Hunt), 121, 122,
    123, 124, 125–7, 128, 140, 214, 256
'Hist! said Kate the Queen'
    (D.G. Rossetti), 20
Histoire de l'art par les monumens (Seroux
    d'Agincourt), 81
History of England (Mackintosh), 152
History of Painting in Italy (Lanzi), 34
Hodge-Podge; or Weekly Efforts, 77, 167
Hogarth, William
    Brown's interest in, 160
    Hunt's interest in, 120
Hogarth Club, 160
Holbein, Hans, 41–2, 151
Holy Family (Siddall), 186, 191
Hooker, Richard, 125
Hopes and Fears for Art (Morris), 206
Hough, Graham, 79, 266
House, Humphry, 266
The House of Life (D.G. Rossetti), 24, 25,
    26, 28, 91, 96, 99, 246–7
The House of the Wolfings (Morris), 209
Houses of Parliament, 33, 63–4, 150–1
Housman, Laurence, 165, 174, 180
'How I Became a Socialist' (Morris), 197
'How We Live and How We Might Live'
    (Morris), 207
Howitt, Anna Mary, 187

Hueffer, Ford Madox (Ford Madox Ford),
    149, 260, 266
Hughes, Arthur, 73, 165, 173, 178, 179, 212,
    236, 253, 258
*A Huguenot, on St Bartholomew's Day,
    Refusing to Shield Himself from Danger
    by Wearing the Roman Catholic Badge*
    (Millais), 133, 139, 140, 145
Hunt, Cyril, 118
Hunt, John Dixon, 266
Hunt, Leigh, 20
Hunt, William Henry, 258
Hunt, William Holman, 116–31. *See also
    names of specific works by Hunt*
    autobiography of, 265, 266
    Brown and, 119–20, 123, 130, 150–1, 153
    Burne-Jones and, 116
    Christian iconography, 64
    contrasted with Burne-Jones, 226
    contributions to *The Germ*, 82
    D.G. Rossetti and, 16, 23, 94, 120
    doctrine of nature, 21, 22
    editing of list of Immortals, 62
    excusing radicalism of list
        of Immortals, 17
    first inclination toward
        Pre-Raphaelitism, 34
    'first principles' approach, 119–23
    first public exhibition, 64
    formal training, 48
    human self-repression, 136
    illustrations for 'The Lady of Shalott',
        22–3, 43
    illustrative and narrative drawing, 56
    influence of early Flemish art, 39
    influence of post-Raphaelite art, 42–4
    interchangeability of past and present,
        127–31
    interest in early Italian art, 36–7
    interest in Keats, 18, 21
    list of Immortals, 10–11, 15, 16
    Millais and, 120, 134, 140–1, 143–4
    mimesis and design, 123–7
    myths and realities of, 116–19
    old masters and, 34, 35
    outline drawing style, 50, 51
    reading Dickens, 19
    realist Protestant painting, 67–71
    recent exhibitions, 268
    religion and, 118, 119, 127–9, 130
    Ruskin's critique of works by, 54
    Siddall's likeness in works by, 193
    Swinburne and, 237

symbolism, 22–3, 226
W.M. Rossetti and, 250, 251, 253, 256, 258
The Hunt in the Forest (Uccello), 37
Hunter, Tom, 269–70
'Hyperion' (Keats), 21
Hypnerotomachia Poliphili, 229–30

'If' (C. Rossetti), 57
If I Can embroidery (Morris), 214
The Illustrated Family Bible, 74
Illustrated London News, 33–4, 37
Illustrated Scrapbook, 77
illustrative and narrative drawing, 49
Immortals, list of, 277–8
    as attempt to unite English and
        continental literary traditions, 17–18
    authors, 77–8
    Hunt's misrecognition of, 16
    as indicator of fractured nature of Pre-
        Raphaelitism, 18
    as indicator of political ideology, 17
    as indicator of sexual politics and
        feminism, 17
    as indicator of religious and intellectual
        background, 62
    overview, 10–11
    reasons behind certain exclusions, 15–16
    star ratings, 15
    writers on, 15–18
Improvisatrice (Landon), 17
'In Prison' (Morris), 199–200
'Introductory Sonnet' (D.G. Rossetti), 96, 97
Isabella (Millais), 21, 36, 37, 64, 107, 134–6, 140, 146, 153, 155, 250
'Isabella and the Pot of Basil' (Keats), 18, 21, 64, 77, 134

James, Henry, 112, 255
Jameson, Anna Brownell, 35, 63, 67, 72
Jasmine wallpaper (Morris), 215, 216, 217
'Jenny' (D.G. Rossetti), 99
Jesus Christ, 62, 64, 67, 74, 127
Jones, Ebenezer, 27
Joseph and his Brethren (Wells), 27
Journals of Travel to Iceland (Morris), 205
Jowett, Benjamin, 237
Le Juif errant (Sue), 19

Keats, John
    doctrine of nature, 21–2
    influence on D.G. Rossetti, 27, 239
    influence on Hunt, 127

influence on Millais, 64
influence on Pre-Raphaelites, 18, 20, 21, 77, 120
influence on Siddall, 184
influence on Swinburne, 239
'Isabella and the Pot of Basil', 18, 134
Keble, John, 24, 72, 167–8
Keightley, Thomas, 28
Kelmscott Chaucer (Morris and Burne-Jones), 17–18
Kelmscott Press, 220
Kennet textile (Morris), 214
'King Arthur's Tomb' (Morris, D.G. Rossetti), 201
King Cophetua and the Beggar Maid (Burne-Jones), 231–4
Kingsley, Charles, 125, 130, 229
The Knight's Farewell (Burne-Jones), 185, 186
'Kubla Khan' (Coleridge), 170

'La Belle Dame sans Merci' (Keats), 77
La Belle Iseult (Morris), 39–40, 186, 212
'La connaissance des peintres préraphaélites anglais en France, 1855–1900' (Lethève), 267
La Pia de' Tolomei (D.G. Rossetti), 240
Lady Affixing a Pennant to a Knight's Spear (Siddall), 183, 185–6
Lady Clare (Siddall), 183, 186, 190–1
Lady Lilith (D.G. Rossetti), 28, 110, 240
The Lady of Shalott (Hunt), 42–4, 56, 136, 188
The Lady of Shalott (Siddall), 188
'The Lady of Shalott' (Tennyson), 22–3
'The Lady's Lament' (D.G. Rossetti), 94–5
Landon, Letitia Elizabeth ('L.E.L.'), 17
Lanzi, Luigi, 34
Lasinio, Carlo, 36–7, 50, 63, 105
'The Lass of Lochroyan', 185
The Last of England (Brown), 148, 158–9
Latham, David, 8–9
Laus Veneris (Burne-Jones), 237–8
'Laus Veneris' (Swinburne), 237–8, 241
The Laws of Fésole (Ruskin), 54, 55
Layard, Austen Henry, 233
Lear, Edward, 159
Leathart, James, 160
Leech, John, 255
Lefevre, Raoul, 220
Legend of Good Women (Chaucer), 230
Leighton, Frederic, 145, 258
'L.E.L.' *See* Landon, Letitia Elizabeth

L'Enfant du Régiment (Millais), 142

Leonardo da Vinci, 35–6, 58, 74

'The Leper' (Swinburne), 241, 245

Les Fleurs du mal (Baudelaire), 239

Lessing, G.E., 81

Lethève, Jacques, 267

Life and Death in Hackney (Hunter), 269–70

The Life and Death of Jason (Morris), 203

Life and Letters of Keats (Milnes), 21

Life of Blake (Gilchrist and Rossetti), 27, 165–6

The Life of Christ (Farrar), 70–1

Life of Mary Shelley (*Mrs. Shelley*) (L.M. Brown), 262

'Life-in-Love' (D.G. Rossetti), 99

The Light of the World (Hunt), 67–9, 71, 117, 127–8, 129, 130, 164, 258

Lindsay, Alexander, 67

Linton, W. J., 27

Lippi, Filippo, 37

list of Immortals. *See* Immortals, list of

Liverpool Post, 255

'living it off', 19–20, 24, 27

Lorenzo Monaco, 37, 107

Lorrain, Claude, 53

'Love Is Enough' (Morris), 203

Love Leading the Pilgrim (Burne-Jones), 238

Lovers Listening to Music (Siddall), 191–2

Lycidas (Milton), 125

Lyell, Charles, 35

Lyrical Ballads (Wordsworth and Coleridge), 251–2

Lytton, Edward Bulwer, 19, 64, 120

Macbeth (ill. by Retzsch), 50

MacCarthy, Fiona, 212

Mackintosh, James, 152

Maclise, Daniel, 53, 151

Macmillan, Alexander, 238

Mademoiselle de Maupin (Gautier), 239

Madonna and Child with an Angel (Siddall), 191

'Madonna Consolata' (D.G. Rossetti), 93–4

'Madonna Mia' (Swinburne), 243

Madonna of the Rocks (Leonardo), 35–6

The Magazine of Art, 41–2

'The Maids of Elfen-mere' (D.G. Rossetti), 57

Mallarmé, Stéphane, 5

Malory, Thomas, 72, 185, 200, 213, 223, 229

Manet, Edouard, 128

Mantegna, Andrea, 35–6, 58, 233

Mariana (Millais), 138–9, 256

Mariana in the South (D.G. Rossetti), 40

The Marriage of Heaven and Hell (Blake), 97–8

Marsh, James, 71

Marshall, Peter Paul, 212

Marx, Karl, 207

Mary in the House of St John (D.G. Rossetti), 73

Mary Magdalene at the Door of Simon the Pharisee (D.G. Rossetti), 41, 57

Masson, David, 3–4, 5

Materials for a History of Oil Painting (Eastlake), 107–8

Maud (Tennyson), 20

Maurice, F. D., 54, 159

Mazzini, Giuseppe, 259

McGann, Jerome, 8, 104, 109, 166, 244, 266

medievalism, 63, 187

  Burne-Jones, 224

  D.G. Rossetti, 23, 41, 96

  Hunt, 123

  Millais, 134, 138

  Morris, 40, 198–9, 200, 201, 206, 213–15, 216–17, 220

  Siddall, 183, 185

  Swinburne, 237, 238–9, 241, 243–4, 245

Medusa (Leonardo), 36

Meinhold, Wilhelm, 242–3

Melencolia (Dürer), 57

Memling, Hans, 35–6, 40–1

Memoir (W.M. Rossetti), 262

Memoirs of the Early Italian Painters (Jameson), 35

Men Playing Checkers (Sweerts), 41–2

The Merciful Knight (Burne-Jones), 223–4

Meredith, George, 93, 239

Metternich, Klemens von, 259

Michelangelo, 34, 58, 63, 111

Millais, Effie (Euphemia Gray), 133, 141–2

Millais, John Everett, 133–47. *See also names of specific works by Millais*

  Brown and, 144, 160

  copying from old masters, 34

  D.G. Rossetti and, 134, 144

  doctrine of nature, 22

  in first *P.R.B. Journal* entry, 3

  first public exhibition, 64

  formal training, 48

  Hunt and, 120, 134, 140–1, 143–4

  illustrations for C. Rossetti's poems, 165

illustrations for 'The Lady of Shalott', 22, 23
illustrative and narrative drawing, 56
influence of early Italian art, 37–8
influence of post-Raphaelite art, 41–2, 44
interest in early Italian art, 36–7
interest in Keats, 18, 21
outline drawing style, 50
recent exhibitions, 268
Ruskin and, 141–2, 143, 144–5
Ruskin's critique of works by, 54
Siddall and, 141
Siddall's likeness in work by, 193
Swinburne and, 237
symbolism, 64, 66
Thackeray and, 19
W.M. Rossetti and, 250, 251, 253, 256
Miller, Annie, 118, 119
Miller, John, 160
Milnes, Monckton, 21
Milton, John, 28, 112, 125
Minotaure, 269
Minstrelsy of the Scottish Border (Scott), 184–5
'A Modern Idyl' (Deverell), 82
Modern Love (Meredith), 239
Modern Painters (Ruskin), 22, 35, 53, 122
'A Moment's Monument: Reflections on Pre-Raphaelite Vision in Poetry and Painting' (J.D. Hunt), 266
Monaco. See Lorenzo Monaco
'The Monochord' (D.G. Rossetti), 92
Morning Chronicle, 83–4
'Morning Sleep' (Scott), 82
Morris, Jane Burden, 109, 111–12, 113, 190, 193, 199, 217, 220, 261
Morris, Marshall, Faulkner & Co. (Morris & Co.), 28, 148, 160, 200, 212, 213, 215, 218, 219, 223, 226
Morris, May, 220
Morris, William. See also names of specific works by Morris
  beauty and the public, 212–17
  Brown and, 212, 219
  Burne-Jones and, 211–12, 213, 219, 220, 223, 224
  colaboration, 217–21
  designs of, 211–21
  D.G. Rossetti and, 201, 211–12, 213, 219
  Faulkner and, 212
  Hogarth Club, 160
  influence of early Flemish art, 39–40
  interest in D.G.Rossetti's drawings, 57

Kelmscott Chaucer, 17–18
Marshall and, 212
Oxford and Cambridge Magazine, 5, 198
'palace of art', 187
realistic poetic style, 93
Swinburne and, 236–7, 238, 240–2, 243–4
Webb and, 212
writings of, 196–209
Le Morte d'Arthur (Malory), 72, 185, 200, 213, 223, 229
Moxon, Edward, 22, 27
Moxon Tennyson, 40, 41, 56, 188, 237
'Mrs. Holmes Grey' (W.M. Rossetti), 94, 251–2
Mulready, William, 158
'The Music Master' (Allingham), 19–20, 57
'Mutual Suicide Association', 19
My Beautiful Lady (Woolner), 25
'My Beautiful Lady/My Lady in Death' (Woolner, ill. by Hunt), 82
'My Sister's Sleep' (D.G. Rossetti), 77, 93, 172–3

narrative and illustrative drawing, 56–60
Nativity (Hughes), 73
nature
  Brown's observation of, 156
  close drawing from (observational drawing), 48, 49, 53–5
  doctrine of (truth to nature), 21–2, 67, 78–9
  inspiration for Morris, 213–17
  Millais' vision of, 141
Nazarenes, 39, 80, 151
The New Life (D.G. Rossetti), 90
The New Path, 84
New Poems (C. Rossetti), 262
'Newborn Death' (D.G. Rossetti), 100
The Newcomes (Thackeray), 19
Newman, Teresa, 149
News from Home (Millais), 144
News from Nowhere: Or, an Epoch of Rest, Being Some Chapters from a Utopian Romance (Morris), 196, 199, 206, 208–9
Nineveh and Its Remains (Layard), 233
Noble, J. Ashcroft, 76, 84
Nocturne in Black and Gold (Whistler), 219
Norton, Charles Eliot, 55, 192
'Notes on Designs of the Old Masters at Florence' (Swinburne), 240
'Notes on Some Pictures of 1868' (Swinburne), 240

Notes on the Royal Academy Exhibition,
1868 (Swinburne), 28
'Notes on the Text of Shelley'
(Swinburne), 240
The Novel on Blue Paper (Morris), 199
Nursey, Claude 'Lorraine', 34

Odes of Horace (Morris), 217
The Odyssey (ill. by Flaxman), 49–50
'Of My Lady in Death' (Woolner), 82
Of the Laws of Ecclesiastical Polity
(Hooker), 125
'Old Pictures in Florence' (R. Browning), 36
Old Water-Colour Society, 223
Olympia (Manet), 128
'On an Old Roundel' (Swinburne), 243
On Heroes, Hero-Worship and the Heroic in
History (Carlyle), 67
'On Refusal of Aid Between Nations' (D.G.
Rossetti), 93
On the Construction of Sheepfolds
(Ruskin), 125
'On the Mechanism of a Historical Picture'
(Brown), 154–5, 156
'On the Nature of Gothic' (Ruskin), 220
On the Origin of Species (Darwin), 69
'The One Hope' (D.G. Rossetti), 100–1
1 Holland Park (Morris & Co.), 219
Ophelia (Millais), 139–41, 193, 214
Orchard, John, 82
The Order of Release (Millais), 144
Orientalism (Said), 129
Our English Coasts (Strayed Sheep) (Hunt),
123, 157, 256
Our Lady of Good Children (Brown), 37
outline drawing style, 48, 49–52
Overbeck, Johann Friedrich, 80, 151
Oxford, 37, 55
The Oxford and Cambridge Magazine, 5
The Oxford and Cambridge Magazine, 84,
196, 198, 199
Oxford Critical and Cultural History of
Modernist Magazines, 267
Oxford Movement, 65, 72, 167
Oxford Union frescoes, 211–12, 213, 223,
236, 237

'The P. R. B.: I' (C. Rossetti), 165
'The Palace of Art' (Tennyson), 187–8
Palgrave, F.T., 255
The Parable of the Boiling Pot (Burne-Jones),
73–4
The Parables of Our Lord (Millais), 56, 73

Paradise Lost (Milton), 112
Paradiso (Dante), 98
'The Parisian Commune, 1871' (W.M.
Rossetti), 259
Parkes, Bessie, 17
Parsons, John Robert, 112, 193
The Passing of Arthur (Siddall), 187
'The Past' (W.M. Rossetti), 259
Past and Present (Carlyle), 159
Pater, Walter
on D.G. Rossetti, 89, 93, 96, 239
on Leonardo, 74
on Morris, 203, 239
Swinburne and, 239
Patmore, Coventry, 3, 16, 17, 20, 192
Pauline (Browning), 20
Peace Concluded (Millais), 142
Peacock and Dragon (Morris), 216–17
Peacock Room (Whistler), 216
La peinture anglaise (Chesneau), 267
Perrault, Charles, 28
The Perseus Series (Burne-Jones), 230
Phyllis and Demophoön (Burne-Jones), 228
'Piangendo star con l'anima smarrita' (D.G.
Rossetti), 93–4
Picasso, Pablo, 269
Pietà (Francia), 36–7
'The Pilgrims of Hope' (Morris), 199, 203
Pimpernel wallpaper (Morris), 216
Pippa Passes (Browning), 20
Pippa Passes (Siddall), 187, 191–2
Pissarro, Lucien, 180
'The Pit and the Pendulum' (Poe), 234
Pitture a fresco del Campo Santo di Pisa
(Lasinio), 36–7
The Plague at Ashdod (Poussin), 36–7
Plint, Thomas E., 159–60, 223
La Plume, 84
Poe, Edgar Allan
illustrations by D.G. Rossetti, 51, 81
influence on Burne-Jones, 229, 230–1, 234
influence on Pre-Raphaelites, 77, 81–2
in list of Immortals, 19
Poems (Scott), 25
Poems (Tennyson), 185
'Poems and Ballads: A Criticism' (W.M.
Rossetti), 243
Poems and Ballads (Swinburne), 238, 240–1,
243, 244–5, 246, 247
Poems by the Way (Morris), 203
The Poetical Works of Christina Georgina
Rossetti with Memoir and Notes &c by
William Michael Rossetti, 262

Polidori, Gaetano, 164
Pontormo, Jacopo da, 234
'The Portrait [On Mary's Portrait]' (D.G. Rossetti), 77, 81
Portrait of Baldassare Castiglione (Raphael), 35
Portrait of Giovanni Arnolfini and his Wife (van Eyck). *See Arnolfini Portrait*
Pound, Ezra, 93, 104, 267
Poussin, Nicolas, 36–7
Powell and Son, 223
'Præraphaelitism' (W.M. Rossetti), 253
'Praise of My Lady' (Morris), 199, 241
PRB Journal (W.M. Rossetti), 250–1
'The Pre-Raphaelite Literary Painters' (Spender), 266
The Pre-Raphaelites exhibition (Stockholm, 2009), 269–70
The Pre-Raphaelites exhibition (Tate, 1984), 149
Pre-Raphaelitism
	artists before antiquarians, 33
	as attempt to break down boundaries between arts, 6–7
	charges against, 6
	composition of original Brotherhood, 2, 16
	drawing, 47–60
	fall from favour and revival, 265–6
	influence of early Flemish and German art, 38–41
	influence of early Italian art, 36–8
	influence of post-Raphaelite art, 41–4
	influential artists, 32–44
	influential literature, 15–28
	as label, 1–2
	place in history, 265–70
	religious and intellectual background, 62–74
	revivalism, 33–6
	revolutionary impact of, 63–6
	segregation of visual and literary arts in studies of, 7–9
	as starting afresh, 5–6
Pre-Raphaelitism and the Pre-Raphaelite Brotherhood (Hunt), 118–19, 123, 149
The Pretty Baa-Lambs (Brown), 156
The Prince's Progress and Other Poems (C. Rossetti), 173, 177–8
Prinsep, Val, 236
The Prodigal Son (Millais), 73
Proserpine (D.G. Rossetti), 111–14
'Proserpine' (D.G. Rossetti), 113

prosody, 90
Prout, Samuel, 54
Pugin, A.W.N., 216
Punch, 33, 34
Purgatorio (Dante), 5, 112–13
'The Purpose and Tendency of Early Italian Art' (Stephens), 80–1

Quarterly Review, 47
Queen Iseult (Swinburne), 237, 241
The Queen Mother (Swinburne), 240–1

Radford, Ernest, 77
Rae, George, 160
The Raising of Lazarus (Sebastiano del Piombo), 135
Raphael, 34, 35, 63, 135
'The Raven' (Poe), 81
The Raven and Other Poems (Poe), 81
Records of the Past (Samuel Bagster & Co.), 233
The Recuyell of the Histories of Troye (Lefevre), 220
Redgrave, Richard, 158
Red House (Morris et al), 40, 217–18
Redon, Odilon, 58
religion
	Biblical criticism, 69, 71–2
	Burne-Jones and, 225
	C. Rossetti and, 166, 168–9
	Catholicism, Collinson's conversion to, 72
	Catholicism, perceived threat of, 65, 66
	D.G. Rossetti and, 72–3
	Hunt and, 64, 67–71, 127–9
	list of Immortals as Creed, 16
	as poetry, 71–4
	Protestant painting, 67–71
	Ruskin and, 72
	Scott and, 74
Rembrandt, 41–2
The Renaissance (Pater), 74
Renan, Ernest, 71–2
'Repining' (C. Rossetti), 82
Retzsch, Moritz, 50
revivalism, 33–4, 35
Reynolds, Joshua, 34, 48, 63, 107, 153, 155
Reznikoff, Charles, 93
Richardson, James, 246–7
Ricketts, Charles, 165, 179–80
Rienzi, Cola di, 64
Rienzi: The Last of the Roman Tribunes (Lytton), 64, 120

Rienzi Vowing to Obtain Justice for the Death of his Young Brother, Slain in a Skirmish between the Colonna and the Orsini Factions (Hunt), 36–7, 120, 123, 128, 250
Roberts Brothers of Boston, 178
'Rococo' (Swinburne), 243
Rolin Madonna (van Eyck), 41
Romanticism, 77–8, 239, 241
'Rondel' (Swinburne), 243
The Roots of the Mountains (Morris), 205
Rosamond (Swinburne), 240–2
Rossetti, Christina, 164–80. *See also names of specific works by Rossetti*
art of the book, 173–80
contributions to *The Germ*, 77, 82
D.G. Rossetti and, 16, 17, 164, 165, 173, 174, 175, 176, 177–8
doctrine of nature, 22
emblem form, 166
interest in Blake, 28
interest in Dante, 23–4
modelling, 164
religion and, 166, 168–9
Siddall and, 193
as 'sister' to the Brotherhood, 3
Swinburne and, 237, 240–1, 243
Tractarian poetry, 167
verbal-visual aesthetic, 166–73
W.M. Rossetti and, 260, 262
Rossetti, Dante Gabriel. *See also names of specific works by Rossetti*
accusation of technical incompetence, 105
Allingham and, 16, 19–20
on Baudelaire, 27
Brown and, 16, 17–18, 150, 154, 155, 158, 161
Burne-Jones and, 57, 73, 223
C. Rossetti and, 16, 17, 164, 165, 173, 174, 175, 176, 177–8
Christian iconography, 64
doctrine of nature, 21–2
double works, 96–101
in first *P.R.B. Journal* entry, 3
first public exhibition, 64
formal training, 48
The Germ, 76–7, 78–80, 81, 83
Hogarth Club, 160
on Hughes, 178
human self-repression, 136
Hunt and, 16, 23, 94, 120
illustrations for 'The Lady of Shalott', 22, 23
illustrative and narrative drawing, 49, 56, 57
influence of early Flemish and German art, 40–1
influence of early Flemish art, 40
influence of early Italian art, 37
influence of Poe, 81
influence of post-Raphaelite art, 41, 44
interest in Blake, 27–8
interest in Botticelli, 32, 269
interest in Browning, 20
interest in C.J. Wells, 18, 26–7
interest in Dante, 23–5
interest in darkness and the Gothic, 19
interest in early Italian art, 36–7
interest in Keats, 21
interest in supernatural, 28
kiss, as sign of consummation between material and immaterial, 26
letter regarding list of Immortals, 10, 15
liberated approach to rhyme, 91–2
Millais and, 134, 144
Morris and, 201, 211–12, 213, 219
novels read by, 19
oil study of bottles, 105, 106, 154
old masters and, 34, 35–6
outline drawing style, 50, 51–2
Oxford and Cambridge Magazine, 198
painting of, 103–14
paintings of women, 109–14
poetry of, 89–101
poetry's transvaluation of the everyday, 19–20
popularity of works by, 109
post-Brotherhood life, 16
realistic and artificial styles, 91–6
recent exhibitions, 8, 268
as relative beginner, 5
religion as poetry, 72–3
Scott and, 16, 19, 24, 107
segregation of visual and literary work in studies of, 7–8
sexual politics and feminism and, 17
Siddall and, 41, 105–6, 109, 165, 184, 189, 191, 192, 193–4, 261
Swinburne and, 27, 28, 236–8, 239, 240–3, 244, 245–7, 248
syllabic verse effect, 92–3
transfiguring woman motif, 24–5
translation work, 89–93
watercolours, 49
web-based archive, 8

W.M. Rossetti and, 250, 251, 252, 253, 255, 260–1
Working Men's College, 54
Rossetti, Gabriel Charles Dante. *See* Rossetti, Dante Gabriel
Rossetti, Gabriele, 89–90
Rossetti, Maria, 23–4
Rossetti, William Michael, 250–63. *See also names of specific works by Rossetti*
  aim of Brotherhood, 63
  Brown and, 255, 258
  C. Rossetti and, 260, 262
  as critic, 253–7
  D.G. Rossetti and, 81, 103, 104, 250, 251, 252, 253, 255, 260–1
  first journal entry, 3
  The Germ, 77, 82–3, 84, 252–3
  as historian and documenter of Brotherhood, 260–3
  Hughes and, 253
  Hunt and, 250, 251, 253, 256, 258
  as international interpreter of Pre-Raphaelism, 257–8
  list of Immortals, 10, 15
  looking back on Pre-Raphaelite movement, 179
  Millais and, 250, 251, 253, 256
  politics and poetry, 258–9
  Ruskin and, 254, 255, 258
  Scott and, 253, 258
  Siddall and, 192
  Swinburne and, 237, 238, 240–1, 243, 252
Royal Academy Schools, 47–8, 54, 65, 116, 117, 119, 120, 160
Ruskin, John
  on *Arnolfini Portrait* (van Eyck), 39
  'the Art Catholic', 166
  Brown and, 153–4, 157–8
  close drawing from nature (observational drawing), 48, 53–5
  as critic and mentor, 16–17
  on D.G. Rossetti's imitation of van Eyck, 107
  doctrine of nature, 21, 156
  first comment on Brotherhood, 1
  illustrative and narrative drawing, 56
  influence on Burne-Jones, 224
  influence on Morris, 207
  interest in Keats, 21
  interest in Sandys, 57
  interest in Tennyson, 20–1
  medievalism, 214, 216, 220

  Millais and, 141–2, 143, 144–5
  phases of Raphael's work, 35
  on reform of art, 63
  religion as poetry, 72
  Siddall and, 56, 191–2
  Swinburne and, 236
  symbolism, 22
  on Turner, 122
  Whistler and, 219
  W.M. Rossetti and, 254, 255, 258

Sacred and Legendary Art (Jameson), 63, 72
Said, Edward, 129
Saint Cecilia (Siddall), 188
Sambrook, James, 265–7
Sand, George, 19
Sandys, Frederick, 57, 165
Sano di Pietro, 37–8
Sass's Drawing Academy, 48, 50
The Savoy, 76
The Scapegoat (Hunt), 226
Schools of Design, 54
Scott, Walter, 19, 184–5
Scott, William Bell. *See also names of specific works by Scott*
  D.G. Rossetti and, 16, 19, 24, 107
  The Germ, 82
  influence of early German art, 40
  kiss, as sign of consummation between material and immaterial, 26
  religion as poetry, 74
  Swinburne and, 236, 237–8, 240–1
  transfiguring woman motif, 25–6
  W.M. Rossetti and, 253, 258
Sebastiano del Piombo, 135
'Second Sunday in Advent' (Keble), 167–8
The Seeds and Fruits of English Poetry (Brown), 151–2
Self-portrait (Siddall), 189, 190, 192–3, 194
Seroux d'Agincourt, Jean-Baptiste-Louis-George, 81
The Shadow of Death (Hunt), 70–1, 117, 124, 126, 127, 130–1
Shakespeare, William, 247
Shaw, George Bernard, 67
Shelley, Mary, 262
Shelley, Percy Bysshe
  D.G. Rossetti's interest in, 27, 90, 239
  Hunt's interest in, 127
  influence on W.M. Rossetti, 259, 262
  Swinburne's interest in, 239, 240

Sibylla Palmifera (D.G. Rossetti), 28
Siddall, Elizabeth Eleanor, 183–94. *See also
names of specific works by Siddall*
archaicizing and medievalizing art, 184–7
death of, 28
D.G. Rossetti and, 41, 105–6, 109, 165,
191, 192, 193–4, 261
image of herself, 192–4
interior spaces, 187–90
introduction to Brotherhood, 5, 83
Millais and, 141
patrons and the public, 191–2
practice of art, 190–1
Ruskin and, 56, 191–2
Swinburne and, 237, 239, 240
Signs of Change (Morris), 206
'Silent Noon' (D.G. Rossetti), 92
Sing-Song: A Nursery Rhyme Book (C.
Rossetti), 173, 178–9
Sir Galahad and the Holy Grail (Siddall), 185
Sir Isumbras (A Dream of the Past) (Millais),
144, 145, 256
*Sir Lancelot Bringing Sir Tristram and the Belle
Iseult to Joyous Gard* (Morris), 217–18
Sir Patrick Spens (Siddall), 240
'Sister Helen' (D.G. Rossetti), 185
'The Sleeper' (Poe), 81
Sleeping (Millais), 146
Smith, Alexander, 19
Smulders, Sharon, 178
socialism
Brown, 148, 159
Morris, 196, 197, 206, 207, 208, 209, 212
W.M. Rossetti, 258
Solomon, Simeon
Babylon Hath Been a Golden Cup, 58, 59
illustrative and narrative drawing, 49,
58–9
recent exhibitions, 268
Swinburne's review of work by, 240
Some Reminiscences (W.M. Rossetti), 260
'Song' (C. Rossetti), 82
Songs before Sunrise (Swinburne), 238
Songs of Innocence and of Experience
(Blake), 28, 178
'Songs of One Household' (D.G. Rossetti),
172–3
Sonnets for Pictures (D.G. Rossetti), 93
'Sonnets for Pictures' (D.G. Rossetti), 245–6
Sordello (R. Browning), 41
Southend (Brown), 156
Souvenir of Velasquez (Millais), 44
Spasmodics, 19

The Spectator, 83, 253, 254, 255
Spender, Stephen, 77, 266
Spring (Millais), 145
St Catherine of Alexandria, 35
St Cecilia (D.G. Rossetti), 41, 56
'St Dorothy' (Swinburne), 243
Stein, Richard L., 269
Stephens, Frederic George, 3, 76, 80–1, 161
Stevens, Wallace, 93
Stillman, W. J., 255
The Stonebreaker (Brett), 40
The Stones of Venice (Ruskin), 55, 220
Stories after Nature (Wells), 26–7
'The Story of Aileen and Basille', 226–7
*The Story of Sigurd the Volsung and the Fall
of the Niblungs* (Morris), 196, 203–4,
205–6
'The Story of the Unknown Church'
(Morris), 198, 209
Stothard, Thomas, 58
Stowe, Harriet Beecher, 244
Strauss, David Friedrich, 71
Strawberry Thief textile (Morris), 216–17
Strayed Reveller (Arnold), 253
Strayed Sheep (Our English Coasts) (Hunt),
123, 157, 256
Sue, Eugène, 19
'Summer Dawn' (Morris), 199
'The Sundew' (Swinburne), 246
'A Superscription' (D.G. Rossetti), 95, 96
'Le surréalisme spectral de l'Éternel Féminin
préraphaélite' (Dalí), 269
Sweerts, Michiel, 41–2
'Sweet Death' (C. Rossetti), 82
Swinburne, Algernon Charles, 236–48.
*See also names of specific works by
Swinburne*
artificial poetic style, 93
Brown and, 237
Burne-Jones and, 236–8, 240–1, 242–3
C. Rossetti and, 174, 237, 240–1, 243
D.G. Rossetti and, 27, 28, 236–8, 239,
240–3, 244, 245–7, 248
femme fatale, 241–3
Hunt and, 237
Morris and, 236–7, 238, 240–2, 243–4
Ruskin and, 236
Scott and, 236, 237–8, 240–1
Siddall and, 237, 239, 240
Wells and, 27
W.M. Rossetti and, 237, 238, 240–1,
243, 252
Swinburne, John, 236

Take your Son, Sir! (Brown), 39
The Tale of Balen (Swinburne), 244
A Tale of the House of the Wolfings
    (Morris), 205
Tennyson, Alfred
    Brotherhood's interest in, 18, 20–1
    influence on Burne-Jones, 224, 232
    influence on Siddall, 184, 185, 186, 187–8
    influence on Swinburne, 237, 239
    'The Lady of Shalott', 22–3, 42
Thackeray, William Makepeace, 19, 40–1
'This Advent moon shines cold and clear' (C.
    Rossetti), 168–9
Thomas, William Cave, 151
The Times, 32, 44, 53
Tintoretto, 22, 35
Titian
    influence on painting of D.G. Rossetti, 110
    influence on painting of Hunt, 121
    influence on Pre-Raphaelites, 35–6, 41, 42
'To Death, of his Lady' (Villon), 243
'Tolling Bell' (Woolner), 26
Tractarian poetry, 167
Tracts for the Times, 167
Transfiguration (Raphael), 135
Trellis (Morris), 217
Trevelyan, Pauline, 236–7
Trevelyan, Walter Calverley, 236
Trilby (du Maurier), 254
Tristram and Isolde (Morris), 28
Tristram of Lyonesse (Swinburne), 28, 238,
    244, 247
The Triumph of the Innocents (Hunt), 124
Tucker, Herbert, 28
'The Tune of Seven Towers' (Morris, D.G.
    Rossetti), 201
Tupper, Alexander, 83
Tupper, George, 83
Tupper, John Lucas, 19, 20, 83
Turner, J.M.W., 53, 122, 143, 157, 255
Twelfth Night (Deverell), 193

Uccello, Paolo, 37
'Ulalume' (Poe), 81
Uncle Tom's Cabin (Stowe), 244
'Useful Work vs. Useless Toil' (Morris), 207

The Vale of Rest (Millais), 145
Valentine Rescuing Sylvia from Proteus
    (Hunt), 193
Van Dyck, Anthony, 41–2
Van Eyck, Jan
    influence on Hunt, 34, 35

influence on Morris, 214
influence on painting of D.G. Rossetti, 36,
    107, 110
influence on painting of Millais, 135
influence on Pre-Raphaelites, 33, 39, 40–1,
    42
Van Gogh, Vincent, 109, 269
Van Hanselaer, Pierre, 150
Velázquez, Diego
    influence on Pre-Raphaelites, 41, 42, 44
    rise of reputation, 32, 44
Venus Verticordia (D.G. Rossetti), 110
Veronese, Paolo, 110
Verses: Dedicated to my Mother (C.
    Rossetti), 164, 180
Victory O Lord! (Millais), 146
Vie de Jésus (Renan), 71–2
Villon, François, 243
Vine wallpaper (Morris), 219
'Viola and Olivia' (Tupper, ill. by
    Deverell), 83
Virgin and Child with Six Saints (di Pietro),
    37–8
La Vita Nuova (Dante), 4, 24, 51, 72, 90, 93,
    100, 103, 104
Voragine, Jacobus de, 220

Waking (Millais), 146
Walpole, Horace, 19
Wappers, Gustaf (Egide Charles Gustave;
    Baron Wappers), 150
Warner, Malcolm, 38, 39, 107
The Water of the Wondrous Isles
    (Morris), 196
Watkinson, Ray, 149
Watts-Dunton, Theodore, 238, 240, 247–8
Waugh, Edith, 118
Waugh, Evelyn, 118, 266
Waugh, Fanny, 118
Webb, Philip, 212, 217, 219–20
Wedding Feast at Cana (Veronese), 110
The Well at the World's End (Morris), 196
Wells, Charles Jeremiah, 18, 26–7
Westminster Cartoon Competitions, 63–4,
    150–1
Whistler, James McNeill, 4, 44, 73, 145,
    216, 219
The White Girl (Whistler), 44
white ground, painting over
    D.G. Rossetti, 107–8
    Hunt, 122
Whitman, Walt, 259
'Who has seen the wind?' (C. Rossetti), 179

Wilenski, R. H., 6
Wilkie, David, 34, 158
William Blake (Swinburne), 238, 239, 240–1
William Michael Rossetti (Cameron), 257
Williams, Isaac, 167
Windermere (Brown), 156
Windus, William Lindsay, 258
'witch' drawing (Siddall), 185
Woman with a Mirror (Titian), 41, 110
Wood, Christopher, 126
The Woodman's Daughter (Millais), 20, 37
'The Woodman's Daughter' (Patmore), 20
'The Woodspurge' (D.G. Rossetti), 93
Woolner, Thomas
    contributions to *The Germ*, 82
    D.G. Rossetti and, 24
    influence of Poe, 82
    kiss, as sign of consummation between
        material and immaterial, 26
    The Last of England (Brown), 158
    Swinburne and, 236

transfiguring woman motif, 25–6
    W.M. Rossetti and, 251, 254
Wordsworth, William, 20, 21, 184, 251–2
Work (Brown), 130, 148, 155–6, 159
Working Men's College, 54
Works of Geoffrey Chaucer (Kelmscott
    Press), 220
The Wrestling Scene in 'As You Like It'
    (Maclise), 53
Wuthering Heights (Brontë), 19
*Wycliffe Reading his Translation of the New
    Testament to his Protector, John of
    Gaunt, Duke of Lancaster, in Presence
    of Chaucer and Gower* (Brown),
    17–18, 151

Yeast (Kingsley), 125
Yeats, William Butler
    artificial poetic style, 93
    influence of Pre-Raphaelites, 267
    rhetoricians versus poets, 101
    rhythm, 247

Cambridge Companions to...

AUTHORS

Edward Albee edited by Stephen J. Bottoms

Margaret Atwood edited by Coral Ann Howells

W. H. Auden edited by Stan Smith

Jane Austen edited by Edward Copeland and Juliet McMaster (second edition)

Beckett edited by John Pilling

Bede edited by Scott DeGregorio

Aphra Behn edited by Derek Hughes and Janet Todd

Walter Benjamin edited by David S. Ferris

William Blake edited by Morris Eaves

Brecht edited by Peter Thomson and Glendyr Sacks (second edition)

The Brontës edited by Heather Glen

Bunyan edited by Anne Dunan-Page

Frances Burney edited by Peter Sabor

Byron edited by Drummond Bone

Albert Camus edited by Edward J. Hughes

Willa Cather edited by Marilee Lindemann

Cervantes edited by Anthony J. Cascardi

Chaucer edited by Piero Boitani and Jill Mann (second edition)

Chekhov edited by Vera Gottlieb and Paul Allain

Kate Chopin edited by Janet Beer

Caryl Churchill edited by Elaine Aston and Elin Diamond

Coleridge edited by Lucy Newlyn

Wilkie Collins edited by Jenny Bourne Taylor

Joseph Conrad edited by J. H. Stape

H. D. edited by Nephie J. Christodoulides and Polina Mackay

Dante edited by Rachel Jacoff (second edition)

Daniel Defoe edited by John Richetti

Don DeLillo edited by John N. Duvall

Charles Dickens edited by John O. Jordan

Emily Dickinson edited by Wendy Martin

John Donne edited by Achsah Guibbory

Dostoevskii edited by W. J. Leatherbarrow

Theodore Dreiser edited by Leonard Cassuto and Claire Virginia Eby

John Dryden edited by Steven N. Zwicker

W. E. B. Du Bois edited by Shamoon Zamir

George Eliot edited by George Levine

T. S. Eliot edited by A. David Moody

Ralph Ellison edited by Ross Posnock

Ralph Waldo Emerson edited by Joel Porte and Saundra Morris

William Faulkner edited by Philip M. Weinstein

Henry Fielding edited by Claude Rawson

F. Scott Fitzgerald edited by Ruth Prigozy

Flaubert edited by Timothy Unwin

E. M. Forster edited by David Bradshaw

Benjamin Franklin edited by Carla Mulford

Brian Friel edited by Anthony Roche

Robert Frost edited by Robert Faggen

Gabriel García Márquez edited by Philip Swanson

Elizabeth Gaskell edited by Jill L. Matus

Goethe edited by Lesley Sharpe

Günter Grass edited by Stuart Taberner

Thomas Hardy edited by Dale Kramer

David Hare edited by Richard Boon

Nathaniel Hawthorne edited by Richard Millington

Seamus Heaney edited by Bernard O'Donoghue

Ernest Hemingway edited by Scott Donaldson

Homer edited by Robert Fowler

Horace edited by Stephen Harrison

Ted Hughes edited by Terry Gifford

Ibsen edited by James McFarlane

Henry James edited by Jonathan Freedman

Samuel Johnson edited by Greg Clingham

Ben Jonson edited by Richard Harp and Stanley Stewart

James Joyce edited by Derek Attridge (second edition)

Kafka edited by Julian Preece

Keats edited by Susan J. Wolfson

Rudyard Kipling edited by Howard J. Booth

Lacan edited by Jean-Michel Rabaté

D. H. Lawrence edited by Anne Fernihough

Primo Levi edited by Robert Gordon

Lucretius edited by Stuart Gillespie and Philip Hardie

Machiavelli edited by John M. Najemy

David Mamet edited by Christopher Bigsby

Thomas Mann edited by Ritchie Robertson

Christopher Marlowe edited by Patrick Cheney

Andrew Marvell edited by Derek Hirst and Steven N. Zwicker

Herman Melville edited by Robert S. Levine

Arthur Miller edited by Christopher Bigsby (second edition)

Milton edited by Dennis Danielson (second edition)

Molière edited by David Bradby and Andrew Calder

Toni Morrison edited by Justine Tally

Nabokov edited by Julian W. Connolly

Eugene O'Neill edited by Michael Manheim

George Orwell edited by John Rodden

Ovid edited by Philip Hardie

Harold Pinter edited by Peter Raby (second edition)

Sylvia Plath edited by Jo Gill

Edgar Allan Poe edited by Kevin J. Hayes

Alexander Pope edited by Pat Rogers

Ezra Pound edited by Ira B. Nadel

Proust edited by Richard Bales

Pushkin edited by Andrew Kahn

Rabelais edited by John O'Brien

Rilke edited by Karen Leeder and Robert Vilain

Philip Roth edited by Timothy Parrish

Salman Rushdie edited by Abdulrazak Gurnah

Shakespeare edited by Margareta de Grazia and Stanley Wells (second edition)

Shakespeare on Film edited by Russell Jackson (second edition)

Shakespeare and Popular Culture edited by Robert Shaughnessy

Shakespeare on Stage edited by Stanley Wells and Sarah Stanton

Shakespearean Comedy edited by Alexander Leggatt

Shakespearean Tragedy edited by Claire McEachern

Shakespeare's History Plays edited by Michael Hattaway

Shakespeare's Last Plays edited by Catherine M. S. Alexander

Shakespeare's Poetry edited by Patrick Cheney

George Bernard Shaw edited by Christopher Innes

Shelley edited by Timothy Morton

Mary Shelley edited by Esther Schor

Sam Shepard edited by Matthew C. Roudané

Spenser edited by Andrew Hadfield

Laurence Sterne edited by Thomas Keymer

Wallace Stevens edited by John N. Serio

Tom Stoppard edited by Katherine E. Kelly

Harriet Beecher Stowe edited by Cindy Weinstein

August Strindberg edited by Michael Robinson

Jonathan Swift edited by Christopher Fox

J. M. Synge edited by P. J. Mathews

Tacitus edited by A. J. Woodman

Henry David Thoreau edited by Joel Myerson

Tolstoy edited by Donna Tussing Orwin

Anthony Trollope edited by Carolyn Dever and Lisa Niles

Mark Twain edited by Forrest G. Robinson

John Updike edited by Stacey Olster

Mario Vargas Llosa edited by Efrain Kristal and John King

Virgil edited by Charles Martindale

Voltaire edited by Nicholas Cronk

Edith Wharton edited by Millicent Bell

Walt Whitman edited by Ezra Greenspan

Oscar Wilde edited by Peter Raby

Tennessee Williams edited by Matthew C. Roudané

August Wilson edited by Christopher Bigsby

Mary Wollstonecraft edited by Claudia L. Johnson

Virginia Woolf edited by Susan Sellers (second edition)

Wordsworth edited by Stephen Gill

W. B. Yeats edited by Marjorie Howes and John Kelly

Zola edited by Brian Nelson

TOPICS

The Actress edited by Maggie B. Gale and John Stokes

The African American Novel edited by Maryemma Graham

The African American Slave Narrative edited by Audrey A. Fisch

Allegory edited by Rita Copeland and Peter Struck

American Crime Fiction edited by Catherine Ross Nickerson

American Modernism edited by Walter Kalaidjian

American Realism and Naturalism edited by Donald Pizer

American Travel Writing edited by Alfred Bendixen and Judith Hamera

American Women Playwrights edited by Brenda Murphy

Ancient Rhetoric edited by Erik Gunderson

Arthurian Legend edited by Elizabeth Archibald and Ad Putter

Australian Literature edited by Elizabeth Webby

British Literature of the French Revolution edited by Pamela Clemit

British Romantic Poetry edited by James Chandler and Maureen N. McLane

British Romanticism edited by Stuart Curran (second edition)

British Theatre, 1730–1830, edited by Jane Moody and Daniel O'Quinn

Canadian Literature edited by Eva-Marie Kröller

Children's Literature edited by M. O. Grenby and Andrea Immel

The Classic Russian Novel edited by Malcolm V. Jones and Robin Feuer Miller

Contemporary Irish Poetry edited by Matthew Campbell

Creative Writing edited by David Morley and Philip Neilsen

Crime Fiction edited by Martin Priestman

Early Modern Women's Writing edited by Laura Lunger Knoppers

The Eighteenth-Century Novel edited by John Richetti

Eighteenth-Century Poetry edited by John Sitter

English Literature, 1500–1600 edited by Arthur F. Kinney

English Literature, 1650–1740 edited by Steven N. Zwicker

English Literature, 1740–1830 edited by Thomas Keymer and Jon Mee

English Literature, 1830–1914 edited by Joanne Shattock

English Novelists edited by Adrian Poole

English Poetry, Donne to Marvell edited by Thomas N. Corns

English Poets edited by Claude Rawson

English Renaissance Drama edited by A. R. Braunmuller and Michael Hattaway (second edition)

English Renaissance Tragedy edited by Emma Smith and Garrett A. Sullivan Jr.

English Restoration Theatre edited by Deborah C. Payne Fisk

The Epic edited by Catherine Bates

European Modernism edited by Pericles Lewis

European Novelists edited by Michael Bell

Fantasy Literature edited by Edward James and Farah Mendlesohn

Feminist Literary Theory edited by Ellen Rooney

Fiction in the Romantic Period edited by Richard Maxwell and Katie Trumpener

The Fin de Siècle edited by Gail Marshall

The French Novel: From 1800 to the Present edited by Timothy Unwin

Gay and Lesbian Writing edited by Hugh Stevens

German Romanticism edited by Nicholas Saul

Gothic Fiction edited by Jerrold E. Hogle

The Greek and Roman Novel edited by Tim Whitmarsh

Greek and Roman Theatre edited by Marianne McDonald and J. Michael Walton

Greek Lyric edited by Felix Budelmann

Greek Mythology edited by Roger D. Woodard

Greek Tragedy edited by P. E. Easterling

The Harlem Renaissance edited by George Hutchinson

The Irish Novel edited by John Wilson Foster

The Italian Novel edited by Peter Bondanella and Andrea Ciccarelli

Jewish American Literature edited by Hana Wirth-Nesher and Michael P. Kramer

The Latin American Novel edited by Efraín Kristal

The Literature of the First World War edited by Vincent Sherry

The Literature of London edited by Lawrence Manley

The Literature of Los Angeles edited by Kevin R. McNamara

The Literature of New York edited by Cyrus Patell and Bryan Waterman

Literature on Screen edited by Deborah Cartmell and Imelda Whelehan

The Literature of World War II edited by Marina MacKay

Medieval English Culture edited by Andrew Galloway

Medieval English Literature edited by Larry Scanlon

Medieval English Mysticism edited by Samuel Fanous and Vincent Gillespie

Medieval English Theatre edited by Richard Beadle and Alan J. Fletcher (second edition)

Medieval French Literature edited by Simon Gaunt and Sarah Kay

Medieval Romance edited by Roberta L. Krueger

Medieval Women's Writing edited by Carolyn Dinshaw and David Wallace

Modern American Culture edited by Christopher Bigsby

Modern British Women Playwrights edited by Elaine Aston and Janelle Reinelt

Modern French Culture edited by Nicholas Hewitt

Modern German Culture edited by Eva Kolinsky and Wilfried van der Will

The Modern German Novel edited by Graham Bartram

Modern Irish Culture edited by Joe Cleary and Claire Connolly

Modern Italian Culture edited by Zygmunt G. Baranski and Rebecca J. West

Modern Latin American Culture edited by John King

Modern Russian Culture edited by Nicholas Rzhevsky

Modern Spanish Culture edited by David T. Gies

Modernism edited by Michael Levenson (second edition)

The Modernist Novel edited by Morag Shiach

Modernist Poetry edited by Alex Davis and Lee M. Jenkins

Modernist Women Writers edited by Maren Tova Linett

Narrative edited by David Herman

Native American Literature edited by Joy Porter and Kenneth M. Roemer

Nineteenth-Century American Women's Writing edited by Dale M. Bauer and Philip Gould

Old English Literature edited by Malcolm Godden and Michael Lapidge

Performance Studies edited by Tracy C. Davis

Popular Fiction edited by David Glover and Scott McCracken

Postcolonial Literary Studies edited by Neil Lazarus

Postmodernism edited by Steven Connor

The Pre-Raphaelites edited by Elizabeth Prettejohn

Renaissance Humanism edited by Jill Kraye

The Roman Historians edited by Andrew Feldherr

Roman Satire edited by Kirk Freudenburg

Science Fiction edited by Edward James and Farah Mendlesohn

Scottish Literature edited by Gerald Carruthers and Liam McIlvanney

The Sonnet edited by A. D. Cousins and Peter Howarth

The Spanish Novel: From 1600 to the Present edited by Harriet Turner and Adelaida López de Martínez

Travel Writing edited by Peter Hulme and Tim Youngs

Twentieth-Century British and Irish Women's Poetry edited by Jane Dowson

The Twentieth-Century English Novel edited by Robert L. Caserio

Twentieth-Century English Poetry edited by Neil Corcoran

Twentieth-Century Irish Drama edited by Shaun Richards

Twentieth-Century Russian Literature edited by Marina Balina and Evgeny Dobrenko

Utopian Literature edited by Gregory Claeys

Victorian and Edwardian Theatre edited by Kerry Powell

The Victorian Novel edited by Deirdre David

Victorian Poetry edited by Joseph Bristow

War Writing edited by Kate McLoughlin

Writing of the English Revolution edited by N. H. Keeble

The Pre-Raphaelites edited by Elizabeth Prettejohn

Printed in Great Britain
by Amazon